Book belongs to Rose Briley

Human Relations in Organizations

THE WEST SERIES IN MANAGEMENT

Consulting Editors:

Don Hellriegel   *Texas A & M University*
John W. Slocum, Jr.   *Southern Methodist University*

Aldag and Brief   *Managing Organizational Behavior*
Burack   *Personnel Management: Cases and Exercises*
Costley and Todd   *Human Relations in Organizations, 2d Ed.*
Daft   *Organization Theory and Design*
Downey, Hellriegel, and Slocum   *Organizational Behavior: A Reader*
Hellriegel, Slocum, and Woodman   *Organizational Behavior, 3d Ed.*
Hrebiniak   *Complex Organizations*
Huse   *Organization Development and Change, 2d Ed.*
Huse   *Management, 2d Ed.*
Kelley and Whatley   *Personnel Management in Action: Skill Building
    Experiences, 2d Ed.*
Mathis and Jackson   *Personnel: Contemporary Perspectives and
    Applications, 3d Ed.*
Morris and Sashkin   *Organization Behavior in Action: Skill Building
    Experiences*
Newport   *Supervisory Management: Tools and Techniques*
Ritchie and Thompson   *Organization and People: Readings, Cases, and
    Exercises in Organizational Behavior, 2d Ed.*
Schuler   *Effective Personnel Management*
Schuler   *Personnel and Human Resource Management*
Schuler, Dalton, and Huse   *Case Problems in Management, 2d Ed.*
Schuler, McFillen, and Dalton   *Applied Readings in Personnel and Human
    Resource Management*
Veiga and Yanouzas   *The Dynamics of Organization Theory: Gaining a
    Macro Perspective*

Human Relations in Organizations

Second Edition

Dan L. Costley
New Mexico State University

Ralph Todd
American River College

WEST PUBLISHING COMPANY
St. Paul • New York • Los Angeles • San Francisco

Chapter Opening Photo Credits: Chapters 1, 2, 3, 5, 6, 7, 8, 9, 10, 11, 12, 14, 15, 16—
Jeffrey Grosscup; Chapter 4—© Magnum Photos, Inc.; Chapter 13—Owen
Franken/Stock, Boston; Chapter 17—Robert George Gaylord; Chapter 18—Agency
for International Development; Chapter 19—Charles Farrow

Production Coordination: Carlisle Graphics

Copyright © 1978, 1983 by WEST PUBLISHING CO.
50 West Kellogg Boulevard
P.O. Box 3526
St. Paul, Minnesota 55165

Printed in the United States of America

Library of Congress Cataloging in Publication Data

Costley, Dan L.
    Human relations in organizations.

    (The West series in management)
    Includes bibliographies and index.
    1. Organizational behavior.   2. Personnel
management.   3. Psychology, Industrial.   I. Todd,
Ralph.   II. Title.   III. Series.
HD58.7.C65   1983   658.3   82-24823

ISBN 0-314-69643-1

Contents

4 Working Together—Leaders and Groups   259

Preface

The productivity of organizations depends on people. This book focuses on the behavior of individuals in organizations. The subject of this book is sometimes called human relations at work, behavior in organizations, or human resources management. Whatever label is used, this book is about people in organizations and the achievement of individual and organizational goals.

A developmental approach is used in combining theory, research, and applications for improving interpersonal effectiveness in organizations. Much of the material grew out of management experiences and is a result of extensive consulting with a variety of organizations. Anyone who works in an organization should find the material in this book helpful in dealing with day-to-day problems associated with interpersonal relations and productivity. The emphasis of this book is on the skills needed for effective leadership, including the ability to communicate, to understand human needs, to cope with conflict and frustration, to motivate others, to use authority, and to increase group productivity.

We discuss the forces affecting individuals in an organizational setting by providing the reader with an opportunity to examine the application of principles or organizational behavior and to develop an understanding of underlying theoretical principles. We have tried to provide an opportunity for anyone interested in human behavior at work to read and learn from material that is understandable, interesting, and enjoyable. To aid the learning process, each chapter begins with a preview and self-evaluation questions and there is a quick review in outline form at the end of each chapter. Discussion questions, case incidents, and suggested readings are provided after each chapter.

The reader is given a variety of viewpoints and approaches in dealing with problems of managing people. This book is designed to present accepted areas of knowledge and to avoid extremes of controversial and argumentative theories of organizational behavior.

Acknowledgments

Many managers, professors, and students have contributed to the development of the material in this book. Even though they are not all mentioned by name, they all have our thanks, especially our students.

Special recognition and appreciation for support is deserved by Rose Byrum for invaluable assistance in preparation of the second edition.

For the second edition our appreciation is expressed to the following reviewers who provided intellectual stimulation and guidance: Leon Adkinson, Taylor University; James Anderson, Fullerton College; David Balkin, Northeastern University; Stephen Branz, Triton College; Ed Fratantaro, Orange Coast College; Michale E. Kolivosky, Hillsdale College; Bill Lacewell, Westark Community College; Robert LeRosen, Northern Virginia Community College; Gene Schneider, Austin Community College; John W. Slocum, Jr., Southern Methodist University; Jeff Stauffer, Ventura College; Dan Underwood, Inver Hills Community College.

For excellent support and assistance, we thank the people at West Publishing Company. We appreciate the assistance of our editors, Richard T. Fenton, Esther W. Craig, and Sherry H. James.

A special thanks to Lynn Reichel of Carlisle Graphics whose support and guidance was of great value.

We are grateful for the unqualified support of our families while we worked on this manuscript. It is to them that this book is dedicated.

Human Relations in Organizations

Organizations 1

1 Understanding People in Organizations

Learning Objectives

After reading this chapter, you should be able to:

1. Understand why human relations is important in organizations.

2. List basic approaches in understanding people at work.

3. Define common theories of human behavior.

4. Describe the effects of organizational environment on human relations.

5. Understand the major management skills needed for effective human relations.

6. Present a philosophy of effective human behavior in organizations.

Chapter Topics

Understanding Behavior in Organizations

Why People Do What They Do

Organizational Trends

The Influence of Organizations

Linking the Individual and the Organization

Motivation and Performance

Working Together—Leaders and Groups

Beliefs and Realities

Change, Values, and Responsibilities

Preview and Self-Evaluation

Employees and managers in work organizations frequently discover that they have different priorities and areas of primary interest. Managers must think chiefly in terms of organizational goals: productivity, quality of service or product, costs, sales, and profits. At the same time, nonmanagement employees may be concerned more with personal human values such as fair treatment, interesting work, appropriate pay, security, and opportunity for advancement.

To get work accomplished, managers must work with and through other people, channeling employees' skills, knowledge, and effort. Unlike machines, however, human beings do not turn on and off at management's command. For many years, and to some extent today, managers believed that people worked for pay and pay alone. However, research indicates that pay is only one element of work. Employees have complex needs. They are influenced not only by their immediate managers, but by other employees, by the type of work to which they are assigned, and by the organizations to which they belong. Understanding human behavior in order to create conditions in which employees can meet organizational as well as personal goals is an essential management skill.

This first chapter introduces a few of the many areas of concern that may help in understanding human behavior in organizations. To test your knowledge of these issues, take the following true-false quiz before reading the chapter. After you have read the chapter, take the test again. You may be surprised at the answers.

Answer True or False

1. Managers and nonmanagers frequently have different priorities but the same interests at work. T F

2. Research indicates that most people work only for the pay. T F

3. Job satisfaction does not always lead to improved productivity. T F

4. Behavioral science is concerned primarily with control of what people do. T F

5. One current behavioral theory states that biologically inherited factors may be as important or more important than environmental factors. T F

6. When people are no longer rewarded for specific kinds of behavior, that behavior gradually disappears. T F

7. The quality of worklife movement is primarily a concern of Japanese management. T F

8. Our perceptions are, for the most part, unlearned. T F

9. Communication in organizations is not limited to the spoken or written word. T F

10. Human relations is chiefly a concern of more advanced societies. T F

ANSWERS: 1. F; 2. F; 3. T; 4. F; 5. T; 6. T; 7. F; 8. F; 9. T; 10. F.

Understanding Behavior in Organizations

Few, if any, areas of knowledge are as important or contain such a complex mixture of fact and fiction as the study of human behavior in work organizations. Decisions affecting people are essential to the success or failure of organizations. Yet managers who are skilled in analysis of data, problem solving, planning, and the "paperwork" of their job are often bewildered by the actions of their employees. Two central questions are always present in a work situation: What causes people to do the things they do? and How can performance be improved? The answers are not always clear. Understanding the major factors affecting people at work and the techniques for implementing major research findings and theories of human behavior in work situations is a powerful management tool.

central questions in work situation

ways we learn about behavior

A major problem encountered in dealing with the actions of people at work is related to the way our understanding of behavior is learned. From infancy, we develop concepts, beliefs, and values concerning our own behavior and that of others. Very young children are sensitive to the moods and feelings of their parents and quickly learn what kind of behavior is rewarded, punished, or ignored. As children grow older, they learn about the behavior of other people as well.

Day-to-day experiences also teach us sets of attitudes, beliefs, and values that affect the way we relate to others. Our own behavior influences to some extent the behavior of the other people we encounter in day-to-day activities. When these relationships are not understood, the potential for "people problems" increases.

search for keys to productivity

From the pioneering work of industrial engineers and organizational analysts in the early part of this century to the contributions of contemporary behavioral scientists, the quest for keys to unlock the productive capacities of people has been a major area of concern. But the sad fact remains that managers and nonmanagement employees have not succeeded in finding those keys. In recent years, productivity in the United States has not risen nearly as rapidly as it has in many other countries, yet we have been leaders in behavioral research regarding people at work. Admittedly, there are many disagreements among different investigators of behavior in work organizations. The relationship between job satisfaction and productivity is a good example of many issues still being debated (see Figure 1.1).

issue of job satisfaction and productivity

Some organizational behavior specialists believe that job satisfaction leads to improved productivity. They cite studies showing that productivity declines when employees become dissatisfied. Other stud-

Which of the following statements is true:

1. Increased job satisfaction leads to higher productivity.
2. Higher productivity leads to increased job satisfaction.
3. Satisfaction and productivity have little or no direct relationship at work.
4. Statements 1, 2, and 3 are true.
5. Statements 1, 2, and 3 are false.

Figure 1.1 An example of a difficult organizational behavior problem.[1]

ies show that as employees become more productive, satisfaction with work improves. Yet because conditions at work such as the speed of machines, the amount of assistance available, and the requirements of specific tasks vary greatly from one organization to another, factors leading to either satisfaction or productivity are neither clearly known nor well understood.

Under some conditions, especially those in which employees can control their work pace to some extent, increased job satisfaction may lead to increased productivity. But it is equally possible that when people are rewarded for their performance, increased productivity may lead to job satisfaction and feelings of competence. Finally, in jobs such as automated manufacturing or processing there may be little relationship between satisfaction and productivity.

However, productivity is only one of many people problems faced by managers at work. Managers are also concerned with issues such as stability of the work force—especially absenteeism and turnover— communication effectiveness; interpersonal conflicts; and day-to-day relationships with employees and other managers who may have conflicting attitudes, values, and beliefs. A primary reason that the study of behavior in organizations is important is to learn to observe, predict, and influence behavior at work. To do this requires a grasp of what people are doing, why they are doing it, and methods for implementing desired changes. When we speculate or guess why people do the things they do, we enter the age-old realm of defining causes of human behavior.

managers and human behavior

Why People Do What They Do

Since the earliest recorded times, philosophers have attempted to explain human behavior. Some thinkers felt that people were naturally aggressive, hostile and greedy and accepted control only to protect themselves from others. A few felt that people were born without knowledge and had to learn all their behavior. But attempts to study and understand behavior scientifically began only about one hundred years ago. Since then, such experimental studies have steadily increased in scope and complexity.

behavioral science a recent field of study

One of the more lasting explanations of human behavior was proposed by Edward Thorndike over seventy years ago.[2] Thorndike stated that we tend to repeat those actions that are followed closely by satisfaction or reward and avoid those actions followed by discomfort or punishment. Thorndike called his theory "The Empirical Law of Effect." Since Thorndike's early studies, many newer, more comprehensive theories of human behavior have been developed. From a practical point of view, however, Thorndike's observations still seem valid. Most people tend to seek rewards and avoid punishments in most of their activities.

Thorndike "Empirical Law of Effect"

But Thorndike's Empirical Law of Effect did not adequately explain much more than casually observed behavior. Newer and more elaborate methods were needed to understand how and why people act as they do.

Behavior Modification

B. F. Skinner has for many years been recognized as a leader in the field of behavior modification with his theory of *operant conditioning*. Essentially, Skinner and other psychologists believe and have demonstrated that people can be conditioned to behave in specific ways. Just as a dog or porpoise will learn to respond to calls and whistles, people also learn from their environment. Skinner took Thorndike's theory one step further by stating that reward and punishment can be used to modify or shape behavior. A dog will learn to obey a specific command because of a potential reward, such as a biscuit or word of praise, or to avoid certain actions because of potential punishment. According to Skinner, rewards (or in some instances punishment) reinforce or strengthen actions. People, like animals, learn to associate potential rewards with certain activities and strive to achieve those rewards. If there is no reinforcement for our behavior, Skinner maintains, it will gradually disappear. As long as occasional reinforcement is present, actions that result in reward will be repeated.

Skinner's techniques have been tried at a number of educational institutions and industries, and they seem to work. For example, Emery Air Freight, one of the country's largest air freight carriers, developed a system that provided feedback to employees on their job performance. Workers could then measure their own improvement and success. Management reinforced the changes with praise and recognition. The program has produced significant cost savings and improved quality, lowered absenteeism, and raised employee morale. According to Emery, work habits developed through the behavior modification process seem to be long lasting.

Cognitive Theories

Cognitive theory examines how people know about the world around them, how people become aware of the world around them, and how they make judgments.

A number of researchers believe that Skinner's behavior modification approaches are useful but do not adequately explain human behavior. Cognitive psychologists find that people interpret the world around them and act on the basis of their expectations. If they believe that a certain action will result in a reward, they will act to achieve it. However, they will not work to gain a reward that has little value to them or one they think is unachievable.

Julian Rotter at Ohio State University has developed research data over many years of experimentation that indicate people are externally or internally oriented. Externally oriented people believe that their lives are controlled by forces outside themselves. They expect others to direct them and be responsible for their success or failure. They also rely on luck or coincidence, as well as authority, for many of their decisions. On the other hand, internally oriented people believe that the individual is largely responsible for his or her own behavior. They rely primarily on their own resources and accept personal responsibility for both success and failure.

More recent cognitive psychologists propose that when something happens (usually represented by the symbol "S") people interpret the event (O) and act in a specific way (B) with certain consequences (C).[3] The consequences then help determine how the event is interpreted if it occurs again. The S-O-B-C approach has gained popularity recently because it recognizes that the results of what people do influence what they will do next.

S-O-B-C approach

Interaction Theory

What a person does is explained in part by S-O-B-C, but it is also necessary to recognize the impact of environmental forces. Albert Bandura,[4] one of the primary advocators of social learning or *interaction theory*, states that people learn not only from their own experiences but from observing others in various situations. A mental image is formed and the person learns to act in a characteristic way. For example, a child may watch how his or her parents act toward their neighbors. As additional observations take place, the mental image may change and behavior will also change. The way, then, a person perceives a situation and its potential consequences strongly influences behavior. In work situations, people are constantly affected by the way they interpret the nature of their jobs, the managers' reactions, and the actions of their peers.

An equally interesting theory is that of the sociobiologist.

interaction theory—learning from observation

Sociobiology

Although the belief that human behavior is instinctive, at least in part, has been discounted by most contemporary researchers, *sociobiology theory* is founded on evidence of unlearned behavior. In his writings on sociobiological behavior, Edward O. Wilson[5] states that characteristics inherited from parents, grandparents, and all of a continuing line of ancestors predispose much of our behavior.

Sociobiologists do not deny that people learn but believe that inclinations and abilities such as mathematics, music, athletics, and art are inherited. For example, unless we inherit tone perception, rhythm, and muscle coordination, we will find it difficult to become pianists. They also believe that we are most attracted to people whose genetic characteristics are similar or superior to our own. Recent studies show that identical twins reared totally apart from each other often make very

sociobiology— inclinations and abilities are inherited

similar life choices such as type of occupation and number of children. They show the same preferences in hair style, clothing, and music. While these studies do not prove sociobiological theory, they do seem to strengthen Wilson's contention that some behaviors are not learned but inherited.

Where Are We Now?

managers must describe, predict, and influence behavior

It is evident that human behavior can be explained by a number of theories, each with its own merits and its own deficiencies. Yet managers of work organizations need a framework to help them not only interpret the behavior of people but accomplish three essential tasks:

1. Accurately describe what people are doing in specific situations.
2. Predict behavior, based on objective descriptions.
3. Influence behavior by creating situations that will in turn lead to desired, predictable behavior.

For instance, a manager notices that some employees respond favorably each time they are given increased responsibility. As a result, he or she can use added responsibility as a predictable factor in getting positive results from these employees in certain specific situations.

employees interact with work, management, peers

While not ignoring the value and contributions of other theories, we believe it is most useful to view employees in an organizational setting as interacting with each other, with what is going on within themselves, with their work, and with their boss.

By *interaction*, we mean that people are continually influencing and being influenced by several major factors. At work, major factors are other employees, the job (situation), and management (see Figure 1.2, page 13). Employees influence and are influenced by their managers and their jobs, most often simultaneously. Managers must begin to understand the principles of achievement-oriented human relations along with the techniques that change theory into practice. Among many vital management skills, understanding people and creating conditions to help maximize employee performance may be the most difficult ones to master.

Japanese (Management) Spoken at Sony, U.S.A.

If American employers are wondering whether Japanese-style management works with American employees, Masayoshi (Mike) Morimoto, plant manager at Sony Electronic Company in San Diego, can answer, "Yes."

The approximately eighteen hundred employees of Sony often outproduce their counterparts in Japan in meeting productivity goals and quality standards. Mike Morimoto believes that American workers, like the Japanese, respond well when they are involved in company decisions, when there is less social distance between themselves and management, and when management loyalty to workers is emphasized as strongly as worker loyalty to management.

Hallmarks of the Japanese approach are evident in many ways. Before major decisions are made or implemented, the plant manager meets with all Sony employees, usually in groups of about 100 workers at a time. Also, the executive dining room is conspicuously absent. Mike Morimoto eats in the cafeteria with other employees and makes a point of sitting with a different group each day. The only private parking space is reserved for the company nurse in event of an emergency. And even when consumer demand for new televisions has dropped, there have been no layoffs.

With all of these factors, it's not difficult to see why the Japanese management style gets results. Through an understanding of employee needs and the ability to predict results, Sony management has been able to influence employee behavior effectively and consistently.[6]

Organizational Trends

quality of worklife

Several major trends have emerged that promise to continue to influence the way organizations will function throughout the remainder of this century. One of the most significant trends is called "*Quality of worklife*" or QWL. In all Western European countries and the United States, management, behavior scientists, and industry experts are analyzing the many factors that contribute to employee productivity and to conditions that foster personally satisfying work experiences— all important to the quality of worklife. At this time QWL is a philosophy of improving conditions of work but not a specific technique. In addition, electronic technology has dramatically changed and will continue to change the very nature of work itself both in the office and in factories. Robots are replacing workers on the assembly line, and offices increasingly rely on computer-linked word-processing equipment rather than on traditional clerical support. Virtually every facet of organizational life is affected by changes in technology and in the ways people are seen at work. Organizations, with their complex people relationships, promise to be very different in the future from those we have known in the past.

influence of electronic technology

Out of the Office and Back to the Home?

Modern work trends may be taking us full circle from cottage industries in the home to the modern factory and office, right back to the home again— courtesy of the computer and telecommunications. At Blue Shield and

Blue Cross in Columbus, S.C., a few women "cottage keyers" process 70 percent of Blue Shield claims on their home computers. They communicate with their supervisors by telephone and never have to visit the company's office. Control Data Corporation of Minneapolis and a number of other companies have similar programs.

People who are employed by traditional companies, yet control their own hours and choose their own work place may be the wave of the future. With access to a telephone and electrical outlets, a worker can do computer-assisted jobs from any location in the country. He or she simply feeds information into the main office and receives assignments in return.

Jack Niles of the University of Southern California estimates that by 1990, 15 to 20 percent of the American work force will work in the home and from other locations—vacation spots, business travel sites, etc. They won't ever need to report physically to a main office or other company facility.

The Influence of Organizations

We begin our study of the ways people relate to each other by examining the influence of organizations on their lives. During what is usually considered a normal working career, many people will change jobs several times; become part of and leave several organizations; and have their attitudes, beliefs, and values at least partially shaped by their work environment.

Organizations influence human relations in many important ways. By *human relations*, we mean the kinds of relationships that occur in work organizations. Effective human relations are management actions and decisions that lead to productivity by all members of an organization.

While it is very important, the formal structure of an organization has less influence on the long-term actions of people at work than do the attitudes, beliefs, and values of managers. Every day managers must communicate with and set examples for nonmanagement employees, other managers, and at times, people outside their immediate organizational unit (section, department, division, etc.). In addition, the skill level, training, and attitudes of individual employees influence the manager's behavior, as well as the behavior of other employees. Finally, the behavior of people at work is influenced by the jobs to which they are assigned. Some jobs require creative application of specialized training, some are paced by machines, some are highly routine and repetitive, and some have a very broad range of activities and responsibilities. These three major forces—the manager's attitudes and actions, the characteristics of the employee, and the type of work—all interact with each other to influence what happens in the work situation.

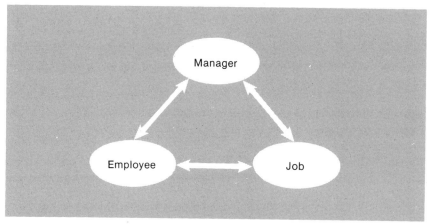

Figure 1.2 The basic organizational relationship. Each factor constantly influences and is influenced by the other two.

Figure 1.2 shows this relationship among job, employee, and manager. Each is constantly influencing the other two. The precise effect of the three-way relationship on performance depends on many complex factors. A bright, ambitious employee who sees his or her job assignment as dull may translate resentment against the job to resentment against his or her manager. That same employee's manager, who sees the assigned job as necessary, valuable, and simple, may interpret the employee's attitude as being typical of those "damn know-it-alls."

Linking the Individual and the Organization

Within any organizational structure, people are constantly acting and reacting to each other and to their jobs. Their behavior is also affected by a wide variety of personal factors not directly job related. People are also guided by less easily identified influences, ranging from the state of the economy to the weather.

Perception

One of the most important aspects of human behavior in any situation is the array of experiences and sensations called perception. *Perception*, as it is used here, refers to the ways we interpret our experiences. It includes those things we have learned to identify through taste, smell, touch, sight, and hearing. Also, feelings, hunches, anything we are aware of is the result of perceptual responses to either external or internal stimulation. The thought of a movie seen last evening, a growling stomach, a feeling of anxiety, or a peak experience are all internal perceptions.

importance of perception

perceptions are learned

Our perceptions are for the most part learned. We are taught what the color red is, what a smile means, and that a hot stove will burn, either through personal experience or through instructions from others, books, television, or simple observation. What we learn creates a set of conditions inside our bodies that leads to highly personalized reactions. A person who, as a child, has fallen from a tall tree may perceive heights as frightening, while another who does not share the same experience will have a different perception. Likewise, what one employee perceives as an attractive and challenging assignment may be dull and ordinary to another.

perception is selective

Perception is also selective. Often we perceive only what is meaningful or significant to us in our world. We tend to ignore those things that have little positive *or* negative value. When we find ourselves part of a group, we are usually aware of only those people or events that for reasons of appearance, speech, or location stand out. We are, in fact, incapable of perceiving all of the thousands of factors in our environment that constantly compete for attention. Temperature, humidity, background noise, light, personal dress, and so forth, are only noticed in the extreme.

The way employee perceptions are selected and interpreted profoundly influences behavior at work. Skilled managers are concerned with developing personal behavior that their employees will perceive as encouraging openness, confidence, and trust. They also try to minimize decisions or actions that employees may perceive as threatening or nonrewarding.

Communication

communication links the individual and the organization

Another important factor linking the individual and the organization is skill in understanding and being understood—the process of communication. Communication is the act of understanding and being understood. It involves sending, receiving, and interpreting messages. All too often, what is said or written, or even shown in pictures or graphic symbols, is not understood. *Communication*, however, is not limited to what is spoken or written. Tone of voice, loudness, and emphasis on certain phrases frequently transmit more real meaning than the words themselves. The ways people stand, sit, dress, and speak, as well as their facial expressions, movements, and mannerisms, all communicate.

An additional stumbling block in effective communication lies in the words themselves. If the simple statement "Sally is fast" is made, it is difficult to know whether Sally is a speedy runner, a true friend, is stuck in one place, completes her work quickly, or has too many men friends. Our language is complicated by common words that can have several meanings.

Although communication is one of the most complex human activities, an understanding of some of its basic processes, difficulties, and techniques is a necessary ingredient of effective organizational life. People at work are constantly relating to each other. With adequate knowledge and skill, managers may direct many of these relationships toward the achievement of organizational goals such as improvement in schedules, costs, quality, and productivity—the basic ingredients of nearly all organizations. Realistic managers know that performance is judged by results.

Motivation and Performance

Few topics have been given as much attention by behavioral scientists as motivation. Many managers feel that employee motivation is an essential key to organizational success. *Motivation* is a word used to describe all of the many causes of human behavior. Three questions are frequently voiced by managers concerning motivation: Can employees be understood? Can their actions be predicted? Is it possible to control or direct employee behavior? While these questions are often hard to answer, workable approaches to increase motivation can be learned. *motivation is a key to organizational success*

In many ways, motivation can be considered the core of human behavior studies. If human behavior is to be accurately predicted and directed toward achievement of organizational goals, its causes must be understood.

But understanding behavior is not easy. Some physiologists believe that behavior is largely determined by complex chemical and electrical changes throughout the body, especially in the central nervous system. Anthropologists and sociologists have demonstrated the influence of culture and environment on the ways people behave. Psychologists have emphasized the influence of learning and perception on motivational patterns. While all of these behavioral research efforts are interesting and valuable, managers want practical, applicable concepts that will help them to get work accomplished. The most valuable theories for managers are those that can be easily translated into meaningful action.

Several useful approaches to motivational problems are available to managers. First, they must understand the needs of employees. All too often, increases in pay, improvement in benefits, and a cleaner, more attractive working environment are seen as the primary tools of motivation. These are important and necessary, but employees have other needs as well.

Yet understanding needs is not the only route to effective motivational program development. Another important factor is the conditions that affect personal adjustment. Frustration and conflict, for example, are unavoidable in most work situations, and they often reduce a worker's effectiveness. The intensity and causes of frustration and conflict are directly related to how well employees, including manag- *personal adjustment* ers, can adjust to the complexities of day-to-day work situations. Stress, burnout, and boredom are major management concerns.

Working Together—Leaders and Groups

People do not work alone in most organizations. They are usually part of formal and informal groups. Leaders, both formal and informal, and other group members strongly influence what individual employees, including managers, do or do not do.

leadership   Most people can recognize leaders, but how do we define leadership? We can say that leaders are people who get others to do things, who show support for causes, or who actively demonstrate beliefs in principles supported by others. But there are many different kinds of leaders. Some are charismatic, dependent primarily on their dynamic personalities for their leadership strength; others are recognized experts that people rely on for information and direction; still others may be quietly competent decision makers, autocratic but effective dictators, deeply philosophical geniuses, or less romantic but invaluable achievement-oriented managers. While leadership is difficult to characterize, there is a great deal of data concerning leadership effectiveness. Leaders are necessary. If not formally designated, they will be chosen by people who feel a particular leader can best help them achieve their personal and group goals. In a sense, leadership springs from followers and not necessarily from the qualities or characteristics of a person designated as leader.

leadership   Leaders to not operate in a vacuum. They are leaders of groups.
springs from   Groups may be either formal or informal and may have both formal and
followers   informal leaders. Effective leaders and managers with leadership qualities recognize that much of what is done or not done springs from group feelings. The strong adherence by many employees to group norms (what most group members believe and expect) is known to be a major factor in the effectiveness of an organization's ability to achieve necessary goals.

groups   Groups are major forces in the lives of work organizations. People are joined together for many reasons. Groups at work are formed, for the most part, of those people who have similar interests, jobs, values, or likes and dislikes. Friendships and alliances with others serve several purposes that an individual alone may find difficult to achieve. As a member of a group, the individual employee is able to enjoy a certain degree of security. He or she can rely on others for support when job difficulties are encountered. Groups protect members in more subtle ways, however, than friendship and support. Over a period of time, work groups frequently develop internal standards or norms. A group that has a high degree of agreement and support among its members may frequently control output far more than its formal managers do.

In fact, a closely knit group can actually countermand a manager's order or production quotas and set its own informal ones.

A key part of this text is concerned with groups and their influence on organizational goals. Managers who understand not only the dynamics of groups (the way they work) but also individual group member characteristics are most effective in helping to create high rather than low norms within the group.

Beliefs and Realities

Other major factors in the growing body of knowledge concerning human behavior at work are the effect management beliefs have on their interactions with employees, the kinds of power and status relationships in an organization, and the managerial skills of those who are in positions of authority.

What managers believe and what actually occurs are sometimes different. A common behavioral problem is that employees are reluctant to let their supervisors know where real problems actually lie: *management beliefs*

The Brown Streaks

A famous soap maker allegedly discovered an unidentified brown impurity in some of its soap. Employees, when questioned, seemed unable to identify its origin or its identity. In desperation, the company hired a consultant who walked through the processing line and quickly learned that a new and eager safety inspector had removed cans from the initial work station as a matter of health and sanitation. The cans were used by tobacco-chewing employees. As a matter of both revenge and convenience, they were getting rid of their tobacco juice directly into the soap mix. Although the mystery was solved, several case lots of soap had to be destroyed.

The late Douglas McGregor, while a professor at the graduate school of management at the Massachusetts Institute of Technology, repeatedly emphasized that employee performance is directly related to manager's assumptions. Managers with low expectations generally get low performance. An employee who is not expected to tell managers where problems exist will avoid volunteering information. One whose management does not expect more than minimum performance, gives minimum performance. McGregor's powerful message is that high-achieving managers are those who have high expectations for themselves and their employees, who lead rather than push their workers, and who include employees in decision making. *expectations affect performance*

Power

power and influence

Power is the degree to which one person or group influences another person or group. In an organization, power relationships exist among differing levels of management, between managers and employees, and among various levels of employees. Some people obtain a degree of influence or power through politics. They become acquainted with those who have legitimate power, they enlist others in their own personal causes, or they become experts and dispense their knowledge to carefully selected persons. Legitimate power is usually proportionate to a person's job or position. The higher an individual is on the organizational ladder, the more power he or she is assigned or expected to have.

In real-life situations, managerial effectiveness is dependent to some degree on the recognition of power, politics, and human behavior on the job. As we shall discuss later, power is not the sole property of management in work organizations; it is shared by many.

Change, Values, and Responsibilities

We live in a world of rapid change. In some cases, to adjust we must find different ways of doing things, reassess our moral values, and evaluate our social as well as our work responsibilities.

change is inevitable

Change is an inevitable consequence of existence. Most changes are difficult to predict and control. In organizations, however, change is frequently planned and results from a known cause. A number of techniques have been developed to encourage orderly and productive change. Some psychological techniques, such as transactional analysis, have gained wider acceptance by management consultants and trainers than by the truly professional behavioral scientist. A few organizations have used behavior modification techniques, popularized by B. F. Skinner, while others have installed long-range organizational development programs. These and many other techniques are used to bring about change that will improve organizational effectiveness. Of course, some changes cannot be accurately predicted or controlled. When confronted with the unanticipated, managers need even greater skills in change management.

moral values

Another organizational concern is the ever-present question of moral values and policy requirements. A company may espouse fairness to customers but have highly selective credit policies, limited warranties, and few consumer policies. Managers, aware of new market developments, may take advantage of "inside" information to enhance their stockholdings or investments. Surplus company materials may be purchased and resold. What is "right" remains an ever-present problem.

Closely related to "rightness" are the social policies of an organization. How much an organization can afford to pay for the welfare of so-

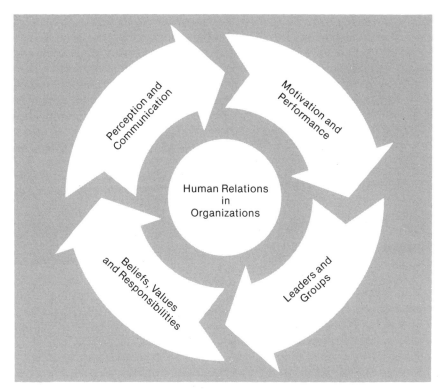

Figure 1.3 Factors affecting human relations in organizations.

ciety as a whole is a pressing problem for many managers. The degree to which companies have responsibilities extending beyond profit, services, and product production is still somewhat unanswered. Do companies need to be concerned with social goals that extend beyond the bounds of the work place? If the answer is yes, then to what degree becomes critically important.

Summary

What, then, can realistically be done to improve managerial effectiveness in its human relations policies and activities? Both theory and practice provide a basis for making rational decisions concerning human behavior in work organizations. As used here, *human relations* is a much broader term than the simple slogan, "Do unto others before they do unto you." It is, we believe, a term describing management actions and decisions that lead to effective performance by all members of a work organization.

    In a very real sense, human relations has been an almost universal concern of humanity from antiquity. Not only places of work, but also

both theory and practice are necessary

whole societies are structured to encourage cooperative, mutually beneficial relationships based on exchange of goods, services, and respect. With few exceptions, most societies recognize that survival is dependent on cooperative effort to achieve common social goals.

Work organizations are dependent on similar conditions. Like societies, they are dependent on employees cooperatively directing efforts toward achieving organizational goals of producing products or services. Management is charged with the difficult responsibility of creating conditions that stimulate effective individual and group performance.

people are dependent on each other It is difficult to overemphasize the necessity for managers to understand the impact of their behavior on others and the way behavior of all people is linked together. The Adinkra tribe of Ghana lives by the slogan "We are linked in both life and death." While the origins of the slogan are lost in antiquity, its meaning is as important to us today as it was to older societies. The Adinkra symbol for human relations is shown in Figure 1.4.

The way employees are linked to each other, their jobs, and their managers involves many complex and frequently misunderstood types of behavior. Managers, with the primary responsibilities for planning, coordinating, organizing, evaluating, and correcting the activities of others, as well as defining the goals that must be attained, frequently have an entirely different point of view than employees. Their concerns encompass more than the immediate job to be accomplished and individual employee problems. Managers tend to be more involved with organizational needs than personal needs. Nonmanagement employees, because of the limits of their authority and responsibility, see their jobs from a much more personal frame of reference. Satisfaction of individual human needs is their primary area of interest.

Figure 1.4 The Adinkra human relations symbol: "We are linked in both life and death."

Effective managers recognize their employees' as well as their own areas of concern. They strive to build relationships of trust, confidence, and understanding that will allow energy to be directed toward achievement rather than conflict.

effective managers are concerned about employee needs

Quick Review

I. Understanding Behavior in Organizations
  A. Knowledge of human behavior at work is made up of both fact and fiction.
  B. Day-to-day experiences teach sets of attitudes, beliefs, and values.
  C. Managers have not yet found the keys to unlock the productive capacities of people.

II. Why People Do What They Do
  A. Association theories are based on the concept that people are conditioned by their environment.
  B. Cognitive theories imply that people not only learn but interpret and choose appropriate responses.
  C. Interaction theories recognize the ways environmental factors affect each other.
  D. Sociobiology centers on the importance of genetic structure and inheritance of abilities.

III. Organizational Trends
  A. Quality of worklife is a major trend throughout the developed world.
  B. Electronic technology is changing the way most work is done.

IV. The Influence of Organizations
  A. During a normal working career, people will have several jobs and will have their attitudes and beliefs partially shaped by their work environment.
  B. The structure of an organization has less influence on behavior than the attitudes, beliefs, and values of its managers.
  C. The skill level, training, and attitudes of the employee and the nature of the job also influence what happens in the work situation.
  D. Job, employee, and manager constantly interact with each other.

V. Linking the Individual and the Organization
  A. Perception can be defined as the way we interpret our experiences.
  B. Our perceptions are, for the most part, learned.
  C. Perception is selective.
  D. Communication also links employees to the organization.

VI. Motivation and Performance
   A. Managers feel employee motivation is a key to organizational success.
   B. In many ways, motivation can be considered the core of human behavior studies.
   C. An understanding of employee needs is a necessary starting point in learning about motivation in organizations.
   D. Frustration and conflict are unavoidable in most work situations.
VII. Working Together—Leaders and Groups
   A. Individual employees are part of both formal and informal groups.
   B. Most people can recognize leaders. There are several kinds of leaders.
   C. In a sense, leadership springs from followers.
   D. Groups, both formal and informal, are major forces in organizations.
   E. Managers who understand group dynamics are more effective than those who don't.
VIII. Beliefs and Realities
   A. Employee performance is often directly related to manager's assumptions.
   B. Power is the degree to which one person influences another person or group.
   C. Power and politics are realities of organizational life.
IX. Change, Values, and Responsibilities
   A. Change is an inevitable consequence of existence.
   B. Companies need managers who have strong skills in managing aspects of change.
   C. Rightness or moral values is a major management concern.
   D. Should companies be concerned with social goals beyond the work place? The issue poses difficult problems for management.

Key Terms

Human relations	Interaction theory	Communication
Behavioral science	Reinforcement	Motivation
Cognitive theories	Quality of worklife QWL	Power
Sociobiology	Perception	

Discussion Questions

1. Why is there such a great deal of wrong information about human behavior?
2. Explain reasons for failure of U.S. organizations to stay competitive with those of Japan and Europe.
3. What factors, in your experience or that of people you know, have led to increased job satisfaction?
4. Are leaders in work situations necessary? Defend your response.
5. How are employees, in most organizations, linked to each other in their jobs?

Case Incidents

Paid to Do Their Jobs

Al Woodward handed a thick folder to Beverly Dunn and breathed a sigh of relief. "Well, it's done and it looks good," he said. Personally, I think it's the best analysis of market trends we've ever done—*and* it's a day ahead of schedule." "Thanks Al," Beverly said smiling, "you did a great job. Tell the crew not only do I appreciate their knocking themselves out over this report, but pizza and drinks will be on the house after work. Wait until Tony Davis sees this!"

"So you finally got it done?" was Tony Davis' first comment when Beverly laid the report on his desk. As marketing director, he relied heavily on Beverly's research section for future sales and advertising planning as well as new product development. "Look Tony, our crew really went to bat over this one, worked overtime, beat the schedule, and did a first-class job," Beverly responded. "Maybe some thanks or appreciation from you is in order." "Now Bev," said Tony, "why baby them? They're paid to do their job, and they did it. I don't see anything special about people doing what they're assigned."

That afternoon Beverly called Al Woodward into her office. "I just told Tony to take this job and fly with it, Al. He didn't give us one word of recognition or appreciation for the future trends report, just like always. It's plain stupidity! In any case, I've recommended you for the job, and I imagine you'll get it." "Don't quit, Bev." Al urged. "We need you." Privately, he made up his mind that if she really left, he'd start looking for another job as well. With his skill, it wouldn't be hard to relocate.

1. Contrast Tony's point of view with Beverly's and Al's. Who was right?
2. Does Tony realize the effect of his attitude on his employees?
3. How do you think Bev's resignation will affect other employees in the market research department?

The Plight of the Promoted

After three hectic years as manager of general employment for Pyrotechnology Corporation's Pine River plant, Patsy Hicks now faces the future with both pride and apprehension. She started with the company as an employment interviewer and was quickly promoted to section supervisor of all nonmangement administrative and clerical employment. Within a year, Patsy was again promoted to manager of general employment. In a large plant with 16,000 full-time employees in many job classifications, it was a demanding, challenging, and sometimes thankless task. Now Bill Murphy, her immediate manager and director of personnel relations, was meeting with her to discuss a needed reorganization.

"We're going to create a new position of general personnel manager," said Bill. "We want you to fill that spot. You can select your successor in the employment department. Five departments now reporting to me will be your new responsibility. One will be your current department. The others are Employee Services and Benefits, headed by Hank Childs; Personnel and Management Development, with Irv Colt; Personnel Records, managed by Sue Green; Personnel Research, headed by Karen Entz; and Professional and Administrative Employment, managed, as you know, by Ken Marty." Patsy took a deep breath. Ken Marty was frequently thought of as the fair-haired boy and in line for the next promotion. "Labor Relations and Wage and Salary Administration will stay with me. Well, what do you think?" asked Bill. Patsy smiled, "It'll be a real challenge and I'm looking forward already to what I'll be doing. Thank you for your confidence in my ability."

After Patsy walked out of Bill's office, she wondered how the news would be received by the other department managers and what kinds of problems she'd be faced with. The more she thought, the larger the problems or reorganization appeared.

1. What do you think Patsy's first major problem will be?
2. What assumptions would you make about Ken Marty's reaction?
3. Although Patsy is not the company's first woman manager at this level in the organization, how do you think employees, both men and women will be likely to react?
4. What do you feel Patsy's first meeting with the department managers reporting to her should be like?

Exercise

Listed below are eight strategies for improving an organization. Rank them in order of importance. Place a *1* by the factor that is most important, a *2* by the factor next most important, and so on. The least important item will be ranked with an *8*.

_____ Hire younger workers who can be easily and quickly trained.

_____ Get rid of older employees and deadwood.

_____ Improve communications between managers and employees.

_____ Develop jobs that are interesting and challenging.

_____ Delegate increased authority and encourage broader responsibility.

_____ Build effective social relationships between managers and employees.

_____ Encourage participation in decision making.

_____ Treat employees fairly, impersonally, and without favoritism.

After you have completed your rankings, compare them with the rankings of other class members, and discuss similarities and differences. How are the rankings related to students' job experiences?

Endnotes

1. Based on a concept developed by D. E. Klinger, *Public Personnel Administration* (Prentice-Hall, 1981).
2. Edward L. Thorndike, *Animal Intelligence* (New York: Macmillan, 1911).
3. Fred Luthans, *Organizational Behavior* (New York: McGraw-Hill, 1981).
4. Albert Bandura, *Social Learning Theory* (Englewood Cliffs: Prentice-Hall, 1977).
5. Edward O. Wilson, *Sociobiology: The New Synthesis* (Cambridge: Harvard University Press, 1975).
6. Adapted from a syndicated news release written by Steve Sonsky of the Knight-Ridder Newspapers, January 1982.

2
Organizations and the Individual

Learning Objectives

After reading this chapter, you should be able to:

1. Understand the concept of interdependence among people and the formation of organizations.

2. Recognize the major forces that influence behavior at work.

3. Realize the impact of organizational size on workers.

4. Define organizational climate and factors that shape climate.

5. Understand the importance of psychological contracts, responsibility, and authority.

6. Recognize the differences in technologies and their effects on people.

7. Describe the difference between executive and associative organizations.

Chapter Topics

People and Organizations

Types of Organizations

Influences of Organizational Structure

Influences of Organizational Size

Organizational Climate

Responsibility, Authority, and Psychological Contracts

Situational Influences

Preview and Self-Evaluation

Major fast food franchisers such as McDonald's, Pizza Hut, and Kentucky Fried Chicken realized several years ago that maintaining consistent quality in thousands of their locations was extremely difficult with independent owner-managers. It became a policy for these companies to buy back franchises, when possible, and to replace owner-operator management with company-trained employees. By doing so, the companies were able to ensure, at least to some degree, that the quality of a hamburger, piece of chicken, pizza, or other food would be nearly identical at each location.

However, even with the most carefully planned controls and ingredients, service, policy, and personnel training, some unwanted differences among company fast food outlets still appear. As Walter McClarin, Personnel Director of the "Blue Diamond" brand of almonds stated, "Most organizations can deal with the technical and material sides of their businesses. It's people that cause problems."

People with their unique personalities and needs are as much a key to the success or failure of an organization as material resources or economic conditions. But the situation is not one way. People influence organizations, yet organizations also change people. Our workplace is one of the most important environments we encounter.

In this chapter we examine some of the characteristics of organizations and how they affect people. Try to answer the following questions before you read the chapter; then, answer them again after you have finished reading.

Answer True or False

1. Most workers today are independent of other employees in the performance of their jobs. T F

2. Employees in small organizations are usually more specialized than those in large organizations. T F

3. As an organization grows, flexibility of individual procedures, decisions, and job methods increases. T F

4. Line organizations are those that contribute directly to an end product or service. T F

5. All work organizations have purposes. T F

6. Organizational climate and morale are the same concept. T F

7. Managers who have high expectations of employee performance tend to support employees' ability to achieve. T F

8. Responsibility and authority are both delegated to employees by higher levels of management or supervision. T F

9. Work relationships between managers and employees are built on what each expects from the other. T F

10. In organizations, power and authority are the same function. T F

ANSWERS: 1. F; 2. F; 3. F; 4. T; 5. T; 6. F; 7. T; 8. F; 9. T; 10. F

People and Organizations

Anthropologists tell us that even primitive human beings banded to- *early group* gether to achieve common goals such as mutual security, gathering and *efforts* distributing food, companionship, and preservation of traditional lifestyles. Early in human history, individuals began to develop specialized skills in making tools, weapons, and pottery, and in healing and storytelling. People learned that survival of the species and, most importantly, an improved and more comfortable life depended not only on their own abilities, but those of others. While the early tribal and extended family organizations were not the same as organizations in which people work today, there is a notable common element: people joining together to accomplish personal and group goals.

most people are interdependent

If we look carefully at organizations, we find that few, if any, people are totally independent of others. Instead, we are interdependent; each person must to some extent rely on others. Most of what we know and what we have is the result of all the knowledge and effort of generations before us. Since organizations seem to be a natural and universal human development, it is helpful to understand some of the characteristics of organizations and their significance to the people within them.

Types of Organizations

organizations influence individuals

When we walk into a library, we automatically lower our voices, talk less, and disapprove of anyone who speaks or laughs loudly. From childhood we have learned that most libraries have rules designed to minimize reader disturbance. We expect people who work in libraries to be quiet, helpful, and by their very actions, to disapprove of noise. Libraries aren't the only organizations that affect behavior in clearly observable ways. People in banks, construction companies, factories, mines, newspaper companies, retail stores, hospitals, or any other of the hundreds of types of organizations, to some extent act, dress, and behave differently. Many factors affect the ways employees act at work. The characteristics of the organization in which they are employed, however, are among the most important influences on their behavior.

coordination and cooperation

In order to understand their influence, it is necessary to examine some of the basic characteristics of work organizations. An *organization* can be defined as a group of people working together in a coordinated effort to accomplish known goals. As used here, the term *coordination* refers to people doing the right things at the right time. *Cooperation* involves the degree to which people help each other achieve the organization's goals. People may be either voluntarily cooperative or cooperative because of rules and direction.

In addition to varying degrees of cooperation and coordination, or their absence, organizations have different primary purposes:

purposes of organizations

1. Product organizations, such as lumber companies, basic chemical producers, toy manufacturers, automobile manufacturers, food processors, and carton manufacturers, to name just a few, are concerned chiefly with converting raw materials into usable forms.
2. Service organizations, typified by stock brokerages, airline companies, and beauty salons, are concerned with assisting, helping, and providing means for more enjoyable or secure living.

3. Some companies provide both products and services through the production of items which they sell, maintain, and train people to use. Prominent exmples are IBM and Xerox.

Another way to look at organizations and some of their complexities is to examine the way an organization actually develops.

Influences of Organizational Structure

After graduating from college with a degree in real estate and passing her state broker's license examinations, Marla Adams decided to go into business for herself rather than seek employment with an established firm. Marla had worked during her college career for two different real estate firms in both sales and office administration. She felt she knew at least the basics of the business. With the help from one part-time employee, Ed James, an accounting major at a local college, Marla had the beginnings of an organizational structure. *Organizational structure*, in this sense, means the arrangement of work in such a way that the objectives of the organization can be effectively accomplished. Structure defines who reports to whom, as well as the major areas of responsibility. Later, we will see that organizational structure has other pupposes as well. A chart of Marla's beginning organizational structure is shown in Figure 2.1.

structure defines relationships

As can be seen, even at this very early stage, several important features of organizational structure are identifiable:

1. Work has been divided in such a way that both people know their primary duties and the duties of the other person in the organization.
2. Both people know what kinds of decisions they are primarily concerned with.
3. A reporting relationship has been established. Each person knows what kind of information the other person in the organization must have to function effectively.
4. From a psychological point of view, Marla and Ed realize that the organization cannot function smoothly unless they both do their jobs well.

Marla Adams	Ed James
Sales	Telephone answering
Financing	Appointments
Contracts	Records
Listings	Bookkeeping

Figure 2.1 Marla Adams' organization: How she and Ed James divide their tasks.

Since Marla and Ed were an effective team, it soon became evident that if there were more people in the organization, the company could increase sales, earn greater profits, and provide broader services to customers. The Adams Realty Company now had three different kinds of objectives, although they were not formally composed or recorded:

1. Operational, defined by the intent to increase sales.
2. Profit, defined by the desire to increase revenue from sales.
3. Service, defined by the desire to provide greater services to customers.

The objectives of Adams Realty, like those of any other organization, have a major influence on the type of structure the organization develops. The life blood of the real estate business is sales. Its organizational structure must support sales activities. The second stage in the development of the Adams Realty resulted in the structure shown in Figure 2.2.

Ed James, after graduating, accepted full-time employment with another firm. Fortunately, Marla was able to convince Carlene Veglia, a trained office management specialist, to join her staff. With the addition of Carlene and new sales personnel, Adams Realty had developed a new structure. Again, we see that work has been divided in two ways: by sales area, to preclude the salespersons from trying to serve the same accounts, and by function. The functions, or activities, performed by the salespeople are distinctly different from those of Carlene or Marla.

When an organizational structure is represented by charts, boxes on the chart (containing names and job titles) define areas of responsi-

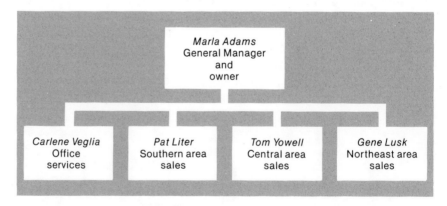

Figure 2.2 Adams Realty: Organizational structure in the second stage.

bility. Lines connecting the boxes represent flow of authority. Both responsibility and authority will be discussed in greater detail later.

Organizations, whether small like Adams Realty or highly complex like IBM, affect the people within them in a number of ways. Research has indicated that the type of organization and skills required to perform a task have strong effects on behavior. Low-skilled jobs where workers are closely supervised and perform repetitive work tend to be less satisfying and may result in high employee turnover. Likewise, many other types of jobs offer little opportunity for personal development of transferable skills and knowledge. In such cases, economic incentives and association with co-workers may be the only attractions of the job. The work itself has little meaning. *influences of type of work*

In contrast, jobs that require substantial training, developed skills, and a large degree of control over assigned work are usually more satisfying. Employees can be strongly attached to their work even if they do not like the organization that employs them. Workers in this category often include computer programmers, nurses, statisticians, law enforcement officers, machinists, accountants, electronic technicians, and other professionals. In all of these fields, the work is controlled to a large extent by the person performing the task rather than by external direction (supervision) or by machines.

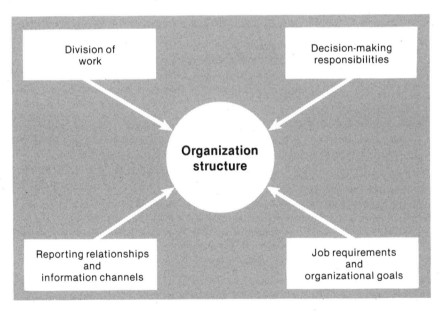

Figure 2.3 Factors affecting the structure of organizations.

The Great Coupon Shuffle

Grocery cooperatives, formed to provide various services for small grocery chains and independent markets, must handle thousands of discount coupons collected from customers by their member stores. Before the coupons can be sent to the issuing manufacturer or processor to be redeemed, they must be sorted according to product and price.

In one major western cooperative, 120 women have the task of sorting these countless coupons into their proper categories. After only six to twelve weeks on the job, most employees quit. People who have worked longer than a year are called "lifers" by other employees.

Management has tried to compensate for the tedious work by raising pay, increasing rest periods, and improving the work stations. These steps have helped slow the rapid turnover, but a worker who has been on the job more than a year is still known as a "lifer."

Influences of Organizational Size

In addition to the type of assigned work, organizational size is another important factor affecting people on the job. If we examine the growth of Adams Realty, we can readily see that Marla's relationship to the people reporting to her changes as the organization grows. Small organizations usually differ from large companies in several ways:

small vs. large organizations

1. Everyone knows everyone else in the organization.
2. Usually, work assignments are highly flexible. Tasks are not greatly specialized.
3. Relationships between managers and employees are more informal.
4. Managers often perform the same types of activities as employees.
5. While there is greater diversity, there is also less opportunity for promotion or the development of highly specialized skills.
6. Small organizations frequently pay less and have fewer employee benefits than do large organizations.

After seven years of operation, The Adams Realty organization shown in Figure 2.4 has 139 full-time employees (number of workers is in parentheses under each major organizational unit). By usual standards, Adams Realty is still a relatively small organization. Because of its increase in size, however, it has developed some characteristics of a larger company:

aspects of larger organizations

1. Increased specialization has occurred.
2. Reporting relationships are more rigidly defined.
3. Marla Adams no longer knows everyone in the organization as well as she could in the beginning.

4. Several of the functions in the organization are ones in which Marla has no expertise.
5. Employees have no need to know and, in fact, have little interest in functions performed by people outside their immediate work group.
6. Each employee is relatively anonymous outside his or her assigned department or section.

There are, however, some positive aspects to larger organizations:

7. There is greater opportunity for promotion by virtue of increased organizational subdivisions.
8. Specialization can lead to increased efficiency within the specialized area as long as employees feel their full potential is being used. Too much specialization leads to dissatisfaction and inefficiency.
9. Employees usually have more complete resources for accomplishing their tasks.

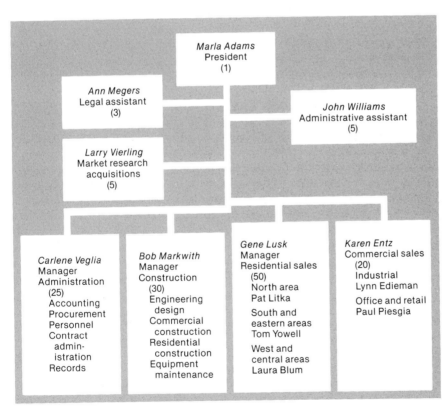

Figure 2.4 Adams' current organizational structure: Numbers in parenthesis represent full-time employees only.

As we can see, the types of activities performed by members of an organization change as the organization grows. When an organization is small, there tends to be greater flexibility in what an individual person does and much less formality than in large organizations. Satisfactions are derived from knowing on a first-name basis everyone in the total work group, and from understanding the functions of other people. If we examine the Adams Realty structure in Figure 2.4, we can see that Marla's tasks have changed dramatically. Even though she may still sell on occasion, she is no longer Marla Adams, real estate salesperson. She is, instead, Marla Adams, manager, concerned primarily with assisting Pat, Tom, Gene, and Carlene in accomplishing their goals and with resolving unusual problems, approving transactions, planning future activities, evaluating and correcting where necessary the performance of her organization as a whole, and projecting through personal contacts her company's image.

Before leaving the structural and size components of the Adams Realty Company, let's take a brief look at the organization from Marla's point of view. As her organization grows, Marla's interpersonal relations with her employees tend to decrease. Any individual employee is only 1/139 of the total organization. Her primary interactions are with her division managers, external contacts (very large accounts, community organization, professional associations, other realtors, etc.), and staff specialists, John Williams and Ann Megers. Organizational units or functions that contribute directly to the primary purpose of the company are called "line" organizations. Those that provide specialized information, advice, or services not directly associated with the end product or service are considered to be "staff." While staff people generally have more daily contacts with the manager, line people have the primary responsibility for achieving the organization's objectives.

From the individual employee's point of view, the organization is, in reality, his or her immediate work unit, including the unit supervisor plus, in some cases, the supervisor's immediate manager. One way to examine this limited employee viewpoint is by the way Ann Stewart, newly employed in residential sales, is affected (Figure 2.5).

As can be seen, Ann is one of 6 people to her immediate supervisor, but to Marla Adams, she is one of 139. In any organization of more than twenty people, there is a certain amount of anonymity. Ann may have seen or perhaps been introduced to Marla Adams, but she does not know a great deal about Marla or other departments of Adams Realty.

A number of inferences can be drawn from the Marla Adams example that are applicable, to some extent, to all organizations:

1. All work organizations have purposes. The purposes, originally defined by the owner or top management, are broadened, interpreted, and developed by others in the organization.
2. "Visibility" of the total organization is difficult for persons at the top and is usually impossible for nonmanagement employees. The

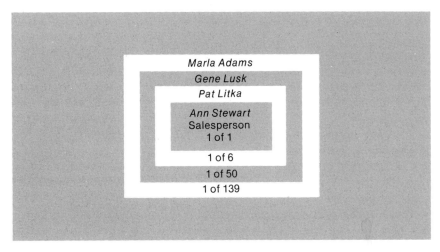

Figure 2.5   Ann Stewart is only 1/139 of Marla Adams staff, 1/50 of Gene Lusk's, 1/6 of Pat Litka's. Each organizational level increases her anonymity in the total organization.

organization is, for the most part, the perceptions an employee has of his or her department. Except at "points of interface," little is known of other segments of the organization.

3. *Points of interface* are those people or functions in other sections or departments that serve as sources of necessary information, material, or approval. If Ann needs information on property appraisal, she calls someone in the property appraisal department for help. The person with whom she communicates her needs (face-to-face, telephone, written memorandum, or indirectly through her immediate supervisor) is a point of interface. Ann's knowledge of the total organization outside her immediate work unit is limited largely to her understanding of the points of interface she uses.

A major difficulty in most large organizations is that employees and many lower-level managers have difficulty understanding the functions of other areas. Employees, like Ann Stewart in sales, may have little knowledge of the contribution employees in procurement, market research, or construction make to the organization's success or failure. They may develop a type of *organizational centrism*, that is, the belief that their part of an organization is the most important one. Maintenance mechanics and their maintenance supervisor may believe that their department is the most essential one in the total organization. No one could work if the maintenance crew failed to replace burned out lights or let waste paper accumulate. Salespeople, technicians, and accountants may all feel the same about their areas. Each thinks his or her department is the glue that holds the entire organization together. In truth, it is held together by all of them.

organizational centrism

Organizational Climate

climate sets the pattern

Most work places develop a distinct personality or climate. Climate may be thought of as the fundamental internal character of an organization that sets the pattern for how things get done. It is the rules of the company game that evolve over the years. Work climate is determined largely by the expectations and attitudes of managers and the reactions of employees to those expectations and attitudes, as the following example shows.

Don Nelson and Alan Yelverton worked part-time for a local brick manufacturer as pallet makers. The pallets were wooden frames on which bricks were stacked for easier loading on and off trucks. Bill Boswell, the pallet area foreman, constantly criticized Don and Alan for not holding their hammers correctly, parking lift trucks too close to their work, and paying too much attention to "them damn college books" during their lunch breaks. Not once did Bill acknowledge that Don and Alan were the best pallet construction team the company had ever employed or that both of them had been just as effective on other assignments in the plant. When pallet lumber arrived one morning, Don and Alan both determined it was three inches shorter than specifications. "O.K., geniuses," said Bill in a loud voice when he saw them discussing the problem, "you guys hop-to." By two o'clock in the afternoon, forty undersized pallets had been constructed. When Bill angrily confronted Don and Alan, they both shrugged and commented, "We were only doing what you told us to do."

organizational climate and individual feelings

If most employees in any part of an organization, whether a section, department, division, or total organization, have similar feelings about the way in which the organization responds to employee needs, we then have a measurement of its organizational climate. Organizational climate encompasses more than individual or group morale, although the two concepts are closely related. Morale is generally considered the extent to which an employee or group of employees feel the goals of the organization are important and the extent to which they are willing to cooperate voluntarily in achieving the organization's goals. Climate concerns the emotional core of an organization. Some

expectations and attitudes affect climate

places of work are cold, formal, and impersonal; some are warm, friendly, and supportive; others are stormy, going from one crisis to another; and still others seem to create a climate of stagnation with no rewards and little punishment. The possible varieties of climate within a work place are almost endless.

However, the major factor in an organization's climate is still management's attitudes and expectations and employee reactions to them. In his early studies of management, Rensis Likert described organizational systems varying from those with little support, employee participation, and trust to those whose basic position involves high degrees of trust, participation, and support.[1] It is our contention that to such positive concepts as trust, participation, and support we must add clarity of objectives and managerial expectations. If, as Douglas McGregor pointed out, managerial expectations and assumptions tend to guide employee feelings about organizations,[2] we can predict critical climate factors by examining the way managerial assumptions and expectations affect employee attitudes and performance.

Managers who have high expectations of employees, based on the assumption that most people are capable, responsible human beings, tend to demonstrate strong support for their employees' ability to achieve. With this type of leadership, employees tend to respond to the positive achievement-oriented climate with both high performance and personal satisfaction.

high expectations tend to result in high performance

Decreases in managerial expectations can result in employees lowering their personal standards; a decrease in trust, supportive supervision, or openness can result in suspicion and hostility. By the same token, the lack of objectives will result in crisis or firefighting organizational climates.

Climate, while important, does not necessarily determine the effectiveness of an organization. External conditions such as the state of the economy, changes in technology, market demands, or relevance of product or service also influence the organization and the effectiveness of its employees. When California's Public Utilities Commission changed its rate structure formula, most customers, especially in rural areas, found their utility bills increasing as much as 300 percent. Within two weeks, Pacific Gas and Electric became the most hated and feared organization in the state. As citizen attacks against the rate hikes in-

Figure 2.6 Factors affecting organizational climate.

creased, employees reacted by becoming very defensive. One mainte-nance mechanic reported, "Yes, we are aware of public opinion. Some of us just don't let anyone know where we work. It's tough to be hated."[3]

mixed climate
common

Under some conditions, a mixed climate is relatively common. Part of an organization may be optimistic, voluntarily cooperative, with an overall "can-do" attitude. Another section or department can be apa-thetic, with little creativity or innovation, yet be able to meet normal job requirements. In a third part of the same organization, we may find general hostility toward work, between managers and employees, and between different functions.

Usually, however, an organization will develop an overall climate generally characteristic of all its parts. A major factor affecting organi-zational climate is the way employees evaluate the status of their as-signments. Also, the degree to which employees are trained and compe-tent can influence organizational effectiveness. Nevertheless, our contention is that the primary organizational lifestyle or climate, while influenced by many factors, is determined primarily by the perceptions employees have of managerial expectations and attitudes, and by their knowledge of the organization's objectives.

Power and Status at the Keyboard

At the independent Data Computing Corporation, computer programmers clearly enjoy the highest status. Their training, skills, and work assign-ments often mean they make key decisions that directly affect customers and other employees. Programmers collaborate with top management and frequently work side-by-side with customers to solve problems. In general, programmers are highly motivated and show strong support for management goals.

At the other extreme, key data entry operators, who type endless reams of statistical data and other material, describe their jobs as tedious and boring, and consider themselves to be in the lowest echelon of the organization.

The most complaints, however, come from computer operators. They continually feed data, monitor production, change tapes and discs, and complete jobs that come to them from programmers. They feel under con-tinual pressure to meet deadlines set by others and claim they are held re-sponsible for errors usually not their fault. Their morale is correspondingly low, and they have little motivation to support company goals.

The climate of each work area within the company is distinctly differ-ent. It is interesting to speculate on the influence of the organization's general manager, who was once a programmer.[4]

Responsibility, Authority, and Psychological Contracts

If we accept an assignment and perform the required tasks, we have acted responsibly. *Responsibility* is a broad term encompassing any act, set of actions, or belief about what we should or should not do. The degree to which we hold ourselves accountable for our actions is one measure of responsibility. In a work organization, responsibilities are defined to a large extent by what we believe the legitimate duties of our job encompass. When we take actions outside either the formally or informally defined areas of our regular assignment, we are assuming responsibilities which may be necessary but which we are not authorized to perform. Some organizations restrict the areas of all employees' responsibilities, while others encourage expansion of responsibilities. To be effective, however, we must also have the authority that is necessary to carry out the responsibilities.

responsibility

Responsibility is tied directly to our own personal value system and the obligations we have accepted. We are limited in exercising our responsibilities unless we also have the authority to obtain necessary resources or assistance. *Authority* can be viewed several ways. In one sense it is the legitimate right to assign work and expect it to be accomplished. Authority can also be viewed as the right to requisition tools and supplies, to sign documents committing the organization's funds, or to delegate actions to others. Often, authority refers to the degree of expertise a person has in a given skill or field of knowledge. There are many definitions of authority, but the common element in all of them is that authority implies influencing the actions or thinking of others. When authority is not recognized or is ignored, there is no influence and consequently no authority. As pointed out by Chester Barnard several years ago, authority, while seeming to flow downward through an organization, also flows upward.[5] It embodies the ancient concept that one can govern only with the consent of the governed.

types of authority

In our society, groups and individuals react to authority in many ways. The traditional "Protestant ethic" stressed, along with hard work, frugality, and individualism, the respect for authority. Even today, large segments of our society stress respect for authority and in many cases, fear of authority. In ancient traditions, the only time a person was involved with higher authority was when punishment or, on rare occasions, reward, was administered. Some managers create the same feelings in employees today, giving rise to fear, suspicion, even hatred of authority. As a reaction to the way authority is often used to subjugate or demean, many employees, especially younger ones, reject and rebel against almost any display of authority. More and more managers are realizing that power and authority, while related, are not necessarily the same. Appropriate use of legitimate authority involves building respect, recognizing organizational functions, and often, de-

reactions to authority

power and authority are not necessarily the same veloping new concepts of managerial roles. Accepting individual differences, recognizing needs, and realizing different employee perceptions all enhance the effective use of authority. Power is derived from the perceived ability to punish, to give rewards, or to influence status, pay, promotion, or longevity.

Psychological Contracts

implied agreements Both employees and employers have certain expectations of each other in the work environment. When an employee knows what the manager expects and the manager knows that the employee understands what is expected, then a psychological contract exists. A *psychological contract* is the unspoken set of implied agreements that relates to a manager's feeling that "if you do your job, you'll be treated as you want to be treated" and an employee's "if you treat me as I want to be treated, I'll do my job."

Work relationships are built on sets of expectations and the degree to which those expectations are fulfilled. In an organization, employees have many expectations:

employee expectations
1. An assignment that demands ability and aptitude.
2. Fair treatment.
3. Acceptance as a person by the immediate supervisor as well as peers.
4. Recognition for accomplishment.
5. Belief in ability to learn, understand, and accept responsibility.
6. High expectations of what can be accomplished given the right assignment, training, and direction.
7. An opportunity to influence decisions through participation or consultation.

Admittedly, not all employees want the same things or have the same expectations. There is, however, strong evidence of needs in a work situation that are closely related to acceptance, self-worth, and personal development, in addition to the desire for material gain. Managers, on the other hand, also have expectations of employees:

what management expects of employees
1. Willingness to perform, to the best of ability, assigned tasks.
2. Voluntary cooperation in identifying and solving problems.
3. Acceptance of personal responsibility.
4. Recognition of legitimate authority.
5. Obedience to established rules and procedures.
6. Ability and willingness to learn.
7. Positive feelings toward the organization and its managers.

42   Chapter 2

Managers, as well as employees, may have other expectations than those listed above. Our concern, however, is that any actions that frustrate either an employee's or manager's expectations will weaken the psychological contract. When expectations of either (or both) parties go unfulfilled, the psychological contract ceases to exist. Absence of the psychological contract results in ineffective work and in feelings of distrust and suspicion on the part of both employee and manager.

As can be readily seen, psychological contracts are closely related to the concept of trust. The degree of trust and confidence employees and managers may have in each other depends on whether each feels the other is supporting the psychological contract. If employees seem unwilling to follow established rules and procedures, accept responsibility, or perform as well as the manager knows they can, the contract is broken; and the manager may no longer trust the employee to complete an assigned task. Managers who are seen as unfair, insincere, unwilling to listen and respond, or as incompetent also break the contract and are not trusted by employees. Without mutual trust and confidence, the primary conditions of an effective psychological contract performance deteriorate. Eventually the organization suffers losses not only in productivity, quality, schedules, and cost, but strong adversarial relationships between managers and employees develop.

trust basis of contract

Some experiments are being made to put psychological contracts into written employee-manager agreements and then require that the two sides meet periodically to see if the contract is working. At this time, such practices are rare. Whether they will become commonplace depends on many changes in the way managers and employees relate to each other. There are indications that in some organizations psychological contracts are discussed but not put in writing. It is a move in the right direction.

written psychological contracts?

Situational Influences

Experience has taught us that the type of technology used, the type of product or service produced, the kinds of people employed, and the attitudes of management all influence the organizational structure and its functions. When viewed this way, organizations are composed of sets of psychological assumptions about the way work should be divided and performed, as well as an analysis of what is necessary to accomplish the organization's tasks. To help managers with their organizational problems, principles have been evolved over the years that apply to most organizations. At one time, it was thought the principles could be used as universal rules. We now know that the type of work and level of employee knowledge and skill, as well as management attitudes and ability, all

psychological assumptions

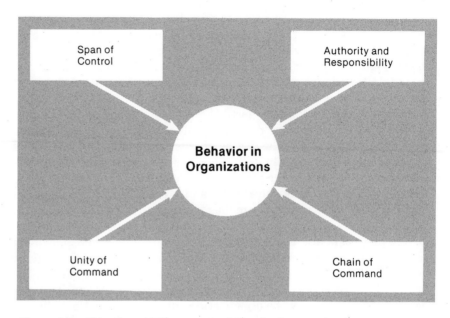

Figure 2.7 Situational influences on behavior in organizations.

affect the way the basic principles are used. Some of the more important organizational principles are listed below:

span of control 1. Span of control refers to the number of people that report to a single manager. The size of a department or section is determined by management's concept of the ideal number of people (or in some cases, functions) one manager can effectively direct. Early management theorists felt that spans of control should be relatively small, in most cases no more than seven to ten employees for each supervisor.

During the past few years, two separate views of span of control have developed. One view advocates a broad span of control or a relatively large number of subordinates reporting to each manager at all levels of an organization. With a broad span of control, individual subordinates are forced to rely to a greater extent on their own decisions and abilities rather than on direction from their immediate superior. Managers with broad spans of control (ten or more subordinates) are forced to rely more on the assumption of responsibility, appropriate exercise of authority, and decisions of individual employees. When spans of control are narrow, managers can interact more directly with their employees and exercise greater control. In either case, the important determinants of span of control remain the nature of the tasks to be performed, the skill and knowledge of employees, and the attitudes of management.

2. Every person in an organization needs to know to whom he or she reports and what that person's scope of authority encompasses as well as the area of responsibility. As organizations increase in size, the number of divisions of work and the number of organizational layers tend to increase. When work is divided into specialized areas, as in Marla Adams's case, and similar functions such as products, services, programs, or processes are grouped together in a logical manner, we see the organizational principle of *departmentation.* If departments are grouped together into divisions, we then have another layer of management. Each layer represents a step in a hierarchy or *scalar chain.* *authority and responsibility*

The position a person holds in the scalar chain represents his or her authority, status, power, and area of responsibility.

3. Unity of command refers to the principle that no employee should be required to report to more than one superior for instructions and evaluation of performance. In modern organizations, employees in many types of assignments find that, although there is a person to whom they administratively report, there are many people whom they must please, take direction from, and respond to in order to accomplish their assigned tasks. Although somewhat altered in its application, the principle of unity of command is still a necessary component of organizations. It provides the stability of knowing where the buck really stops as far as individual work is concerned. *unity of command*

4. Among the many other principles defined by early management students are chain of command, or lines of reporting and accountability; delegation to the lowest level capable of making the correct decision or taking the correct action; and organization balance, the concept that each organizational segment should have equal influence if not equal size with other organizational units. Perhaps most important, however, is the concept that the organization must have clearly defined and well-known objectives. *chain of command, delegation, organizational balance*

Current management thinking does not invalidate any of the early or classical principles but applies them with selective emphasis dependent on the type of work, objectives, skill, and knowledge of employees, and beliefs of the organization's managers. As conditions change, so do organizational formats and their influence on the organization's core of existence, its employees.

A Final Thought

Dr. Austin Gerber, dean of the School of Business at Sacramento State University, has pointed out that organizations ultimately develop an *executive* or *associative style.*[6] Executive organizations are those that *executive and associative organizations* stress control, precision, and direction from the top. Associative companies, on the other hand, tend toward participation, individual responsibility, and reliance on informal systems. Both systems work. The effectiveness and conditions under which each operate are the subject of later discussions. We feel that modern management, however, is constantly torn between the philosophy of each system. As organizations grow in size and complexity, philosophical decisions about which systems help employees become more effective are increasingly difficult to make.

We have seen that organizations vary in size, purpose, complexity, and design. Yet it is through organizations that most meaningful work is accomplished. It is through the common efforts of people working together that the world is supplied with its needs and is changed. Whether we, as individuals, like or dislike the organizations with which we are associated is immaterial. The fact remains that these directed group efforts enable us to survive.

In an era that is witnessing the growth of new technologies—such as the automated office, increasingly sophisticated communication technology, robotics in nearly all phases of routine work, combined with massive social and economic change—work organizations require employees to be more adaptable, creative, and innovative than ever before. We live in an exciting and challenging historical period of organizational life.

Quick Review

    I. Types of Organizations
       A. The way people act at work is influenced by the type of organization to which they belong.
          1. Societal expectations, job demands, public image, and peer acceptance help shape behavior in organizations.
          2. Type, size, structure, methods of control, authority relationships, and climate are all important organizational characteristics.
       B. Major types of organizations include those that produce products, those that provide services, and those that provide both products and services.
    II. Influences of Organizational Structure
       A. Organizational structure is defined as the way work can be arranged to accomplish the objectives of the organization.

B. Some of the important structural considerations include:
  1. Division of work
  2. Decision-making level
  3. Reporting relationships
  4. Everyone knowing his or her job and reporting relationship
C. Organizational objectives include those that are operational, profit oriented, and service oriented.
D. On an organizational chart, boxes represent areas of responsibility; lines represent the way authority is delegated.
E. Organizations can be structured according to geographic area, type of product, customer, process, or programs.
F. Variations of organization are almost endless.

III. Influences of Organizational Size
A. As organizations grow larger, they change in several ways.
B. Staff refers to advisory, informational, or specialized services to management. Line refers to the segments of the organization that actually produce products or service.
C. All organizations have purposes.
D. Employees have "visibility" and recognize points of interface.

IV. Organizational Climate
A. Organizational climate includes more than morale.
B. Organizational climate includes managerial expectations, trust, support and openness, and clarity of objectives.

V. Responsibility, Authority, and Psychological Contracts
A. Responsibility involves acceptance of an obligation to perform.
B. Authority involves the right to act, decide, or delegate without prior approval.
C. Psychological contracts involve the expectations of the employee interacting with the expectations of management.
D. Both managers and employees have expectations. Unfulfilled expectations can weaken or nullify the psychological contract.

VI. Situational Influences
A. Classical principles include span of control, departmentation, scalar chain, chain of command, organizational balance, and development of clear objectives.

B. No two organizations apply organizational principles in precisely the same manner.

VII. Final Thought

A. Organizations evolve into primarily executive or associative patterns. Both work.

B. Meaningful work and, indeed, human survival is dependent upon organizations.

Key Terms

Organization

Coordination

Organizational structure

Objectives

Points of interface

Line and staff functions

Organizational centrism

Organizational climate

Responsibility

Authority

Psychological contracts

Departmentation

Scalar chain

Executive and associative styles

Discussion Questions

1. Describe some major differences between two organizations with which you are familiar.
2. Why are organizations different in their style and structure?
3. What influence does the chief executive of an organization have on the organization's climate?
4. Explain the difference between authority and responsibility in work organizations.
5. How will increased utilization of computers affect employees in small businesses?

Case Incidents

The Right Ingredients for Success

Nancy Ribody and John Crago had become acquainted during an evening management class at a local college. They were both experienced in bakery operations and, after some discussion, pooled their resources to open a small store specializing in French, Belgian, and Swiss pastries. John cooked, waited on walk-in customers, and with part-time help ran the bakery while Nancy concentrated on sales to restaurants and hotel dining establishments.

As their outside and in-house sales increased, they realized they could easily double their business by hiring more permanent employees, opening new locations, and perhaps expanding into other cities. Since their first venture was successful, obtaining additional money was not a problem.

Their primary concern was to maintain the quality that had built their company's reputation and established long-lasting relations with their customers. To achieve their goal, they were required to do some careful planning.

1. What are Nancy and John's first planning steps?
2. How can they ensure that their quality standards will be met in new stores?
3. What types of problems will they probably encounter?

Your Replacement

Dorothy Curtis is a branch manager for the city credit union with two assistant managers working for her. She is to be promoted to a position in the main office as soon as she can find a person to fill her position. Dorothy's boss has told her that she should select one of her assistant managers. In her opinion, neither of her assistants has shown any leadership ability or desire to manage on his own. When she talks to her assistants, each indicates that he is not interested in assuming the responsibility for decisions that the branch manager's job requires. They enjoy their current positions and do not have any desire for promotion.

1. Why would an employee not want to be promoted?
2. Would it be desirable for Ms. Curtis to try to convince one of them to take the job, even though she thinks he is not qualified, so that she may be promoted.
3. Why would her boss want her to select one of her employees?
4. Should she try to convince her boss that her employees are not capable and do not want the position? If so, how?
5. Other than promoting her subordinates, what alternatives could she suggest to her boss for filling the position?

The Employee Who Can't Make Decisions

Louis Alvarez supervises six tellers in a savings and loan company. The tellers handle opening accounts, deposits, withdrawals, and loan payments. Since the tellers are in constant contact with customers, they can have a substantial effect on customer satisfaction. Almost all of the complaints that Mr. Alvarez receives are about the way Don Holt, one of the tellers, treats customers.

When a customer asks Don a question, he goes to Mr. Alvarez to check on the answer. If Mr. Alvarez is busy, Don keeps the customer waiting until he can check with someone else. Don checks with Mr. Alvarez even on minor details related to his job. Don's dependence on Mr. Alvarez has been increasing, and he wants approval for decisions that other tellers can make on their own. Don is consuming a great deal of Mr. Alvarez's time by checking and double checking to see that everything is being done exactly the way it should.

Don appears to have a strong desire to do a good job. He is always at work on time, is very polite, dresses exceptionally well, and tries to cooperate with everyone.

1. What are some possible explanations for Don Holt's dependence on Mr. Alvarez to make decisions?
2. Would it be desirable for Don Holt to be moved to a different type of job?
3. What can Mr. Alvarez do to help Don make decisions on his own?
4. Is this situation an individual problem or an organizational problem?

Exercises

1. List the kinds of organizations represented by members of your class.

2. Which of these organizations are liked or disliked the most by the employees?

3. On the basis of other students' experiences, what factors can you identify that make some organizations more satisfying to employees than others?

4. List three jobs you think would be interesting and three you would dislike, then ask three other students to do the same. Compare their lists to your own. Are there any similarities? Any major differences?

Endnotes

1. Rensis Likert, *The Human Organization* (New York: McGraw-Hill, 1977).
2. Douglas McGregor, *The Professional Manager* (New York: McGraw-Hill, 1967).
3. *Time*, 22 March 1982, p. 58.
4. Based on interview with manager of Independent Data Computing Company (fictitious name, facts are correct), February 1982.
5. Chester Barnard, *The Function of the Executive* (Cambridge, Mass.: Harvard University Press, 1938).
6. Based on speech delivered to California Business Educator's Association. Lake Tahoe, April 14, 1980.

3 Management and Organizations

Learning Objectives

After reading this chapter, you should be able to:

1. Describe how organizations influence the lives of individuals.

2. Discuss changing attitudes toward work and resulting problems for organizations.

3. List the characteristics of bureaucratic organizations.

4. Describe the advantages and disadvantages of bureaucratic organizations.

5. Identify challenges faced by organizations and the type of actions required to meet the challenges.

6. Discuss the responsibilities of management.

Chapter Topics

The Influence of Organizations

People Problems in Organizations

Employee Attitudes

Challenges Faced by Organizations

Management Responsibility

Preview and Self-Evaluation

Louis Salazar had been a supervisor in the computer center of a large state university for five years. The university's rigid procedures and regulations became so frustrating that he decided to look for a position in private business. With his outstanding experience and educational background, he obtained a job supervising the data processing for a bank. After a month on the new job, he stopped by the university to see a management professor that he had frequently complained to about the bureaucratic operation of the university. Louis said, "I left the university to escape restrictive rules and unreasonable procedures, but my new job is even worse. The bank's operating procedures are an end in themselves rather than a means to achieve objectives. I spend all my time fighting red tape while trying to develop an effective data processing system. I thought it would be different in private business."

Louis's complaint is one commonly heard from employees who feel they must "fight" the organization to do an effective job. In order to understand the factors that influence Louis's attitude toward organizations, it is necessary to examine the managerial approaches and organizational policies that shape the work environment. Chapter 3 reviews some of the influences and problems that are encountered by employees and managers.

Before reading this chapter, try answering the true-false questions to test your perceptions. After reading the chapter, check the questions again and see if your perceptions are the same.

Answer True or False

1. Even though organizations satisfy many needs, we are actually becoming less dependent on organizational structures. T F

2. The effectiveness management has in organizations has no direct impact on our quality of life. T F

3. There are some management systems that work in every type of situation. T F

4. The desire of employees to be involved in decisions about working conditions has been continually decreasing. T F

5. The emphasis on satisfying the psychological needs of employees will probably decrease in the future. T F

6. The bureaucratic model originally was developed as an improvement over earlier management systems. T F

7. Although efficiency is an element in productivity, it is often achieved at the expense of individual motivation and pride in work. T F

8. In bureaucratic organizations there is usually very little specialization by individuals. T F

9. A narrow view of responsibility sees management focusing on day-to-day problems and responding to immediate crises. T F

10. The social-psychological changes occurring in organizations have a greater impact than mechanical and technical changes. T F

ANSWERS: 1. F; 2. F; 3. F; 4. F; 5. F; 6. T; 7. T; 8. F; 9. T; 10. T

The Influence of Organizations

It is one of the central features of an industrial society that most of its productive work is carried out in organizations. There is a real discontinuity in our complex society between the places where we work for a living, and the places where we find our recreation, social activities, and family life. Our productive labor is, almost without exception, carried out in some kind of organization as owner, manager, or employee.[1]

Everyone's life is continually influenced by organizations. Each day individuals have contacts with numerous organizations with varied purposes and functions. The organizations that make up our society are large and small, formal and informal, and those with widely varied objectives, such as religious, economic, educational, governmental, social, military, and political organizations.

contributions of organizations

Organizations have made possible many of the major advances in civilization. It has been through organized effort that we have achieved better health care and extended the human life span. Organizations make it possible to provide an ever-expanding range of goods and services, from automobiles and professional sports to fire and police protection. We work and play in an environment that is dominated and continually influenced by organizations. People are, at least partially, products of the organizations that influence them. Organizations affect the way people dress, what they eat, where they travel, their attitudes and values, and their individual aspirations. The effectiveness of the management in organizations has a direct impact on our quality of life.

people are an organization's greatest asset

An organization's greatest asset can be its people. One of the primary responsibilities of management is to create conditions that will maximize the productivity of people. In business, government, and nonprofit organizations, human resources are often not used effectively. Many organizational problems can be traced to people and people problems.

Contemporary man was man-in-organizations. If the 19th century was the age of the individual, then the 20th century is essentially concerned with the emergence of organizations. Modern man is only too aware of the ambivalent sensation of living and working in an organization, of being organized and organizing.[2]

People Problems in Organizations

Skill in human relations has increasingly become an essential ingredient for effective management. The emphasis on satisfying the psychological needs of employees will probably become stronger in the future. The desire of employees to be involved in decisions about working conditions has been continually increasing.

There are many approaches that can be taken in managing people in the work environment. There is no known management approach or system that will work with everyone or in every type of situation. As has been pointed out,

no one type of management is best for all situations

> you should be wary of "getting religion" or adopting one managerial approach and rejecting the rest. If you find yourself doing this, it will be because you are paying more attention to your own experiences (or problems) than you are to the study of various alternatives for a particular organization with which you must deal in the future. There is not now, nor probably ever will be, any one technique of management which is best over periods of time and for diverse organizations.[3]

More people than ever before seem to believe organizations are becoming their masters. Many people resent the power and influence of organizations and feel they threaten individual freedom and dignity. Problems of the effective use of human resources will always be a concern of managers.

are organizations becoming our masters?

Robert Townsend, former president of Avis Rent-A-Car Company, provided the following comment on the problem of the use of people in organizations:

> In the average company the boys in the mailroom, the president, the vice-presidents, and the girls in the steno pool have three things in common: they are docile, they are bored, and they are dull. Trapped in the pigeonholes of organization charts, they've been made slaves to the rules of private and public hierarchies that run mindlessly on and on because nobody can change them.[4]

Even with all the problems that face organizations today, we are using organizations to satisfy more of our needs, and we are becoming more dependent on complex organizational structures. "It has been demonstrated throughout human history that most individuals can achieve more of their goals or achieve them faster, easier, more completely, or more efficiently through organizations."[5]

we use organizations to satisfy our needs

John D. Rockefeller concisely stated the importance of skill in human relations when he said, "I will pay more for the ability to deal with people than any other ability under the sun."[6]

To be effective, managers must understand human behavior in organizations and must be aware of approaches that will maximize the productivity of people. While the effective use of human resources does not constitute the entire area of management, it is a vitally important aspect of any manager's job.

Employee Attitudes

One of the most critical problems faced by many organizations is the changing attitude toward work. This change in attitude is demonstrat-

*changing
attitudes toward
work*
ed by the experience of a personnel manager in a large manufacturing company. While interviewing a recent high school graduate who had expressed an interest in going to work, he asked the graduate what type of work he wanted. The graduate replied, "What's available in management?" The interviewer indicated that there were no positions open in management, but that there were openings for production workers. The individual expressed his rejection of the possibility of working in production by replying, "No thanks, man. Those are nothing jobs." Managers are finding that an increasing number of individuals refuse to accept what *they* define as "nothing jobs."

unsatisfied needs
Many managers face the problem of developing methods to motivate employees *they* have classified as stubborn, apathetic, and unproductive. Although some problems in productivity result from younger workers questioning traditional work values, productivity problems can also be attributed to organizational practices, as is pointed out by Steers.

> ". . . it appears that younger workers have not lowered the value they place on hard work. Instead, they generally want to contribute to organizations in meaningful ways and get frustrated by what they perceive as bureaucratic or needless hurdles to their effective job performance."[7]

"Problem employees" are trying to tell management something, but often they feel that management is not listening. When management does listen, employees may believe that management is not willing to take any action. These employees are usually *not* asking to "do their thing without contributing to the organization"; they are *not* asking for a "nice and polite supervisor." Their major unsatisfied needs will not be met by more fringe benefits. Many employees are saying, "Let me be involved in achieving meaningful and challenging goals," "Use my time and ability well," and "Let me do responsible and meaningful work."

"nothing jobs"
The number of "nothing jobs" appears to be increasing in many organizations. These jobs may have been designed to develop more efficient production in industries making use of rapidly expanding technology. Under pressure to reduce costs, the efficiency experts may break jobs down into smaller and smaller units, creating the "nothing job." The *nothing job* exists where the individual has no planning or controlling functions. Often, these functions are stripped away from the job under the assumption that this will lead to more efficiency. In many cases, however, there is an increase in efficiency without an increase in the overall effectiveness of the organization.

efficiency
Likewise, it is often assumed that efficiency is the key to achieving organizational objectives and making higher "profits." Managers are trained to plan and control the performance of workers. Although effi-

ciency is an element in productivity, it may be achieved at the expense of employee motivation and pride in work done. Ineffective use of human resources may result in increased turnover, a lower quality of workmanship, a lower output, and increased downtime. The effective organization maximizes the use of individual abilities (effectiveness) rather than simply attempting to make individuals more efficient.

Efficiency or Effectiveness?

A well-known story tells of Henry Ford's experience with an efficiency expert he hired to evaluate Ford Motor Company.

After analyzing the company operations, the efficiency expert made a very favorable report to Henry Ford with the exception of the activity of one individual. The expert reported, "There's a man down the hall who's wasting your money. Every time I've gone by his office, he's just sitting with his feet on the desk."

Henry Ford's reply to the expert was: "That man once had an idea that saved us millions of dollars. At that time his feet were right where they are now."

The Bureaucratic Model

The concept of the *bureaucratic model* was formed during the Industrial Revolution. Early in the revolution, "management" was criticized for nepotism, cruelty, and whimsical and subjective judgments. Thus, the need for order in the organizations and the workers' demands for impartial treatment shaped the bureaucratic model. The purpose of the bureaucratic model is to provide a framework for organizing and directing various business activities. The bureaucratic model stresses the following features:

characteristics of bureaucratic organizations

1. A rigorous chain of command, usually structured as a pyramid.
2. Extreme specialization and division of labor in all tasks.
3. A set of procedures and rules specifying actions for all situations related to work activities.
4. Selection and promotion of employees based on technical competence.
5. General impersonality in regard to human relations.

This model leads to the development of well-defined functional specialization with control exercised through the formal hierarchy of authority. The bureaucratic organization tends to have rigid structures developed to provide better control and to promote efficiency. The characteristics of the bureaucratic organization can lead to the following negative results:

- limiting the organization's ability to meet changing conditions because it lacks flexibility and adaptability.
- reducing inventiveness and creativity.
- developing functional specialists who may become isolated without making effective contributions to the achievement of organizational goals.
- increasing downtime because the formal control by the hierarchy forces employees to wait for a decision to be passed down from the top.

advantages of bureaucratic hierarchy

The hierarchy of the bureaucratic model has certain well-accepted advantages, as shown in Figure 3.1. Discipline is usually good and routine procedures are well controlled. If the top manager is exceedingly strong, he or she can make the whole organization respond quickly. The hierarchy takes time to develop, but once established, is exceedingly effective for controlling large numbers of people.

disadvantages of bureaucratic hierarchy

Figure 3.1 also lists bureaucratic weaknesses. "Grave disadvantages" of the hierarchy are cited by Anthony Jay in *Management and Machiavelli*. One disadvantage is "its depressing effect on the human spirit."

> A man strives for promotion and reward and success up to a certain point, but, earlier or later, almost all realize that whatever they do they are not going to get much further. They then change from aiming at the maximum possible to the minimum excusable; their ingenuity and energy are converted from the task of getting more power and money to that of giving less time and effort.[8]

A second disadvantage cited by Jay is that the hierarchical system grows rigid with time:

> The hierarchic system enshrines and sanctifies the qualities that brought that success in the past, and continues to search for and promote men with those qualities even when circumstances have changed and different qualities are needed.[9]

Such a system has a tendency to inhibit and discourage flexibility, adaptability, and change. It is this environment that may produce the "problem" employee.

motivation problems

As problems of motivating employees arise in a bureaucratic organization, often the response is to develop fixed systems of rights, duties, and procedures. These fixed systems limit the individual's freedom on the job and in many cases reduce commitment to the job and to

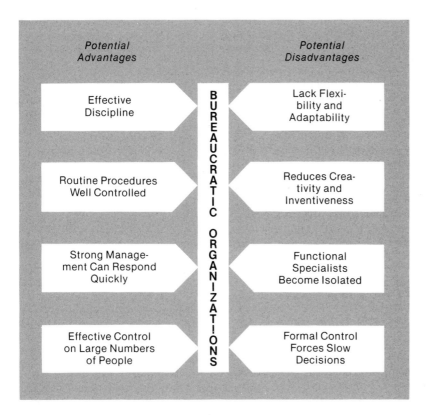

Potential
Advantages

Potential
Disadvantages

Effective
Discipline

Lack Flexi-
bility and
Adaptability

Routine Procedures
Well Controlled

Reduces Crea-
tivity and
Inventiveness

Strong Manage-
ment Can Respond
Quickly

Functional
Specialists
Become Isolated

Effective Control
on Large Numbers
of People

Formal Control
Forces Slow
Decisions

BUREAUCRATIC ORGANIZATIONS

Figure 3.1 Potential advantages and disadvantages of
bureaucratic hierarchy.

the organization. Under the fixed system, individuals "go by the book"
and have no incentive to improve methods for reaching organizational
goals.

The Conflict Between Individuals and Organizations

One approach taken to deal with the problems of individual versus organization in the bureaucratic model is to develop an impersonal approach to human relations. Managers become impersonal in their dealings with employees and attempt to ignore individual differences and
focus on the task accomplishments. This leads to individual dissatisfaction, because the employees feel that the organization is impersonal
and is using them like a machine. Under these conditions it is almost
impossible to obtain cooperation and coordination among individuals
and groups within the organization.

   Creating more bureaucratic organizations does not seem to be a
fruitful approach in using and challenging the potential of human be-

*an approach to
deal with conflict*

new approaches
are needed to
develop human
potential

ings. New approaches and different models are needed if organizations are going to become more effective. More productive organizations must be based on more productive individuals. Some poeple are realizing that organizations have not used them well. They are refusing to accept the role of a machine-like object to be used as a factor of production. In a changing social and psychological environment, organizations are faced with individuals who are demanding that their importance as human beings be recognized. Individuals are examining their roles in society and in organizations. They are questioning whether they are using their potential for creativity, productivity, and achievement. In the absence of opportunities to use their potential, employees may engage in unproductive behaviors.

It is not difficult to find examples of undesirable behavior in organizations. Where there is a lack of respect for employees, energy may be devoted to "playing games" rather than achieving objectives and solving problems. Individuals become status seekers, and the status seekers become status symbol seekers. Politicking turns into a game of destructive competition that prevents effective achievement.

management
attitudes

Many difficulties in motivating individuals in organizations can be traced to management assumptions that people are inherently bad. When organizations develop tight controls to limit, push, check upon, inhibit, and punish individuals, these controls are usually based on the assumption that people are evil, lazy, destructive, and irresponsible. Employees will recognize these attitudes and may behave very much in the way the manager assumed they would. As a result employee behavior may arise partially from management expectations and partially from resentment.

To help prevent lazy, destructive, and irresponsible behavior, managers must change their attitudes about the nature of their employees and the manner in which the organization influences on-the-job behavior.

Challenges Faced by Organizations

The conflict between the changing values toward work and adherence to the bureaucratic model points to the need for change in management practices. This conflict, coupled with the rapid state of technological growth, is forcing most organizations to change their structures, management practices, and work procedures.

competition

The problems for organizations using outdated machines and production processes are heightened by more intense competition. Competition is increasing for both the customer's dollar and for skilled workers. Also, the cost of labor has been rapidly accelerating, which places additional pressure on organizations to use their human resources effectively.

These *social-psychological* changes occurring are now having a greater impact on many organizations than mechanical and technical changes. Organizations are becoming more involved in the total environment in which they operate. Pollution, housing, education, civil rights, and other problems of the quality of life are becoming major concerns. These challenges will become increasingly important in the future. Organizations must deal effectively with the emerging challenges if they are to remain viable in a rapidly changing society. The challenges faced by organizations are illustrated in Figure 3.2.

challenge of rapid change

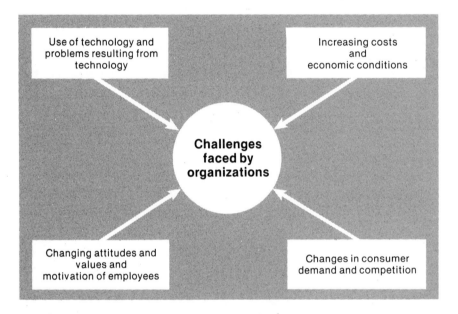

Figure 3.2 Challenges faced by organizations.

The Effective Organization's Reaction to Challenges

To meet the challenges of the future, organizations will need to use creative planning approaches. To meet the demands of rapid change, managers must effectively use both short- and long-range planning. Managers need to approach all plans with the attitude that critical analysis must be made from time to time. It is clear that fixed plans for a five- or ten-year period may not be valid without continuous revisions.

planning

Systems of organization must be developed that foster cooperation with organizations. To obtain cooperation and commitment within the organization, managers need to develop methods that will involve employees in more planning and organizing activities. Management must ask itself, Is the organization related to individual employees in such a way to produce meaningful goals and objectives that can lead to long-term commitments by the individuals in the organization?

communication Successful motivation of individuals in organizations requires the establishment of continual and open communication among individuals and between groups. To achieve organizational goals, individuals need to be able to communicate across organizational lines without being blocked by rigid structures and status barriers.

adaptation Most organizations are extremely complex systems that deal with complex problems. Instead of looking for "quick-fix" solutions to problems, managers must identify and solve their underlying causes. It is better to deal with real causes than to try to simplify management processes to a set of "management rules." Searching for absolute principles of management that will work in every situation does not lead to more effective management. Effective management requires that knowledge about organizations be adapted to specific situations to meet the requirements of complexity and change (see Figure 3.3).

> More effective organizations are made about interested and able people; in small, freely communicating, face-to-face groups; under articulated and dedicated leadership; deeply committed to a clear and challenging objective and thoroughly involved in solving the problems which stand in the way of achieving the objectives.[10]

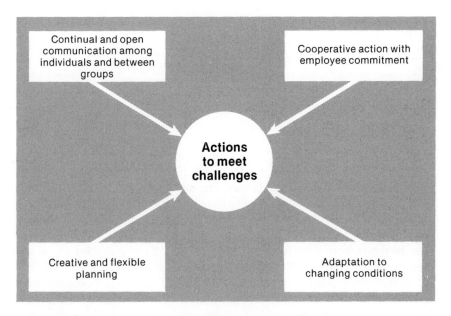

Figure 3.3 Actions to meet organizational challenges.

Management Responsibility

There are those who hope that the area of management responsibility will someday stabilize into a set of well-defined activities. It might be desirable if the manager's role and responsibilities were simple to understand and easy to communicate. Presently, the hope for such universally agreed upon definitions appears to be an unrealistic dream.

As long as changes are taking place in the environment within which organizations operate, there will be corresponding changes in responsibility that management must assume. Social and legal changes taking place in society force the modification of management's responsibilities both inside and outside the organization.

change is continual

A narrow view of responsibility sees management performing specific activities, such as solving day-to-day problems or completing weekly production reports. The broader view of responsibility sees management creating opportunities and anticipating future problems.

Responding to Needs—A Narrow View of Responsibility

A "respond to needs" approach assumes that management's responsibility is limited to regulating and controlling the activities that take place within the organization. The purpose of regulation is to promote efficiency in the accomplishment of tasks. This implies a sound decision-making approach to recurring problems. When problems arise in the organization, management responds by defining and implementing corrective measures. This "reactive" approach concentrates on eliminating activities that violate organizational policies and procedures. In short, management's primary responsibility is to make employees more productive by eliminating problems as quickly as they present themselves.

Management views its role *as the result of* economic development and financial conditions. A narrow view of responsibility encourages management to be primarily or exclusively concerned with the economic activities involved in making a profit or meeting budget requirements. Of course, management must meet the economic and financial responsibilities required by the organization, but the manager who is concerned only with financial activity has defined management narrowly.

The range of activities that a manager is responsible for varies in different organizations and in different positions within an organization. A manager's responsibility may range from directing the accomplishment of known and well-defined tasks to the broadest possible responsibilities of creativity and innovation.

Creating Opportunities—A Broad View of Responsibility

Management's responsibility may be broadly defined to include the achievement of organizational objectives relating to internal operation and the external effects the organization has on society. A broad definition of management's role would include responsibility for the "quality of life" in the organization. Improving the quality of life in an organization would include responsibility for adapting the organization's structure to the needs, aspirations, and potential of individuals.

management should create opportunities

Management can be viewed as a subculture with its own systems of values and beliefs. If the management subculture's values are broad in scope, there is a focus on innovation and creativity, such as the discovery and application of new knowledge to increase productivity.

Rather than merely responding to situations as they occur, management would concentrate on creating opportunities in the environment in which the organization functions. Economic and social development in our society are the result of the management of the organizations that we depend on for goods and services. Table 3.1 summarizes both broad and narrow approaches to defining management responsibilities.

Table 3.1 Management responsibilities

Narrowly defined (responds to needs)	Broadly defined (creates opportunities)
Responsible for economic and financial activity	Responsible for the "quality of life" in an organization
Responsible for responding to changes in economic and social conditions	Responsible for the economic and social impact of the organization
Responsible for directing employee activity to provide goods and services	Responsible for discovering and applying new knowledge to increase the quality and quantity of output
Responsible for solving problems that occur in the organization	Responsible for designing creative and innovative systems that prevent problems from occurring
Responsible for adapting and training individuals to serve organizational needs	Responsible for development of the organization to utilize the potential of individuals

Employee Relations Philosophy at Nucor Corporation

Employee relations, general management methods, and productivity bonuses at Nucor Corporation have sparked the company's spectacular growth. From 1974 to 1980, sales have increased by 600 percent while profits have risen a whopping 1,500 percent. A multi-million dollar steel manufacturing firm, Nucor has developed a philosophy of employee relations based on four primary components:

1. First and foremost, management must provide employees with the opportunity to earn according to their productivity.
2. The company must be managed so that employees will feel that if they are doing their jobs properly they will have a job tomorrow.
3. Employees must feel that they are being treated fairly.
4. Employees must have an avenue of appeal if they are being treated unfairly.

Nucor's philosophy is reflected in many ways through its management policies. For example, all employees from the president down have the same benefit plan in areas of insurance, vacations, and holidays. The success of Nucor's employee relations has been attributed to the high degree of mutual respect and confidence between employees and managers. As recognition of Nucor's success, it was selected by NBC to be included in a 1980 documentary on productivity entitled, "If Japan Can, Why Can't We?"

The experience of Nucor is a demonstration of the willingness of American employees to work, and the effects of a progressive human relations management policy.[11]

Easier Said than Done

Practices and techniques of management are relatively easy to write about, but effective implementation is difficult and time-consuming. Philosophies and theories of management are more highly developed than are the procedures and methods for their implementation in organizations. For the effective operation of any management system, it is necessary that organizational environment be supportive of management systems and practices. One of the most difficult problems in management is to develop practices and policies within an organization that are consistent with each other. With economic, political, and social changes requiring rapid changes in organizational policies, inconsistencies can easily occur. Effective management requires that practices be flexible enough to be adapted according to the changing requirements of the organization.

effective management requires flexibility

The potential for more effective management is unlimited. Most organizations find that they must continually adapt and modify their management practices to meet the challenges of an ever-changing environment. The future effectiveness of organizations will depend on the application of a broad spectrum of management concepts and practices.

Quick Review

I. The Influence of Organizations
   A. Organizations continually influence everyone. They have many purposes and are formal as well as informal, large as well as small.
   B. Organizations have made possible much of human progress. They affect most aspects of our lives.
   C. People are a major asset, expense, and source of problems for managers of organizations.

II. People Problems in Organizations
   A. There is no known management style or system that works equally well for all people in every type of situation.
   B. Organizations are becoming more complex, and people are increasingly dependent on organizations to satisfy their needs.
   C. Effective human relations is a vital part of successful management.

III. Employee Attitudes
   A. Employees want meaningful work with more responsibility and more challenge.
   B. Managers develop "nothing jobs" to achieve efficiency and thus kill motivation and pride.
   C. The bureaucratic model of organization, with its emphasis on hierarchy and authority, while effective in controlling, is usually ineffective in development of individual initiative.
   D. To help prevent lazy, destructive, and irresponsible behavior, managers must change their attitudes about both people and organizational influences.

IV. Challenges Faced by Organizations
   A. Social-psychological as well as technical and competitive changes provide important challenges to managers.
   B. New and creative management approaches are necessary for effective adaptation to organizational changes.
   C. There are no set of rules or principles that will help management as much as open-minded examination of everyday realities and adaptation to complexity and change.

V. Management Responsibility
   A. The narrow view of management responsibility is largely "reactive." It views management as responding to day-to-day needs and activities.
   B. A broad view of management responsibilities focuses on innovation and creativity—prevention as well as cure.
   C. While it is easy to write about management problems, the realities of the work environment are very complex. A broad spectrum of concepts and practices are necessary for effective management.

Key Terms

Nothing jobs
Efficiency
Bureaucratic organization model

Bureaucratic hierarchy
Management attitudes

Social-psychological changes
Management responsibility

Discussion Questions

1. What are the most direct influences of organizations on your life?
2. Give an example of a way effective or ineffective management has directly affected you.
3. Are organizations "becoming our masters"?
4. What are the most important problems of change and uncertainty currently facing managers of organizations?

5. What do you feel are the major demands that employees will make on management in the next five years?
6. What are the advantages and disadvantages of the "bureaucratic model" of management?
7. What do you consider to be the characteristics of an "ideal" job?
8. What are the characteristics of effective organizations?

Case Incidents

The "No-Match" Rule

The Top-Line Paint Company had two serious fires and put into effect the following regulation: "No matches, lighters, or other fire-producing devices are permitted inside the plant. Violation of this rule will mean automatic and permanent dismissal for any employee." The new rule was posted on the bulletin board at each entrance to the plant.

Previously, many employees had brought matches and cigarette lighters into the plant. The old "no-smoking" rule had been respected, and there was no evidence that any fires had been caused by employees' smoking in the plant.

Tom Neal had worked for Top-Line for twenty years and was considered one of the best processing inspectors in the plant. Two weeks after the no-match rule went into effect, Tom was climbing up to inspect a mixing vat when a book of matches fell from his pocket. They landed at the feet of Mr. Christy, Tom's supervisor.

Mr. Christy picked up the matches and told Tom, "I'm going to have to report these matches, and it'll mean your job."

Tom climbed down from the vat without saying a word. He looked at Mr. Christy and said: "I did nothing that created any safety hazard. If you try to fire me, I'll sue you for every penny you have."

1. If you were Mr. Christy, what would you do? Why?
2. Was there anything wrong with how the rule was worded?
3. Did the company effectively communicate the new rule?
4. How could this situation been handled more effectively?

Let Betty Do It

Betty Call recently became the manager of a well-established flower shop. The shop has a large number of steady customers and an excellent reputation in the community.

Betty is highly skilled in flower arrangement and can prepare orders faster than any of the other employees. Since becoming manager, she has prepared most of the orders herself and has insisted on checking everything before it leaves the shop. Betty has become so involved in the preparation and checking of arrangements that she has no time to order supplies or maintain records. Because she feels she has to check the work of twelve employees, Betty is neglecting some of the responsibilities of managing the shop. The other employees are developing the attitude of "let Betty do it."

1. Is Betty functioning as a manager or as a technical specialist?
2. What should Betty do to be a more effective manager?
3. How could Betty help her employees feel more responsible for their work?

Conflict Situation

Mike Garcia graduated in the top five percent of his college class with a degree in management. He accepted a job as a section supervisor in the training department of a government agency. Mike's supervision reflects the agency's policies on how jobs are to be done. He explained to the employees that agency policies and procedures were to be followed in accomplishing all work. Even with repeated explanations, there were some employees who insisted that they be allowed to do the job their "own way," not according to agency policies.

Mike told Ed Andrews, one of the employees who continually refused to cooperate, "You are going to have to do the job according to agency procedures."

Ed replied, "No, you have to buck it back up the line and tell the agency that they're wrong; we don't want to do it that way."

Mike responded, "I am not going to do that. You either do it the way I told you, or you'll be replaced."

Ed retaliated with, "If you knew anything about management, you'd realize that you should support employees. We can get the job done best when we do it our own way."

1. Should Mike Garcia strictly enforce agency policy or should he allow employees to do the job in their own way?
2. What reply should Mike Garcia have made to Ed Andrews?
3. Could Mike Garcia have handled this situation more effectively? How?

Exercise   *The Ideal Organization*

Most people have very definite ideas about the type of organization in which they would like to work. Using the following categories, describe the characteristics of the ideal or best possible organization. Your descriptions should indicate the conditions you personally feel would be the most desirable.

Most Desirable Physical Working Conditions:

Most Desirable Psychological Conditions: (behavioral & emotional factors)

Most Desirable Characteristics of the People You Would Work with:

Economic Benefits Most Desired:

Most Desired Characteristics of Management:

Most Desired Type of Work (the nature of the job):

(You might find it interesting to compare your responses with those of someone else in the class.)

Endnotes

1. Robert Dubin, *Human Relations in Administration* (Englewood Cliffs, N.J.: Prentice-Hall, 1974), p. 31.
2. Joe Kelly, *Organizational Behavior* (Homewood, Ill.: Irwin-Dorsey, 1969), p. 1.
3. David Hampton, Charles E. Summer, and Ross A. Weber, *Organizational Behavior and the Practice of Management* (Glenview, Ill.: Scott, Foresman and Company, 1973), p. xviii.
4. Robert Townsend, *Up the Organization: How to Stop the Corporation from Stifling People and Strangling Profits* (Greenwich, Conn.: Fawcett Publications, 1970), pp. xi–xii.
5. Herbert G. Hicks, *The Management of Organizations: A System and Human Resources Approach* (New York: McGraw-Hill, 1967), p. 16.
6. John D. Rockefeller as quoted in Garret L. Berten and William V. Hangley, *Organizational Relations and Management Action* (New York: McGraw-Hill, 1966), p. 3.
7. Richard M. Steers, *Introduction to Organizational Behavior* (Glenview, Ill.: Scott, Foresman and Company, 1981), p. 9.
8. Anthony Jay, *Management and Machiavelli* (New York: Holt, Rinehart and Winston, 1967), p. 70.
9. Ibid.
10. J. P. Jones, "People the Independent Variable," in *Organization Theory in Industrial Practice*, ed. I. M. Hairs, (New York: John Wiley & Sons, 1962), p. 550.
11. John Savage, "Incentive Programs at Nucor Corporation Boost Productivity," *Personnel Administrator*, August 1981, pp. 33–36, 49.

Communication 2

4 Perception

Learning Objectives

After reading this chapter, you should be able to:

1. Describe the perceptual process and its effect on behavior.

2. Explain how people selectively perceive information.

3. Discuss how people's expectations affect the way they interpret information.

4. Identify the ways individuals organize perceptions.

5. Describe how an individual's frame of reference influences the selection, organization, and interpretation of information.

6. List the effect of individual needs on perception.

7. Identify how the perceptions of managers and employees differ.

8. Explain how managers can apply knowledge of perception to improve employee performance.

Chapter Topics

Perceptual Process

Selective Perception

Perceptual Organization

Frame of Reference

Interpretation of Perceptions

Stereotypes

We Perceive What We Need

Differing Perceptions of Managers and Employees

Preview and Self-Evaluation

A cafeteria manager told this true story: "One of my biggest problems is the way people taste things. One customer will complain that the soup is too highly seasoned. Another will protest just as loudly that the soup is not seasoned enough. The cook says it's just right. No two people seem to taste the soup or anything else alike." Nor do any two people see, hear, feel, understand, or interpret the world around them in the same way. Perception, the way we interpret our experiences, is one of the most fascinating and troublesome facets of human behavior. Its importance to employees and managers is far greater than most people realize. When managers and employees have differing perceptions regarding quality, quantity, schedules, and the importance of a given task, accomplishing meaningful objectives is nearly impossible. In Chapter 4, perception is discussed from several vantage points.

Before reading this chapter, try answering the following true-false questions to test your perceptions. Then after reading the chapter, check the questions again to see if your perceptions are the same.

Answer True or False

1. All perception involves interpreting what is perceived.   T   F

2. An individual's perceptions influence job performance and human relations.   T   F

3. Perception is a creative process by which individuals construct a unique view of the world. T   F

4. All information available to an individual in the environment becomes part of the individual's conscious experience. T   F

5. The intensity and frequency of a message increase its chances of being accurately received. T   F

6. We often see what we expect to see and not what is actually there.   T   F

7. Much of the dissatisfaction in organizations occurs because managers do not hear what employees are saying, but only what managers expect them to say. T   F

8. Whether an object is judged to be heavy or light depends totally on the weight of the object. T   F

9. Stereotyping is a way of describing people's individual characteristics.   T   F

10. Managers and union leaders tend to underestimate the importance of social and psychological needs of their employees. T   F

ANSWERS: 1. T; 2. T; 3. T; 4. F; 5. F; 6. T; 7. T; 8. F; 9. F; 10. T

Perceptual Process

> If one's concern as a supervisor . . . is to try to effect some change in the behavior of other people, . . . then it is critical that one seek to understand their perceptions if one is to understand the circumstances under which their behavior might change.[1]

The effective manager realizes that views of work, the world, and jobs are not necessarily shared and agreed upon. But, as numerous studies of perception show, many people assume that others see the

we do not all have the same view of the world

world in the same way they do. These same studies show that the best supervisor is the one who can accurately estimate employee perceptions. Since there are no formulas to help managers understand what is on another's mind, they are left to their own inventiveness and sensitivity.

perception is a creative activity

Peception involves the process by which people select, organize, and interpret sensory stimulations such as seeing, hearing, and smelling into meaningful information about their environment. Figure 4.1 illustrates the perceptual process in a somewhat simplified form. Perception, therefore, is the starting point for all behavior. It is the process by which one begins to understand what is going on in the surrounding world. There can be no behavior without individual perceptions because it is not the physical stimulation of the senses that completes the perceptual process, it is the interpretation of those sensations by the receiver.

However, if behavioral situations are viewed only in terms of stimulus and response, the key factors involved in individual perception are omitted from the resulting interpretations. When an individual is confronted with information, at least three perceptual processes take place: selection, organization, and interpretation (Figure 4.1)

Most people assume that everyone perceives things in the same way. After all, we do live in the same world, see the same sun, and drive

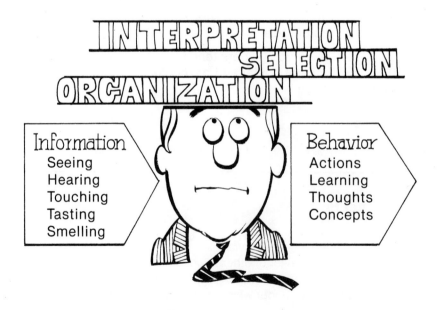

Figure 4.1 The perceptual process.

the same highways. But do we see things in the same way? The best evidence suggests that perception is a creative process by which individuals construct a unique and relatively private view of the world. Individuals begin creating their images of the world early in life and continue to form them until death.

Each employee brings to the organization a unique storehouse of perceptions. It is important for managers to understand the employee's pattern of perceptions that affect how the individual views the job, the supervisor, fellow workers, and the organization. An employee's perceptions influence job performance, attitude, and interpersonal relationships.

perceptions influence job performance

Selective Perception

Much of the information that is available to an individual is not perceived and made a part of that person's conscious experience. *Selective perception* involves deciding to pay attention to some things and to ignore or avoid others. The employee who decides to listen to the union representative and to avoid talking with the supervisor is involved in selective exposure.

selective exposure

The selective nature of perception also involves *selective awareness* in which people are able to filter out information they do not want

selective awareness

How Many F's?

Read the following sentence and see how good you are at counting the F's in the sentence.

- -

FOULED UP FILES ARE THE RESULT OF FOOLISH NEGLECT AND FINISHED FILES ARE THE RESULT OF SCIENTIFIC STUDY COUPLED WITH THE EXPERIENCE OF MANY YEARS.

- -

How many F's did you count? If you did not find *nine* F's try again. Why did you miss some of the F's?

It is easy not to perceive the F's in the words "of." Most people "select out" a third of the F's and count six F's. Perception is often influenced by what we think is important. If you did not think *of* was important you probably did not count all the F's.

---

to be consciously aware of. Students are able to ignore noise made by others in a class when they are concentrating on what the instructor is saying. Employees are able to tune out the constant noise of machinery on the production line. While reading a book, an individual may be unaware of smells, noises, and pressures on the skin.

Much of the information available in the environment does not become a part of conscious experience because of the selective nature of perception. Your nose provides an example of selection that is with you all of the time. Close your left eye and you see your nose with the right eye; close your right eye and you see your nose with your left eye; open both eyes and your nose disappears.

Perceptual selection is affected by an individual's needs, expectations, interests, and the characteristics of the information.

Intensity

If messages are loud or bright, there is a greater chance that people will select them. As the volume of the radio is increased, there is a greater likelihood indiviuals will "hear" it. This does not mean the desired interpretation of the message will be created, but merely that there is a greater chance that the individual will attend to the information. *Intensity* functions to increase chances of selection. Common examples of intensity are the volume of the speaker, the size of a billboard, or the brightness of a color. Attempts to achieve desired responses from individuals through intensity alone will probably be disappointing. Intensity does not increase the accuracy of perception; it only increases the probability that the information will be selected.

AS THE VOLUME INCREASES, THERE IS A GREATER LIKELIHOOD THAT THE MESSAGE WILL BE SELECTED BY THE RECEIVER

Frequency

The more often information is presented, the greater the chance of selection by the individual. Sometimes effectiveness is attributed to the amount of information alone. There is no guarantee of achieving desired results by just repeating information. Repeatedly telling employees to work harder is not likely to result in increased individual effort.

Confusing information repeated frequently is still confusing information. *Frequency*, in and of itself, does increase the probability of selection by receivers, but it does *not* increase the chance that the receiver will accurately interpret and organize the information.

repeating confusing information increases confusion

Frequency can inhibit desired behavior when the information is transmitted so often that the receivers become bored or irritated. It is possible for an increase in frequency to result in a feeling of being "talked down" to, and the receiver may respond negatively.

Expectations

Read the phrases printed within the triangles below.

Did you see what was really in the triangles? Or did you see what you expected to see?

Most people will report what they expected to see. In the case of "Bird in *the the* hand," they report seeing "Bird in *the* hand," omitting one of the words in the phrase (there are two the's). We never expect to find two *the's* next to each other. As we perceive, we select, organize, and interpret the information to conform with our expectations. When reality differs from our expectations, it is often easier to change our perceptions of reality than to grapple with the difference between our expectations and the information.

The context in which information appears affects our *expectations* and structures the interpretation of the message by receivers. Let's take the simple sentence, "I went to the bank and wrote a chack." When most people hear this sentence, they repeat it back by saying, "I went to the bank and wrote a check." We develop a set of expectations by setting the scene in a bank, where under normal circumstances one would expect a check to be written. But in this case we have introduced *chack* in an incongruent context which the individual automatically reinterprets to fit the context or surrounding.

context affects our expectations

We could use the term *chack* in another sentence and get quite a different interpretation: "I went out to a chicken farm to show my children the baby chacks." When people interpret this sentence, they convert *chack* to *chick*.

explanation of information
In evaluating information it is not a question of what the information says; it is a question of what the individual expects the information to say. Much of the dissatisfaction within organizations occurs because managers do not hear *what* employees say, but what they expect them to say. The same is true of message transmission from managers to employees; the employee does not hear what the manager says but what is *expected*.

sandwich technique
Often, attempts are made to change behavior by criticism. A frequently used method of criticism is referred to as the sandwich technique: First tell the individual something nice, something desirable, or something good. Then criticize the individual. Follow with something positive at the end of the conversation. The effectiveness of this technique is questionable because it develops a set of positive expectations—"We're talking about nice things and everything is going fine." Suddenly the context is changed, and the individual is expected to immediately switch expectations to deal with criticism. Often, the individual does not change expectations to deal with criticism, the criticism is ignored, and no change results.

How do your expectations affect your perception? Do you think you can follow directions? Take the 3-minute test that follows and see how you rate?

READ EVERYTHING BEFORE DOING ANYTHING

How to Follow Instructions

1. Put your name in the upper right-hand corner, last name first.
2. Circle the word *name* in sentence one.
3. Underline the words *upper right-hand* in sentence one.
4. Now draw a circle around the word *how* in the title.
5. Sign your name under the title.
6. In sentence three, draw a circle around the word *underline*.
7. Draw an *x* in the lower left-hand corner.
8. Draw a circle around the *x* you just drew.
9. If you think you have followed instructions to this point, write *I have*.
10. Close your eyes and raise your left hand over your head.
11. Write the name of your occupation:
12. *Count out loud* in your normal speaking voice backwards from ten to one.
13. Now that you have read the instructions carefully, do only what sentence three asks you to do. Ignore all other directions.

Perceptual Organization

Each individual has to try to organize a sensible and coherent world out of an environment which may not make sense in itself. This tendency is often referred to as *perceptual organization*. A never tells B everything when they talk. B, of course, fills in the gaps. A common result is that B's response to the message may be quite different from A's expectation. Behavior depends on the image. *individuals organize perceptions*

Try the following problem: Below are nine dots. Join all nine dots by drawing four straight lines. You are not allowed to lift your pencil from the paper, and every time you change direction of a line (turning or retracing), it counts as another line.

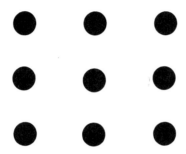

Most people try to solve the problem by staying inside a square defined by the dots. Many people even "perceive" the instructions as saying that they must stay in a "square." But there is no square! The dots provide an environmental stimulus which may be organized into a square by the perceiver—and this blocks successful task performance. (Solution on next page.)

How would you describe the following?

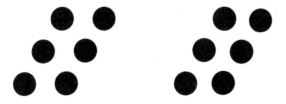

Most people say there are two sets of six dots; practically no one will respond by saying twelve dots. To summarize the data by saying you see two sets of six dots is a rather harmless and trivial selection from the basic description of the information that appears. The phenomena occurring is one of organization and grouping of the data on *grouping*

the basis of nearness. This factor is almost always involved in perception and interpretation. Things which are close are perceived as alike.

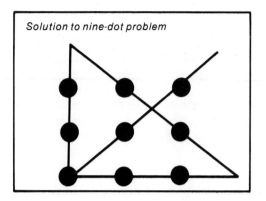

Solution to nine-dot problem

Association

association   In many cases, grouping results in a phenomenon referred to as *association*. Let's assume we have an employee who is classed as "lazy," who "doesn't work hard," and who "puts out very little effort." We now hire a new employee who eats lunch with the lazy employee, rides with him to work, and frequently associates with him on the job. It would not be hard to draw the conclusion that both employees are lazy. Association or reality?

How would you describe the following to someone?

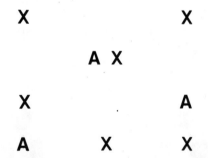

Most people say there are six X's and three A's. Why? Why not nine letters?

Closure

we desire   When we perceive information, we tend to organize it into whole and
complete   continuous patterns. If the pattern is incomplete, we tend to fill in the
information   missing elements. The incomplete "circle" must be completed. The perceptual process involved in completing figures is referred to as *closure*.

The need for closure may apply to many activities. For example, it may apply to the tension that accompanies the interruption of a task and the satisfaction and relief that come from its completion. Task completion is in essence the attainment of the whole figure.

Now let's consider another characteristic of perception that is not so directly tied to social perceptions.

Reproduce the following figures:

Did you introduce any systematic distortions or change? Most people do. These figures are usually changed, in the process of being reproduced, as follows:

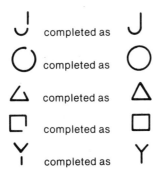

The perception of things as belonging to common groups is achieved by the use of grouping according to similarity and proximity and by attaining closure. We structure information by putting similar concepts together and attempting to provide a "complete story." *we structure information*

One of the most generalizable propositions about behavior is that *people respond neither to individual elements one at a time nor to the sum total of individual elements; they respond to the relationship among the elements.*

When we *think* we have the complete picture or the whole story, we stop looking and listening.

How do you react to ambiguous information? People were shown a series of simple ambiguous drawings and were asked to reproduce a labeled figure. Each picture was preceded by a word indicating what was to be drawn. The redrawn pictures were distorted from the original stimulus according to the label attached. The labels attached were systematically varied so that the same word did not always precede the drawing. Examples of some of the results are shown in Figure 4.2. *ambiguous information*

Reproduced figure	Word list I	Stimulus figure	Word list II	Reproduced figure
	Curtains in a window		Diamond in a rectangle	
	Two		Eight	
	Hourglass		Table	
	Eyeglasses		Dumbbells	
	Seven		Four	
	Pine tree		Trowel	

Source: Leonard Carmichael, H. P. Hogan, and A. A. Walter, "An Experimental Study of the Effect of Language on the Reproduction of Visually Perceived Form" *Journal of Experimental Psychology* 15 (1932): 73–86.

Figure 4.2   The effect of language on the reproduction of symbols.

Frame of Reference

External *and* internal influences interact to shape the processes of selection, organization, and interpretation of information. We develop a personal *frame of reference* which includes all the internal and external factors that affect behavior at a given time.

major reference points   Any accurate analysis of behavior must examine an event in the appropriate frame of reference. This does not imply that all influences operating at a given time have equal effects on our behavior. Within any situation there are major reference points which weigh more heavily in shaping the outcome of an event. Major reference points may be in external situations or internal influences, depending on the interrelationships of factors at the time.

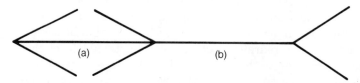

Which of the horizontal lines is longer? Did you measure them?

Take any two lines of *equal* length. Add inward-pointing arrows to one line and outward-pointing arrows to the other. The lines no longer look equal. In our experience they are *not the same lines* because the frame of reference is different. Each line and its arrows are part of a perceptual unit. Architects have long utilized this type of phenomenon to create impressions of height, spaciousness, and curves in the form of buildings. Why is it the moon looks so much larger while ascending—when seen just over the top of horizon trees?

Are the center circles the same size or different? Which of the two center circles in the illustration below looks the largest?

 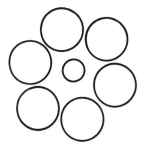

Even simple objects like these two circles are experienced in a relational way. In the complex and dynamic area of human relations, where individuals interact with one another, it is not at all surprising that the relational effects become even more important.

Although the center circles are the same size, most people don't see them as equal because of the circles around them—their frame of reference. To perceive the size of the circle accurately, we can change the frame of reference by removing the surrounding circles.

perception involves relationships

In some situations it is possible to increase the accuracy of perception by changing the frame of reference. In most cases, communication must succeed within the existing frames of reference even though they are constantly changing.

What is wrong with the question, Which one is larger? Often, all you can tell is which one *looks* larger. We don't ask an individual what *appears* to be the best; we ask it as if it is an absolute. In this sense, the better question would be; Which circle *appears* to be the larger?

how accurate is your perception?

Interpretation of Perceptions

The way anything is interpreted depends on its surroundings or the context in which it appears. What happened with the dots occurs with all perception. The context in which information appears affects what you think you see or hear.

Suppose the same message is given to the employees by the company president and by the union president. Ask the employees to interpret it and you will get two different interpretations. *The context always affects interpretation.*

all judgments involve comparisons

The simplest judgment of physical objects to the most complex social judgments involves making comparisons. In order to judge or interpret, there must be some basis for comparison. Time and space judgments require comparison within a frame of reference. If there are no objects available for a point of reference, it is not possible to determine the location in space or whether something is moving or standing still.

Adaptation Level

What is normal? Small? Large? What feels heavy? What feels light? What appears to be effective or ineffective depends on a series of comparisons and who is viewing an object or event. Human perceptual judgment occurs within the particular background an individual brings to a situation. *Adaptation level* refers to the perceptual changes that occur as an individual makes a series of comparisons. There is no absolute relationship between the perceived magnitude and the actual "physical magnitude." People develop "adaptation levels" with regard to any given evaluation of magnitude (e.g., temperature, light intensity, size, etc.). Evaluations are based on a series of perceived comparisons. An orange tastes sweet after eating a lemon, but sour after eating candy.

The important implication of the adaptation phenomenon is that judgments are not simply intellectual evaluations; they are the result of perceptual comparisons. Whether objects feel heavy or light and whether individuals appear intelligent or stupid depends on a series of comparisons. Individual responses will vary depending on the individual's background and the context in which the judgment occurs.

When a manager is evaluating employee productivity, his or her judgments are based on an evaluation scale that has been developed through experience. As a result of observing a number of people involved in accomplishing tasks, the manager has acquired a personal scale for rating employee productivity.

perception involves evaluation

Stereotypes

Stereotypes are attitudes that serve as shorthand guides to characterizing groups of people. The term *stereotype* was originally used in printing to refer to a plate that printed the same image over and over again. Stereotypes exist for religious groups, racial groups, occupational groups, and nationality groups. People select characteristics to identify groups of people and attribute those characteristics to each person in the group.

What characteristics come to mind when you think about lawyers, protestants, blacks, truck drivers, professors, or football players? Each of these terms probably calls to mind a mental picture containing characteristics that stereotype the group. The stereotype one has of a group will usually strongly affect the way one perceives an individual who is seen as a member of the group.

stereotypes affect perception

The use of stereotypes makes it possible to describe people within simple and well-organized categories. Stereotypes save the time and effort required to find out what a person is really like. There is the implication that all the people belonging to a group are alike: "When you've seen one, you've seen them all."

Stereotypes limit the ability to perceive other people accurately. They can result in individuals being seen only as a part of a group. Stereotyping can prevent people from finding out how a person is unique and different from a "group."

An Exercise in Stereotyping

Identify a "group" described by each of the following sets of characteristics.

Absent-minded, unrealistic, impractical_____

Artistic, impulsive, passionate _____

Emotional, weak, gentle _____

Witty, quick-tempered, quarrelsome _____

Strong, logical, aggressive _____

Lazy, clannish, superstitious _____

Hard-working, dependable, honest _____

Mercenary, shrewd, industrious _____

Quiet, careful, patient _____

Compare your answers with someone else's.

We Perceive What We Need

Although communication is possible because of similar interpretation of experiences, neither individual experiences nor interpretations of them are identical. Even when two people look at the same thing (object, person, movie, etc.) from nearly the same spot, their interpretations differ. Our needs, desires, wishes, dislikes—our frame of reference—are the boundaries surrounding our perceptions.

A family visits a department store and browses around together. As they leave, they discuss what they saw. The father noticed lawn mowers and power tools; the mother, fur coats and dishwashers. The daughter noticed bathing suits and cosmetics; the son, a candy counter.

Did they visit the same store? Although the "physical reality" was the same, the information perceived by the individuals was not. Because they had different needs and wants, from a perceptual point of view they visited different stores.

Examine what people report they've heard after listening to a political speech. Their needs directly affect their perceptions. For example, the farmer heard about farm-price supports, the teacher heard
about support for education, and the construction executive heard
about plans for a new highway.

*individual needs
alter perceptions*

Our needs alter our perceptions. In one experiment, people looked
at cards through a screen that blurred the pictures. People who had not
eaten for nine hours before looking at the pictures described more of
them as food items than did people who had recently eaten.

In another experiment, children were asked to estimate the size of
coins. Poor children tended to estimate all coins to be physically larger
than did children from higher income brackets.

In our daily search for order and certainty, we interpret according
to our expectations and work from these to predict future responses.
How can we know enough about human nature or an individual's experiences to infer how he or she might react? We develop expectations as
we come to know an individual and we empathize. We project our
thoughts to other people. Part of our time is spent in estimating the
other person's feelings and thoughts and tempering our remarks to provide the most effective stimulus or response.

*can we predict
behavior?*

A person needing directions   A person needing a loan   Someone who is late
for an appointment

Figure 4.3   Individual needs alter perceptions.

Those oblivious to external cues about others' internal experiences are not taking full advantage of the feedback possibilities that contribute to more effective communication. Through our ability to "feel out people," we learn to adjust to new situations and environments and increase our ability to communicate.

How Position in an Organization Influences Perceptions

The effect on perception of a person's position in an organization was demonstrated in a classic study of managers by Dearborn and Simon.

A group of twenty-three executives of a large manufacturing company were asked to read a factual case often used in college business administration courses. The case described the problems of a medium-sized manufacturing company that produced seamless steel tubes. Each executive was asked to identify the most important problem facing a new president in that company. Which problem should be addressed first?

Six of the executives were sales managers, five were production managers, four were accounting managers, and eight managed staff functions such as legal, public relations, industrial relations, and medical. The researchers wanted to find out if the executives would perceive the key problem in terms of their own positions and the activities of their department.

The results of the study indicated that, indeed, the managers' positions did influence their perception of the most important problem facing the new president. Sales executives saw sales as the most important problem. Production executives identified production problems as most urgent. Public relations and industrial relations executives saw human relations as the company's biggest problem.[2]

Differing Perceptions of Managers and Employees

*perceiving
employee needs*

Accurate perception of the needs of employees is an important aspect of a manager's job. If managers do not accurately perceive the relative strength of employee motivation, their efforts to improve productivity through motivation will be ineffective. Managers may be appealing to needs that are already satisfied or are unimportant to employees.

R. L. Kahn's study of management perceptions of employee needs revealed that management greatly overestimated the importance employees attached to high wages.[3] In the study, only 28 percent of the employees ranked wages as most important, while 61 percent of the managers perceived that wages were the most important for employees. The study showed that management underestimated the importance of the social and psychological needs of their employees.

The problem of accuracy of management perception of what employees want from their jobs is also apparent in research reported by Paul Hersey and Kenneth Blanchard.[4] The research involved supervisors who were asked to put themselves in the position of their employees and to rank the importance of a series of items describing what they wanted from their jobs. Supervisors ranked good wages, job security, and promotion as most wanted by employees. The workers themselves ranked the most important items as full appreciation of work done, to be "in" on things, and sympathetic understanding of personal problems. The results of this study indicate the inaccuracy of management perceptions.

accuracy of management perceptions

The results of these and similar studies are especially important for management, because both managers and employees act on the basis of their perceptions. If management perceptions can be brought closer to the reality of employee perceptions, it may be possible for managers to increase their effectiveness in working with individuals.

we behave on the bases of our perceptions

Two researchers compared managers' and labor leaders' perceptions of employee needs with the employees' report of their needs.[5] They found that both union leaders and managers held inaccurate perceptions of employees wants. They overemphasized the importance of material rewards and working conditions and underestimated the importance employees placed on getting along with supervisors and co-workers. It is interesting to note that in this study managers considerably overestimated the employees' evaluation of the union's importance.

Because the process of motivation always takes place within the framework of employee perceptions of the situation, employees act in ways that make sense to them based on what they perceive to be important. An important implication for management is that the employee's perception of the relationship with the boss is critical. As Rensis Likert pointed out: "An individual's reaction to any situation is always a function not of the absolute character of the intervention, but of his perception of it. It is how he sees things that counts, not objective reality.[6]

Quick Review

   I. Perceptual Process
      A. Effective managers realize that all individuals have differing perceptions.
      B. There is a tendency for people to assume others perceive as they themselves do.

C. There are no formulas for piecing together what is in another person's mind.
D. Perception involves the process by which a person selects, organizes, and interprets sensory stimulations.
E. Perception is the starting point of all behavior.
F. Employee perception influences performance, attitude, and interpersonal relations.

II. Selective Perception
A. Perception tends to be selective. Much of the information around us is not perceived.
B. Selective exposure involves paying attention to some things and ignoring others.
C. Selective awareness refers to filtering out information we do not want to be consciously aware of.
D. Perceptual selection is affected by several characteristics of the stimulus.
    1. Intensity is the strength of the stimulus, such as loudness, brightness, size, movement, etc.
    2. Frequency refers to repetition of the same stimulus.
    3. Expectations involve the tendency to react to things as we expect them to be rather than as they are.

III. Perceptual Organization
A. We tend to organize things in such a way that they make sense to us.
B. One way of organizing is by grouping similar stimuli.
C. Closure, the tendency to perceptually complete the incomplete, is another method of organizing perceptions.
D. People respond to the relationship between elements of a stimulus rather than to the individual elements.
E. Three perceptual processes involve selection, organization, and interpretation.

IV. Frame of Reference
A. External and internal influences of perception constitute a person's frame of reference.
B. Major reference points influence behavior and perception more heavily.
C. Communication must succeed within constantly changing frames of reference.

V. Interpretation of Perceptions
A. Adaptation level refers to perceptions based on comparison with other similar but different stimuli. (A baseball player will swing two bats so the one actually used "feels" lighter.)

B. Stereotyping involves the assignment of characteristics to a whole group based on belief or observation of only one or two representatives of that group.
VI. We Perceive What We Need
   A. Individual needs alter the way we perceive information and events.
   B. We interpert data according to our expectations and use this information to predict future responses.
   C. Such feedback can help us develop more effective communication.
VII. Differing Perceptions of Managers and Employees
   A. Incorrect managerial perceptions lead to ineffectiveness.
   B. Studies indicate that managers and union leaders tend to perceive employee needs incorrectly.
   C. Motivation always takes place within the framework of what employees perceive as important.

Key Terms

Perception
Perceptual process
Selective perception
Selective awareness
Intensity

Expectations
Frequency
Perceptual
   organization
Association

Closure
Frame of reference
Adaptation level
Stereotypes

Discussion Questions

1. How do employees usually want to be perceived their first day at work?
2. Describe a personal experience involving incorrect perceptions. What caused the errors?
3. Jumping to conclusions is a form of perception based on inadequate information. Why do people "jump to conclusions?"
4. How do our perceptions help and hinder problem solving?
5. Based on personal experiences, describe ways frames of reference can differ. Give real life examples.
6. List some conditions to which most people become perceptually adapted. Example, normal background noises in restaurants, schools, or work.

7. How can stereotypes be changed?
8. Explain why, once formed, perceptions of people or events are difficult to change.

Case Incidents

Different Perceptions of Performance

Ann Cord is the supervisor of the purchasing department on a military installation. Leo Morales, a specialist in the purchase of electronic equipment, has worked for Ms. Cord for three years. Leo has a bachelor's degree in electrical engineering and has actively continued his education by taking graduate courses and attending professional training programs. Leo's work has been outstanding, and he is highly respected by everyone who works with him.

Ms. Cord rated Leo outstanding on the annual performance evaluation and justified the high evaluation by citing Leo's specific accomplishments. When Ms. Cord's boss reviewed Leo's evaluation, he said it was too high. Ms. Cord's boss felt Leo could not be considered outstanding because he did not participate in the "official" social activities. Leo had not attended the reception held by the installation commander for employees, he did not come to the purchasing department picnic, and he had avoided other social activities.

Ms. Cord's boss made it clear that she had the right to refuse to change the evaluation, but he would consider it a serious error in judgment on her part.

1. How do Ms. Cord and her boss differ in their perception of what constitutes "outstanding performance?"
2. Do their positions in the installation affect what they perceive as important in employee behavior? Explain your answer.
3. If you were Ms. Cord, would you advise Leo Morales to start attending the social activities? Why or why not?
4. If Ms. Cord refuses to change Leo's evaluation, how do you think her boss's perception of her performance will be affected?

What Did I Say?

Roger Peck, salesman for an aircraft manufacturer, reported the results of his trip to the sales manager, Mr. Fest: "Well, I got the order for five twin-engine model 243C's from the Vito Corporation. They sure gave me a bad time. I had to make one demonstration after another. I must have answered a million questions for half of the company officers. They didn't give me a minute's rest for the whole week. It seemed like I was there a month. They even had a meeting scheduled for me every night. I sure don't like these pressure sales situations with customers that are impossible to please. I hope I never see another sales job like that. It was ridiculous."

Mr. Fest turned to Roger and said, "Great, now let's go to work on how you can wrap up the International Company order."

1. What was Roger trying to say?
2. How did Mr. Fest perceive Roger's message?
3. What reaction do you think Roger had to Mr. Fest's reply?
4. If you were Mr. Fest, how would you have replied?
5. What basic problems in perception are illustrated by this situation and what can be done to prevent them in the future?

The Rumor

A municipal hospital was experiencing a severe financial squeeze. Occupancy was lower than had been forecast and collections were slow. Equipment costs were running higher than expected and the cost of supplies was rising.

As the year ended, there was increased discussion among the hospital's 200 employees about the effect of the current financial situation on salaries for the next year. A rumor began to circulate that there would be no salary raises and that personnel reductions were very possible. Employees were shocked by the extent of the financial problems indicated by the rumor.

They began to ask their supervisors, "Does top-level administration agree with this rumor or not?"

The administrators made no comment, refusing to confirm or deny the rumor. The information in "official" communication from administration was that "the matter was under study." While employees waited for word on pay increases and wondered if they might be laid off, their morale dropped lower and lower. Most employees began to believe there would be no pay increases.

The administration finally announced that no employees would be laid off and that pay raises would average 4 percent. The employees were delighted when they received the announcement.

The administration was pleased with the employee reaction, since six months before there had been demands for 10 percent pay increases and a reduction of work loads.

1. Was the acceptance of work loads and the lower pay raise better than it would have been if the rumor had not started?

2. Should the administration have taken any action when the rumor was circulated?
3. What are possible long-term effects of this type of situation?
4. What guidelines should management use in dealing with rumors?

Exercise   *What Are Your Perceptions?*

We all develop perceptions of the characteristics of occupational groups and the traits that are typical of people in different occupations.

Indicate the traits, behaviors and characteristics that describe your perceptions of people in the occupations listed below. Use the words or phrases that first come to mind to describe the people in the occupation.

OCCUPATION   CHARACTERISTICS

Managers

_____

Nurses

_____

Autoworkers

_____

Accountants

_____

College Professors

_____

Janitors

_____

Lawyers

Secretaries

Engineers

How are your perceptions of individuals affected by their occupation?

How would your perceptions of an occupation affect your relationship with a person in that occupation?

How did you develop your perceptions of occupational groups?

Do your perceptions reflect or reinforce stereotypes you hold?

Endnotes

1. Harold J. Leavitt, *Managerial Psychology*, 2d ed. (Chicago: University of Chicago Press, 1964), p. 35.
2. D. C. Dearborn and H. A. Simon, "Selective Perception: A Note on Departmental Indentification of Executives," *Sociometry*, 1958, 21, p. 142.
3. R. L. Kahn, "Human Reactions on the Shop Floor," in *Human Relations and Modern Management*, ed E. M. Hugh-Jones (Chicago: Quadrangle Books, 1959).
4. Paul Hersey and Kenneth H. Blanchard, *Management of Organizational Behavior*, 2d ed. (Englewood Cliffs, N.J.: Prentice-Hall, 1972), pp. 38–40.
5. Ury M. Gluskinos and Bruce J. Kestlemen, "Management and Labor Leaders' Perception of Worker Needs as Compared with Self-Reported Needs," *Personnel Psychology*, Summer 1971, pp. 239–46.
6. Rensis Likert, "A Motivational Approach to the Modified Theory of Organization and Management," in *Modern Organization Theory*, ed. Mason Haire (New York: John Wiley & Sons, 1959), p. 161. For additional examples of perceptual differences see John Senger, "Seeing Eye to Eye: Practical Problems of Perception," *Personnel Journal*, October 1974, pp. 744–51.

5

The Process of Communication

Learning Objectives

After reading this chapter, you should be able to:

1. Discuss the importance of communication in human relations.

2. Describe basic models of communication.

3. Explain how language usage can determine the effectiveness of communication.

4. Identify barriers to effective communication.

5. Describe what an individual can do to be a more effective listener.

6. Explain how nonverbal communication affects human relations in organizations.

7. List the major nonverbal dimensions of communication.

Chapter Topics

The Importance of Communication

Models of Communication

Language and Meaning

Separating Facts from Inferences

Barriers to Effective Communication

The Process of Abstracting

Effective Listening

Guides for Listening Improvement

Nonverbal Communication

Preview and Self-Evaluation

Human beings interact with each other through the process of communication. Although understanding and being understood are very basic activities, the complexities of communication are still not fully explored. In management-employee relations, no single behavior is as important as the process of communication. In Chapter 5, we examine some of the more important aspects of communication in the work place.

Before reading this chapter try answering the true-false questions below to test your perceptions. Then after reading the chapter, check the questions again to see if your perceptions are the same.

Answer True or False

1. Available research indicates that as much as 70 percent of all business communications fail to achieve their intended purpose.   T   F

2. The first obstacle any message must overcome is to be selected from all the messages competing for the receiver's attention.   T   F

3. Communication consists of the transmission of meanings.   T   F

4. People can use language as they wish, with no reference to the real world. T F

5. When we report on an observed event, we abstract and report only the characteristics that are important to us. T F

6. Most people retain 25 percent or less of what they hear. T F

7. By analyzing facial expressions it is easy to distinguish between emotions such as anger, fear, grief, and despair. T F

8. Most people will move physically closer when communicating with individuals they like and will maintain more distance from those they dislike. T F

9. Most people can make accurate judgements about an individual's personality by observing the person's voice qualities. T F

10. People tend to avoid information which conflicts with their own attitudes and beliefs. T F

ANSWERS: 1. T; 2. T; 3. F; 4. T; 5. T; 6. T; 7. F; 8. T; 9. F; 10. T.

The Importance of Communication

"Managers are speaking, reading, writing and listening beings who spend 70 to 80 percent of their time in some form of communication."[1] Management must communicate to gain understanding, to motivate, and to obtain cooperation from employees. Every aspect of management is related in some way to the process of communication. Unfortunately, it does not appear that managers are as effective in communication as they need to be because "available research indicates that as much as 70 percent of all business communications fail to achieve their intended purpose."[2]

A manager must communicate effectively in order to achieve personal success in an organization. Managers are judged by their ability to communicate with superiors, subordinates, and others at their own level in the organization. Promotions and job assignments are affected by management's evaluation of individual abilities to communicate. Much of the need satisfaction that individuals achieve in organizations is through communicating with others.

effective communication is necessary for success

Communication is the vehicle through which human abilities and physical resources are combined to produce outputs and attain objectives.

Achievements often depend on the use of symbols. What difference can words make? What difference can one word make?

the difference one word made

An interpretation of the Japanese word *mokusatsu* destroyed thousands of lives and changed millions more. The word has two commonly used meanings: (1) to ignore and (2) to refrain from comment. In July 1945, the Japanese emperor was ready to end the war and had the power to do so. The members of the Japanese cabinet were prepared to concede to the Allies' ultimatum but wanted more time to discuss the terms. A press release was issued announcing a policy of *mokusatsu*, with the no-comment implication. But, through a choice in translation, it was transmitted on the foreign wires with the "ignore" implication. To recall the release would have resulted in an apparently unthinkable loss of face. Had the meaning the Japanese government intended been interpreted correctly, the cabinet might have backed the emperor's decision to surrender. What difference did it make? There probably would have been no atomic bombs dropped on Hiroshima and Nagasaki, no Russian armies in Manchuria, and maybe no Korean War to follow. One word . . .and tens of thousands of lives.[3]

Although it is possible to send messages around the world and to astronauts on the moon, management and labor often have difficulty communicating with each other across a table. Our technical ability to transmit messages is highly developed, but person-to-person communication is often ineffective.

we can't pay attention to all available information

We are all surrounded by more messages than we can possibly pay attention to, much less interpret. The first obstacle any message must overcome is to be selected from all the messages competing for the receiver's attention. Once selected for interpretation, the message content may be accepted or rejected. Acceptance depends on the receiver's interpretation and how the message fits with his or her values and beliefs. Part of the process of acceptance may be rational; part, emotional; and part, below the level of conscious thought.

Models of Communication

There is no single model of human communication that takes into account all the elements that may be involved in a specific situation.

Figure 5.1 Basic communication model.

Chapter 5

Communication models are not as complex as the communication situations they attempt to predict. All models of communication include at least three basic elements: *a source, a message,* and *a receiver.* The source may be an individual or a group. The message may be in the form of ink on paper, sound waves, a gesture, or any other signal capable of being interpreted. The receiver or destination may be an individual or group.

The complex process of communication can be reduced to a fairly simple model. The model in Figure 5.1 presents the major elements in the communication process.

message transmission

The individual desiring to send information starts with some concept or idea that is in his or her mind. The individual decides to share the information with someone else. The information must be *encoded* or put in a form that makes transmission possible. This can involve words, symbols, sounds, or expressions that can be transmitted. Transmission may involve face-to-face conversations, written messages, drawings, the telephone, or other methods of getting information to a receiver. The message is received (through the senses of hearing, sight, etc.) and the receiver *decodes* the message. The receiver interprets the decoded message and assigns meaning to its symbols. Figure 5.2 shows a difference in sender and receiver interpretation of a message.

For communication to be effective, both the source *and* the receiver must understand the code system being used. The source can encode and the receiver can decode only in terms of the experience each has had. The source and the receiver must have had similar experiences for communication to be effective. By using information about the receiver's past experience, the source can encode the message so it relates to that experience.

Figure 5.2   Both sender and receiver must share the same code.

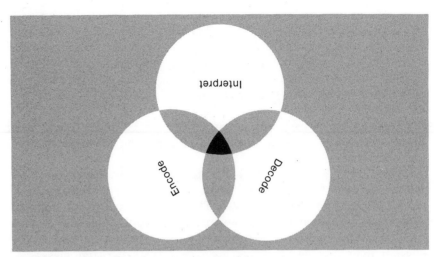

Figure 5.3 Encoding, decoding, interpreting process.

code system

Shared knowledge of the code does not necessarily mean that messages will produce the desired responses. The message is more than the code system. When a painter applies oils to canvas according to rules of perspective, we "see" a clear lake nestled among the mountains. The lake is in neither the oil paints nor the rules governing their application to the canvas. The effect results from the combination of the message elements.

We can draw some conclusions from this basic approach to communication:

1. If the source doesn't have adequate or accurate information, the message generated has little chance of producing desired responses.
2. The receiver, not the source, determines whether the message is encoded fully, accurately, and effectively.
3. The attitudes, experiences, and motivations of the receiver determine whether the message is decoded in a way that corresponds to the source's intent.

encoding and decoding

Each person in a communication situation both encodes and decodes. *Encoding* is the process by which an individual's ideas are converted into symbols that make up a message. To put ideas into words is encoding. *Decoding* is the process of interpreting symbols contained in a message by determining what the symbols refer to.

Individuals can receive and transmit information simultaneously. Either the sender or the receiver in a human communication system can be represented in the way shown in Figure 5.3.

We are constantly decoding information from our environment, interpreting this information, and encoding information. As information passes *through* us, it is changed by our interpretations, and it changes us. The inputs always affect the outputs in some way.

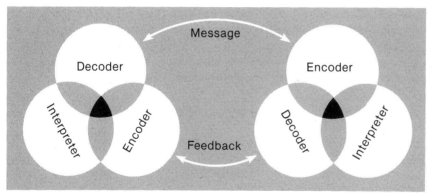

Figure 5.4 The message/feedback process in communication.

In a conversation between two people, there is constant communication. The process involves feedback indicating how our messages are being interpreted. This process is shown in Figure 5.4.

An important element in the communication process is the *channel*. In face-to-face communication, many people consider only the voice transmission channel. But other channels, such as facial expressions, posture, gestures, and intonation patterns, are often more important. These channels gain importance as a result of two things: (1) increased experience with a particular person and (2) increased sensitivity to nonverbal communication.

communication channels

Messages are seldom transmitted by means of a single channel. In a speech communication situation, sound may be the primary channel. Others are the expressions on the speaker's face, his or her gestures, the lighting in the room, the feel of the seats, and the information communicated by the nature of the audience.

When we communicate, we are trying to satisfy our felt needs (Figure 5.5). Communication is one of the tools available to us to affect be-

Figure 5.5 Communication is a way of satisfying needs.

havior and achieve objectives. We use communication to inform, to interpret, and to motivate. Regardless of the specific form of behavior we want from a receiver, we are basically trying to obtain a behavioral response that will satisfy our felt needs. Communication is most effective when the receiver knows what we mean and reacts in the way we desire.

Language and Meaning

Assumption: Meanings are in words.

Reality: Meanings are in people (see Figure 5.6). Without people, there are no meanings.

Assumption: Because there is a word, the thing the word represents must exist.

Reality: There can be words that do not represent reality. This assumption leads to confusing words with things. It can also result in the creation of verbal monsters. The boogieman created by a child or the nonexistent irate customer can become verbal monsters. The imagined threat of loosing one's job can become a verbal monster.

Assumption: Communication consists of the tramsmission of meanings.

Reality: We cannot transmit meanings—only messages. Meanings are in the mind of the message receiver.

These assumptions give us a starting place in dealing with symbolic processes.

Is the Word the Thing?

Physical things have both a functional value and a *symbolic value.* Often, it is the symbolic value which leads us to accept or reject a specific

Figure 5.6   Only people have meanings.

object. While food has functional value, for example, how and with whom we dine can be symbolic. Special foods may symbolize festivals and special occasions. Clothes are selected not only for functional values, but also for symbolic values reflecting taste, wealth, or social position. When buying a house, your choice is not based totally on functional value or an "economic good buy." You also take into account the symbolic value of a "good address."

Language is a highly developed and complex system. Most of the desirable and undesirable qualities of language result from that characteristic. There is no necessary connection between the language symbol and what it symbolizes. We can say that something is beautiful when we have actually judged it ugly. Our feelings are expressed through language, and in turn, feelings are generated by the language we use. We often begin to feel about the word as we have felt about the object the word represents. When we do this, we treat the symbol as if it were the thing symbolized.

Is it more important to have the symbol than the thing it stands for? For some students and teachers, the symbol of learning (the grade) is more important than learning itself.

The manager functions in a verbal and symbolic environment. They are bombarded with communications from employees, other managers, salespeople, customers, and so forth. Through the use of words and other symbolic arrays, managers create the symbolic world they live in. They are free to try to create any type of verbal world they desire.

we can create a verbal world

We *can* construct language as we wish, with no reference to the "real" world. This construction causes no harm as long as we are able to recognize fiction as fiction. The problem is we often do not attempt to distinguish between words and what they stand for.

Fact, Fiction, or Inference?

Can *all* statements be judged true or false? Can *any* statement be judged true or false? Are there some statements that we know are false by the nature of the statements? Language is a powerful tool for analyzing many dimensions of reality. Though words won't keep you dry in a rainstorm and wordless beavers build dams, a modern jet aircraft could not have been conceived or manufactured without the use of symbols and language.

"*Reasoning*" from observation is *inference making*, and we are continually making inferences. Most of the statements we make are *not* reports of observations, but *inferences*. To make no inferences is impossible, yet we often treat our statements as if they were observations of absolute accuracy. We may observe an individual *doing* something— throwing a book, pounding on a desk, or kicking a chair. But we may not observe that the individual is "mad." An individual's state of mind can only be inferred.

inferences

We make inferences quickly and automatically. A: "Look at that drunk." B: "Did you see a drunk?" A: "Well, I saw a man in messy clothes weaving down the street." B: "Well, he looked (I inferred) drunk."

inferences are necessary

The question is not whether we make inferences, but whether we are aware of the nature of the inferences we make. All situations contain a degree of uncertainty about the nature of what we experience or observe. Often, we cannot predict with complete accuracy what will happen next.

Managers responsible for policy decisions and program implementation do not always have all the factual evidence they would like to have to make decisions. They often must deal with inferences selectively passed along to them. It isn't surprising that the inferences are sometimes treated as factual evidence. This practice may be a highly effective technique for gaining power, because making organizational decisions in the face of uncertainty demands assurance.

observations

Observational statements are referred to as "denotative." This implies that we think what we have said is highly representative of some event or thing. When we use language to describe reality, we are dealing with a symbol-to-object *relationship*. Problems occur when we forget that meaning is a relationship between an individual and reality. Meaning is not a characteristic of an object. We use words that have clear references for us but not necessarily for our receivers.

How can we clarify reports? How can we be "accurate"? Point to the object, or if you can't point, approximate pointing by using models or pictures of objects. We often overlook this very simple approach to clarifying meaning. Remember that completely denotative definitions require the presence of the symbol *and* the object.

separate facts from inferences

When we fail to recognize that we have made an inference, we take an uncalculated risk. We behave, however, as if we were not taking a risk at all. All inference situations involve some uncertainty. When we fail to recognize this uncertainty, we do not bother to evaluate the probabilities of the outcome. This means we can be caught off guard when unexpected consequences occur.

Communication involves the transmission of symbols and messages from source to receiver. Meanings are attached to the symbols by the receiver. We do not transfer meaning as we would transfer milk from a pitcher to a glass; we transmit only symbols and messages that, hopefully, elicit meanings in receivers (see Figure 5.7).

Let's take a look at a series of statements:

meaning

To use words properly, you must know their meanings. Right or wrong? Wrong, of course. To use words properly, you must be able to estimate the approximate meaning that will be elicited in the receiver. The accuracy of communication is the degree of similarity between what the source wants the receiver to think and what the receiver thinks.

Figure 5.7 We do not transfer meaning—only messages.

The purpose of writing is to transmit meaning. Right or wrong? Wrong. The purpose of writing is to transmit symbols and messages which we hope will elicit or evoke meaning.

I hear a noise that sounds like thunder; that means rain soon. That means nothing soon. The receiver implies and creates meaning from the sounds reaching him. Interpretation of messages provides additional inputs for an individual. Communication is not an action/reaction system, but a feedback system in which we can adapt and change meanings according to the situation.

When we have experienced similar situations, we develop similar meanings for them. Consistency in response to symbol situations is the result of learning similar meanings.

communication depends on similar meanings

Communication does not require identical meaning in both sender and receiver. Two people will usually not have exactly the same meanings for anything. Effective communication depends on whether there is enough similarity between source-intended and receiver-elicited meaning for understanding to occur.

Barriers to Effective Communication

We do not react to a message in isolation; we react to the relationship created by the situation, the message symbol, and the individual. Focus on the sender's meaning for the word, not on the word itself. Our

The Process of Communication   113

meaning for an object does not include all the characteristics of the object but only selected characteristics. In developing and changing meaning, we consider features of the situation: our expectations and previous experiences, our motives and desires.

Process of Abstracting

we cannot communicate every detail

Experiences cannot be communicated directly. A headache or an emotion, whether joy or sorrow, cannot be directly transferred to a receiver. We use language to represent experiences and feelings.

Communication involves the process of *abstracting*. When we report on an observed event, we abstract by reporting only the characteristics that seem valuable to us. These are often more a product of inference than of observation. We observe only partially. As we attempt to convert observations into language, we further abstract by using general rather than specific terms.

Using language involves leaving out details. We cannot communicate *every* detail of any given event. We are forced by the limitations of observation to leave out those details we cannot observe. If we tried to *completely* describe a simple object, such as a table, we would fill volumes and still not succeed. It is easy to see the limitations of language. We may become frustrated when we attempt to describe in detail a complicated process because of our inability to complete the description.

levels of abstraction

In language, there is a movement from lower to higher levels of abstraction. A simple example of choosing a level of abstraction would be moving from a term such as *transportation* to the more specific term *motor car* to an even more specific term, *automobile,* and continuing to *four-door sedan* and a description of make, color, year, accessories, and so on. As we move from the abstract to the more specific, we increase the probability of obtaining the desired response from the receiver.

Proceeding from lower to higher levels of abstraction and back again can occur continuously. Varying levels of abstraction are most effective when the variation is adjusted to the needs of the receiver. The more concrete, the lower the level of abstraction. We attempt to increase our effectiveness by determining what level of abstraction has the highest probability of obtaining the desired response. In the example above, we could have shown someone the automobile referred to. This method of communication, however, can be extremely time-consuming and expensive; and it does not guarantee the desired response. It only increases its probability. Although two people view the same object, they may not interpret it in the same way.

adjust to the receiver

Abstracting, interpreting, and drawing inferences from our interpretations is a personal process. People vary in their ability to deal with abstractions. The level of abstraction must be adjusted to the receiver in order to achieve maximum effectiveness. If we are too specific, we may become boring. If we are too general, operating at too high a level of abstraction, our messages may become meaningless. A message that can mean anything means nothing.

Abstracting may result in generalizations with weak connections to reality. We may become lazy in our usage and depend heavily on highly abstract and general terms, stereotypes, labels, and pigeonholing. When operating at a high level of abstraction, we may use terms which lump dissimilar characteristics into one highly abstract group. We must generalize, but we should not be surprised when a generalization does not produce the desired response from the receiver.

It is wise to realize that we can never communicate with total effectiveness. No matter what attempts we make for precision, we are doomed to some degree of failure; consequences cannot be predicted with complete accuracy.

Confusing Symbols with Realities

A communication barrier involves confusing *symbols* with things or processes. The inability to distinguish between the word and the thing it stands for makes it difficult to compare the communication of an individual with the realities of the physical world. An example of this tendency is the social taboo attached to the use of some obscene and sacred words. The words are regarded as the objects for which they stand. It is easy to overlook the fact that a word is but a symbol. It is *not* the thing for which it stands.

words and things

Words may be considered as pointers, indicators, or forms of representation intended to correspond to anything whatsoever that may exist or be experienced. To oversimplify, we can say there is a world of words and a world of not-words. The universe of discourse is not the universe of direct experience. A word is not a complete representation—if it were, it would not be a word but a nonverbal fact. Words can be manipulated independently of any nonverbal event or fact. No *inner* necessity governs the use of words in their relationship to things, feelings, and circumstances. We can use language to distort, lie, write fiction, or tell fables. Words can be used according to the whim of the user. Language cannot force a user to adhere to actual facts. Every receiver of messages should attempt to determine whether or not the verbal statements correspond to realities.

world of words and world of not-words

Awareness of the different characteristics of symbols and what they stand for should lead to the understanding that messages should be *neither* blindly rejected nor blindly accepted. We should be conscious of the possibility of structural dissimilarity between words and things.

Experience and Expectations

The way people live influences their manner of thinking, feeling, and acting. People have experiences which result in a set of expectations concerning communication situations. These experiences and expectations give meaning to our language. One basis for effective communication is the similar experiences and expectations people attach to similar language symbols. The farmer whose experiences and expectations differ from those of the factory worker, the doctor, or the banker finds it as hard to understand them as they do to understand him.

Our expectations in a specific situation affect our interpretations of messages. For example, when individuals are exposed to ambiguous messages or words (e.g., *chack*) they respond in terms of their expectations. When expecting the name of an animal, the interpretation is *chick*. When expecting a term related to money and banking the interpretation is *check*.

Attitudes and Values

People tend to interpret messages so they are consistent with their attitudes and values. When forced to deal with individuals and events beyond individual experience, people tend to fill in the gaps according to their attitudes. Thus, from a limited knowledge of Germans, a person can build a complete description of them.

The process of interpreting information so that it is consistent with existing attitudes and values often characterizes our thinking. In the absence of *any* relevant experiences, our attitudes and values may be the basis for our judgments. Attitudes and values may have an emotional basis which makes them very resistant to fact and logic. Emotionally loaded attitudes often result in stereotypes that are extremely difficult to change.

attitudes and values satisfy needs

Many studies have shown that attitudes are not necessarily abstractions from personal experience. They are often learned from others.

Attitudes and values serve personal needs. In some cases the content of the attitude is wish fulfillment. Studies have shown that anti-Semitic attitudes are strongest among persons dissatisfied with their own achievements. These studies argue against the notion that all attitudes are rationally founded. Attitudes are seldom revised under the impact of new factual evidence if they are providing need satisfaction for the individual. The attitude will not be modified until the individual finds another way of satisfying the need.

Individual Differences

It would be easier to overcome psychological barriers to communication if there were no individual differences—if we all had common abilities, experiences, and environments. Because we are different in so many ways, however, we distort the intended meaning of messages according to our predispositions. Individual psychological differences are some of the greatest barriers to communication (see Figure 5.8). Our communication is affected by our needs and interests.

Figure 5.8 When people have different experiences, they develop different meanings.

After a tour of a company's newly acquired department store, three corporate managers sat down to discuss needed improvements. Their discussion quickly became an argument over each manager's perception of the "real" problems in the store. The marketing manager saw major problems in the display of merchandise and the way salespersons were serving customers. The finance manager saw major problems in the way sales slips were completed and the use of the cash register. The maintenance manager saw major problems in the operation of the escalator and the fire protection system. It seemed as if they were talking about different department stores. The communication problem in this situation resulted from the selected perception of the managers.[5]

effect of needs and interests

Effective Listening

Functioning effectively in an organization requires the ability to listen. On the average, 45 percent of our communication time is spent in listening.[4] Since we spend such a large percentage of our time listening, we should be concerned about improving our listening ability. Successful communication depends as much on the ability to receive messages as it does on the ability to send messages. When a person speaks and no one listens, there is obviously no communication. If managers listened effectively to co-workers and employees, they could substantially increase their success as managers.[5]

How Well Do We Listen?

Most people do not listen very well. Research indicates that an average individual retains about 50 percent of the main content of a ten-minute speech immediately after listening to it. After forty-eight hours the retention drops to about 25 percent of the original content.[6] A number of other studies have found basically the same results. A conservative estimate would be that most people retain 25 percent or less of what they hear. Everyone has observed situations where there was a communication failure because of poor listening.

it is difficult to listen effectively

As individuals go about their daily activities, they are often preoccupied with their own problems, which makes it difficult to listen effectively. Better listening means paying attention to what is said. A total focus on one's own concerns results in psychological deafness.

The lack of good listening is one of the major communication problems in organizations. If individuals would listen attentively, misunderstandings and conflicts could be drastically reduced.

neglected skill

No communication skill has been more neglected in the education system than listening behavior. Most individuals are continually taught the skills of reading, writing, and speaking throughout the educational process. Rarely are individuals taught how to listen effectively. Listening that results in accurate comprehension requires concentration and hard work. There are no easy approaches or shortcuts to improving listening.

Sperry Corporation Promotes the Importance of Listening Skills

The following quote from a Sperry Corporation advertisement in *Business Week* illustrates the importance businesses place on effective listening.

"A listener loose in a world of talkers has one unbeatable edge: the flow of new ideas through his ears to his mind never stops.

It has been said there's at least one thing to learn from everyone one meets. Provided one bothers to listen.

Unfortunately for most people, no one ever bothered to teach us how. Which is why listening is available to Sperry employees, worldwide.

Helping our people become better listeners helps make us a better corporation.

For one thing, it eliminates the enormous costs of simple listening errors.

But more than that, it's making our employees better thinkers. Better problem sovlers. And ultimately more open to the original and unexpected."[7]

Barriers to Effective Listening

Individuals are not born with good listening habits. Like all other communication skills, effective listening must be learned. Bad habits must be eliminated and more effective listening behaviors must be developed. The following bad habits form barriers to effective listening.

Daydreaming or Creative Distractions   Poor listeners often lose the speaker's words by concentrating on their own train of thought. Daydreaming may involve thinking about pleasant past experiences or anticipating some desirable future event. A student may replay last night's party rather than listen to the lecture in a class. An employee may visualize a forthcoming fishing trip rather than listen in the meeting on safety procedures. Individuals can also create distractions by worrying about problems. A student may fail to listen to the 8:00 class because he or she is worrying about a test in the 10:00 class. An employee may worry about overdue bills rather than listen to the manager's instructions.

daydreaming

Mentally Arguing with the Speaker   Instead of listening to what someone is saying, the poor listener often begins to disagree mentally and starts planning a rebuttal. Mentally arguing with the speaker often involves making assumptions about what is going to be said. Developing arguments before comprehending the total message usually leads to misunderstanding and conflict. Individuals may develop arguments because their emotions have reduced their objectivity. Conclusions reached before a speaker is finished are often inaccurate.

If a speaker uses emotionally loaded terms, the poor listener may mentally argue with the use of the terms. The poor listener may attempt to censor the message rather than try to understand it. The listener may try to rebut or discredit the speaker who uses loaded terms such as *pig* for police officer or *broad* for woman. Effective listening takes place when the speaker is allowed to finish before evaluations and judgments are made.

emotionally loaded terms

Desire to Talk   Frequently, individuals are poor listeners because they are preoccupied with talking. They may use "listening time" to rehearse what they are going to say when it is their turn to talk and fail to hear what the speaker is saying. Many individuals feel more active, more useful, and more important when talking. They must have a strong desire to listen if they are to resist the need to talk.

impatient to talk

lack of interest   *Indifference and Lack of Interest in Message Content*   Those who assume that a message is going to be dull and boring will be poor listeners. Once a listener becomes indifferent to the message, there is little a speaker can do to recapture attention. When viewed objectively, it is difficult to identify a subject that is totally uninteresting. If the listener concentrates on the message, there is usually information that is meaningful and useful. A good listener will look for useful information in any message. Good listeners expose themselves to messages that broaden their interests and develop their abilities. To decide a message is going to be of no value means listening stops before it begins.

Negative Reactions to the Speaker's Appearance or Delivery   You cannot listen effectively if you are mentally responding to the speaker's dress, voice qualities, or mannerisms. Listeners may fail to comprehend important and useful information if they react negatively to the characteristics of the speaker. It is often easy to focus on a mannerism to the point that the message content is secondary to the style of delivery. To the effective listener, the message content is much more important than characteristics of the speaker.

Guides for Listening Improvement

To improve listening requires a commitment to communication. The following are practical guides for more effective listening. They do not provide an easy way to better listening—you will have to work at improving you skills.

1. Stop talking. You can't listen while you are talking.
2. Empathize with the speaker. Try to put yourself in the speaker's place. Try to determine how the speaker feels about the message. Try to understand the speaker's point of view, taking into account his or her attitudes, values, and background.
3. Ask questions. This shows that you are interested and it encourages the speaker. Ask questions to further your understanding, not to embarrass or show up the speaker.
4. Concentrate on what the speaker is saying. Actively focus your attention on concepts, ideas, attitudes, and feelings related to the message.
5. Show the speaker that you want to listen. Look and act interested. Listen to understand, rather than to argue. Try to put the speaker at ease. Don't be antagonistic; the speaker may then conceal his or her true ideas, attitudes, and feelings. Try to evaluate the effect you are having on the speaker.
6. Control your emotions and your temper. Anger usually leads to distortion and misinterpretation. Try to put worries, fears, and problems aside; they interfere with good listening. Try not to get emotional about what is said.

7. Get rid of distractions. Put down papers, pencils, and other objects that may distract you. If you are in an office, shut the door. Eliminate as many outside distractions as you can.

8. Look for areas of agreement. Mentally developing arguments sets up a barrier to understanding. Listen for areas of common interest and agreement. A speaker may be "turned off" if he or she perceives disagreement.

9. Avoid jumping to conclusions and making evaluations. Try to listen nonevaluatively, without making judgments about what is being said at the time. Making evaluations and drawing conclusions usually results in getting ahead of the speaker and "hearing" things that are not said. It is difficult to understand what the speaker is saying if you concentrate on what you think is going to be said. Don't assume that the speaker is distorting the truth because you disagree with his or her views. Listen to understand the conclusions and evaluations that the speaker is making.

10. Listen for the main points. Concentrate on the speaker's main ideas and the material used to support them. Sometimes we hear only the illustrative material, the examples, stories, and statistics. It is easy to miss the main points if we listen for minor details. Don't allow your reactions to distract you from the key concepts.

To become better listeners, individuals must be genuinely interested in what others have to say and less preoccupied with themselves.

Open-Door Policy at COBE Laboratories, Inc.

COBE Laboratories, a Colorado manufacturer of medical therapeutic systems, has found a way to encourage greater employee participation and involve more workers and managers in the decision-making process.

COBE's open-door policy promotes the discussion of problems, criticisms, and suggestions as they arise. If an employee feels dissatisfied with a supervisor's response in a particular case, the employee has a direct line to the next higher level of management. The open-door policy makes it possible to bypass the normal chain of command; if necessary, employees can even take their concerns directly to the president of the company.

Generally, COBE encourages employees to solve problems with their immediate supervisors. Yet going to a higher level of management does not necessarily mean that the immediate supervisor cannot handle the problem. The problem or suggestion may simply require the knowledge and experience of more people. For those supervisors threatened by the open-door policy, management counsels them to listen to and ask for employees' opinions more often. All supervisors meet with top-level management every two months to discuss concerns in their areas.

COBE has found that its open-door policy has improved the quality of input on company problems and facilitated better decision making.[8]

Nonverbal Communication

One of the most important keys to understanding communication is to realize that much of it is never put into words. A nonverbal message can be transmitted by a nod of the head, a frown, an enthusiastic tone of voice, leaving one's office door open or closed, or arriving late for an appointment.[9]

actions and words
Much of the communication that affects people is never verbalized. People communicate by the way they look at another person or by the gestures they make. A *nonverbal message* can be transmitted by a handshake, a pat on the back, a smile, a frown, or any observable behavior. The most important expressions of emotional states usually are communicated on the nonverbal level.

Managers who tell employees that they are interested in their suggestions but ignore their ideas and information are communicating a lack of interest. The statement, "Actions speak louder than words" is especially true for communication in organizations as shown in Figure 5.9. Employees are influenced more by managers' actions than by their words.

Individuals often spend a great deal of time and thought preparing verbal messages. It is usually assumed that writing or speaking effectively requires conscious thought and real work, learning how to spell, to write sentences, to read, and to make speeches. Nonverbal communication behaviors, on the other hand, are usually learned by imitation. As a result, people tend to be less aware of the nonverbal messages they transmit and receive. This lack of awareness can lead to problems

silence communicates
in communication. Silence is an example of a type of nonverbal communication that is often not consciously considered. Employees may feel that their efforts are unappreciated if managers fail to compliment them on outstanding work.

Five major nonverbal dimensions that directly affect communication are: (1) kinesics, or body language; (2) proxemics, or spatial relations; (3) chronemics, or the use of time; (4) paralanguage, or the use of the voice; and (5) artifacts, or object language.

Kinesics (Body Language)

Kinesics is the study of body movements and the visual aspects of behavior. Included in the study of kinesics are the effects of posture, facial expressions, movement, and gestures. Body language can support and supplement verbal communication. Body language can also be used to attempt to hide attitudes and feelings. You probably have told someone that you like his new clothes when you really didn't like them. To support your verbal statement of "liking," you may have attempted to look pleased by smiling and nodding with approval.

Body language also contradicts verbal statements when an individual says, "I am interested in what you have to say" while looking out the window, tapping her fingers on the desk, and continually glancing at the clock. The more the individual fidgets, the stronger the nonverbal message, "I am not interested and want to leave."

body language

Figure 5.9 Actions speak louder than words.

The Process of Communication   123

Because of individual differences, it is easy to misinterpret body language. An individual who is yawning could be anxious, fatigued, or bored. Judgments about the meaning of body movements must be made carefully. Although facial expressions provide information about emotional states, it is difficult to distinguish between emotions such as anger, grief, and despair.

The study of kinescis has not been extensive enough to determine direct relationships between specific body movements and meaning. The following are some of the preliminary conclusions that may help increase awareness of body language.

increasing awareness of body language

- Orienting the body or crossing the legs toward another person may indicate a desire to include the other in communication.
- Leaning forward and facing a person may indicate a favorable attitude toward the individual.
- Turning the shoulders and legs away from a person may indicate dislike.
- As the intensity of an emotional state increases, the individual tends to increase body movements.
- Positioning of the shoulders and legs toward one person and away from another may indicate, "I am with you and against the other person."
- Raising the head and shoulders may indicate assumption of a superior role position or higher status. Lowering the head and shoulders may indicate assumption of an inferior role position or lower status.
- Direct eye contact may indicate attraction and interest. Avoiding eye contact may indicate a rejection or lack of interest.

No single body movement, however, should be considered as an absolute indication of individual's attitudes, feelings, or emotions.

Proxemics (Spatial Relations)

Proxemics is the study of how individuals structure and use space. Important spatial relations include the distances maintained between people during communication and the use of space in houses, offices, cities, and buildings. Individuals learn what is considered to be the appropriate distance to maintain in communication situations. The appropriate distance for communicating with friends may not be the same as the appropriate distance for talking with the boss.

space speaks

Giving an employee a private office conveys a nonverbal message of that individual's importance to the company. Most employees are concerned about the space in which they work. The amount and type of space in an office, the office location, and the way it is furnished can represent authority, status, position, and protection. Although the amount of space is not an absolute indication of status, it is usually a sign of importance. The location of an office may also function as an indication of importance. Executive offices are usually located on the top floors of a building.

Most people will move physically closer when communicating with individuals they like and will maintain more distance from those they dislike. If someone gets too close (according to the individual's distance standards) the individual will become uncomfortable and probably move away. If the receiver moves too far away, the communicator tends to move toward the receiver to reestablish the desired spatial relationship.

Individuals usually maintain a greater distance from people with high status. For example, an employee may stand in the doorway of the manager's office to talk, while the manager's boss will walk up to the edge of the desk.

The higher the status of individuals, the more right they usually feel to invade the space of those with lower status. The president of the company can invade the space of managers by barging into their office at any time, but it is not acceptable behavior for the managers to barge into the president's office. A teacher can invade the space of students by looking over their shoulders as they write an exam. Students cannot return the invasion by looking over the teacher's shoulder while the exams are being graded.

The use of space is a significant aspect of any communication situation.

Chronemics (Use of Time)

An important but often overlooked element of nonverbal communication is the use of time, or *chronemics.* Time is often viewed as a commodity that can be spent, saved, earned, or wasted. American society is very time-conscious as reflected in our dependence on clocks and time schedules. In business one frequently hears that "time is money." Attitudes toward time are communicated by the ways individuals deal with it.

time talks

The importance of time in organizational communication can be seen everywhere. We set completion dates for projects, use time clocks, establish specific pay periods, schedule meetings, and negotiate working hours. Specific times are often established for coffee breaks and lunch periods. Completing a project within a specific time period may be a major consideration in an employee's performance evaluation. The employee who is frequently late to work will most likely be communicating disorganization, disinterest, and unreliability to management.

Much of the communication of the use of time involves arrival times. When an individual arrives ahead of time for a meeting it may communicate interest and respect for the person holding the meeting. To arrive late for a meeting may communicate disinterest and disrespect for the person holding the meeting.

Whether an arrival at a meeting or appointment or party is considered early, on time, or late depends on beliefs about acceptable arrival times. When invited to a cocktail party at 7:00 P.M., the expected arrival time may be 7:30 P.M. or later. An appointment with the boss at 9:00 A.M. may involve an expectation that the employee arrive ten minutes early in case the boss is "running ahead of time." It is usually expected that employees will never arrive late for an appointment with the boss. However, it is usually acceptable for the boss to arrive late for an appointment with an employee or to keep an employee waiting. Most organizations develop definite standards to be observed in the use of time. The standards may vary as a result of job function, status in the organization, and the nature of the situation; but failure to observe the standards communicates nonverbal messages that can reduce the individual's chances for success in the organization.

Paralanguage (Use of the Voice)

Paralanguage is concerned with how something is said rather than what is said. The meaning of a sentence can differ significantly depending on which words are stressed. Consider the following variations:

- *How* did he do the job?
- How *did* he do the job?
- How did *he* do the job?
- How did he *do* the job?

By shifting the emphasis, the sentence can convey different meanings. The way the voice is used is an important element in understanding messages. Individuals can "read between the lines" of written messages, and they can "hear between the words" of spoken messages.

Paralanguage can be broken down into the following four major elements: (1) *voice qualities*, which include tone, rhythm, resonance, and tempo; (2) *vocal characteristics*, which include crying, laughing, whispering, sighing, yelling, yawning, and so forth; (3) *vocal irregularities*, which include nonfluencies (em,uh-hum, ers, etc.) and silent pauses; and (4) *vocal qualifiers* of intensity (how loud or soft), rate (how fast or slow), and pitch (how high or low). It is the combination of these elements that results in each individual having unique speech patterns.

Most people are quick to make judgments about another's personality based on a combination of paralinguistic characteristic. In some cases the judgments turn out to be accurate; in some cases, inaccurate. The number of times these judgments are accurate or inaccurate does not seem to affect the frequency with which the judgments are made. Some of the common personality stereotypes based on voice characteristics are:

- Individuals with nasal voices are nagging, whiny, and unpleasant.
- Men with deep throaty voices are mature, sophisticated, and well adjusted, but women with deep and throaty voices are boring, dull, and ugly.
- Women with high-pitched and breathy voices are feminine, pretty, shallow, and petite. Men with high-pitched and breathy voices are artistic, unrealistic, and "unmanly."
- Individuals who speak in a monotone are cold, withdrawn, and have little interest in life.

stereotypes based on use of the voice

These judgments about personality made from voice characteristics are not generally supported by research evidence. A variety of studies have found very mixed results on the accuracy of using voice characteristics to predict personality traits.[10]

Studies of paralanguage have demonstrated that individuals vary in their ability to determine the emotions of a speaker from vocal cues and that individuals also vary in their ability to express their emotions through the use of the voice.[11] It appears that some emotions are much easier to distinguish than others. For example, it may be easy to distinguish between sympathy and hate but difficult to distinguish between anxiety and fear.

The rate or speed with which individuals speak may be an indication of their emotional state. It has been found that faster rates, short comments, and frequent pauses indicate anger, stress, or fear; slower rates, longer comments and less frequent pauses indicate grief or depression.[12]

Artifacts (Object Language)

Object language or *artifacts* refers to the communication that results from the display of material things. Some of the objects that frequently influence communication are clothes, furniture, methods of transportation, and architectural arrangements. Individuals attempt to enhance their personal object language by purchasing items such as clothes, lipstick, eyeglasses, hairpieces, and false eyelashes. A person's office furnishings and their arrangement also convey messages about the individual. The arrangement of furniture in a conference room can affect the communication patterns that occur in a meeting. A work environment's architectural style, furnishings, equipment, color, and attractiveness are all important elements in organizational communication.

Physical settings convey information about the kind of activities that are to take place and the kind of behaviors that are acceptable. The restaurant that wants quick turnover has bright lighting, "less comfortable" chairs, and tables placed closely together. If the desire is to encourage customers to stay longer, the lighting is dim, the colors are subdued, and the furniture is comfortable. The benches in shopping malls are usually hard, encouraging people to circulate among the shops rather than sit. The manager who has hard plastic chairs for visitors may be trying to discourage them from staying too long.

messages from objects The furnishings in an office can be used to communicate the status of the occupant. A large wooden desk and an executive swivel chair indicate more status than a small metal desk and a straight chair. Carpeting may indicate a status level, and awards and pictures placed on office walls may convey status or prestige. Each object in an office delivers its message about the occupant.

The way furniture is arranged in an office can affect the communication that takes place there. A desk placed between a manager and an

Figure 5.10   Actions need to be consistent with words.

employee may be a psychological barrier as well as a physical barrier because it represents authority and power.

The nonverbal communication of a manager's clothing, personal mannerisms, and office all affect the total message that employees receive.

Objects in the environment both communicate and affect other communication processes. The way an individual uses objects tells others a great deal about the user.

Conclusions

Our perceptions and interpretations of messages are shaped by our individual needs and desires. The message is *not* only what you want to say and how you say it; it is also what the other person *wants* to hear.

It is difficult to communicate with people who do not already agree with the position expressed by a message. We tend to avoid information which conflicts with our own attitudes and beliefs; consequently, people who are *not* already in favor of the content of a message are difficult to reach. The people who may "need" the message most may be those least likely to hear it.

Knowledge about communication will always be important to anyone who wants to function more effectively in an organization. Communication is the vital link between people that makes it possible for an organization to function. It is never easy to develop effective communication and there are no cure-alls for communication problems. Effective communication requires more than knowing techniques or mastering skills. It must be based on cooperation, trust, and confidence among people.

In recognition of the difficulties involved in gaining understanding, a manager placed the following sign on his desk:

> I know you believe you understood what you think I said, but I am not sure you realize that what you heard is not what I meant.

Quick Review

I. The Importance of Communication
  A. About 70 to 80 percent of a manager's time is involved in communication. All aspects of a manager's job are accomplished through communication.
  B. Our ability to understand others has lagged far behind our technical accomplishments in communication transmission.

C. The first obstacle in any communication is the process of selection.
II. Models of Communication
   A. While no communication model is complete, all communications involve a source, a message, and a receiver.
   B. Once coded and sent, a message is beyond control of the sender.
   C. For communication to occur, both the source and receiver must understand the same code systems.
   D. Communication involves a constant interlocking feedback cycle of encoding, decoding, and interpretation.
III. Language and Meaning
   A. Words link together all human activities.
   B. Words are symbols. We tend to confuse symbols with things.
      1. Meanings are in people, not in words.
      2. Because there are words does not mean there are things. Some words exist for which there are no things.
      3. We cannot transmit meanings—only messages.
   C. Physical things have both symbolic and functional values.
      1. Food is functional. We must eat. With whom we eat, where we eat, how it's prepared, and what is considered edible or inedible is often symbolic.
      2. A real connection between the symbol and what is symbolized does not necessarily exist.
      3. We often feel the same about the word (symbol) as we do about the thing symbolized.
   D. From observations we draw inferences regarding our perceptions of what has taken place. Inferences are not observations but conclusions drawn from observations or reported observations.
   E. Denotative statements are those based on actual observation.
   F. Because we often confuse our observations with inferences and treat inferences as if they were observations, we are led to incorrect conclusions.
   G. Inferences cannot be avoided. We can, however, be aware of inferences.
IV. Barriers to Effective Communication
   A. We do not react to a message in isolation but to the

relationships of situation, message, symbol, and individual.

    B. To encode observations, we abstract parts of them and transmit only our abstractions and inferences.

    C. We must be aware of abstraction and inferences in order to develop effective communication.

    D. Change is always taking place. We have a tendency to freeze our abstractions as if a dynamic, on-going event is frozen in time.

    E. We must keep in mind that:

        1. The word is not the object.

        2. The word does not represent all of the object.

        3. We use language to describe language.

    F. Experiences and expectations often cause us to interpret the world around us in widely differing ways.

    G. People tend to interpret messages in a way consistent with their values and attitudes.

    H. Our tendency to select what we see, hear, and understand is based on our individual psychological differences.

  V. Effective Listening

    A. The lack of good listening is one of the major communication problems in organizations.

    B. Barriers to effective listening include:

        1. Daydreaming or creative distractions.

        2. Mentally arguing with the speaker.

        3. Preferring to talk rather than listen.

        4. Indifference or lack of interest in message content.

        5. Negative reactions to the speaker's appearance or delivery.

  VI. Guides for Listening Improvement

    A. Stop talking.

    B. Empathize with the speaker.

    C. Ask questions.

    D. Concentrate on what the speaker is saying.

    E. Show the speaker you want to listen.

    F. Control you emotions and your temper.

    G. Get rid of distractions.

    H. Look for areas of agreement.

    I. Avoid jumping to conclusions and making evaluations.

    J. Listen for the main points.

  VII. Nonverbal Communication

    A. The most important expressions of emotional states usually are communicated on the nonverbal level.

B. The lack of awareness of nonverbal messages can result in ineffective communication.
C. Five major dimensions of nonverbal communication are:
    1. Kinesics, or body language.
    2. Proxemics, or spatial relations.
    3. Chronemics, or the use of time.
    4. Paralanguage, or the use of the voice.
    5. Artifacts, or object language.

Key Terms

Communication
Source
Encoding
Receiver
Decoding
Message
Communication
   channels

Symbolic value
Inferences
Levels of abstraction
Symbols
Nonverbal
   communication
Kinesics
Proxemics

Chronemics
Paralanguage
Artifacts

Discussion Questions

1. How can communication models be used to improve the effectiveness of communication?
2. How is an individual's position in a social system important in communication?
3. Discuss the effect of group pressure on communication.
4. Comment on the following assumptions about language and meaning.
   a. Meanings are in words.
   b. Because there is a word for it, a thing must exist.
   c. Communication consists of the transmission of meaning.
   d. All statements are either true or false.
5. What are the characteristics of an inference?
6. Does communication require identical meaning in both sender and receiver?
7. How do people learn meanings?
8. Give an example of a low-level abstraction and a high-level abstraction.
9. Discuss the following barriers to effective communication.
   a. Confusing symbols and facts.
   b. The influence of expectations.
   c. Selective perception.

10. Discuss the major barriers to effective listening.
11. What advice would you give an individual who wants improved listening ability?
12. Why is nonverbal communication important to a manager?
13. Describe a situation in which an individual's motivational state was communicated nonverbally.

Case Incidents

No More Reminders

Alan Moore, the shipping supervisor for mail orders in a large department store, must see to it that customer orders are accurately and promptly filled. Alan does not have the authority to make substitutions for items not in stock or to adjust for errors in advertised prices. For these decisions, Alan must go to the warehouse manager.

When Alan asks the warehouse manager for a decision on filling an order, Alan is usually told that the decision will need to be checked with the store manager, who has final authority. Often it is weeks before Alan can ship the order. In an effort to get decisions faster, Alan started reminding the warehouse manager each day of the decisions that were pending. After two weeks, the warehouse manager told Alan, "You mind the shipping, and I'll take care of the decisions. I don't need any more of your reminders."

Alan now has to wait for decisions again, which continues to delay shipping orders. When customers complain to the store manager, the manager blames Alan for the delayed shipments and lets him know in no uncertain terms that getting orders out promptly is his responsibility.

Alan has tried to explain his problem with the warehouse manager, but the store manager simply cuts his explanations short. "Don't give me any more excuses, your job is to see that the orders get out."

1. Will the orders now get out promptly? Will the situation improve? Why or why not?
2. What are the important nonverbal communications in this situation?
3. What should each of the three managers do to improve communication and increase the effectiveness of the shipping department?

For Me or Against Me?

Mr. Cook, production manager, began his weekly meeting with supervisors by stating, "The new production control system will eliminate our current problems of excessive cost due to rejects that do not meet quality standards. I want every supervisor to make this system work."

Before he could continue, James Belt, a senior supervisor who had been with the company fifteen years spoke up. "Mr. Cook, I've met with the other supervisors, and we have a list of twelve changes that have to be made in the new system before it can operate effectively."

"Now Jim," replied Mr. Cook, "on implementing this new system, either you control costs or you don't. I am not going to argue about the system. The industrial engineering staff has assured me that it will work, because it's worked at other plants."

"But Mr. Cook," Belt persisted, "I think we need to work out a few problems before we try to implement the system."

At this, Mr. Cook became angry. "Belt, you're obviously against my system and my attempts to cut excessive costs. I don't want any more discussion on this!"

He then turned to the entire group of supervisors and asked, "Are there any questions?"

Not surprisingly, there were no questions and the meeting was adjourned.

1. What communication problems are illustrated by this situation?
2. How do you think James Belt and the other supervisors felt after the meeting? Did the meeting help develop a commitment on the part of the supervisors to help make the new system work?
3. Could the communication have been handled more effectively by Mr. Cook? If so, how?

Who's Cheating?

In a manufacturing company producing sporting goods, machine operators were paid on an incentive system, which provided a bonus for output in excess of standards set by industrial engineers. The operators were continually tampering with the counters on their plastic molding machines, turning them forward to indicate more units than were actually produced.

Management had been aware of the problem for over six months, but had ignored it at first because the increases averaged less than 5 percent over actual production.

The increases later reached an average of 25 percent. The manufacturing manager called in the supervisor and instructed him to "stop the cheating on the molding machines and punish the cheaters."

The supervisor secretly installed counters in his office that measured the actual production on each machine. None of the operators had any knowledge of the system. The supervisor kept track of the daily production of each operator for two weeks and compared it with the reports taken from the counters on the machines. He made up the payroll report from his secret records of production.

The supervisor then called all of the operators into his office and told them, "We have measured the actual output on the machines and that is what you got paid for. You cheaters are lucky I didn't fire all of you. The next one of you I catch cheating on the production count will be laid off without pay for a week."

Bill Thompson, the newest operator asked, "How do you know anyone is cheating on the production count?"

The supervisor replied, "None of your business. You are paid for production. I'm paid to make sure you don't get paid for more than you actually produce. Is that clear?"

The next day the operators went to the production manager's office. They said that they were not going back to work until the supervisor apologized for his accusation that they were "cheaters."

The production manager called the supervisor in to discuss the problem with the operators. The supervisor told them about the secret counters and emphasized that "my count is 100 percent accurate and it proves you are all cheaters."

The operators freely admitted that they had turned the counters forward, but they insisted it was not cheating. "We only turned the counters forward when we could not get production because the machine was down through no fault of ours."

1. If you were the production manager, how would you handle the situation?
2. What were the characteristics of the communication between the supervisor and the operators?
3. Could the supervisor have handled the problem more effectively? How?
4. Why did the operators turn the counters forward when they felt they were due more production rather than go to the supervisor?
5. What does the term "cheater" mean to both sides in this situation?

Exercise   *Nonverbal Communication*

Most people do not analyze how nonverbal messages affect them. This exercise gives you an opportunity to discover how you react to nonverbal communication.

For each of the five major dimensions of nonverbal communication, think of a specific situation that illustrates it. Describe the specific message (or event) for each dimension, how you interpreted the message (what did it mean to you), and how you responded or were affected by the message.

BODY LANGUAGE (posture, facial expressions, gestures, eye contact, etc.)
Description of message or event:

What did it mean to you?

How did you respond or how were you affected by the message?

SPATIAL RELATIONS (distances between people, use of space in houses, offices, etc.)
Description of message or event:

What did it mean to you?

How did you respond or how were you affected by the message?

USE OF TIME (schedules, time requirements, people arriving early, late, etc.)
Description of message or event:

What did it mean to you?

How did you respond or how were you affected by the message?

USE OF THE VOICE (voice qualities, vocal characteristics, etc.)
Description of message or event:

What did it mean to you?

How did you respond or how were you affected by the message?

OBJECT LANGUAGE (display of material things)
Description of message or event:

What did it mean to you?

How did you respond or how were you affected by the message?

Endnotes

1. James J. Cribbin, *Effective Managerial Leadership* (New York: American Management Association, 1972), p. 161.
2. Ralph W. Reber and Gloria E. Terry, *Behavioral Insight for Supervision* (Englewood Cliffs, N.J.: Prentice-Hall, 1975), p. 138.
3. For a more detailed account, see W. J. Coughlin, "The Great Mokusatsu Mistake: Was this the Deadliest Error of Our Time?" *Harper's*, March 1953, p. 31.
4. Ralph G. Nichols, "Do We Know How to Listen? Practical Helps in a Modern Age," in *Communication Concepts and Processes*, ed. Joseph A. DeVito (Englewood Cliffs, N.J.: Prentice-Hall, 1971), p. 206.
5. Mason Haire, *Psychology in Management* (New York: McGraw-Hill, 1964).
6. Phillip V. Lewis, *Organizational Communications:* The Essence of Effective Management (Columbus, Ohio: Grid Publishing Co., 1980), p. 146.
7. *Business Week,* January 18, 1982, p. 50.
8. Management Review, November 1979, p. 48.
9. Dalmar Fisher, *Communications in Organization* (St. Paul, Minn., West, 1981) p. 118.
10. Mark L. Knapp, *Nonverbal Communication in Human Interactions* (New York: Holt, Rinehart and Winston, 1972), pp. 151–55.
11. Joseph A. DeVito, *The Interpersonal Communication Book* (New York: Harper & Row, 1976), p. 362.
12. D. C. Barnlund, ed., *Interpersonal Communication: Survey and Studies* (Boston: Houghton Mifflin, 1968), p. 529.

6

Communication Effectiveness in Organizations

Learning Objectives

After reading this chapter, you should be able to:

1. Identify recent changes in management practices and their impact on communication.

2. Describe the characteristics of power-oriented and achievement-oriented approaches to communication.

3. State the causes for ineffective communication in organizations.

4. List practices to improve communication in organizations.

5. State how managers can increase productivity by effective communication practices.

Chapter Topics

Changing Management Concepts in Communication

Managerial Approaches to Communication

Practices to Improve Communication

Preview and Self-Evaluation

Successful communication in organizations depends on more than a knowledge of principles and pitfalls. Before the most effective communication technique can be selected, it is necessary to develop sensitivity to people, change in organizational environment, and forces external to the work organization. Of all human activities, communication is one of the most used and, in many ways, least understood. What is effective in one set of circumstances may be entirely ineffective in another. Chapter 6 explores the applications of communication principles to behavior in work organizations.

Before reading this chapter try answering the following true-false questions. Take the test again after reading the chapter. Are there any differences in your responses?

Answer True or False

1. If managers communicate in an organized, clear, and concise manner, they will always obtain employee agreement.   T   F

2. To improve organizational communication often requires changes in management styles or organizational policies.   T   F

3. The most effective way for managers to change employee behavior is to use threats or punishment.   T   F

4. Communications studies have found that the credibility of the source has more impact than the content of the message.   T   F

5. When work activities are controlled by the speed of machines, this can communicate to employees that management feels equipment is more important than individuals.   T   F

6. The quality of interpersonal communication improves when the use of status symbols is reduced.　　T　　F

7. To improve communication managers should be required to put all communication with employees in writing.　　T　　F

8. The use of jargon and technical terms can be a major cause of ineffective communication.　　T　　F

9. An effective approach to improve the quality of communication in an organization is to have employees participate in analyzing and solving job-related problems.　　T　　F

10. Individuals are most affected by messages that provide information on how they can satisfy their needs.　　T　　F

ANSWERS: 1. F; 2. T; 3. F; 4. T; 5. T; 6. T; 7. F; 8. T; 9. T; 10. T.

Changing Management Concepts in Communication

Successful communications to and among corporate employees cannot be a duty delegated to an individual or an organization with a fancy title and then forgotten. Employee information is everyone's job and when it isn't, the consequences can be formidable.[1]

A great many factors affect employee and managerial performance. Among the most important are verbal and nonverbal communication. Anything one person does or is believed to do can communicate to others and can affect their performance.

any behavior can communicate

Managers are faced with increasingly difficult problems in achieving effective communication with employees. Communication problems have resulted from such factors as changes in technology, social values, and in individual expectations of work.

Effective communication requires more than improving the form and style of communication. It requires more than good speech presentation, clear writing, and well-organized meetings. Clarity and organization of communication are important factors, but they do not ensure effectiveness. Many of the difficulties in communication involve organizational practices and procedures and the nature of management's relationships with employees. A supervisor may communicate in an organized, clear, and concise manner yet still be seen as incompetent or unfair by employees. As long as he or she is perceived as either incompetent or unfair, communication with employees will be generally unsuccessful.

changes in management practices

Management practices and procedures designed to improve interpersonal relations can have long-range positive effects. In other words, effective communication depends upon good interpersonal relations between management and employees. Although it is difficult to predict the final outcome of recent changes in management practices and their impact on communication, here are some types of activities being used to improve the quality of organizational communication:

interaction with employees

1. An increasing number of managers are attempting to involve employees in solving problems on their jobs. In changing their approach, management attempts to interact with employees to achieve better planning and a higher quality of job performance rather than focus on selling employees on practices and procedures. Examples of this approach were reported in October 1976 issue of *Fortune* by Alfred S. Warren, Jr., director of Personnel Development for General Motors.[2] In one General Motors plant glass breakage rose to 46 percent of the glass handled. Management tried all the traditional methods of persuading, selling, and threatening to convince employees to be more careful, but nothing worked. The problem of determining the causes of breakage was then turned over to the employees. The glass installers began talking with employees doing other body work about problems that resulted in glass breakage and ways of correcting them. As a result of the improved interaction, glass breakage in the plant almost ceased.

employee participation

2. Managers have traditionally concentrated on developing clear and concise ways of communicating information and instructions to employees. This emphasis on the downward flow of information is changing to an approach which involves developing two-way communication between management and employees directed toward achieving organizational objectives. Such management practices emphasize employee participation and interaction. M. Scott Myers cites the following example of employee participation with management to achieve company objectives: Assemblers were given the opportunity to help their company solve a problem: the company was losing money on the production of radar units. Management shared information with the assemblers concerning costs, delivery schedules, and production requirements. Management also worked with the employees to develop methods of reducing costs and creating more efficient assembly. In a year, using the employees' ideas, the number of

hours of labor required to assemble a radar unit was reduced from 138 to 41.[3] This example illustrates the potential for increased productivity by employee participation and interaction.

3. Verbal communication has always been important in organizations, but management actions are also an extremely important form of communication with employees. To increase the effectiveness of human interaction, managers are attempting to structure jobs so that the work is seen as more meaningful. When employees' jobs are controlled by the speed of an assembly line, workers may receive the message that management sees individuals as less important than equipment. If employees can make decisions independent of machine actions, management may be seen as having trust and confidence in the workers' abilities.

the job communicates

4. Managers are increasingly recognizing that communication is strongly affected by employee attitudes and feelings about management practices. In addition to the factual and logical content of communication, emphasis must be placed on the ways communication affects employees' attitudes and feelings.

attitudes and feelings

Managerial Approaches to Communication

Some of the newer and more successful management practices involve using different approaches to communication. These changes can be characterized as moving from a power-oriented approach toward an achievement-oriented approach to communication.

Power-Oriented Approach to Communication

A *power-oriented approach* assumes that management alone regulates and controls the flow of information in an organization. Regulating information is seen as an efficient method of controlling performance. When poor work occurs, power-oriented management attempts to direct the flow of information toward corrective actions. With a power-oriented approach, communication problems are frequently major causes of poor performance.

The power-oriented manager relies on persuasion and force to improve morale and establish stable communication. Telling people what to do becomes a method of coping with problems. Verbal messages are sent where they are felt to do the most good. Communication with employees focuses on "remedial" approaches and concentrates on stopping violations of organizational policies and procedures. Management communication with employees often focuses on persuading employees to believe they are getting a good deal from management. Information often becomes distorted in management's attempt to sell people on the organization. This approach may involve "propaganda" attempts, which result in employee suspicion and distrust.

Achievement-Oriented Approach to Communication

communication is a tool used in all aspects of management

An *achievement-oriented approach* assumes that effective communication is a necessary part of productive work. Communication difficulties are seen as symptoms or indications of organizational and managerial problems. Communication is *not* seen as an independent function of the organization, but as a tool that is used in all aspects of management.

The achievement-oriented approach does not require "special communication programs," because information is communicated to employees through the job and involvement with management. Individuals at all levels in the organization communicate in planning and controlling functions related to their jobs. The management practices in an achievement-oriented approach attempt to develop communication among individuals as a part of the job.

The assumption underlying achievement orientation is that effective communication results from people having meaningful jobs and doing challenging work related to their personal goals.

Improvement in the quality of communication can be achieved by rearranging work groups, changing organizational patterns, reorganizing jobs, and creating different person-job relationships. To help employees achieve goals the manager changes behavior rather than verbal communication.

language of the job

Most managers realize that no matter how well they listen, how effectively they speak, how clearly they write, or how often they hold meetings, in the end the most powerful effect on communication in an organization is the language of the job. Improvements in communication often require changes in the nature of jobs, management styles, or organizational policies.[4]

It is desirable to create conditions in which the focus of communication is on achievement through problem solving, obtaining information, and expressing feelings. If communication follows the demands of the work situation, it will help to create trust. Managers who rely on actions as well as words to communicate are frequently more effective. When something goes wrong, however, effective managers concentrate on obtaining as much information as they can—they stop telling and start listening. Table 6.1 summarizes the characteristics of power-oriented and achievement-oriented approaches to communication.

Practices to Improve Communication

There are many valuable methods of improving communication in organizations. Although communication is emphasized, the practices of

Table 6.1 Communication orientations

	Power-oriented approach	Achievement-oriented approach
Purpose	Persuasion to control employee behavior	Problem solving to achieve organizational objectives
Focus	Control flow of information to employees	Development of trust and openness with employees
Content	Concentration on verbal communication	Management action to create productive environment
Direction	Downward, one-way communication by management	Interaction among management and employees
Effects desired	Knowledge of procedures and logical carrying out of instructions	Positive attitudes and feelings and achievement of objectives

broad-based management approaches attempt to maximize the use of human resources.

More effective communication can be developed by trying to identify the problem before attempting to find the answers. We must be able to identify why communication is not effective before looking for additional information to transmit.

The Sender Must Accept Responsibility

One problem in communication is the "I told you so" fallacy. The statements, "The employee didn't pay attention" and "I told them, but they didn't listen" are frequently heard in organizations.

"I told you so" fallacy

One company changed its inspection procedures to require inspection of every unit produced. The chief inspector told his group, "I want you to inspect every unit." He had transmitted the message; however, what the inspectors heard was, "We will still sample and inspect every other unit as we have done for the last five years." When the chief inspector found a defective unit that had not been inspected, he blamed the inspectors for not listening. The problem, however, was the chief's assumption that "to tell" is all that is necessary. He did not find out if the inspectors understood what action to take.

The effectiveness of communication can be increased if the person transmitting information accepts responsibility for understanding. When this responsibility is not accepted, the "I told you so" fallacy frequently results.

Communication Effectiveness in Organizations

For the sender to accept responsibility *does not* reduce the responsibility of the receiver in the communication process. Effective communication requires a mutual acceptance of responsibility by sender *and* receiver.

Use Simple and Direct Language

technical terms and jargon

We have all been in situations in which we were unable to understand what people were saying because of their use of technical terms or *jargon*. Lawyers, for example, use different terminology from farmers or dentists. Some writers have labeled this jargon "gobbledygook." Technical jargon can often be found in government agencies, courts of law, universities, and hospitals.

An example of jargon is the phrase Herman Kahn used in describing a war policy as ". . . a policy which emphasized the threat that we could hit the Soviet Union with a counterforce-countervalue 'spasm' attack . . ." *Counterforce* refers to an attempt to degrade or destroy the enemy's offensive capability. *Countervalue* refers to an attempt to damage things which the enemy values. *Spasm* is meant to imply that the first attack is total and a reflex reaction.

Problems associated with jargon can be reduced *by using abbreviated phraseology distinguished for its lucidity*; that is, using simple and direct language (see Figure 6.1). Using "big words" such as those italicized in the preceding sentence may prove you have a large vocabulary, but it does not necessarily increase understanding.

Effective communication depends on language adapted to the vocabulary of the receiver. The purpose of communication is *not* to test the receiver's vocabulary; it is to develop mutual understanding.[5]

Use Positive Motivational Appeals

Most of us have attempted to change the behavior of others by using threats of punishment. In most cases it is not the most effective method of changing behavior.

A prime example is a pack of cigarettes bearing the message: "Warning: The Surgeon General has determined that cigarette smoking is dangerous to your health." The same message is seen often in newspapers along with information linking smoking to lung cancer and heart disease. Because of the threatening nature of this information, many people quit reading, listening, and watching the ads. A more effective approach in motivating people to change their behavior involves concentrating on rewards rather than threats, fear, and punishment.

threats result in avoidance

A major problem in using threats is that people may want to avoid the sources of the threats and the places in which the threats occur.

Threats usually tell people what not to do. They seldom lead to positive, goal-oriented actions. Communication is more effective if it focuses on positive and rewarding courses of action.

Examples of using positive motivation to correct problems usually dealt with by threats and punishment have been summarized by Harry Wiard.[6] One of the more interesting examples was a steel plant that

Figure 6.1 Use simple and direct language.

gave trading stamps to the families of employees who had uninterrupted periods of attendance. Absentee rates were considerably reduced. The traditional approach of reducing absenteeism involves some form of punishment for "unexplained" absences. In another example cited by Wiard, employees were provided with an extra break whenever they could increase production. If they completed a specified number of units in a given hour, the rest of the hour could be used as they wanted. Production, as hoped, improved.

The Receiver Must See Benefits

satisfy needs Individuals are most affected by messages providing chances to satisfy needs. They are attentive to messages which are potentially rewarding and tend to disregard those having no reward value. The receiver rather than the sender defines whether the message contains possible rewards. Effective managers are "receiver oriented" and have developed the ability to analyze whether messages provide incentives for the receiver to listen, understand, and act to achieve organizational goals.

Provide the Receiver with Complete Information

Often messages are transmitted without all the information required for a complete message. Incomplete messages leave room for the receiver to fill in missing information and distort the intended meaning. When rumors transmitted through organizational grapevines are analyzed, one of their main characteristics is that they started as incomplete messages. Messages become rumors when information is added or deleted as the message is transmitted from one person to another.

complete messages One way to help combat distortions is to ensure that *who, what, when, where, why* and *how* are included in every message transmitted. Communication will usually not be 100 percent accurate, because there will be some changes in the information as it is transmitted from person to person. However, one company saved thousands of dollars simply by printing the words *who, what, when, where, why,* and *how* on all scratch pads, phone message pads, and memo pads. Messages were far more complete than they would have been otherwise.

Messages transmitted to employees should explain how the information will affect them and their jobs. If all essential elements of a message are included, the chance of distortion is reduced.

Management Guidelines for Dealing with Rumors

1. Define the rumor.
    a. What is the specific content of the rumor?
    b. Why was the rumor started?
    c. Rumors result from uncertainties. Identify these uncertainties.

2. Evaluate the rumor.
   a. Is it important enough for management to deal with?
   b. Has the impact of the rumor affected productivity?
   c. Does the rumor have the potential to affect productivity in the future?
3. When providing information or answers be sure information is factual and is supported with specific details.
4. Evaluate the available methods to inform employees.
   a. Consider whether the grapevine and informal channels should be used.
   b. Use official methods of communication such as memos, meetings, and letters.
   c. Suit the method of communication to the situation.
   d. Use face-to-face communication whenever possible.
5. Be sure to use a credible source of information—sources employees will believe.
6. Be sure to answer questions directly and specifically whenever possible. When impossible, admit uncertainty and explain the causes of uncertainty.
7. Management should try to involve employees in the problem-solving process or when changes are being considered.

Obtain Feedback

A problem in organizations is that communication is often one way—without feedback. *Feedback* involves checking responses to communication to determine if messages are understood. The basis of advanced electronic communications systems is feedback. In most advanced technological systems, two-thirds of the system is used to check reliabilities, to feed back information on system operation, and to check and double-check the accuracy of the transmission of information.

feedback

Unfortunately, human beings often ignore the basic principles of feedback. To avoid misunderstandings, the sender must obtain, by observing the reactions of the receiver or by asking appropriate questions, the receiver's interpretation of the message. To ensure action-oriented communications, it is necessary to have feedback.

In some cases management has a *closed-door policy*, although the stated policy is that of an open door. When an employee walks in, the closed-door manager starts looking at the clock or tapping on the table. The manager asks the employee to hurry up, keep it important, keep it relevant, and make it quick. The message is that the manager's time is important. Feedback received by the employee in such cases is largely negative.

Managers need feedback to evaluate whether information is being effectively received, as Figure 6.2 illustrates. An essential ingredient of effective human interaction is two-way communication.[7]

"Open-Line" Programs to Improve Communication

Many organizations claim to be concerned about two-way communication between employees and management, but some companies like Sun Oil, IBM, and Bank of America are actually doing something about it. These firms have established what are known as "open-line" communication programs. The technique is characterized by confidentiality and candor.

Basically, the program establishes a confidential channel between employees and management. The channel can be used by any employee who wants to submit a problem, complaint, opinion, or suggestion to management. To ensure confidentiality, communications are directed to a coordinator, who is the only one aware of the writer's identity. The program guarantees that a confidential, written reply from management will be sent to the employee's home.

The open-line program can help an organization compensate for managers who lack strong communication skills or who do not encourage two-way communication with their employees. One of the major advantages of these programs is that concrete suggestions to improve company operations can be channeled directly to top management.

The open-line program conveys the nonverbal message to employees that management believes communication is a two-way street and is working to make it clear and direct.

Figure 6.2 Without feedback there is a loss of information.

Eliminate Noise Through Message Isolation

Another problem that occurs in organizations is lack of *message isolation*. Frequently, employees are bombarded with so many messages it is difficult to tell what is important (see Figure 6.3). Consequently, they tend to ignore much of the information. Managers buried with reports and memoranda often spend time shuffling papers from one side of the desk to the other, moving from the *in* basket to the *out* basket, from the *out* basket to the file. Information and reports are often not read but merely moved around or filed.[8]

Psychological noise or *interference* involves not accurately receiving a message because of preoccupation with other things. After an emotional or traumatic experience, an individual is especially susceptible to psychological interference. An employee walked into the supervisor's office and said, "I've got to tell you about this problem I have at home." The supervisor replied, "Just a minute, wait until I explain a new safety procedure." In this case, the employee pointed out the psychological interference that needed the manager's attention before safety procedures could be discussed. Supervisors are more effective in such situations when they deal with psychological interferences before talking about procedures or other work-related matters.

psychological interference

If an employee's problems are of such magnitude that he or she can't pay attention to the job, effective management may consider allowing the employee to take care of the problem the same way sick leave is provided. Employees with pressing personal problems are often susceptible to injury and may cause injury to those around them. They also have difficulty concentrating on their assigned tasks and are generally ineffective.

Figure 6.3 Lack of message isolation creates communication problems.

An important factor in eliminating psychological noise is the careful timing of messages. Many organizations hold important meetings just prior to lunch or quitting time. These are two of the worst times to try to communicate. Employeees may be worried about missing a ride home, running an errand, or other pressing personal needs. In addition, lower energy levels during these times of day often result in inattention and irritability.

Use Multiple Channels

In order to transmit messages effectively, one can use *multiple communication channels* to stimulate more than one sense in a receiver. When more sensory perceptions are used, such as sight, smell, or touch, the brain receives more stimulation; and the possibility of understanding and retaining messages is greater.

eliminate interference

The use of multiple channels provides a variety of reinforcing messages and helps eliminate interference. If the individual sees the message as well as hears it, there will be less interference from seeing other information. If other senses are also involved, interference will be further reduced.

Use Face-to-Face Communication

involvement and participation

One advantage of *face-to-face communication* is that immediate feedback from the receiver is possible. Face-to-face communication uses multiple channels of communication with ease and efficiency and makes it possible to obtain message isolation. Involvement and participation can be developed in face-to-face interaction much more readily than through any other media such as telephone calls, correspondence, reports, or charts.

Face-to-face communication is sometimes avoided because it takes more time than other methods or because the situation can be uncomfortable. The immediate feedback of interpersonal interaction can reveal misunderstanding, ineffective communication, and feelings that neither the sender nor receiver wish to expose. A useful technique is to approach all face-to-face interactions with three goals: (1) to obtain information, (2) to give information, and (3) to establish a relationship of trust and confidence.

Advisory Panels to Improve Communication

The Equitable Society has increased communication between top management and employees by the use of a series of Rotating Advisory Panels. Each panel is composed of twelve people who meet with the president and other executives at least four times a year. Panel members are selected by the personnel department and management in each area of the company. The panels represent a wide range of employees, including minorities, women, and management.

A facilitator works with the panel to organize the agenda for each meeting. Panel members are periodically changed to obtain a variety of viewpoints.[9]

Develop Empathy

Effective human interaction requires a sensitivity to the world of the receiver—the receiver's attitudes, emotions, and feelings. Developing *empathy* with an individual involves putting yourself in the other person's shoes. Messages can then be more effectively constructed and you can determine the best approach to ensure understanding. Part of the process of developing empathy is to understand how others see us. We can gain this knowledge by encouraging others to give us direct and meaningful feedback about our behavior and our communication. This requires a climate of trust and confidence. No technique, however, can substitute for careful observation and sensitivity to the way others react to our verbal and nonverbal messages.[10]

world of the receiver

Develop Credibility as a Source of Information

Communication studies have shown that the *credibility* of the source of information often overrides a message's real value. If receivers believe the source of the information is credible, they are likely to pay attention to the message and to be affected by the content. Messages from sources lacking credibility are frequently ignored, even though the content may be perfectly valid.

credibility vital to communication

Evaluation of the source's credibility depends on the perceived competence and trustworthiness of the source. These factors are not the "property" of the source but are determined by receivers. Credibility is "in the eye of the beholder."

trust and competence

The perceived credibility to perform a task and make task-related decisions depends on the source's qualifications, expertise, or competence. Individuals perceived as having high credibility are usually seen as possessing some desirable combination of experience, training, education, skill, ability, information, and intelligence.

Trustworthiness tends to be a general credibility factor covering the total range of an individual's behavior. Trust of a person is not limited to a job or an area of influence. Trust involves being perceived as having characteristics such as honesty, fairness, justice, ethics, and dependability. Trustworthiness has an influence in all communication situations.

Fortune magazine described an interesting experiment on source credibility. A cartoon chart of "the Four Goals of Labor" was clipped from a union newspaper and photostated. A new source of the goals was attached at the bottom: "From June 3, National Association of Manufacturers Newsletter" (a management publication). Twenty union members were then shown the ad and asked if they thought it was a fair presentation of labor's goals. Four grudgingly said it was and two couldn't make up their minds. The responses of the remaining fourteen included "patronizing," "loaded," "paternalistic," and "makes me want to spit . . ."[11]

Reduce Status Awareness and Social Distance

status symbols One of the barriers to effective communication is the social distance among people that arises when there are status differences. Although status differences will probably always be with us, communication can be made more effective by reducing or eliminating the status symbols which heighten existing social differences. Some of the status symbols which reduce communication are titles, forms of dress, reserved parking spaces, special privileges, office furniture and fixtures, the executive dining room, and so on. Most people possess *status awareness* when they realize that these symbols communicate a variety of nonverbal messages about power, prestige, and position. While status symbols are difficult to avoid, many organizations have dramatically reduced the most objectionable ones and have improved interpersonal relations.

Use Direct Communication Whenever Possible

too many links Communication in an organization is often characterized by messages passing through a number of people and organizational layers before reaching their destinations. In other words, there are frequently too many links in the communication process. The more individuals the message goes through, the greater the chance of systematic distortion. Whenever possible, it is highly desirable to communicate directly with the individuals who must take the action.

Reinforce Verbal Communication with Action

actions and words Much of the communication that directly affects our behavior is nonverbal; that is, actions interpreted by other people. A simple example of this phenomena in operation was a supervisor who tried to influence employees to stop taking company-owned items out of the plant. The supervisor gave a thirty-minute speech and successfully made his point. Then, he went back to his office, picked up two boxes of the company's drawing pencils and walked out of the plant, passing by the same employees to whom he had just lectured. At this point, some of the employees were asked, "What did you think of the speech; will it have any effect on your behavior?" They said it would not affect what they did at all since the supervisor was still stealing pencils. In such cases, nonverbal behavior overrides any verbal communication. Many times, the things that irritate individuals and block effective communication are the nonverbal elements. It is often said that 65 percent of our face-to-face communication is nonverbal. As shown in Figure 6.4, people react more to our actions, our tone of voice, and our manner of delivery than to our message.

Conclusions

Concepts and techniques of communication are relatively easy to write about, but their effective implementation is difficult and time-consuming (see Figure 6.5). Philosophies and theories of communication are much more highly developed than are the procedures and methods for their implementation in organizations.

Figure 6.4 Actions are the message.

Communication Effectiveness in Organizations 155

The effective implementation of any system or procedure to improve communication requires organizational support, particularly from top management. Effective implementation always requires flexibility so procedures can be adapted to meet requirements of the organization.

The potential rewards of more effective communication are unlimited. For most organizations the traditional and conventional concepts and practices are no longer sufficient to meet current challenges. The future of the richly varied and complex processes of organizational communication will require application of a broad spectrum of new concepts and practices.

Figure 6.5 Steps in effective communication.

Quick Review

I. Changing Management Concepts in Communication
   A. Changes in technology, social systems, values, and individuals entering the work force all affect communication in organizations.
   B. Some general directions of managerial changes toward communication include:
      1. Changing from emphasis on management's use of threats and persuasion to emphasis on motivating employees to participate in analyzing and solving their own job problems.
      2. Changing from emphasis on control of flow of communication to emphasis on establishing employee participation and interaction with management.
      3. Changing from emphasis on merely getting employees to do their jobs to emphasis on structuring the job so it is more meaningful to them.
      4. Increasing emphasis on the way communication affects employees' attitudes and feelings.
II. Managerial Approaches to Communication
   A. In power-oriented approaches, managers assume the responsibility of regulation and control of information. They focus on remedial concerns and propaganda.
   B. In achievement-oriented approaches, managers assume that effective human interaction is an intrinsic component of productive work. Communication problems are seen as symptoms of managerial inadequacy.
   C. Problems in communication are, basically, organizational problems.
III. Practices to Improve Communication
   A. The sender must accept responsibility for the effectiveness of the communication.
   B. Simple, direct language is most effective.
   C. Positive motivational appeals are stronger than those based on fear.
   D. The receiver must see benefits in the communication.
   E. The receiver must be provided with understanding, including the *who, what, where, when, why, and how* of the subject being discussed.
   F. Feedback or two-way involvement is necessary for understanding.
   G. Through message isolation, "noise" or extraneous messages can be minimized.

H. Multiple channels of communication should be used when possible.
I. Face-to-face communication is superior to letters, memoranda, or telephone communication.
J. Empathy is a necessary component of all successful communication.
K. Development of credibility is mandatory for successful communication.
L. Status awareness and social distance are barriers to communication and should be reduced.
M. Direct communication is more effective than communication passed through several layers of organization.
N. Actions reinforce verbal communication.
IV. Conclusions
A. Effective implementation of organizational communication is difficult, time-consuming, but rewarding.
B. Communication practices, to be effective, must have the support of all levels in the organization.
C. Traditional concepts and practices no longer meet the challenges of creating effective organizational communication.

Key Terms

Power-oriented communication
Achievement-oriented communication
"I told you so" fallacy

Jargon
Message isolation
Feedback
Empathy
Credibility

Face-to-face communication
Psychological noise
Status awareness
Multiple channels

Discussion Questions

1. What do you believe will be the most critical issues involving organizational communication in the future?
2. What are the major differences between a power-oriented approach and an achievement-oriented approach to communication?
3. Comment on the statement, "Communication problems are basically problems resulting from the environment created by the organization."
4. How can the "I told you so" fallacy be avoided?
5. How can you determine what information will be important to an individual?

6. What elements are necessary for a message to be complete and to reduce the chance for message distortion?
7. What are possible advantages and disadvantages of an "open-door policy"?
8. What action can a manager take to reduce "psychological noise"?
9. How would you determine your credibility as a source of information?
10. Discuss a specific situation where the verbal communication of an individual was *not* consistent with the individual's actions.
11. Why is the effective implementation of new communication concepts and techniques difficult?

Case Incidents

Too Much Paperwork?

Mary Richards is the laboratory supervisor in a 1,500 bed, city-owned hospital. She has complete responsibility for personnel, supplies, equipment, scheduling work, and providing reports of laboratory tests to the doctors. The hospital personnel who use the laboratory feel it is efficiently managed and upholds high professional standards. The only complaints are from patients who must sometimes wait 30 to 45 minutes to have tests run.

The hospital administrator seldom visits the lab and does not discuss problems or performance with Mary face to face. When a patient complains about having to wait for lab tests, the administrator writes Mary a memo and requires her to make a written response. Also, the administrator has been requiring weekly reports on use of supplies and materials; these reports previously were made only once a month.

Lately Mary has become so bogged down with the required paperwork that she cannot adequately supervise her laboratory. She has reached the point of considering looking for another job if the "put it in writing" policy of the administrator continues.

1. Does the administrator's policy of depending on written memos and reports promote effective communication?
2. What would you advise the hospital administrator to do to improve communication with Mary Richards?
3. If you were in Mary Richards' position what could you do to improve communication with the administrator and reduce the time spent on paperwork?

4. Excessive paperwork is a common complaint by people in organizations. What approaches can be used to reduce or more effectively handle paperwork?

The Open Door

Tom Wood is the owner and president of T. W. Enterprises, which operates six carryout food establishments as its major business. The food store's main product is fried chicken. The six stores are all located within twenty miles of each other in a West Coast city.

Mr. Wood started the business over fifteen years ago and almost all improvements and changes have been initiated and directed by him. He usually refers to the stores as "his stores." Some of the store managers and central office staff have complained to Mr. Wood that improvements need to be made in the stores and some new equipment is needed. Mr. Wood's typical reply is, "When we have the money we will spend it on the most essential items." When asked what he felt were the most essential items he replied, "I will decide that when we have the money."

Over the past three years, the profit percentage of sales and return on investment of T. W. Enterprises has been gradually declining. Mr. Wood attributes the decline in profit to increased competition and rising costs. The six-month financial report of the controller projects a loss for the year unless something is done to increase sales or reduce costs for the next six months.

To obtain ideas on ways to increase profit, Mr. Wood set up a meeting with the six store managers, the controller, and the maintenance manager. Mr. Wood began the meeting by explaining the financial situation the company was in and announcing, "I have always had an open-door policy. I want you to bring me any ideas you have on how to cut costs. You should feel free to come to see me on any problems you have."

During the next month, the store managers were in the central office several times a week, but no one mentioned any ideas for cutting costs or brought up any problems. On several occasions Mr. Wood overheard store managers discussing ways to increase sales and reduce costs with the controller and maintenance manager.

1. Why weren't store managers going to Mr. Wood with ideas and problems?
2. What could Mr. Wood do to increase feedback and make his "open-door" policy work?
3. If you were in Mr. Wood's position in this situation, what course of action would you have taken? (Be specific and explain why.)
4. What guidelines should a manager follow to develop feedback which would identify problems and provide ideas on increasing sales and cutting costs?

Is Anybody There?

Jerry Osborn is an outstanding salesman for a computer manufacturer. His quarterly total sales in dollar value consistently place him in the top ten percent of all company salesmen. The company has consistently recognized his effectiveness over and above his sales commissions. He has received expense-paid trips to Paris and Hawaii, free tickets to numerous sports events, and citations and plaques, which are displayed in his office.

There is only one part of the job Jerry does not like—the paperwork. A required monthly report on each account must be completed. The reports average six pages for each account. An additional report on sales prospects is required and must include an explicit strategy for closing sales or reasons why the project should be dropped. It takes Jerry at least two days a month to complete the reports.

He often says, "I can see the company's point of view. The reports can be very helpful to a new salesperson, but they are of no value to an experienced one." One month, about a year ago, he did not send in the report. Two weeks passed before formal notices began coming from the company, including a very critical letter from the vice-president for marketing. Jerry decided it was not worth fighting the system and sent in the reports each month.

As he filled out the reports it occurred to him that the only time he had received any feedback on his monthly reports was when he failed to turn them in. At no other time had anyone commented on the reports. About halfway through the report on a sales prospect he wrote, "If anyone has read this far in this useless report, I will personally buy them a steak dinner."

He did not have to buy a single steak dinner.

In the middle of a report the next month, he wrote, "Mr. Edward Howard is a dirty old man who could not tell the difference between a computer and an elephant." (Mr. Howard was the company president.)

After hearing nothing about his report for over a month he concluded that "nobody" read the monthly reports. "They just let you have it if you don't turn one in." Jerry proceeded to describe his experience with the reports to every company salesperson he saw.

1. How do you think the experience with the reports affected Jerry's attitude toward the company and his job?
2. If you were the vice-president for marketing and found out about Jerry's behavior relative to the reports, what would you do?
3. Do you think the report system should be changed? If so, how?
4. What basic guidelines should be followed in the design and operation of a report system?

Exercise What Do Management Actions Communicate?

Below are various management behaviors. Describe what each behavior would communicate to you if you were an employee of the organization. What message would you receive about the manager and how the manager expected employees to behave?

1. The manager covers for his or her boss when the organization's policy on expense accounts is violated. The manager makes out receipts for nonexistent expenses when the boss has exceeded the allowable expenses for meals or travel so the boss can get reimbursement for what was actually spent.

2. The manager protects employees from daily administrative frustrations by doing paperwork for employees and reducing to a minimum the information they must provide for reports.

3. The manager blames innocent employees for errors that higher level management is concerned about.

4. The manager involves employees in decisions that affect them and their jobs. The manager asks employees for their ideas and suggestions on how to improve working conditions.

5. The manager divulges confidential information about employees to other employees.

6. The manager is always available to answer questions and discuss problems with employees.

7. The manager falsifies quality and quantity reports that go to higher level management.

8. The manager establishes specific priorities and time limits for the work to be done by each employee.

9. The manager accepts gifts and favors from employees in exchange for preferential treatment.

10. The manager makes a genuine effort to understand employees and tries to match individuals to the jobs for which they are best suited.

11. The manager takes credit for employees' ideas and suggestions and presents them to higher levels of management as his or her own.

12. The manager violates the organization's policy by using the company car for family vacations.

Endnotes

1. John A. Howland, "Talking at or Talking With?" *Bell Telephone Magazine*, March–April 1971, pp. 4–9.
2. Max Ways, "The American Kind of Worker Participation," *Fortune*, October 1976, p. 176. Also see "Workers: Eager for Responsibility," *Nations Business,* November 1980, p. 38.
3. M. Scott Myers, *Every Employee a Manager* (New York: McGraw-Hill, 1970), p. 49.
4. For a detailed example see Jeremy Main, "How to Battle Your Own Bureaucracy," *Fortune*, June 29, 1981, pp. 54–58.
5. For analysis of how people improve communication skills see Gary T. Hunt, *Communicative Skills in the Organization* (Englewood Cliffs, N.J.: Prentice-Hall, 1980).
6. Harry Wiard, "Why Manage Behavior? A Case for Positive Reinforcement," *Human Resources Management*, Summer 1972, pp. 15–20.
7. Lyle Sussman and Paul D. Krivonos, *Communication for Supervisors and Managers* (Sherman Oaks, Calif.: Alfred Publishing Co., 1979).
8. More is not always better is illustrated in Charles A. O'Reilly III, "Individuals and Information Overload in Organizations: Is More Necessarily Better?" *Academy of Management Journal,* December 1980, pp. 684–96.
9. *Personnel Administrator*, January 1980, p. 19.
10. See Otis W. Baskin and Craig E. Aronoff, *Interprersonal Communication in Organizations* (Santa Monica, Calif.: Goodyear Publishing, 1980).
11. "Is Anybody Listening?" *Fortune*, September 1950, p. 82. Also see J. L. Di Gaetani, "The Business of LIstening," *Business Horizons,* October 1980, pp. 40–46.

Motivation and Performance **3**

7 Motivation Concepts

Learning Objectives

After reading this chapter, you should be able to:

1. Discuss the importance of motivation in organizations.
2. Explain the process of motivation and the basic characteristics of human motives.
3. Describe the need hierarchy theory and its implications for management.
4. Identify the characteristics of individuals with high achievement motivation.
5. Describe how managers can promote achievement motivation.
6. Explain how affiliation motivation can be satisfied.
7. Describe the types of power motivation and how they affect management styles.
8. Explain expectancy theory of motivation and how it can be applied to improve performance.

Chapter Topics

Motivation and Management

Definition of Motivation

Characteristics of Motivation

The Process of Motivation

Maslow's Need Hierarchy

Achievement Motivation

Affiliation Motivation

Power Motivation

Expectancy Theory of Motivation

Preview and Self-Evaluation

Three areas of human behavior—perception, learning, and motivation—have been studied more than all others. While all three are important, none is more central to organizational effectiveness than motivation. Motivation deals with the fundamental question, Why do people act as they do? Perhaps more important to managers is the question, What can be done to help employees become more productive in their jobs? There are many theories of motivation, ranging from purely mechanistic behavioral approaches to those that are almost mystical in their view of human activity. In Chapter 7, we take a pragmatic, understandable view that has been useful to many people in developing insights into behavior. Nearly everyone has a personal theory of human motivation.

Before reading this chapter try answering the true-false questions. Then after reading the chapter, check the questions again to see if your responses are the same.

Answer True or False

1. Eating, talking, and operating a machine are motivators.   T   F

2. The goal an individual is trying to achieve controls the individual's behavior.   T   F

3. How needs are satisfied depends largely on the choices that the individual perceives to be available.   T   F

4. Achievement of a single goal may satisfy several different needs of the individual.   T   F

5. When a need is satisfied, the individual is no longer motivated.   T   F

6. When management places extreme emphasis on job security, the effect on employee behavior will be to increase creativity.   T   F

7. Individuals with high-achievement motivation prefer situations where success depends on luck.   T   F

8. For individuals with high affiliation motivation, task accomplishments are usually more important than social relationships.   T   F

9. An organization cannot function without people who have the motivation to obtain power and influence behavior.   T   F

10. For individuals to improve performance, they must expect that their efforts gain them a desired reward.   T   F

ANSWERS: 1. F; 2. F; 3. T; 4. T; 5. F; 6. F; 7. F; 8. F; 9. T; 10. T

Motivation and Management

People usually do things for an organization because the organization does things for them. When management asks employees to provide something for the organization, the employees expect to receive rewards for their efforts.

employee needs

When an organization is managed so that employees can satisfy their individual needs by achieving organizational objectives, they exert full effort on the job. If employees perceive management as hindering their need satisfaction, they reduce their efforts or, in extreme cases, even fight the organization.

The most productive organizations are those in which people can satisfy personal needs while contributing to the achievement of organizational objectives. The most effective managers make sure that employees have an opportunity to satisfy their needs on the job.

Because people are unique, their behavior in complex organizations is not easily understood. There is enough similarity in the basic needs of individuals, however, to make it possible for organizations to provide satisfaction. Understanding motivation in organizations is difficult since individual behavior is affected by various interactions that take place between people in an organization.

motivation affects
productivity

Individual motivational patterns affect productivity in work organizations. But problems of employee motivation do not necessarily stem from lack of personal motivation. Motivational problems exist when behavior is focused on other goals than organizational ones or at a level far below an employee's capability.

Definition of Motivation

The term *motivation* has a variety of meanings. There are numerous, lengthy definitions of motivation that go into great detail regarding internal systems and discuss the interaction of factors such as needs, drives, and motives. These detailed psychological analyses are not dealt with here. Instead, we will summarize and abstract material on motivation that will be helpful in understanding behavior in organizations.

As a beginning toward understanding work behavior, we will use the definition of motivation provided by Bernard Berelson and Gary Steiner: "A motive is an inner state that energizes, activates, or moves (hence "motivation"), and that directs or channels behavior toward goals."[1] From this definition, several factors should be kept in mind.

motivation is an
inner state

First, motivation deals with internal conditions that are not actually observed and cannot be isolated for physical analysis. Motives such as hunger, security, sex, and recognition cannot be seen. What we do observe are the behaviors that result from the internal motives. Eating, drinking, talking, operating a machine, or making a sale can be observed; but the motives that lead to these behaviors can only be inferred. In other words, we attempt to make educated guesses as to why specific actions occur. Our primary purpose for studying motivation is to increase the accuracy of our inferences concerning people in work situations.

Second, many of the discussions of motivation involve the construction of models and terms describing processes that have not been observed. Most of our analysis of motivation depends on observing a set of conditions confronting an individual, observing the resulting behavior, and hypothesizing why the behavior occurred.

Third, the result of motivation is always activity. People respond to internal motives by activities directed toward goals they believe will produce satisfaction. When the internal motivation is hunger, for example, a person responds by actively seeking food.

Fourth, motivation and behavior are not the same. Motivation is an important factor in determining behavior, but there are also other influences, such as biological, social, cultural, and organizational factors, perception, and so forth.

In some cases it is impossible to infer a specific motive behind the observable behavior of an individual. The differences in eating behavior illustrate that the motive for selecting food and a place of eating is not always simple hunger. Eating behavior may also be connected with satisfying the need for status or prestige. The rising executive who "must" eat lunch at the country club may be motivated more by status needs than by hunger. A single behavioral act may involve several complex underlying motives (see Figure 7.1).

a behavior may involve several motives

Characteristics of Motivation

Human behavior is *not* random. All behavior is the result of some internal motivation. This does not mean that all human behavior is predictable, but that there is some cause for it, known or unknown. In observing a busy street we note all the people going their diverse ways. As observers, we do not know where they are going or what prompts their movements, but surely there are reasons. The observed movements are in some way, perhaps only indirectly, the result of people fulfilling unsatisfied needs.

all behavior is motivated

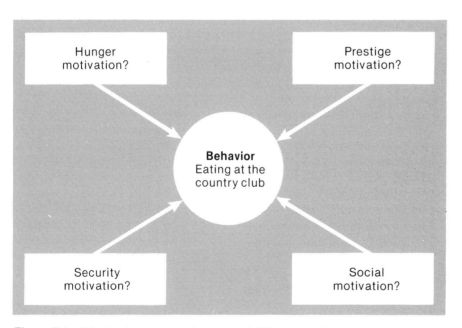

Figure 7.1 A behavior may involve several different motives.

Individuals do not always understand their own motivations. They may not understand the reasons for their actions or the needs they are trying to fulfill. Suppose a person, apparently without reason, decides to hop in her car and take a ride. She has no destination in mind, and the drive may appear pointless. Just by driving around, however, the individual can be fulfilling a number of needs. In a rather low-key way, she may be fulfilling social needs by interacting with people on the roads. Esteem needs may be partially fulfilled by the very act of driving; the driver may be manifesting competence and knowledge of driving. Another possible motive may be a demonstration of affluence or daring by the model of car being driven. It could be any, all, or none of these reasons that prompted the drive. But the driver was motivated in some way, even though she did not recognize the specific motives involved.

behavior is directed toward goals
Human behavior is directed toward obtaining goals. It is assumed that personal needs will be satisfied when the goals are reached. An employee with strong social needs may feel that the way to obtain friends in the office is to become a supervisor. This develops into a dominant goal, and the employee's behavior is directed toward achieving a promotion.

It is important to keep in mind that goals do not *control* behavior. Goals *influence* behavior and give an individual direction in the attempt to satisfy needs. The attractiveness of the goal is related to the amount of frustration produced by unsatisfied needs. Running five miles a day, for example, may not sound attractive; but as an individual goal it may be very satisfying. It can satisfy a safety need for a police officer who wants to be in good condition. It can satisfy an esteem need for an individual who perceives the ability to run five miles a day a challenge. Whatever the goal, it derives its attractiveness from the needs it fulfills.

As soon as one need is satisfied, however, another appears. People are in a never-ending chain of need fulfillment, always striving to improve and perfect their existence.

a satisfied need is not a motivator
A satisfied need is not a motivator. After a need has been satisfied, we have no motivation to direct behavior toward goals related to it. Air is a basic physiological need. When an individual's supply of air is threatened or cut off, the need for oxygen becomes a prime motivator. Normally, we are not motivated by the need for air; we take it for granted. If you went to an employer for a job and he offered as salary all the air you could breathe, you would probably think he was crazy. It is a commodity we already have; why should we work for it? When a need is satisfied it does not motivate.

The Process of Motivation

The process of motivation begins with the internal need creating a state of tension which results in an individual selecting a goal and striving to achieve it. If the actions are successful and the goal achieved, the need has been satisfied (or partially satisfied) and the tension reduced (see Figure 7.2). The tendency to return to a state of less tension, or physical and psychological balance, is called *homeostasis*.

In the process of need satisfaction, difficulties can be encountered in any of the following areas: (1) the individual may not be able to identify a goal that is seen as being related to the need, (2) the individual may not be able to identify a form of behavior (method) to achieve a goal, (3) the individual may identify a behavior but not be able to successfully perform the behavior to accomplish the goal, and (4) the individual may achieve the goal but find that it doesn't satisfy the need. *difficulties in need satisfaction*

The relationship among needs, goals, and behaviors to achieve goals is extremely complex. At any one time, an individual has a number of needs that exist at different levels of intensity. We experience simultaneous needs for food, friendship, achievement, rest and security, and so forth. The intensity of the needs we experience is in a constant state of change as a result of some needs being satisfied and other needs increasing in intensity. *the intensity of needs change*

The goals that individuals select to satisfy needs depend upon the individual's perception of the expected satisfaction to be obtained from a specific goal, the availability of goals in the environment, and the individual's estimate of ability to achieve the goal. An individual will attempt to select goals that can be achieved and that will provide the greatest need satisfaction. Almost any goal that is chosen will satisfy some needs while at the same time prevent the satisfaction of others. In developing behavior patterns, individuals tend to choose goals that they have found to be rewarding in the past. They will tend to avoid goals that they have not been able to achieve or that they found to be unrewarding once achieved. Goal selection is also influenced by the social norms, values, and codes of behavior that are believed to be acceptable.

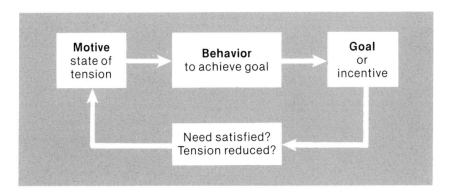

Figure 7.2   Motivation process.

After a goal has been selected, a number of forms of behavior usually are available to achieve it. The particular pattern of behavior selected is affected by the individual's evaluation of abilities and an estimate of the most effective form of behavior in achieving the goal. When choosing behavioral patterns, individuals tend to repeat those patterns that have been most successful in the past.

goal-directed *behavior*   The simplest behavioral model of motivation involves the process of people selecting goals they believe will satisfy needs and then selecting behaviors they believe will lead to successful attainment of the goal. Although the model of the motivation process illustrated in Figure 7.2 is simple and straightforward, the relationships involved are extremely complex. As shown in Figures 7.3, 7.4 and 7.5 goal-directed behavior involves the following factors:

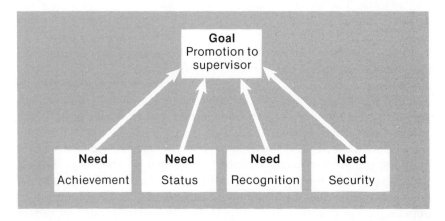

Figure 7.3   A single goal may satisfy several needs.

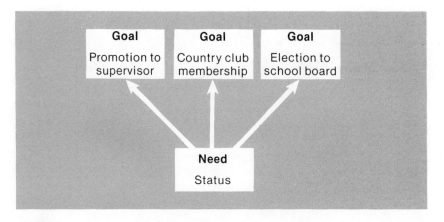

Figure 7.4   Several goals may satisfy the same need.

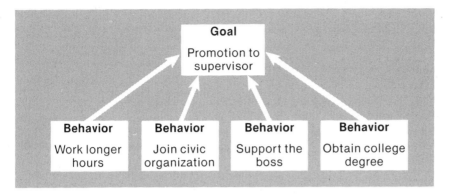

Figure 7.5 Several behaviors may be used to achieve a goal.

1. A single goal may satisfy many different needs.
2. A number of different goals may contribute to satisfaction of the same need.
3. There may be a number of different behaviors which can lead to the achievement of a goal.

It is important to keep in mind that what we observe is an individual's behavior. We cannot observe the internal motivation that leads to the behavior. In many cases, we must infer the "real" goal that the individual is trying to achieve since it may not be directly observable.

Classification of Needs

There are many systems and methods of categorizing human needs. Any of the systems that have been developed may have value for a given individual or for dealing with specific problems. But each system of classifying needs has the problem of individual differences. No descriptive system could be completely accurate or applicable to every individual or every situation. The classification systems that have been developed stem mostly from the areas of psychology, social psychology, and sociology. Most of these systems are similar. The primary differences are usually the degree of detail and number of categories used. There are, however, differences of opinion concerning types of needs and the importance of various need categories. The basic classification of needs discussed here is based upon observable goals and behavior. Needs are grouped on the basis of similarity of goals rather than on the similarity of inferred needs. This is the most widely applied approach to motivation, and it appears to be the most useful for managers.

Since behavior is directed toward goals that will satisfy felt needs, the manager has two basic choices in attempting to increase productivity by "motivating" employees. First, the manager can attempt to "create" felt needs within the employees. Second, the manager can offer the *motivating employees* possibility of satisfying needs already felt by the employees. With either approach, the use of a system of categorizing needs is necessary.

Maslow's Need Hierarchy

A. H. Maslow developed the concept of a hierarchy of needs.[2] It has been extensively applied to managerial situations. Before discussing the specific categories involved in Maslow's need hierarchy, the basic underlying assumptions of his system should be understood.

assumptions
underlying need
hierarchy

1. Motives are highly complex, and no single motive affects behavior in isolation. A number of motives are always in operation at the same time.
2. There exists in each individual a hierarchy of needs which requires, in general, that lower-level needs must be partially satisfied before higher-level needs affect behavior.
3. A satisfied need is not a motivator. When a need is satisfied, another need emerges, so that the individual always remains in a motivated state.
4. Higher-level needs can be satisfied in a greater variety of ways than can lower-level needs.

As shown in Figure 7.6, needs may be classified into five major groups.

Physical or Physiological Needs

physical needs The lowest and most basic level on the need hierarchy is composed of universal physiological needs. People generally concentrate on meeting physiological needs before concerning themselves with higher-level needs. *Physiological needs* include the need for food, water, oxygen, temperature control, reproduction, and shelter.

In our society, the satisfaction of physiological needs is usually associated with money. In this sense, individuals use money to satisfy basic motivations. It is not money itself, however, but what money can buy that satisfies physiological needs. Money can play an important role in obtaining need satisfaction at all levels of the hierarchy.

For individuals who are starving, higher-level needs are relatively unimportant; their behavior is directed toward the satisfaction of hunger needs. However, once physiological needs are relatively well satisfied, other needs become more dominant.

Safety or Security Needs

safety needs The second level consists of needs for safety and security. Safety needs relate to protection from physical harm. Individual motivation involves developing protection from a wide variety of threatening events including accidents, injuries, sicknesses, and a multitude of unknowns. Safety and security needs in the work place involve worker safety and job security factors. Safety needs do not result in the necessity for absolute security, but in the knowledge that reasonable precautions are being taken to minimize risk. Safety programs, job security guarantees, and fair disciplinary procedures are examples of management attempts to satisfy safety needs. To provide additional protection and security, many organizations have some form of job tenure and provide various types of health and accident insurance for employees.

Some writers have suggested that many organizations tend to overemphasize the satisfactions of safety and security needs by providing unnecessarily elaborate programs of fringe benefits in the areas of health and accident insurance and retirement plans. When management places extreme emphasis on satisfying security needs, it may affect employee behavior by reducing initiative as employees follow man-

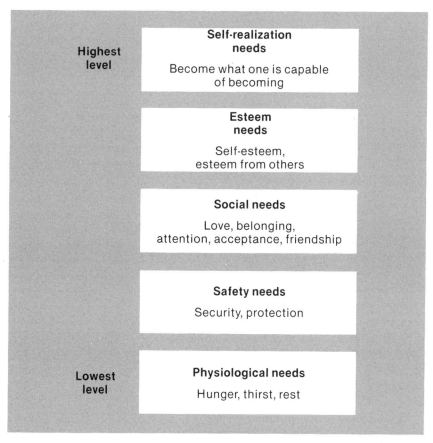

Figure 7.6 Need hierarchy.

agement's lead and focus on their concern for security. In cases where security needs are negatively influenced by fears of being fired, laid off, or demoted, employees may become extremely cautious and defensive.

Social or Belonging Needs

social needs
Social needs can be satisfied only by contacts between individuals or individuals and groups. Such needs include affection, affiliation, companionship, and belonging. Most people are concerned about their social relationships and want to belong and be accepted by others. Relationships, both on and off the job, satisfy social needs. The satisfaction of social needs begins with the family and expands to include social and work groups. Managers must expect that employees will want to satisfy the need for social relationships on the job. If the satisfaction of social needs is hindered, individuals may become antagonistic, uncooperative, and even aggressive toward the organization.

Belonging to a group helps satisfy social needs. Individuals seek affiliation because they desire to have their values and beliefs reinforced by group members. In the process of satisfying social needs, individuals tend to seek out groups that support their strongly held beliefs. If they are deprived of social needs, people will seek them as intensely as a hungry person seeks food.

Esteem or Ego Needs

esteem needs
Esteem needs relate to individuals achieving the confidence and respect they desire in themselves and want to be accorded by others. Most individuals want to have a high level of self-esteem. Esteem needs can be satisfied by gaining knowledge, developing abilities, and successfully accomplishing tasks. When physiological, safety, and social needs are met, individuals usually channel their behavior toward developing higher levels of self-esteem. When esteem needs are satisfied, feelings of independence and confidence usually result. Satisfaction of esteem needs involves the internal factor of individuals' self-perception and the external factor of acceptance and recognition by others. On-the-job esteem needs are expressed in the desire for promotion, achievement, accomplishment, prestige, and status. Failure to satisfy these needs can lead to feelings of inferiority and helplessness, which may lead to passive and apathetic behavior.

Many jobs offer little opportunity for the satisfaction of esteem needs. Most of these jobs are found in the lower levels of organizations in which work has been highly specialized. Such jobs involve the repetition of very simple tasks and allow only minimal use of ability. Individuals holding these jobs are often frustrated, because they cannot use their abilities to satisfy ego or self-esteem needs.

Self-Actualization or Self-Realization Needs

The highest level of needs in Maslow's hierarchy involves the development of full potential. Little is known about the effect of *self-actualization needs* on an individual's behavior. People satisfy needs at this level in many different ways. In addition, self-actualization is often difficult to identify and analyze. Two specific areas linked with self-actualization needs are competence and achievement.

self-actualization needs

Functioning at this highest need level requires a psychologically healthy state. Many individuals never become self-actualized because they are unable to adequately satisfy needs at lower levels. People operating at this level have an accurate perception of reality, are able to accept themselves and others, are creative in their endeavors, and are continually involved in self-development. Self-actualized people want to use their capabilities to the fullest and continue to grow.

Implications of Maslow's Need Hierarchy for Management

Maslow's theory of human motivation includes two basic premises that have important implications for any manager. First, human needs are arranged in a hierarchy of importance. Higher-level needs do not become important in motivating behavior until lower-level needs are relatively well satisfied. This means that people are continually attempting to satisfy needs. When needs in one level have been satisfied, people move to the next higher order of needs. If lower-level needs are not satisfied, the individual may never be motivated by higher needs. For example, if a person's security needs are not being satisfied, the individual will not be motivated by the higher-level needs of esteem and self-actualization. Security needs will continue to dominate the individual's behavior. If management appeals to employees' higher-level needs when lower-level needs have not been satisfied, workers will not be motivated to increase their efforts.

Second, satisfied needs are not motivators. One of the most important points for management to keep in mind is that employees are motivated by needs that are *not* satisfied. In other words, it is what people are seeking that is motivational, not what they already have. As lower-level needs are satisfied, they retain less motivational value in an individual's behavior. A need doesn't have to be completely satisfied, however, before the next level of needs emerges. An individual may move from security needs to social and esteem needs when the security need is "80 percent satisfied." One difficulty in analyzing motivation and using the need hierarchy concept is the individual variability in the amount of satisfaction required before moving from one category to another. Managers must determine which needs are relatively unsatisfied in order to influence the behavior of employees.[3]

it is what people are seeking that is motivational

Is No News Good News?

When Marie Lee stormed into Mike Smith's office, he was both startled and concerned. Before he could react, Marie burst out, "You've got to get me away from that no-good foreman." As personnel representative for the Comptop Data Equipment Company, Mike has rarely encountered such strong emotions. "Why don't you sit down," he said, "and tell me the problem." "Well," Marie blurted in a somewhat more controlled voice, "George Wright, my foreman, never talks to me, never tells me what to do or what not to do—he just barely says hello." Her voice rose again, "It makes me furious—he just never talks to me no matter how hard I work. He just totally ignores me. I can't stand it."

Later that day, Mike called George Wright, Assembly Foreman, into his office, "George, Marie Lee is one of your crew. What kind of worker is she?" asked Mike. "Excellent," George responded. "She comes in on time, does her job, and goes home. I never have to say a word to her. She just does her job."

Achievement Motivation

Everyone has observed that some individuals seem to have a great desire to achieve. We observe individuals in every field who seem to have more drive and more commitment to reach the top than others.

The process of achievement motivation has been extensively studied by David C. McClelland.[4] For over twenty years, McClelland and his associates have studied *achievement motivation* in both laboratory settings and organizational environments. Their studies have led to the identification of achievement motivation as a distinct human need that varies in intensity among people. An extremely important contribution in this area of study has been the ability to measure the amount of achievement motivation possessed by individuals and its effect in specific situations.

challenging and attainable goals   One of the significant aspects of the behavior of individuals with high achievement motivation is that they choose goals which are both challenging and attainable. This behavior was illustrated by McClelland in an experiment in which individuals were asked to throw rings over a peg at any distance they chose. Most individuals varied the distance, throwing some rings from very close and some from very far away. Those with high achievement motivation chose distances that they thought would make success both challenging and attainable—not too close to make the task extremely easy and not too far away to make it extremely difficult or impossible. We observe this form of behavior frequently when employees on a job begin to establish higher but realistically attainable goals. The individual in sales who continually increases sales objectives so that it is necessary to "stretch" to reach them may be exhibiting high achievement motivation.

McClelland's research has indicated that individuals with high achievement motivation are *not gamblers*. They prefer work situations where they can directly affect the outcome. Whenever possible, they choose to work on problems where chance has a minimal effect on the outcome. People without high achievement motivation may tend to be extreme in their approach to risk situations, either favoring highly risky gambles or attempting to minimize any chances of loss.

gambling is not achievement motivation

People who favor a "gamble" tend to choose high-risk situations where the outcome doesn't depend on individual ability or effort. The individual is provided an easy out to avoid personal responsibility for objectives that are not achieved.

Those who avoid risk taking are able to make small achievements that are almost certain. High satisfaction of security needs is provided and the probability of anything going wrong for which the individual could be blamed is avoided.

Individuals with high achievement motivation are, in essence, taking a middle ground position that involves a degree of risk and a high probability of obtaining goals. Such a position can provide high levels of satisfaction because success is heavily influenced by the individual's ability and effort. This characteristic of individuals with high achievement motivation has been referred to as *aggressive realism*.

aggressive realism

Another characteristic of individuals with high achievement motivation is that they are more concerned with the achievement itself than with any rewards that result from their success. Rewards that may result from achieving goals are not seen as essential to the motivation for accomplishment. They do not refuse to accept rewards, but they obtain greater satisfaction from solving a problem than from receiving monetary rewards or praise. The value of money for people with high achievement motivation is in its representation of a measure of accomplishment. Usually, people with high achievement motivation do not modify their behavior to directly seek additional status, recognition from superiors, or pay raises.

success more important than rewards

Since those with high achievement motivation are primarily concerned with individual accomplishment, they tend to have a desire for specific feedback on how successful they are in reaching objectives. Achievement-motivated individuals with a strong desire for job-related feedback are often salespeople or operators of their own businesses. They are not only concerned with the amount of feedback received, but also with the nature of the feedback. They respond most favorably to information concerning their productivity on the job. They usually consider feedback irrelevant if it deals with how coopertive they are, how helpful they are, their physical appearance, their personality, or any of

feedback

a wide range of "social" attitudes. Figure 7.7 illustrates the conditions that promote high achievement motivation.

Individuals with high achievement motivation spend more time thinking about performing high-level accomplishments than do individuals with low achievement motivation. McClelland's research has found that when people begin thinking in terms of achievement, their levels of achievement increase. High achievement motivation results in the individual's concentrating on higher levels of accomplishment and focusing behavior on reaching objectives.

Development of Achievement Motivation

levels of
expectation
The level of an individual's achievement motivation can be affected by the expectations of individuals they associate with. Levels of expectation that parents have for their children affect the levels of achievement motivation the child develops. In the same way, the level of employee achievement motivation can be affected by the expectations of management. If managers expect their employees to show initiative on the job and solve work-related problems, the employees tend to develop higher levels of achievement motivation. In this respect managers often tend to make two types of errors.

First, the manager may expect too much too soon from employees, leading to their withdrawal from problem solving and decision making on the job. Expecting too much too fast tends to develop employee be-

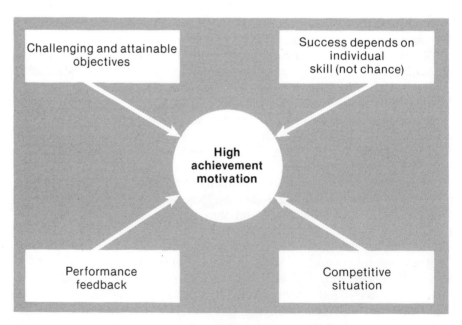

Figure 7.7 Conditions that promote high achievement motivation.

havior patterns that are characterized by a defeatist attitude as well as by passive and indifferent behavior. In many cases, this behavior results when employees fail to achieve the objectives that managers set for them.

Second, management may assume that employees cannot function independently or cannot solve any problems without management's direct supervision. This extreme produces an environment of overprotection and restricts employee behavior. In an overprotective environment, there is little chance to develop challenging objectives, and employees become excessively dependent on management.

Current research indicates that achievement motivation can be developed and increased in individuals. Many training programs have been successful in increasing the achievement motivation of both managers and employees. An organizational environment that offers opportunities for individuals to set and pursue challenging and attainable objectives, and offers supportive management behavior are important in developing achievement motivation.

achievement motivation can be increased

Affiliation Motivation

The need for affiliation—for human companionship and reassurance—produces a desire to interact with people. All indications are that everyone has affiliation needs; they experience some desire to give and receive attention. The intensity of *affiliation motivation* varies among individuals. Some people have very high affiliation motivation while others have relatively low levels.

everyone has affiliation needs

Satisfaction of Affiliation Motivation
The ability to satisfy affiliation needs is affected by the environment and the individual's interpersonal skills. The means available to an individual for satisfying affiliation needs are influenced by social and cultural factors. In organizations individuals often concentrate on satisfying affiliation needs by interaction with other employees. Individuals expect to provide friendly support to other employees and to receive support when needed. These needs are satisfied when there is acceptance from other employees and there is dissatisfaction when rejection occurs. Some jobs provide greater opportunities for satisfaction of affiliation needs than others.

giving and receiving support

For individuals with high affiliation motivation, social relationships will usually take precedence over task accomplishment. Trying hard to get along with others and enjoying the company of others are indications of high affiliation motivation.

Behaviors which result from affiliation motivation are friendliness, high levels of interaction, participation in group activities, coordination of people's efforts, and sensitivity to the feelings of others. Individuals with high affiliation motivation will tend to organize and participate in group activities such as meetings, parties, bull sessions, and reunions. In their interactions with others, they are often involved in helping solve personal problems, coaching, consoling, and sympathizing. They are concerned about the well being and happiness of others.

Individuals can satisfy their affiliation needs in organizations by (1) receiving approval and reassurance from employees and managers, (2) conforming to the desires of work groups and management, (3) helping and supporting others in the organization, and (4) having frequent interpersonal contacts and good interpersonal relations (see Figure 7.8). Individuals with strong affiliation motivation tend to take jobs characterized by a high level of interpersonal interactions, such as public relations, personnel, sales, and teaching.

benefits to
organizations

The satisfaction of employees' affiliation needs can be beneficial to an organization. Research findings indicate that when employee's affiliation needs are satisfied by association with others on the job, there is a decrease in absenteeism and turnover. When there are cooperative work group affiliations, productivity tends to be high and costs low. Most individuals dislike being isolated and desire to have contact with other people.

There are individual differences in the desire for contact with others. It is desirable for organizations to provide individuals with oppor-

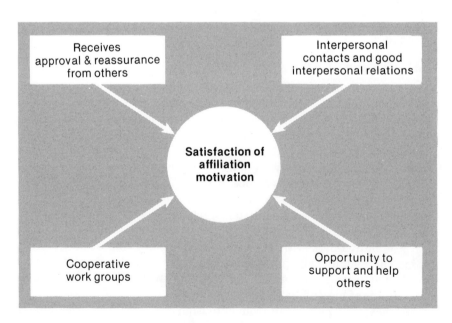

Figure 7.8 Satisfaction of affiliation motivation.

tunities to satisfy their affiliation needs but not to force employees into social situations. Managers should try to create a reassuring and cooperative work environment. Individuals should receive positive feedback when they achieve organizational objectives so that higher productivity results in satisfaction of affiliation needs.

Power Motivation

The need for power produces a desire to influence others and control one's environment. *Power motivation* is specifically related to an individual's relationships with other people. Everyone has some concern for the impact they have on others and would like to have a degree of control in interpersonal relations. In the simplest terms, the goal of power motivation is to feel powerful.

desire to influence

Obtaining power may help an individual satisfy other needs and achieve personal objectives. People also seek power as a primary objective in order to be dominant and forceful. Power is an important factor in the operation of any organization. An organization cannot function without people who have the motivation to obtain power and to influence the behavior of others. A manager's job involves getting things done through the effort of others, and he or she must be motivated to influence other people. Leadership and power appear to be two closely related concepts.

Satisfaction of Power Motivation

The need for power can be satisfied in a variety of ways involving the control of resources, the control of information, and the control of people. As shown in Figure 7.9, it is possible for power motivation to result in individuals trying to own prestige items, such as expensive cars, clothes, houses, or collections of rare objects. Satisfaction of the need for power may result in destructive or constructive behavior. In an organization, destructive results of power motivation could be attacks on others, destruction of property, promoting conflict, or theft. In its most positive form, power motivation can result in accepting responsibility, promoting effective team efforts, and developing productive organizations. Power motivation is neither "good" nor "bad." The way needs for power are satisfied by individuals in an organization can be a major factor affecting the quality of human relations.

power motivation can be satisfied in a variety of ways

the ways power needs are satisfied affect human relations

Power motivation may be expressed in interpersonal relations in a number of forms ranging from making suggestions and stating opinions to using persuasion techniques to win an argument. Individuals may try to influence others by providing information, trying to teach others, attempting to inspire, giving commands, or demanding. Power motivation can result in a desire to be in a superior position and may lead to behaviors such as "telling someone off." Individuals with high

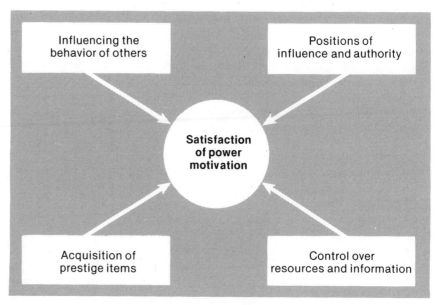

Figure 7.9 Satisfaction of power motivation.

power motivation may appear to be pushy and domineering or to be strong leaders with a high sense of responsibility.

Power and Management Styles

Research by David C. McClelland[5] indicates that power motivation of managers can result in two very different management styles identified as *personal power* and *institutional power*. Personal power can be thought of as "power over" and institutional power as "power with" others.

personal power style   Managers with a personal power style try to be dominant. They can be inspirational and gain strong personal loyalty from employees. The personal power style can result in the manager being overbearing and interfering with the work of others because of their own need to dominate. They may reject organizational responsibility and focus on their desire to be in a superior position. Personal power has been associated with being aggressive, acquiring prestige symbols, and developing dominance-submission relationships. Managers with a personal power style want employees to be loyal and responsible to them personally, not to the organization.

institutional power style   The institutional power manager is concerned with organizational problems and actions that will result in attaining organizational objectives. Managers with this style concentrate their efforts on influencing others to make commitments to effective task performance. They do *not* try to obtain personal submission or to dominate individuals. The manager with institutional power style wants loyalty to the organization and is concerned with group goals. Helping people to identify and achieve group goals, and providing support for individual effort, are characteristics of the institutional power style.

According to McClelland, individuals with a high institutional power orientation have the following characteristics: (1) they feel responsible for developing an effective organization; (2) they like work and doing things in an orderly way; (3) they are willing to sacrifice some of their self-interest for the welfare of the organization; (4) they believe people should receive just rewards for their efforts; and (5) they are more mature and willing to get advice from others.

Organizations have one of their greatest challenges in providing constructive means for individuals to satisfy power needs. Problems can arise from the fact that individual desires for power vary and the way individuals choose to satisfy power needs differ. Not everyone wants a great deal of power, and some who want power do not use it effectively. In providing employees with opportunities to satisfy power needs, managers should determine the employees' actual need for power and their ability to use it well. Both formal and informal authority can satisfy power needs.

challenge for organizations

Expectancy Theory of Motivation

Several *expectancy theories* of motivation have been developed, all founded on the assumption that people choose behaviors based on their expectations about the outcomes.[6]

expectations affect behavior

In other words, the effort a person puts into his or her performance is a function of the value placed on the possible rewards *and* the perceived probability that the effort will be successful (see Figure 7.10). The basic concept of all expectancy theories is that the individual's motivation depends on what the individual expects to receive for his or her efforts.

Valence

According to expectancy theory, motivation begins with the individual's desire for something (i.e., a pay raise, promotion, more responsi-

desire for rewards

Motivation		Valence		Expectancy
(Performance effort)	=	(Value placed on rewards)	✖	(Probability that effort will result in desired rewards)

Figure 7.10 Basic expectancy formula.

bility, recognition, etc.). The strength of a person's preference for a particular outcome such as a goal or reward is referred to as the *valence*. The valence can be positive (desired) or negative (not desired). Valance can vary from -1.00 to $+1.00$. For example, the valence for a promotion would depend on the strength and direction of the individual's preference for the promotion. If the individual had a very strong positive desire for advancement, the valence would approach $+1.0$.

The valence is a result of the individual's internal desires, which are affected by past experiences. The valences for specific goals (or rewards) will vary greatly from person to person.

Expectancy

will effort result in rewards? The individual's probability estimate that a behavior will result in a specific outcome is referred to as *expectancy*. This is the perceived relationship between effort and rewards. Since expectancy is a probability, it can range from 0 to $+1.0$. Regardless of the accuracy of the individual's perception, expectancy influences whether a person will increase the level of effort.

For example, how certain are you that working harder will result in a promotion? If you believe that harder work would almost certainly result in a promotion, your expectancy would approach $+1.0$. If you believed that no matter how hard you worked it would probably not result in a promotion, the expectancy would approach 0.

Expectancy and valence are multiplied to determine the amount of motivation. If expectancy *or* valence is zero, motivation will be zero. If the individual has a high desire (high valence) for promotion *but* does not believe that better performance would result in promotion (low expectancy) there would be no motivation for better performance.

There are several expectations that an individual may take into account when deciding how much effort to expend and how to behave (see Figure 7.11). For example, for an individual to be motivated by the possibility of a promotion, he or she must have at least the following three expectations:

three key expectations

1. The individual must expect that he or she has the capability to improve performance. This may include expectations about individual ability, opportunity to improve, and resources needed to perform.
2. The individual must expect that improved performance will actually result in promotion. Because a reward is said to be available does not mean an individual believes the reward will actually be received.
3. The promotion must be desired by the individual. The individual must expect the promotion will satisfy felt needs such as recognition, status, achievement, etc.

If managers want to affect employee behavior by applying expectancy theory, they should ask three basic questions:

1. Are the potential rewards for the behavior highly valued by the individual?
2. Will the individual feel the rewards are worth the effort required?
3. Does the individual really believe the reward will be received if he or she behaves as desired?

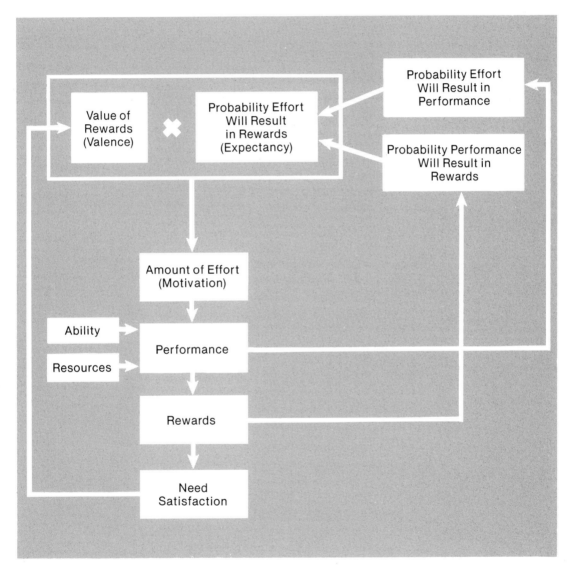

Figure 7.11 Expectancy model of motivation.

What Must an Individual Believe Before Changing Behavior or Increasing Effort?

1. There is a high probability the behavior (or effort) will lead to the desired performance.
2. There is a high probability that as a result of the performance a desired goal (or reward) will be obtained.
3. There is a high probability the goal (or reward) will satisfy important needs.
4. The goal (or reward) has high enough value to be worth the effort required.
5. If the probability of getting the goal (or reward) is low, the value of the goal (or reward) must be very high.

Managerial Implications

application of expectancy theory

Managers can apply the concepts of expectancy theory to improve employee motivation to achieve organizational objectives. The following are specific suggestions on the use of expectancy theory to influence employee behavior.

1. Observe, listen, and ask to determine what goals and rewards are important to each employee.
2. Communicate management's objectives and expectations. Employees should understand the behaviors that are desired.
3. Reward desired performance with rewards that are important to the employee.
4. Increase expectations that desired performance will be rewarded. Tie rewards to desired performance and make reward visible to employees.
5. Provide adequate training and resources to increase the probability that individuals can achieve desired performance. Managers can use guidance and coaching to ensure that efforts will result in desired performance.

Quick Review

I. Motivation and Management
   A. People usually do things for an organization because the organization is doing things for them.
   B. The most productive organizations are composed of people who are satisfying personal needs while

contributing to the achievement of organizational objectives.

    C. Problems of employee motivation do not necessarily stem from a lack of personal motivation.

II. Definition of Motivation

    A. A motive is an inner state that energizes, activates, or moves a person and that directs or channels behavior toward goals.

        1. Motivation deals with internal conditions not actually observed.

        2. The result of motivation is always some type of activity.

        3. Motivation and behavior are not the same.

III. Characteristics of Motivation

    A. Human behavior is not random.

    B. Individuals do not always understand their own behavior.

    C. Behavior is goal directed.

    D. Goals do not control behavior.

    E. As soon as one need is satisfied, another appears.

    F. A satisfied need is not a motivator.

IV. The Process of Motivation

    A. Motivation begins with an internal need creating a state of tension.

    B. Difficulties in the need satisfaction process arise because:

        1. The individual may not be able to identify a goal as being related to the need.

        2. The individual may not be able to identify a form of behavior to achieve the need.

        3. The individual may not be successful in accomplishing the goal.

        4. The goal, once attained, may not satisfy the need.

    C. Individuals tend to select goals that are both achievable and satisfying.

    D. Goal-directed behavior involves the following:

        1. A single goal may satisfy different needs.

        2. A number of goals may satisfy the same need.

        3. A number of behaviors may achieve a desired goal.

V. Maslow's Need Hierarchy

    A. Four basic assumptions underlie Maslow's system:

        1. Motives are highly complex; no single motive affects behavior in isolation.

        2. Lower-level needs must be at least partially satisfied before higher-level needs affect behavior.

        3. A satisfied need is not a motivator.

4. Higher-level needs can be satisfied in a greater variety of ways than lower-level needs.
B. The levels in the hierarchy, beginning with the lowest level needs, are: (1) physiological needs, (2) safety needs, (3) social needs, (4) esteem needs, and (5) self-realization needs.
C. Maslow's need hierarchy has several implications for management:
   1. Human needs are arranged in a hierarchy of importance.
   2. A satisfied need is not a motivator.
   3. Managers must concentrate on unsatisfied needs to influence employee behavior.
VI. Achievement Motivation
A. People's achievement needs vary in intensity.
B. High-achievement people choose goals that are both challenging and achievable.
C. High achievers are not gamblers. They want to affect the outcome of their efforts.
D. High-achievement people are more interested in achieving a goal than receiving external rewards for their efforts.
E. Managerial behavior can depress achievement motivation:
   1. Managers may expect too much too soon.
   2. Managers may assume employees cannot function without direct, close supervision.
F. Managers should set challenging yet attainable goals for themselves and their employees.
VII. Affiliation Motivation
A. The need for affiliation produces a desire to interact with others.
B. The means available to an individual to satisfy affiliation needs are influenced by social and cultural factors.
C. Social relationships will usually take precedence over task accomplishment for individuals with high affiliation motivation.
D. Affiliation needs can be satisfied in organizations by:
   1. Obtaining approval and reassurance from employees and managers.
   2. Conforming to the desire of work groups and managers.
   3. Helping and supporting others in the organizations.
   4. Having frequent interpersonal contacts and good interpersonal relations.

VIII. Power Motivation
   A. The need for power produces a desire to influence others and control one's environment.
   B. Power motivation can be satisfied in a variety of ways involving the control of resources, information, and people.
   C. Two very different types of management can result from power motivation:
      1. Personal power managers, who try to be dominant.
      2. Institutional power managers who are concerned with organizational problems and objectives.
 IX. Expectancy Theory of Motivation
   A. The basic concept of all expectancy theories is that people choose behaviors based on their expectations about the outcomes.
   B. Motivation (effort) is a function of the value placed on possible rewards (valence) *and* the perceived probability that effort will lead to the reward (expectancy).
   C. Some of the key expectations affecting motivation and effort are:
      1. The individual has the capacity to achieve a goal.
      2. There is a strong probability that increased effort will result in the desired reward.
      3. The reward will satisfy a felt need.

Key Terms

Motivation
Need satisfaction
Need hierarchy
Physical needs
Safety needs
Social needs
Esteem needs

Self-actualization needs
Achievement motivation
Affiliation motivation
Power motivation

Personal power motivation
Institutional power motivation
Expectancy theory
Valence

Discussion Questions

1. Explain the meaning of the statement, "There is *no* random behavior."
2. Discuss the relationship among needs, goals, and behavior to achieve goals.

3. What are the implications of Maslow's need hierarchy for a supervisor?
4. Explain how a manager could use Maslow's need hierarchy to increase the productivity of employees.
5. Give an example of a situation in which individuals were able to satisfy their needs and at the same time achieve organizational objectives.
6. How could an organization provide the opportunity for individuals to satisfy self-realization needs?
7. Discuss the characteristics of individuals with high-achievement motivation.
8. How can management's expectations affect employees' levels of achievement motivation?
9. How can affiliation motivation be satisfied in an organization to improve the achievement of organizational objectives?
10. Describe how power motivation can result in constructive *and* destructive behavior.
11. How do expectancies affect the motivation of employees?
12. What can a manager do to improve performance by increasing expectations?

Case Incidents

The Inspection Department

The inspection department of a food processing company has three shifts of inspectors with ten inspectors and a shift supervisor for each shift. The supervisor reports to a chief plant inspector. All of the supervisors have been promoted from line inspectors primarily on the basis of seniority.

Although the inspectors know that they can advance to management positions, most of them are dissatisfied with their present jobs. Most of the inspectors hired try to transfer to another department after only six months in inspection. Much of the dissatisfaction seems to stem from the supervisors' treatment of the inspectors. The major complaint is that supervisors are too restrictive and do not treat inspectors fairly.

For example, the supervisors in the inspection department always take disciplinary action when an employee is absent or tardy without an exceptionally good reason. The chief inspector continually stresses perfect attendance. If inspectors are late, every minute of tardy time is recorded on their records, which decreases their chances of receiving approval for a transfer.

Also, supervisors continually push for error-free inspection. They consider it unsatisfactory if one defective item out of a thousand gets past an inspector. In addition, inspectors feel that while their supervisors may listen to suggestions, they never act on them. The inspectors have continually suggested modifying work procedures to increase effectiveness, but in the past two years the supervisors have never replied to their recommendations.

On the other hand, the supervisors repeatedly complain to the chief inspector and to personnel that their employees lack proper motivation and interest to do an effective job.

1. What is the motivation for individuals to request a transfer from the inspection department?
2. Is the supervisors' complaint about their employees justified?
3. How would you evaluate the current attempts to motivate the inspectors?
4. What other approaches might the supervisors take to motivate the inspectors?

The Office Slob

Joan Mantrell recently became the manager of financial planning for a public utility. There are eighteen people who work in the financial planning office, including statisticians, accountants, engineers, and secretaries.

From the first day Ms. Mantrell became manager, people in the office have been making subtle complaints about the appearance of Tom Gibson. He has been a statistician for the company for the past fifteen years and is involved in determining electric rates. He appears with management in rate hearings before city commissions.

Ms. Mantrell has noticed that Mr. Gibson's clothes are often soiled and wrinkled. His hair is never combed, he comes to work without shaving, and his clothes seldom "go together." His office is also a mess.

He is referred to as the Office Slob. The other employees avoid him and continually make jokes about his appearance.

1. How would you analyze the motivation for Tom Gibson's behavior?
2. What do you think is the motivation behind the employee complaints about Tom Gibson's appearance?
3. Should Ms. Mantrell try to change Tom Gibson's behavior? If so, how?
4. How should Ms. Mantrell respond to other employees complaints about Tom's behavior?

The Climber

Tom Manning is the head of the appliance department in a discount store. Gary Holt, one of his employees, is continually socializing with the store manager. Gary arranges to have coffee breaks with the store manager and plays golf with him whenever possible. Gary is always getting information from the store manager that he should be getting from Mr. Manning. The other employees in the department openly refer to Gary as Mr. Climber.

1. What do you think is the motivation behind Gary Holt's behavior?
2. Does Tom Manning have a problem?
3. Should the store manager continue to socialize with Gary Holt?
4. How could Gary Holt's behavior affect the motivation of the other employees in the department?
5. What action, if any, should Tom Manning take?

Exercise   Employee Motivation

How could the following be "used" by a supervisor to increase *or* decrease employee motivation?

1. Physical working conditions.

2. Supplies, materials, and equipment.

3. Support personnel.

4. Opportunity for learning.

5. Interpersonal relations with other employees.

6. Work schedules.

7. Quality and quantity of work.

8. Recognition.

9. Delegation of authority and responsibility.

10. Information.

Endnotes

1. Bernard Berelson and Gary A. Steiner, *Human Behavior* (New York: Harcourt, Brace and World, 1964), p. 240.
2. A. H. Maslow, *Motivation and Personality* (New York: Harper and Row, 1954), p. 13.
3. For detailed review of motivation theories see Kae H. Chung, *Motivational Theories and Practices* (Columbus, Ohio: Grid, Inc., 1977) and Terence R. Mitchell, "Motivation: New Directions for Theory, Research, and Practice," *Academy of Management Review*, January 1982, pp. 80–88.
4. David C. McClelland, J. W. Atkinson, R. A. Clark, and E. L. Lowell, *The Achievement Motive* (New York: Appleton-Century-Crofts, 1953) and *The Achieving Society* (Princeton, N. J.: Van Nostrand Reinhold, 1961); David C. McClelland, "Business Drives and National Achievement," *Harvard Business Review,* July–August 1962, pp. 99–112.
5. David C. McClelland, "Power Is the Great Motivator," *Harvard Business Review*, 1976, 54 (2), pp. 100–10.
6. For reviews of expectancy theory see D. P. Schwab, J. D. Olian-Gottlieb, and H. G. Heneman, III, "Between Subjects Expectancy Theory Research: A Statistical Review of Studies Predicting Effort and Performance," *Psychological Bulletin,* 1979, 86, pp. 139–47 and Terence R. Mitchell, "Expectancy-Value Models in Organizational Psychology," in N. Feather, ed., *Expectancy, Incentive and Action* (New York: Erlbaum and Associates, 1980).

8 Increasing Performance Effectiveness

Learning Objectives

After reading this chapter, you should be able to:

1. Describe the process of relating employee needs to the achievement of organizational objectives.

2. Discuss the motivation-maintenance theory of motivation and its applications in organizations.

3. Identify the principles of work redesign and job enrichment.

4. Describe how organizations use job enrichment and work redesign to improve motivation and productivity.

5. State why motivational programs fail to improve productivity.

6. Discuss effective approaches to motivation that will improve productivity.

Chapter Topics

Motivation and Productivity

Motivation-Maintenance Theory

Effect of Maintenance and Motivation Factors

Job Enrichment

Work Redesign

Reasons Why Motivational Programs Do Not Work

Workable Approaches to Motivation

Preview and Self-Evaluation

Both managers and organizations want employees that are motivated to achieve organizational objectives. This chapter discusses applications of motivation theory to increase productivity in organizations. Although there are no simple "how to" approaches, on-the-job research has begun to provide meaningful guidelines for motivating people to higher levels of productivity. Current research illustrates approaches that make it possible for employees to satisfy their needs by contributing to the achievement of organizational objectives. Ways in which managers have successfully applied motivation theories are reviewed in this chapter.

Before reading this chapter, test your knowledge by answering the following true-false questions. Then after reading the chapter, check the questions again to see if your perceptions are the same.

Answer True or False

1. Every relationship a manager has with employees affects their motivation. T   F

2. The ability of an organization to provide need satisfaction for employees is usually unlimited. T   F

3. One of the strongest motivators for employees is recognition for contributions to the organization. T   F

4. Motivational factors produce high levels of job satisfaction and motivation. But if they are not present, they produce dissatisfaction.

T   F

5. Poor working conditions often produce negative job feelings, but good working conditions are seldom a reason for positive feelings about the job.

T   F

6. When employees feel good about their job, it is usually due to the nature of the work itself.

T   F

7. The purpose of job enrichment is to provide motivation by training employees to become committed to the organization.

T   F

8. Individuals who work under very close supervision seldom develop a desire to accept more responsibility.

T   F

9. To develop high levels of motivation, managers must design jobs that provide employees with responsibility and challenging work.

T   F

10. Most employees want to be productive.

ANSWERS: 1. T; 2. F; 3. T; 4. F; 5. T; 6. T; 7. F; 8. T; 9. T; 10. T.

Motivation and Productivity

> People are motivated by a variety of personal needs, not by some external technique. The best results come from knowing what these needs are and giving subordinates room to satisfy them while achieving company goals.[1]

motivation essential to productivity

Motivation is an essential element in achieving productivity in any organization. The essence of managing people is to develop conditions that result in employees being motivated to achieve organizational objectives. Successful management depends on developing and maintaining conditions in the organization that integrate employee efforts with the physical and financial resources necessary for success of the organization. It is the efforts of people that determine whether the use of physical and financial resources will result in organizational achievement.

Regardless of the size of the organization or its activities, managers are concerned about the level of motivation in the organization. *Ev-*

ery relationship a manager has with employees affects their motiva-tion. Management's behavior must be analyzed in terms of the direction and degree of motivation. Motivating employees to achieve organizational objectives is a continual management responsibility.

Employee motivation depends on the perceived degree of need satisfaction. When workers perceive that performance will be personally rewarding, they are usually motivated to achieve high levels of productivity.

Relating Employee Needs and Organizational Objectives

employee motivation The process of relating employee need satisfaction to the achievement of organizational objectives is shown in Figure 8.1. It involves the following steps:

1. *Make an evaluation of the needs employees are trying to satisfy.* It is necessary for a manager to determine employees' strongest needs. Since needs are internal and cannot be directly observed, managers must infer the strength of needs from behaviors. It is often difficult to determine these needs accurately.
2. *Determine the goals and activities that employees feel will satisfy their needs.* Different employees have different needs and will

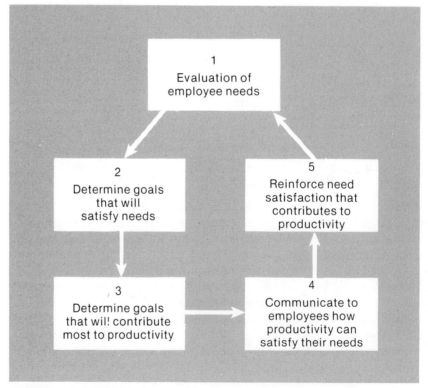

Figure 8.1   Process of relating employee needs to productivity.

develop desires for different goals. The goals of individuals change over time. Some employees will simply tell their goals to managers when asked. Other employees may not be able to specify goals or may not be willing to tell management. By observing the enthusiasm with which employees engage in activities, a manager should be able to distinguish the rewarding from the unrewarding activities.

3. *Determine the employee needs that can be satisfied in the process of achieving organizational objectives.* The ability of an organization to provide need satisfaction for employees is never unlimited. The means available for employee need satisfaction should be evaluated in terms of their contribution to achieving organizational objectives. For most organizations, the purpose of satisfying employee needs is to achieve productivity.

4. *Inform employees of the opportunities available for need satisfaction.* Managers often "overlook" informing employees of opportunities that are available within an organization. In some cases, informing employees may involve making them aware of the possible rewards for desired behaviors. To integrate organizational and individual needs, it is necessary to communicate to employees how achievement of organizational objectives can result in satisfaction of their own needs.

5. *Reinforce employee satisfaction of needs that contribute to organizational productivity.* The reinforcement of desired employee behavior can result in additional needs being satisfied and increase the chances of the behaviors being continued. At the most basic level, this involves giving people credit for doing a good job. One of the strongest reinforcements for an employee is recognition for contributions to the organization.

No One Asked Me

At a prominent Southeastern Iowa dairy, the manager called his staff together to tell them, "We're getting complaints from everyone. The milk's spoiling faster than it should. Consumers, store owners, and restaurant managers are all yelling." After an exhaustive study by qualified experts, the problem remained unsolved. One day, in complete exasperation, the manager walked through the processing section vainly searching for a clue. He stopped momentarily by a pasteurizing unit being repaired by a somewhat shy but industrious older mechanic. "If I only knew where to look for the trouble," the manager murmured. The mechanic looked up and said, "Your experts didn't check the old vent we sealed off when we installed the new processing unit. Maybe it's leaking a little and bacteria are finding their way in." The manager immediately called the chief of maintenance and asked if the vent had been checked. "No sir," he replied, "there's no old vent on the plans." "Well check it anyway," snorted the plant manager. A few days later after the old unrecorded leaky vent was repaired and the early spoilage problem solved, the manager called the maintenance worker to his office. "Why," he queried, "didn't you tell anyone about this sooner?" The answer came promptly. "No one asked me, and if I told them, they probably wouldn't believe me."

Motivation-Maintenance Theory

motivation-maintenance theory

One of the most widely used approaches for analyzing the organizational factors that affect employee motivation is motivation-maintenance theory. Frederick Herzberg conducted the original research that led to the formulation of the theory.[2] It is often referred to as the two-factor theory of motivation, because it describes two sets of factors that are independent but not opposite each other.

Maintenance factors are those factors that make people unhappy or dissatisfied with their jobs. *Motivation factors* are those that make people happy or satisfied and lead to motivation on the job. The basis of the theory is that maintenance and motivation factors are essentially independent of each other and affect behavior in different ways. The opposite of job satisfaction is not dissatisfaction but *no* job satisfaction. The opposite of job dissatisfaction is not satisfaction but *no* dissatisfaction.

It was found in one study that when maintenance factors were not present on the job, employees became dissatisfied. When maintenance factors were present, however, employees were not motivated to high levels of performance.

Motivational factors were found which produce high levels of job satisfaction and motivation. But if they are not present, they do not produce dissatisfaction.

Maintenance needs are generally equivalent to Maslow's lower-order needs in the physical, safety, and social categories. Motivation factors generally relate to Maslow's higher-order needs for esteem and self-realization (see Table 8.1).

Maintenance Factors

dissatisfaction

In interviews with employees, Herzberg found that when people felt dissatisfied about their jobs, they were concerned with the conditions that surrounded the jobs. These maintenance factors involved the environment and conditions in which work was accomplished. Maintenance factors do not involve the nature of the work itself and are not an intrinsic part of a job. Maintenance factors include physical working conditions, job security, company policies and administration, social and interpersonal relations, and pay and economic benefits.

Table 8.1 Comparison of Maslow's need hierarchy and Herzberg's motivation-maintenance theory

Maslow	Herzberg
Self-realization needs	**Motivation factors** Achievement Recognition
Esteem needs	Work itself Responsibility Advancement
Social needs	**Maintenance factors** Interpersonal relations Company policy &
Safety needs	administration Salary Working conditions Supervision
Physiological needs	Job security

If any of these factors are not present to the "liking" of employees, the result is dissatisfaction, which may be expressed in ways that hinder the achievement of organizational goals. Providing for maintenance factors does not produce increases in employee output but prevents losses due to reduced worker performance. Herzberg found that "poor" working conditions were often a factor in negative job feeling, while "good" working conditions were seldom a reason for positive feelings about the job. M. Scott Myers summarized the effect of maintenance factors by stating that "maintenance factors are characterized by the fact that they inspire little positive sentiment when added, but incite strong negative reactions when removed."[3] The following are specific maintenance factors that are usually important considerations in an organization.

Physical Working Conditions   These factors involve the quality of the physical environment in which the individual performs the job. The lighting, temperature control, ventilation, and noise levels are physical factors that directly affect the work environment. Working conditions are also affected by the availability of employee facilities such as parking, restrooms, and cafeterias. When physical working conditions are undesirable, employees tend to focus their attention on these problems and productivity suffers. What is expected by employees as "desirable" working conditions varies depending on the nature of the job.

working conditions

The secretary who gets a new electric typewriter will probably respond favorably and appear to be motivated. Within a few weeks, however, what appeared to be motivation will level off to a condition better described as the absence of dissatisfaction. If a typewriter does not

Increasing Performance Effectiveness 205

function properly, the result is dissatisfaction and lower productivity. When the broken typewriter is repaired, the complaints will stop and the dissatisfaction will go away.

feelings of
security

Security   When individuals feel certain about their continuation in a job, security needs are usually being met. In a work situation, feelings of security are affected by whether individuals believe they are protected by a "fair" and "just" system. For most employees, security needs are most affected by how workers perceive the behavior of their immediate supervisor. A supervisor who is reassuring, supportive, consistent in decisions, and easy to talk with strongly reinforces employees' feelings of security. The importance of security is reflected in employee concern for seniority rights, disciplinary action, review processes, and complaint procedures.

procedures and
rules

Organization Policies and Administration   For many employees, dissatisfaction frequently revolves around the policies and administrative procedures of the organization. It is common to hear complaints about the "red tape" and excessive paperwork in an organization. An organization's goals, policies, procedures, practices, and rules can be dissatisfiers when they are perceived by employees to be inadequate or unfair. For example, promotional policies are often a source of dissatisfaction when they seem to place artificial barriers in the employee's way. Other policies, and their administration, cover a wide range of activities, such as vacations, overtime work, safety rules, and dress requirements.

group interaction

Social and Interpersonal Relationships   An important part of the work environment is the social interaction that takes place among employees. Social needs are satisfied in organizations through both formal and informal group interaction. However, interpersonal relations can cause conflict and dissatisfaction when workers clash over job-related factors such as work load, pay, and advancement. Conflict and dissatisfaction can also result from disagreement about issues not related to the job, such as religion, politics, and other personal matters. Factors affecting social maintenance needs include coffee-break groups, professional groups, committees, lunch groups, parties, car pools, and recreational activities.

compensation

Pay and Other Economic Factors   Any direct or indirect compensation for performing a task can function as an economic maintenance factor. These include wages, salaries, and increases in benefits which are received automatically as a result of being in a position. The benefits that "go with the job," such as social security, sick leave, unemployment compensation, retirement benefits, paid vacations, health insurance, paid holidays, and educational benefits, are maintenance factors. Maintenance factors do *not* include compensation or benefits that are received as a result of outstanding performance.

Figure 8.2 summarizes factors that can result in job dissatisfaction.

Motivation Factors

When employees feel good about their jobs, it is primarily due to the nature of the work itself. Factors which lead to positive feelings and motivation include achievement, recognition for accomplishment, responsibility, and personal growth. The presence of these factors leads to job satisfaction and employee commitment to higher levels of performance.

Motivation factors lead to high levels of satisfaction and increased productivity when they are present, but their absence does not lead to significant dissatisfaction. For example, responsibility leads to feelings of satisfaction about a job, but the lack of responsibility seldom causes dissatisfaction and "bad" feelings.

When motivation factors are present, they not only serve to increase productivity but also to develop greater employee effectiveness.

Achievement   As a motivational factor, achievement is present when employees have feelings of personal accomplishment or the need to accomplish. For achievement motivation to be present, it is necessary that the job be challenging. Two factors are important in analyzing on-the-job achievement motivation: (1) the level of achievement motivation and (2) the ability to perform a specific job. *personal accomplishment*

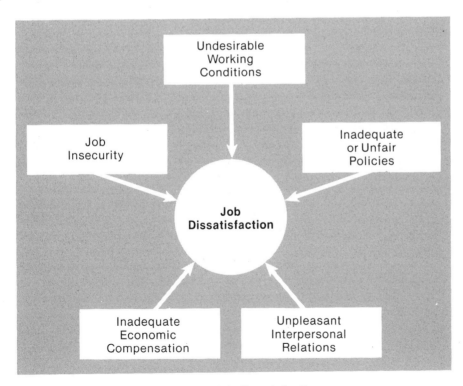

Figure 8.2   Factors contributing to job dissatisfaction.

Since individuals differ in terms of their need for achievement, jobs that offer opportunities to achieve tend to attract people with high achievement motivation. Jobs with few such opportunities tend to attract people with low achievement motivation who are looking for satisfaction of maintenance needs such as security, desirable working conditions and a favorable social environment.

opportunity, ability, and desire

For achievement to occur on the job, the individual must be able to succeed, which requires the ability to solve job-related problems and perform effectively. If a person is to be successful in writing a book, he or she must know how to write. For achievement to be a motivator, a person must have opportunity, ability, and desire.

Factors that can increase the opportunity for on-the-job achievement include delegation of authority and responsibility, involvement in planning and goal setting, availability of information concerning performance, and individual control of the quality of job performance.

Recognition   To function as a motivator, recognition must be the result of accomplishment. Recognition can come from the organization, managers, fellow employees, customers, or the public. For many employees, their jobs form only a small part of an organization's total activity, and recognition is the only way they can evaluate their achievement and contribution to organizational objectives.

forms of recognition

Recognition may take many forms, from verbal or written recognition to pay increases and bonuses. Regardless of the form, the motivational value of recognition does not last very long. Frequent reinforcement is necessary for it to be of continuing motivational value.

Recognition not related to accomplishment is *not* a motivational factor but may satisfy status, security, and social needs. This type of recognition often takes the form of friendliness from others or conversations and discussions that involve the employee's personal interests. Unearned recognition may serve to satisfy maintenance needs by making the environment more pleasant, but it is not a substitute for recognition of accomplishment.

close supervision vs. responsibility

Responsibility   When individuals accept responsibility for decisions affecting their work, they develop a commitment to the job. If responsibility is to be a motivational factor, individuals must have the opportunity to accept responsibility. As responsibility is accepted, external control can be reduced. Individuals who work under very close supervision seldom develop the desire to accept responsibility. In other words, increased job freedom and responsibility go hand in hand. When some jobs are closely examined, it is discovered that the individual is responsible only for "following instructions." To state it more strongly, some jobs have been structured in such a way that employees' sole responsibility is to act like robots.

A study by M. Scott Myers of Texas Instruments revealed that a sense of responsibility is a function of level and supervisory style in the organization.[4] People in top management positions had a higher sense of responsibility than did employees at lower levels. There was an even stronger relationship between accepting responsibility and the style of supervision. The employees' sense of responsibility was higher when their supervisor helped them develop by providing information, delegating responsibility, and encouraging risk taking.

Growth Individual growth takes place through development of new skills and abilities and acquisition of additional knowledge. Growth is motivational for employees and advantageous for the organization since it increases the effectiveness of its human resources. Opportunities for individual growth can involve formal or on-the-job training made available by an organization. The involvement of employees in problem solving and decision making is one of the most effective ways of providing opportunities for growth and, at the same time, increasing the effective use of human resources.

In order for growth to take place on the job, it is necessary that employees receive timely, accurate, and specific feedback on the quality of their performances. Managers can promote growth by helping employees learn how to evaluate personal performance and determine areas in which additional skills or knowledge are needed. By encouraging self-evaluation and performance improvement, management can create the conditions for continual individual growth. The most visible opportunities for growth are through promotion, transfers, and job rotation. *growth and feedback*

Figure 8.3 presents a summary of maintenance and motivation factors.

Effect of Maintenance and Motivation Factors

Research on motivation-maintenance theory has extended to every level of an organization, from hourly employees to top-level executives. Myers concluded from his studies that the motivation-maintenance theory "is easily translatable to supervisory action at all levels of responsibility."[5]

Research on the motivation-maintenance theory indicates that when people do *not* have motivational opportunities, they become preoccupied with maintenance factors. When employees are not able to obtain need satisfaction in the performance of their job, they tend to become "maintenance seekers" and try to reach a point where there is an absence of all dissatisfiers. If employees focus on elimination of dissatisfiers, they tend to look for and find undesirable elements in their environment.

In situations where employees are satisfying motivational needs, there is usually a reduced concern for maintenance factors. When they are involved in meaningful achievement, their behavior may be little influenced by dissatisfactions arising from the lack of maintenance factors. Some of the effects of maintenance and motivation factors are shown in Table 8.2.

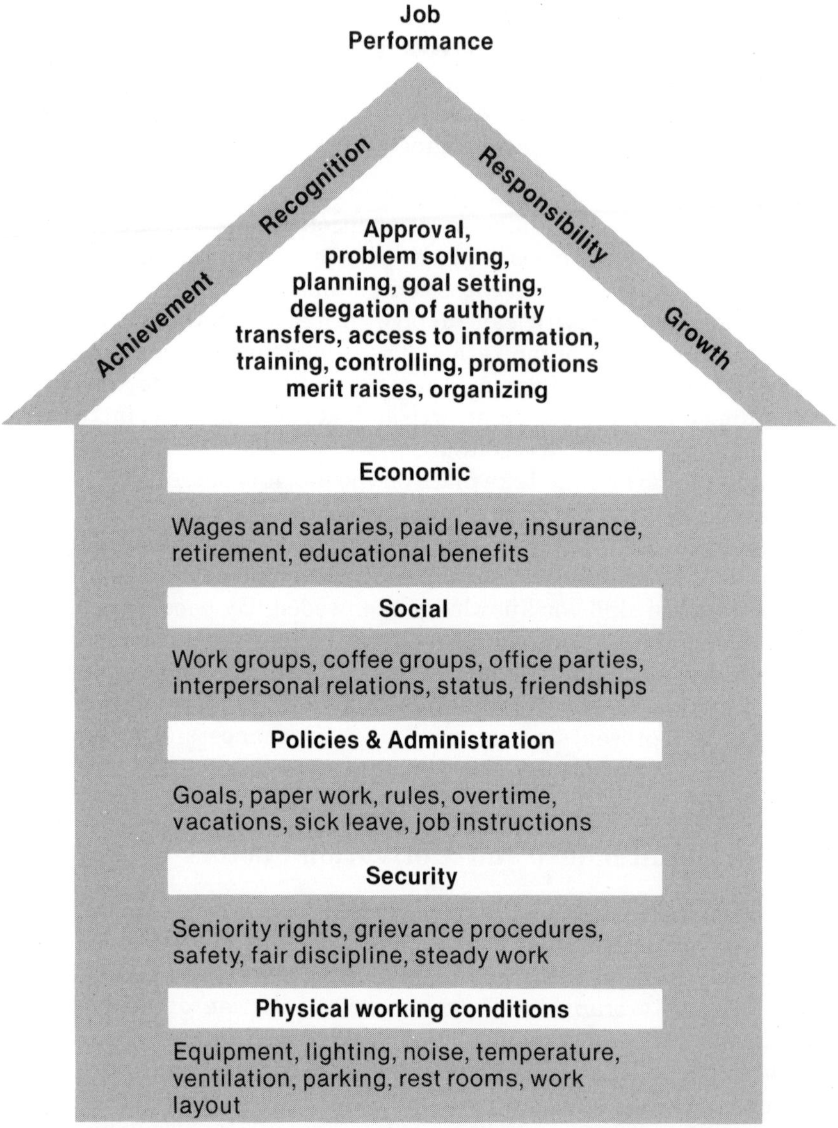

Job
Performance

Recognition   Responsibility

Achievement   Growth

Approval,
problem solving,
planning, goal setting,
delegation of authority
transfers, access to information,
training, controlling, promotions
merit raises, organizing

Economic

Wages and salaries, paid leave, insurance,
retirement, educational benefits

Social

Work groups, coffee groups, office parties,
interpersonal relations, status, friendships

Policies & Administration

Goals, paper work, rules, overtime,
vacations, sick leave, job instructions

Security

Seniority rights, grievance procedures,
safety, fair discipline, steady work

Physical working conditions

Equipment, lighting, noise, temperature,
ventilation, parking, rest rooms, work
layout

Figure 8.3 Maintenance and motivation factors that affect job
performance.

Some Implications for Managers

The most basic implication of the motivation-maintenance theory is
that in order to maximize human productivity it is necessary to satisfy
employees' maintenance needs and provide the opportunity to satisfy
their motivation needs. To develop high levels of motivation, managers
must design jobs that provide employees with challenging work in
which they can assume responsibility for achieving objectives. In
many situatioins it is possible to structure jobs to provide increased
opportunities for achievement, responsibility, growth, and recognition.

Table 8.2 Effects of maintenance and motivation factors

	Satisfaction on the job	No satisfaction on the job
Maintenance needs	No job dissatisfaction; losses due to employees restricting productivity are prevented	Job dissatisfaction; activities which hinder achievement of organizational goals may occur
Motivation needs	Job satisfaction and motivation for higher levels of performance	No job satisfaction and no incentive to increase the quantity or quality of performance

The manager's skill in organizing and planning can be a major influence on the employee's ability to perform effectively on a job. If management has not organized and planned, there can be confusion and lack of coordination resulting in wasted time and effort. The effectiveness of day-to-day supervision of job-related activities can have a major impact on the employee's ability to accomplish tasks. If materials are not available for the individual who is assembling a product, it is obvious the job cannot be performed.

The role of the manager in providing conditions for motivation includes developing an atmosphere of support and approval, communicating all necessary job-related information, encouraging individual goal setting, and providing recognition for achievement.

Job Enrichment

The degree of job dissatisfaction and its impact on many industries has been carefully studied and documented.[6] Classic cases of dull, boring and demotivating job situations have been highly publicized by the press. Job dissatisfaction is one of the major problems management faces today.

To solve many of the problems of motivation and productivity, managers must recognize that the nature of the job has a powerful effect on employee motivation. One approach to increase motivation and productivity is to make basic changes in the nature of jobs. One of the most prevalent approaches being taken to improve motivation on the job is the application of *job enrichment* techniques.

To apply job enrichment, it is necessary to create jobs that are characterized by increased responsibility, personal advancement, recognition, and individual growth. An enriched job involves providing meaningful feedback and allowing employees to participate in decision making, problem solving, and goal setting. Job enrichment does not mean just assigning additional duties to an employee.

The following principles of job enrichment are useful in restructuring jobs (see also Figure 8.4).[7]

Increasing Performance Effectiveness   211

principles of job
enrichment

1. *Remove some controls*. Restructure jobs by removing some of the day-to-day control over the individual, with accountability being retained. For example, one company restructured jobs by allowing employees to decide how their jobs should be done instead of having job methods dictated to them.

2. *Increase personal accountability*. Restructure jobs to increase the accountability of individuals for their own work. As an example, the job of employees assembling electrometers at Corning Glass Works was restructured so they also inspected the meters and were personally accountable for quality.

3. *Provide complete natural units of work*. Natural units of work are jobs complete enough so that workers feel a sense of worthwhile achievement. This usually involves combining "before" and "after" operations into complete jobs. For example, Indiana Bell Telephone company allowed employees to compile the thinner telephone books personally and completely, with their own verification. This made one book "owned" by one employee and combined fourteen steps of work into one unit.

4. *Delegate additional authority to employees*. Restructure jobs so employees are provided with more freedom of action in their jobs. For example, Precision Castaparts allows employees to decide what information they need to do the job and to seek out the information for themselves without having to go through all the formal channels.

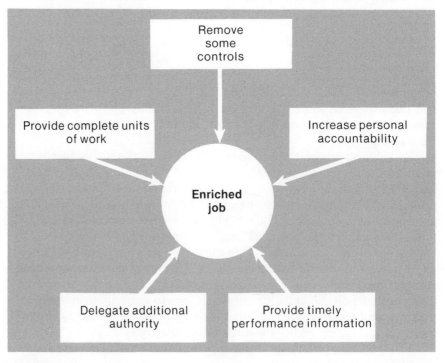

Figure 8.4 Key concepts in job enrichment.

5. *Provide employees with direct and timely performance information.* Restructure communication to provide information directly to the employees instead of having them go through the normal, formal channels of their supervisor. Donnelly Mirrors reports company information on sales, production, inventories, and profits directly to employees.

At a basic level, job enrichment changes the structure of the job so that individuals are planning and controlling as well as performing their work. The great advantage of job enrichment seems to be that it changes the message communicated to employees by the nature of their job. Employees feel they are important and vital assets of the organization. Job enrichment involves employees in decision-making processes and relies on felt needs for responsibility, achievement, and recognition. Many nonenriched jobs seem to communicate that management feels employees are irresponsible, unmotivated, and incapable of learning or growth on the job. The nonverbal communication resulting from the nature of the job can easily override verbal messages transmitted by management in attempting to motivate employees.

job enrichment adds planning and controlling functions

Some examples of successful job enrichment programs may help in developing an understanding of the processes involved.[8] Many of the typists at the Banker's Trust Company of New York had repetitious jobs recording stock transfers. The quality of work was poor, production was low, employee attitudes were negative, and absenteeism and turnover were high. To help change the organizational climate, the typists were involved in altering their work tasks to enrich their jobs. The following changes were made: (1) the typists made their own corrections on computer output tapes rather than having "specialists" make the changes, (2) each typist was responsible for a specific group of customers, (3) the typists checked their own work and eliminated the need for a checker, and (4) the typists scheduled their own work. These changes resulted in an annual savings of $360,000, improved attitudes, and greater employee satisfaction.

examples of job enrichment

Motorola restructured an assembly operation so that each employee would assemble a combination of eighty different components. With the previous assembly methods, an employee worked on one or two components of the total product. The employee's name was put on the units he or she assembled and each employee became personally responsible for the quality of the units assembled. Any units that did not meet testing requirements were repaired by the employee who assembled them.

Additional training was required to enable the employees to assemble complete units. The total assembly operation also required 25 percent more employees. But these increased costs were offset by higher productivity, the need for fewer inspectors, reduced repair costs, improved quality, and less turnover.[9]

A Kaiser Aluminum plant was faced with a problem of low productivity of maintenance employees. Morale was low, and there had been

Increasing Performance Effectiveness

walkouts and slowdowns. To improve productivity, the following changes were introduced: (1) time clocks were removed and employees kept their own time records, (2) direct supervision was virtually eliminated, and (3) the employees decided what maintenance jobs were to be done and in what order. As a result, morale improved, and employees did better work and took pride in it. Maintenance costs were reduced by 5.5 percent.

Work Redesign

Redesign of work can go well beyond the basic concepts of job enrichment. The redesign of work has provided some promising results in productivity and motivation. Although extensive work redesign is still in an experimental stage, there are systems in operation that have resulted in increased employee satisfaction and, at the same time, reduced costs.

Most of the efforts in work redesign have been confined to small work groups. Work redesign in a large setting was implemented in the General Foods manufacturing plant in Topeka, Kansas. The existing plant had had high product waste, expensive recycling, and acts of sabotage; and employees worked effectively only a few hours each day. A new plant was designed to provide a high quality of work life, develop strong employee involvement, and achieve high productivity.

Management, with the advice of employees and consultants, developed the following approach to plant operation.[10]

an innovative approach to work redesign

1. *Self-managed work teams.* Work teams of eight to twelve members were formed and given collective responsibility for segments of the production process. The team members decided who would perform the tasks, and most members learned all tasks in the team. Group meetings were held for decision making and coordination.
2. *Support functions included as a part of each team's responsibilities.* The teams were responsible for quality testing and maintaining quality standards. The team was responsible for functions typically performed by maintenance, quality control, custodial, industrial engineering, and personnel.
3. *Challenging job assignments.* Dull or routine jobs were eliminated wherever possible. Every set of tasks was designed to require responsibility and to challenge employees. The nonchallenging tasks that could not be eliminated were divided among the employees. For example, custodial activities were included in every assignment to avoid having anyone who did nothing but cleaning.
4. *Rewards for learning.* The objective was to have each set of tasks require unique skills that were equally challenging. There were pay increases for mastering an increasing number of jobs.

Individuals were rewarded for learning more aspects of the total manufacturing system. There was no limit to the number of jobs employees could receive pay increases for mastering.

5. *Facilitative team leadership.* There were no supervisors who planned, controlled, and directed the work of team members. A team leader position was created to facilitate decision making and team development.

6. *Managerial decision information provided to operators.* Production decisions that would normally be made by management were made at the operator level. The operators were provided with the necessary economic information and the managerial decision rules.

7. *The plant democratically governed.* Rules affecting employees were developed from collective experience rather than specified in advance by management.

8. *Physical and social settings developed to encourage interactions among employees.* Differentiating status symbols were minimized. There was one parking lot for all employees. Everyone used the single entrance to the plant and office area. A common decorating scheme was used in all areas, from offices to the locker rooms. The plant facilities were designed to promote informal communication among employees during working hours. The informal communication provided an opportunity to coordinate work and inform employees about each other's jobs.

The results of the work redesign at the General Foods plant were impressive. Standard methods of industrial engineering had indicated that 110 employees would be needed to operate the plant. With the application of the team concept it took fewer than 70 employees. Quality rejects were 92 percent below the industry norm, and the absenteeism rate was 9 percent below. Reductions in variable manufacturing costs resulted in annual savings of $600,000.

Reasons Why Motivational Programs Do Not Work

1. Clear and measurable objectives for improvements in productivity may be lacking. Time and effort is spent on removing the symptoms of employee dissatisfaction. The basic reasons for employee needs not being satisfied are not dealt with.

    why programs to improve productivity fail

2. "Canned" approaches to motivate employees are often ineffective, because they are not adapted to meet employee needs or the characteristics of the organization. "Canned" approaches often ignore the highly personal nature of motivation and the specific conditions that exist in the organization.

3. People are always motivated by something. Problems in productivity result from the motivation not being directed toward achieving organizational objectives. When "motivation

programs" attempt to convince employees that they "lack motivation," they resent the implication of deficiency and react in a defensive manner.

4. The motivational impact of the organizational climate is not adequately considered. Often, too much emphasis is placed on gimmicks or procedures to "quickly" motivate employees to increase productivity.

Workable Approaches to Motivation

effective
approaches to
improve
productivity

1. Most employees want to be productive. Yet barriers in the work environment often keep employees from being as productive as they could be. For improvement to occur, either the nature of the job must be changed or the employee must modify behaviors to adapt to the work environment more effectively. In most situations it is more effective to increase productivity by changing the work environment to fit the individual rather than by trying to change the individual.

2. Programs to improve productivity need to focus on the emotions and needs of employees as well as the "logical" and mechanical aspects of productivity.

3. Management's behavior tends to have more effect on employee motivation than messages urging more productivity. Managers must pay careful attention to the way employees perceive management behavior.

4. Increased productivity in an organization does not start somewhere "down the line." The most effective efforts to improve motivation and productivity start with top-level management.

5. Organizational policies, procedures, and techniques to improve motivation must be adapted to meet the needs of individuals and situations. An effective approach is to involve individuals closest to problems in developing solutions that can be implemented in the situation.

6. It is not effective to try to force people to increase their motivation. The best approach is to support employees by making it possible for them to work through problems, develop alternative solutions, and evaluate the results of their actions.

Guidelines for Human Relations to Improve Productivity

Treat People as Individuals

- Most people consider their greatest asset to be their individuality.
- Most people consider their abilities, skills, and personality as unique.

Make the Best Use of Each Person's Abilities

- Look for abilities that may not be in use.
- Attempt to develop unused abilities.
- Reward people who are using their abilities effectively.

Tell People How They Are Getting Along

- Let people know what you expect of them.
- Encourage people on their strong points.
- Train people to overcome weak points.

Give Credit When Due

- Show appreciation when an individual does an outstanding job.
- Compliment individuals in front of others.
- Compliment individuals while the incident is still fresh in their mind.

Tell People in Advance About Changes That Will Affect Them

- Give people as much background about the change as you can. Explain why the change is being made.
- Explain the advantages of the change.
- Get the information about changes to people in the organization first.

Be Sure to Keep Your Promises

- Don't promise anything you cannot deliver.
- Keep promises to a minimum.

Use Authority with Sound Judgment

- Don't substitute your authority for reason.
- Lead, don't drive.

Quick Review

I. Motivation and Productivity
   A. The essence of management is the development of conditions that help motivate employees to achieve organizational objectives.
   B. Every relationship a manager has with employees affects their motivation.
   C. Employee needs can be related to organizational objectives by:
      1. Making an evaluation of the needs employees are trying to satisfy.
      2. Determining the goals and activities employees feel will satisfy their needs.

3. Determining employee needs which can be satisfied in the process of achieving organizational objectives.
4. Informing employees of opportunities available for need satisfaction.
5. Reinforcing employee satisfaction of needs that contribute to organizational productivity.

II. Motivation-Maintenance Theory
   A. Herzberg's two-factor theory describes motivation and maintenance as two sets of conditions that are not opposites of each other.
   B. The absence of maintenance factors leads to dissatisfaction.
   C. The presence of motivational factors leads to satisfaction.
   D. Maintenance factors include physical working conditions, security, organization policies and administration, social and interpersonal relationships, and pay.
   E. Motivational factors include the nature of the work itself, achievements, recognition, responsibility, and personal growth.

III. Effect of Maintenance and Motivation Factors
   A. Achievement is reduced by dissatisfaction with maintenance factors.
   B. When employees are satisfying motivational needs, there is reduced concern for maintenance needs.
   C. Job design, organization, and planning all influence employee effectiveness.

IV. Job Enrichment
   A. To apply job enrichment, it is necessary to create conditions characterized by increased responsibility, personal advancement, recognition, and individual growth.
   B. Job enrichment principles include:
      1. Removing some controls.
      2. Increasing personal accountability.
      3. Providing complete natural units of work.
      4. Delegating additional authority to employees.
      5. Providing employees with direct and timely performance information.

V. Work Redesign
   A. Work redesign involves not only redesign of the task but of the total system in which work is accomplished.
   B. Experiments in work redesign seek to provide high quality of work life, employee involvement, and high levels of productivity.

VI. Reasons Why Motivational Programs Do Not Work
   A. Lack of clear measurable objectives.
   B. "Canned" approaches not characteristic of the organization.
   C. Lack of consideration of organizational climate.
   D. Lack of direction toward organizational objectives.
VII. Workable Approaches to Motivation
   A. Removing of barriers in the work environment.
   B. Focusing on emotions and needs as well as mechanical aspects of productivity.
   C. Emphasizing employees' perceptions of management behavior.
   D. Starting motivational programs at top echelons of the organizations.
   E. Designing policies, procedures, and techniques to meet individual needs.
   F. Supporting employees, developing alternative approaches, and helping them evaluate the results of their actions.

Key Terms

Motivation-maintenance theory

Maintenance factors

Motivation factors

Job enrichment

Natural units of work

Work redesign

Discussion Questions

1. Describe the process of relating employee need satisfaction to the achievement of organizational objectives.
2. How would you determine the activities that individuals feel will satisfy their needs?
3. What methods are available to a supervisor to reinforce employee need satisfaction?
4. What are the basic differences between maintenance factors and motivation factors?
5. Why do you think motivation-maintenance theory has become popular with managers?
6. What are examples of organizational policies that are sources of dissatisfaction?
7. How would you increase the opportunities to satisfy motivation needs on a job you are familiar with?

8. Comment on the statement, "When individuals are not able to satisfy motivation needs they tend to become maintenance seekers."
9. Describe the characteristics of an "enriched" job.
10. What are the potential advantages of job enrichment?
11. Describe how the following jobs might be enriched: (a) service station attendant, (b) city garbage collector, (c) high school teacher, and (d) secretary?
12. Is it possible for a program of work redesign to increase productivity in one organization and decrease productivity in a different organization? Why?

Case Incidents

The City Manager's Assistant

Ron Seely, city manager of a midwestern suburb, realized that one of his new managers in the finance department was not developing quickly enough into a productive member of the team. He decided to help the young man, Bill Thompson, by making Bill his assistant and assigning him special projects to complete on his own. When Bill seemed reluctant to accept the new assignment, Ron merely put it down to the young man's lack of self-confidence.

But as Ron gave more projects to Bill, the young manager could accomplish less and less of his own work—budget analysis and financial planning. Soon other managers began to slow down on completing projects assigned to them by the city manager. Their reasoning was, "Why should we work hard when all Thompson does is sit around and keep the city manager happy?"

The slowdown in productivity was not noticed when city revenues were high, but lately the financial situation has deteriorated. Cuts in Federal funding and higher unemployment in the area are putting increasing pressure on management to make city services more efficient and cost effective.

Ron has encouraged his managers to cut costs and increase their work load. He has also decided that some managers will have to be laid off. In preparation, he has asked each manager to evaluate the others in terms of the most and least valuable individuals. After collecting their reports, he found that each division head had named Bill Thompson as the least valuable manager.

In talking with Bill, Ron was surprised to learn that the young man agreed with the evaluation. "I never wanted to be your assistant," he said. "I was satisfied with my other position in finance. I only took this new job because I felt it was my duty to accept whatever the city manager wanted."

1. What are the motivation and productivity problems in the city management?
2. How could the city manager have prevented the problems from occurring?
3. What would have been an effective approach to improve the productivity of Bill Thompson?
4. What should the city manager do *now* to motivate the managers to cut costs and make their departments more efficient?

Super Efficient

Henry Lane is the supervisor of a shipping department with seven employees. The packers put calculators in individual boxes and place them in cartons for shipping. Each packer works individually to complete his or her share of the calculators to be boxed each day. Betty Rogers finishes her work in about half the time required by the other packers. Because she finishes her work faster, Betty takes longer breaks for coffee and more time for lunch than the other packers. After completing her work for the day, Betty often reads magazines until quitting time. All the packers receive the same pay and there is no extra pay for greater output.

The other packers frequently complain about Betty's longer breaks and her reading to Mr. Lane. They have suggested that she should slow down or be assigned more work.

1. What are possible explanations for Betty's completing her work in about half the time required by the other packers?
2. Since all the packers do the same amount of work and get the same pay, why have the other packers complained about Betty's longer breaks?
3. What are possible results of Mr. Lane assigning Betty more work or asking her to slow down?
4. What action should Mr. Lane take in this situation?

The Problem of the Temporary Employee

The southwest regional warehouse of Allen Variety Stores provides the merchandise for the company's retail stores in ten states. As the orders for Christmas stock began to come in, Tom Reid, the warehouse manager, requested temporary help from the Regional Administration Center.

This year the regional manager selected Vic Johnson to be temporarily assigned to the warehouse. Before Vic reported to work, Mr. Reid was informed by one of his shipping clerks that Vic Johnson was considered a problem employee because he was "lazy." Mr. Reid decided that he should take action to prevent problems when Vic began working in the warehouse.

The day Vic reported to work, Mr. Reid gave him the orders that he was to fill and the amount of time it would take to fill each one. At

2:00 on the first day, Vic told Mr. Reid that he would not be able to get the orders out on time. When Mr. Reid asked why, Vic explained that the method used to cross-check the accuracy of the orders was slowing him down. Mr. Reid felt he had heard enough. He told Vic, "I want you to realize I will not tolerate any more delays or excuses— now get to work."

Vic replied, "I was not trying to make excuses. I wanted to suggest a faster way of cross-checking."

"Vic, if there were a faster method of cross-checking, we would be using it. Your job is to cooperate with the other employees and get the orders out."

During the next week, work assigned to Vic went very slowly. The other employees began to complain that Vic was not doing his share. In response to the complaints, Mr. Reid took Vic off filling orders and assigned him to clean-up duties. This only created another problem, since there was not enough clean-up to keep Vic busy. The employees now complained that Vic was disrupting their work by trying to carry on conversations while they filled and checked orders.

1. Was the action taken by Mr. Reid the day Vic reported to work the best way to attempt to motivate Vic?
2. How would you have replied to Vic's reason for not being able to get the orders out within the specified time and his desire to suggest a faster method for cross-checking?
3. Do you feel that Mr. Reid was taking an appropriate course of action by assigning Vic to clean-up?
4. What course of action would you take if Vic were now assigned to the warehouse permanently?

Exercise   *Actions to Improve Productivity*

Your department's productivity has dropped more than 20 percent in the last two months. Your boss has informed you that unless you get the productivity level up you may be replaced.

Evaluate the Following List of Proposed Actions
Which actions would you take? Which would you take first?

1. Call a department meeting. Release the productivity information and make it clear that you expect immediate improvement.
2. Discuss the decreased productivity with each employee privately. Be specific with each employee about the ways to improve productivity.

3. Say nothing to employees about the productivity problem. Put on pressure for more productivity by your actions. Be strict in discipline.
4. Start immediately to correct all unacceptable behavior through private conferences with employees. Be pleasant but firm.
5. Avoid contact with employees until they feel sorry for you and, as a result, start to solve the problem.
6. Begin involving employees in problems that you previously handled yourself.
7. Have a party for employees and develop off-the-job relations with employees.
8. Provide each employee a written report on the problem and request written feedback on solutions.
9. Go to other supervisors and ask for help in solving the problem.
10. Go to higher level managers and ask for help in solving the problem.

Endnotes

1. Hensleigh Wedgewood, "Meatballs and Motivation," *Supervisory Management,* May 1970, p. 2.
2. Frederick H. Herzberg, "One More Time: How Do You Motivate Employees?" *Harvard Business Review,* January–February 1968, pp. 53–62.
3. M. Scott Myers, *Every Employee a Manager* (New York: McGraw-Hill, 1970), p. 72.
4. M. Scott Myers, "Conditions for Manager Motivation," *Harvard Business Review,* January–February 1966, pp. 58–71.
5. M. Scott Myers, "Who Are Your Motivated Workers?" *Harvard Business Review,* January–February 1964, pp. 73–88.
6. *Work in America: Report of a Special Task Force to the Secretary of Health, Education and Welfare* (Cambridge, Mass.: M.I.T. Press, 1973); H. L. Sheppard and Neal Q. Herrick, *Where Have All the Robots Gone?* (New York: Free Press, 1972).
7. For a more detailed discussion of job enrichment concepts see Frederick H. Herzberg, "One More Time: How Do You Motivate Employees?" *Harvard Business Review,* January–February 1968, pp. 53–62, and Robert N. Ford, "Job Enrichment Lessons for AT&T," *Harvard Business Review,* January–February 1973, pp. 96–106.
8. These examples were drawn from an appendix to *Work in America* that summarizes thirty-four cases studied involving job enrichment.
9. For a more detailed description see Walter B. Scott, "Participative Management at Motorola—the Result," *Management Review,* July 1981, pp. 26–28.
10. Richard W. Walton, "How to Counter Alienation in the Plant," *Harvard Business Review,* November–December 1972, pp. 70–81.

9 Conflict, Frustration, and Stress

Learning Objectives

After reading this chapter, you should be able to:

1. Describe the types of motivational conflict experienced by individuals.

2. Discuss the nature of frustration and how it affects people.

3. Identify the constructive and disruptive effects of frustration.

4. Describe the nature of defense mechanisms and the types of defense mechanisms.

5. Discuss the implications of defense mechanisms for effective human relations.

6. Describe the causes and consequences of stress.

7. Identify individual courses of action to reduce stress.

8. List courses of action an organization can take to control job stress.

Chapter Topics

Preview and Self-Evaluation

William James, the father of American psychology, observed that it is not work that really tires people but the burdens of unmade decisions. The longer we take to decide on a course of action, the more likely we are to experience anxiety, tension, and physical symptoms of stress such as headaches, digestive disturbances, and emotional upsets. Philosophers have said that if a mule is placed precisely between two equal bales of hay, it will starve to death rather than make a choice. Conflict, the inability to choose between two or more alternatives, is an integral part of the human condition. Inability to resolve conflict or to achieve a goal once a course of action has been determined leads to frustration, along with aggression, withdrawal, and stress. In this chapter, we review the problems of conflict, frustration, and stress management and offer suggestions to alleviate these problems on the job.

Before reading this chapter, try answering the following questions. Check the questions again after reading the chapter to see if your perceptions are the same.

Answer True or False

1. When a person works to achieve a goal, a number of different motives are usually involved.   T   F

2. Choosing between two rewarding goals is less difficult and takes less time than choosing between two negative goals.   T   F

3. People experience conflict when they are attracted to an object or activity and, at the same time, want to avoid it.   T   F

4. Frustration is always accompanied by tension.   T   F

5. It is not possible for frustration to arise from imagined problems.   T   F

6. For an individual to choose a different goal can be a constructive result of frustration.   T   F

7. All defense mechanisms involve a degree of distortion of the true relationship between the individual and external reality.   T   F

8. A dull and boring job that has little challenge can be highly stressful.   T   F

9. Situations which produce undesirable levels of stress for one individual may be the source of major satisfaction for another.   T   F

10. The goal of stress management is to use stress as a natural and productive force.   T   F

ANSWERS: 1. T 2. F 3. T 4. T 5. F 6. T 7. T 8. T 9. T 10. T.

Motivational Conflict

The complexity of human behavior is reflected by the many motives that simultaneously affect an individual's behavior. People must continually make choices when attempting to satisfy needs. When a person works to achieve a goal, a number of different motives are usually involved.

    It should be kept in mind that an individual may not be aware of the motives leading to a specific behavior. A person who expresses no

people must make choices

interest in being recognized by other people but continually tries to attract attention is probably influenced by recognition needs.

When goals cannot be obtained, an individual may be forced to choose between satisfactions. The motives themselves are not in conflict; the goals or the methods to obtain goals are incompatible. Conflict then develops.

In the simplest situation for analysis, two conflicting desires will result in three basic types of conflict situations. Psychologists usually call them approach-approach, approach-avoidance, and avoidance-avoidance.

Approach-Approach Conflict

The *approach-approach situation* forces the individual to choose between two different courses of action, each leading to satisfaction. Two different goals or objects are involved, but the individual can obtain only one (see Figure 9.1).

choice between two rewarding goals

In the approach-approach conflict situation the individual must choose one course of action and reject another. The choice is often forced because of limited resources such as time or money. The individual may want both a new car and a new boat, but cannot afford them.

Choosing between two rewarding (positive) goals becomes more difficult and takes longer when they are seen as having equal value. But in most cases of approach-approach conflict, the decision is relatively easy because both alternatives are rewarding. Approach-approach conflicts usually do not result in high levels of tension and frustration. An example of such conflict is having two good job offers and finding them both attractive. A choice must be made between them.

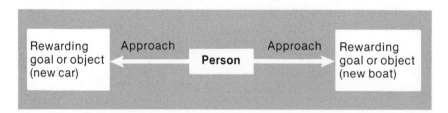

Figure 9.1 Approach-approach conflict.

Approach-Avoidance Conflict

goals can have positive and negative characteristics

In the *approach-avoidance conflict* an individual is attracted to an object or activity and, at the same time, wants to avoid it. The conflict occurs because the goal has both positive and negative features. Approach-avoidance conflict occurs in the case of the offer of a job that pays well but involves living in an undesirable location. The approach-avoidance conflict is diagrammed in Figure 9.2.

Chapter 9

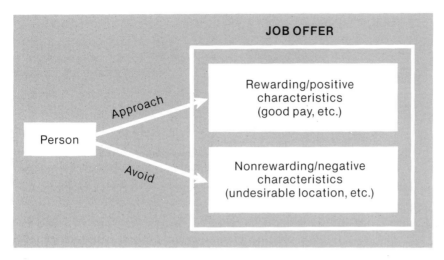

Figure 9.2 Approach-avoidance conflict.

Approach-avoidance conflict often occurs when an individual makes a purchase. The object purchased may have attractive characteristics but its cost is often a negative factor. The decision to approach or avoid involves evaluating the gain versus the losses. Most decisions involve an element of approach-avoidance conflict; few objects, activities, or goals are without some negative aspects.

Approach-avoidance conflict may occur when the goal is positive but the behavior required to achieve the goal has negative characteristics. Receiving additional pay may be a positive goal for an individual, but working overtime to obtain the pay is a nonrewarding activity.

In some situations, the positive goal is obtained but undesirable consequences follow. For example, missing work to go fishing means a loss in pay and, possibly, disciplinary action from the boss.

Avoidance-Avoidance Conflict

Avoidance-avoidance conflict occurs when an individual is forced to choose between two undesirable alternatives. The individual would like to avoid both alternatives (see Figure 9.3).

For example, a student may want to avoid both studying and making a low grade. An individual may be required to choose between transferring to an undesirable city and resigning from the company. There are many sayings that reflect the existence of the avoidance-avoidance conflict: "between a rock and a hard place," "from the frying pan into the fire," "between the devil and the deep blue sea," "the lesser of two evils," and so on.

Because two undesirable alternatives are present in the avoidance-avoidance conflict situation, it is *unlike* the approach-approach situation and the approach-avoidance situation, which contain possibilities

choice between two undesirable alternatives

Conflict, Frustration, and Stress   229

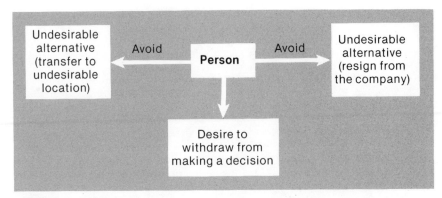

Figure 9.3 Avoidance-avoidance conflict.

for need satisfaction. *In the avoidance-avoidance situation there is typically a desire to escape, either physically or psychologically.* If the alternatives are extremely negative and the individual can't escape, he or she may turn to aggression and attack.

When a person tries to induce others to do something disagreeable or threatening by imposing punishment as an alternative, the procedure can be only as effective as the perceived strength of the punishment. If people operate on avoidance-avoidance conflict for a prolonged period of time, they may become psychologically ill.

Frustration

barriers to need satisfaction

When an individual is unable to attain a goal because of a perceived barrier, frustration results. *Frustration* takes place when efforts to satisfy a need are blocked before the desired goal is reached. The barrier may be in the situation or environment (external to the individual), such as the typewriter that breaks in the middle of typing a term paper. The barrier may be personal to the individual (internal barriers), such as a tendency to procrastinate when faced with a difficult deadline. Frustration is an individual condition based on individual perception and not a characteristic of the external environment.

There are many possible reactions to frustration. When individuals are unable to attain desired goals, they may engage in constructive efforts such as working harder to achieve their goals or redefining their objectives. Other behaviors can be disruptive, such as aggressive behavior directed at a real or imagined barrier.

tension

Frustration is always accompanied by tension. Tension develops when needs are not being satisfied. It is inevitable that, at one time or another, all individuals involved in human organizations will experience feelings of personal frustration. As individuals work toward achieving personal goals, they often find that barriers exist which make it difficult or impossible for them to reach a desired goal. Individual barriers can result from an inaccurate estimate of physical or mental abilities. A young man who has career goals that require a college education but lacks the mental aptitude for college work has overestimated his abilities.

A woman who wants a promotion to a job she is capable of but who lacks the confidence to try for it has erected an individual barrier by underestimating her ability. It is not uncommon that employees attempt to reach goals and quit in the process because they underestimate their abilities to succeed. If an employee *perceives* a goal to be beyond his or her abilities, then the barrier is real to the individual. *perceived barriers are real*

The work environment can produce barriers that result in frustration. An employee may desire to achieve high production, but is blocked by the machine breaking down frequently. A manager who wants to make a good impression on top management by getting a report in ahead of time may be frustrated by a typist who makes so many errors that the report is late. On-the-job barriers may involve the quantity or quality of physical, financial, and human resources.

Most on-the-job frustration appears to result from conflicts between individual wants and the restraints imposed by the organization. In any human organization there are attempts to balance individual needs and organizational needs. As individuals become part of an organization and accept its methods and procedures, the area of conflict shifts from outside to within them. *conflicts between individual needs and organizational needs*

Constructive Results of Frustration

Frustration is often regarded as undesirable because of its destructive effects. These effects frequently occupy our attention, and we tend to overlook those situations in which frustration results in positive outcomes. Frustration can cause individuals to become more effective in attaining personal and organizational goals. Figure 9.4 illustrates some constructive effects of frustration.

Increasing Efforts

As tension increases in the individual, there is a tendency to focus on goal attainment and to eliminate irrelevant and distracting behaviors. In some cases, frustration is part of the challenge of attempting to attain a goal. *frustration is part of the challenge*

One constructive effect of frustration may be an increase in the effort required to reach a goal. If this type of behavior is to take place, the goal must be seen as attainable, and there must be a perceived method to overcome the barrier. Most individuals can tolerate the mild levels of frustration which result from goals being challenging and attainable.

Figure 9.4 Constructive results of frustration.

However, if the barrier cannot be overcome by the individual, behavior will usually be redirected to another method or goal.

Trying Other Methods

search for alternative methods

One of the most frequent redirections of behavior is to choose another method of reaching an existing goal. As tension increases because underlying needs are not satisfied, the individual may notice previously ignored elements in the situation. For example, if an employee wants a promotion and does not achieve it by putting in extra hours of effort, he or she may try another method, such as doing personal favors for the boss.

Choosing Another Goal

Another commonly observed reaction to frustration is a search for alternative goals that are more easily achieved. As tension increases because a barrier cannot be eliminated, alternative goals usually begin to appear more attractive.

change goals or environments to avoid frustration

In the most extreme cases the individual may attempt to change environments, which may mean a change in jobs. When the situation is perceived as producing the frustration, most individuals consider the problem to be in the situation and look for another environment.

A person's view of the environment may change when comparing it with other situations. For example, an employee may investigate other job openings and decide that the current job "isn't so bad after all." This redefining of situations may cause a person to lower the level of aspiration and find ways to satisfy needs in the present job.

Disruptive Effects of Frustration

If constructive efforts to reach goals and satisfy needs are not effective, tension will continue to increase. The tension can reach levels where its effects disrupt goal-directed activity.

When the tension level becomes high, the individual may concentrate so completely on the unsuccessful attempt to reach the goal or on the goal itself that other methods and goals are not considered. The individual may become extremely "emotional" and panicky and lose the ability to deal constructively with the situation.

people react emotionally to frustration

The amount of tension that is experienced as a result of frustration depends on the individual and the nature of the situation. Some individuals can handle more tension than others. The ability of an individual to deal with frustration partially depends on previous experience with similar situations and on the anticipated outcome of the issue. It is possible for a person to tolerate a high degree of frustration for a long time without losing control. Some individuals are able to perform well under pressure and can make realistic and rational choices in situations where most people would panic and lose control. Since most management jobs involve more pressure and frustration than nonmanagerial positions, managers must have the ability to tolerate frustration.

When the individual's tolerance level is exceeded, major disruptive effects may occur. Two of the most frequent responses to prolonged frustration are aggression and withdrawal (see Figure 9.5).

Aggression

Aggression in its simplest form involves a direct attack upon the perceived barrier to achieving the goal. If possible, the individual will direct aggression against the person or object that is perceived as the

attack the barrier

Figure 9.5 Disruptive effects of frustration.

cause of the frustration. Direct aggression may involve physical or symbolic attack, or both. The employee who "cusses" out his supervisor for not approving a transfer is exhibiting a direct symbolic attack. A frustrated employee who thinks that a manager is the "barrier" preventing goal attainment may verbally or physically attack the person or may attempt, by rumors or other means to "get revenge." Aggression can take many forms, including antagonistic behavior, theft, disobedience, sabotage, absenteeism, and interference with the work of others.

displaced aggression   Aggression may be displaced toward an object or a person who is not directly involved in the situation. For example, an employee whose supervisor will not recommend a pay raise may displace an aggressive response toward his or her family. There are numerous forms of displacement, from slamming a door to kicking a dog. Usually, the target of displaced aggression is something or somebody not able to return the aggression.

When an individual cannot clearly identify a barrier, generalized aggression toward objects and persons may result. As frustration increases and its sources become more difficult to identify, the generalized aggressive behavior may increase. In extreme cases, the individual may begin to attack everyone and everything within reach.

There may be many reasons why an individual cannot direct aggression toward the source of the frustration. For example, if an employee were to direct aggression toward the "boss" the worker could get fired.

Withdrawal

A general behavioral reaction to intense frustration of one's efforts is *withdrawal* from the frustrating situation. An employee who cannot decide which of two transfers to take may withdraw from making a decision by staying on the current job.

physical withdrawal   Withdrawal may reduce tension, but it is usually not functional since the goal cannot be attained. This type of withdrawal is not the same as the escape reaction that results when individuals are in dangerous situations. The individual may withdraw from a situation by physically leaving, as is the case when an employee quits a highly frustrating job. The physical withdrawal may be temporary, as in the case of "putting off" writing a term paper until the last minute.

The employee who has been turned down for promotion several times may ask not to be considered for future promotions, thus physically withdrawing from a frustrating situation. Other ways in which employees may physically withdraw include absenteeism, taking sick leave when not sick, increasing the length of coffee breaks, and coming to work late and leaving early.

Withdrawal may also be psychological, as in situations where the individual develops an "I don't care" attitude. For example, a student originally wanted to get an A in a course. After making D's on the first two tests, however, the student decides that simply passing the course will be good enough. Employees who "daydream" on the job may be withdrawing psychologically from a frustrating work environment. Since the work situation seems to be beyond the employee's control, he or she will do the least amount of work necessary to keep the job, not caring if it is done correctly.

psychological
withdrawal

Defense Mechanisms

When someone continually uses forms of withdrawal to deal with frustration, withdrawal becomes a part of their personality. It is no longer a simple withdrawal from a frustrating situation but a *defense mechanism*. The use of defense mechanisms makes it possible for a person temporarily to reduce his or her tension level and its accompanying feelings of anxiety. All defense mechanisms involve a degree of distortion of "true" relationships between the individual and external reality. Although defense mechanisms provide some relief from tension and anxiety, they do not satisfy underlying needs. Individuals learn defense mechanisms at an early age and continue to use those mechanisms that have "worked" for them in the past.

all defense
mechanisms
involve distortion
of reality

Defense mechanisms affect the way individuals relate to each other in organizations and the way they understand and adapt to their environments. Since problems of conflict and frustration are everyday occurrences, the use of defense mechanisms is also common. Everyone uses them to help cope with the barriers that arise in trying to achieve goals. Individual behavior patterns are partially determined by the types of defense mechanisms used and the extent of their use.

Rationalization—"Everybody Does It!"

Rationalization involves a process of justifying behaviors and feelings that are undesirable or inconsistent by providing explanations that make them acceptable. The employee who takes company property for personal use may rationalize the theft by saying "everybody does it."

justifying
behaviors

Rationalization involves developing a "good" reason rather than dealing with the real reason for behavior. In developing rationalizations, individuals usually distort the effects of emotions and motivational factors to maintain their self-esteem and avoid frustration. The individual who says, "I don't quit smoking because I would gain weight if I did, and that would be worse for my health" is rationalizing when the "real" reason for not quitting is that the individual "can't break the habit."

Rationalization can take many forms. When people experience personal failure or violate "moral principles," they can be very creative in developing "good reasons" for their behavior. "I failed the exam because the questions were unfair." "I did not get the report done because the library was too noisy." "I did not make an A in the course because I'd rather get an education than make grades."

sour-grapes   Two of the most common forms of rationalization are popularly referred to as "sour grapes" and "sweet lemons." Sour grapes involves convincing oneself that something is not worth having when one finds it cannot be obtained. When you discover you can't afford a Cadillac, you "decide" they aren't any good because they have a lot of maintenance problems (or any other reason you choose). The employee who did not get a promotion may say, "I really didn't want it because it would require more travel and longer hours." A student may drop a course he or she is failing and tell others, "The material wasn't worth knowing."

sweet-lemons   Sweet lemons involves convincing oneself that something one is forced to accept is really desirable. The sales manager who did not meet sales goals says, "It's just as well that sales were low, because they'll listen to my requests for more advertising money and give me more sales help." Another form of sweet lemons occurs when employees identify their jobs by more prestigious titles, as in the case of elevator operators who are referred to as "transportation specialists."

Rationalization can involve a complex set of reasons used to explain a behavior. With a number of reasons available, the individual has defenses in depth, so that if one rationalization "does not work," others are still available. The employee accused of damaging a machine may say, "Someone else was the last to use the machine," or "The machine had not been working properly for some time," or "The machine has never been repaired properly by maintenance, and besides this type of machine is not a quality product anyway."

Limited use of rationalization can be beneficial in reducing frustration and helping individuals in tension-producing situations to function effectively. However, if rationalization is used to extreme, an individual can become so entangled in unreal justifications that any realistic problem solving is avoided.

Repression—"Motivated Forgetting"

putting it out of conscious memory   *Repression* involves "forgetting" painful and frustrating information by unconsciously putting it out of one's memory. As a result, the individual is not able to recall the original incident. Repression is a type of "motivated forgetting," but at an unconscious level.

The "deliberate" suppression of painful or unpleasant information is a frequent form of behavior, but it is not repression. Repression is not a deliberate act; it occurs as a defense reaction to threatening information. An employee who "forgets" a responsibility that, when assigned, triggered fears of failure *may* have repressed the assignment. Feelings and experiences which produce a sense of guilt may result in repression. For example, an employee may "forget' to tell the boss about an embarassing argument with a customer.

Reaction-Formation—"Methinks the Lady Doth Protest Too Much"

Reaction-formation occurs when the individual reacts to a desire or behavior by exhibiting opposite attitudes and behaviors. The repression of strong tension-producing desires can be accompanied by behavior that is the opposite of the repressed desire.

exhibiting opposite behaviors

The manager who represses the desire to have an affair with his secretary may go on a crusade against such type of "sinful" activity by employees. The real desire has been repressed and his behavior changed by denouncing his own feelings as perceived in others. Another example of reaction-formation is the mother of an "unwanted child" who becomes over-protective to "prove" to herself and others that she has no negative feelings toward the child.

An employee's extreme obedience to the boss could really be a reaction of "hate" for the boss. In this situation, reaction-formation may create tension and frustration that could eventually cost the employee a job.

Just because we have a little knowledge of reaction-formation, we should not develop a skeptical attitude toward people's motives. Reaction-formation does illustrate that behaviors can sometimes reflect the opposite motivation of what the behavior seems to be. In specific cases it may be difficult to determine the "real" motivations of an individual. You will need to know a great deal about the person and the particular circumstances before you can accurately interpret an intense attitude or behavior such as reaction-formation.

Projection—"It's All Your Fault"

Through the use of projection, individuals protect themselves from awareness of their own undesirable characteristics and feelings by attributing them to others. *Projection* allows an individual to "hide" feelings by projecting them onto another person. The employee who feels hostility toward the supervisor might use projection to hide the feeling by attributing hate to the supervisor. The individual may say, "The supervisor is out to get me, but I'll get something on the supervisor first." Individuals who have been unsuccessful in obtaining promotions may project their feelings and believe that others are "out to get them" or they may attempt to block the promotion of others in the organization.

protection from undesirable feelings

Individual security or insecurity on the job may have an effect on the use of projection. As pointed out by Sick, insecure employees tend to project their inadequacies onto others. "Those who are well adjusted and secure perceive positive traits in others, while those who are insecure and unable to recognize and accept their shortcomings tend to perceive others as having the same characteristics."[1]

The supervisor who has a production "crisis" because equipment is breaking down and tells employees, "Don't panic, don't panic, don't panic!" may be using projection. The supervisor has redefined the situation by projecting the undesirable feelings of "panic" onto employees. Individuals are using projection when they attempt to avoid dealing with unacceptable feelings or unsuccessful behaviors by blaming others or attributing their own characteristics to others.

Identification—"Hero Worship"

sharing in another's success

Individuals are using *identification* when they pattern their behavior after others. Identification can involve assuming the values, attitudes, and behaviors of someone else. By identifying with someone, it is possible to "share" in the success of another individual. The achievements of a successful person can become satisfactions for the individual frustrated by failure.

An employee may adopt the values and behaviors of a respected and admired manager. This may be carried to the point where the employee adopts the mannerisms, speech, dress, hobbies, and eating habits of the admired person.

An employee may make no attempt to develop abilities through education, training, or experience but obtain satisfaction by identifying with people who are famous, rich, and successful. Identification with "heroes" can become the most important aspect of an individual's life.

Failures as well as successes are shared in identification. An individual may feel "real" pain and disappointment when a "hero" is injured or fails. Conflict can occur when an administrative assistant identifies with the boss to the extent of assuming not only some mannerisms but also the authority and responsibility of the boss. Secretaries are frequently observed identifying so closely with their bosses that they make the boss's decisions and assume the authority of the boss's position.

Regression—"Disneyland Here I Come"

becoming a child again

Regression involves responding to frustration by reverting to earlier and less mature forms of behavior. The individual may revert to "childish" behavior or attempt to "go back" to an earlier and more comfortable time.

Regression may take the form of participation in activities that are usually "reserved" for children. An individual may escape a frustrating situation through regression by going to an amusement park and becoming a child again. There are many activities that reduce tension, including building model airplanes, flying kites, playing with model railroads, and other such activities. Forms of "play" may allow individuals to escape the realities of responsibility and accompanying frustration.

Regression may also take the form of less mature and possibly destructive behavior. Temper tantrums as a response to frustration can be a form of regression. When frustrated on the job, regression may be reflected in pounding the desk, hitting a machine, horsing around, throwing a report on the floor, storming out of a meeting, or crumpling up a letter of complaint. The manager who cannot get approval for an additional secretary might begin typing, filing, and doing other activities more appropriate for subordinates.

The individual exhibiting regressive behavior may want the manager to assume the role of a parent in dealing with the situation. Regression is seldom helpful in achieving goals and solving problems because it does not focus on the present. It is based on the past and a return to "earlier" and less responsible behaviors.

Implications for Human Relations

This review of defense mechanisms has not covered all of those which could be identified or described. It has focused on the more prevalent mechanisms. *All defense mechanisms lead to a degree of distortion in order to preserve one's self-image and reduce tension.*

Because direct satisfaction of needs is not always possible, defense mechanisms are used by everyone. Our human relationships are characterized by a complex interaction among underlying motives, individual goals, and behaviors. The conscious or apparent reasons for any behavior may not be the "real" reasons. Behaviors, attitudes, and feelings are not always what they appear to be. Our interpretations of observed behavior may also be inaccurate when we try to draw conclusions about the underlying motivation. The use of defense mechanisms serves to illustrate that individuals do not always understand their own behavior or the relationship between their behavior and the underlying motivation.

behaviors may not be what they appear

Even though there is always a relationship between underlying motivation and behavior, it is not one that is simple or easy to determine. It's possible that the expressed feelings and attitudes toward another person are in fact the "real" ones. But it's also possible that the expressed feelings and attitudes do not reflect the internalized motivation.

Since we develop and use defense mechanisms to protect ourselves, they are a consideration in any human relationship. Because the development and use of defense mechanisms is neither recognized nor understood by the individuals using them, they are often difficult for individual comprehension. In other words, for a defense mechanism to be effective, it must "fool" the person who is using it. It is not really important that other people may also be fooled.

The defense mechanisms that an individual uses are those that have been effective in the past in protecting the individual's self-image. People do not always use the same defense mechanisms over and over. An individual may vary the frequency with which any specific defense mechanism is used. The methods individuals develop for protecting their self-image produce distinctive patterns of behavior that seem to persist over long periods of time. Those defense mechanisms that are used in on-the-job situations are usually ones that have been developed very early in the individual's life.

people need defense mechanisms
All people need defense mechanisms to cope with the frustrating situations which arise in any organization. Most people face many situations in which they can develop no realistic defense, and without the use of defense mechanisms the tension level can become incapacitating. The continual use of them, however, is undesirable.

Everyone can think of situations in which individuals are observed using defense mechanisms as a reaction to frustration. Any individual operating in an organization should find it useful to understand these mechanisms, because they help us understand our own behavior and the behavior of others. It's important for the manager to view the use of defense mechanisms by employees as a symptom of possible work-related problems rather than as behavior to be somehow "stamped out." In many situations, the use of defense mechanisms may be the result of an incompatibility between the nature of the job and an individual's personality. The employee who frequently comes to work late may be exhibiting avoidance reactions toward a job that is dull, boring, and unchallenging. In situations such as this, the most desirable managerial action is to eliminate the "cause" of the frustration rather than to discipline the employee harshly.

By evaluating the frequency with which employees use defense mechanisms, managers may gain insight into the degree to which employees are fulfilling their needs. It is then possible for management to help reduce frustration resulting from job-related barriers and to help employees accomplish their goals.

Stress Management

Stress management recently has become a subject of intense interest. While research on the cause and effect of stress has increased dramatically, there is still much that is not known.[2] For most people, dealing with conflict and overcoming frustration produce high levels of stress. Everyone experiences stress or pressure as they cope with the day-to-day problems. Employees must deal with stress that results from the demands of their job and their managers.

everyone experiences stress
Job-related stress can result in undesirable effects for both organizations and individuals. Mild forms of stress may produce discomfort,

indigestion, fatigue, and headaches. High levels of stress can contribute to severe conditions, such as ulcers, strokes, heart attacks and high blood pressure. However, avoiding all stress would be undesirable, if not impossible. In fact, moderate amounts of stress tend to increase performance and result in higher levels of achievement. Stress that is effectively managed by an individual is a positive force. Otherwise it can result in undesirable or unproductive behavior. The amount and type of stress that is most desirable depends on the individual's ability to handle pressure situations. As a result, the goal of stress management is to use stress as a natural and productive force.

What Is Stress?

Stress is the nonspecific response of the body to any demand made upon it that results in the individual preparing to take action. In everyday terms, people know the feelings that result from stress—racing heart, damp hands, dry mouth, and tension. Conflict and frustration produce stress as the individual attempts to adapt to pressures. Stress is the normal reaction of the individual to adapt to the demands of the environment. It is a necessary part of life; without it there are no challenges, no learning, and no achievements.

stress is a normal reaction

If you learn that you are being fired *or* that you are receiving a promotion, your *physical* stress response is the same even though you would evaluate these situations differently. Either situation will produce feelings of pressure, stimulating the nervous system. As a result, the body reacts by increasing the pulse, the lungs take in more oxygen, muscle tension increases, blood pressure goes up, pupils of the eyes dilate, and perspiration increases. In short, the body prepares to meet the challenge. These physiological reactions of the body occur to some degree every time a stressful situation occurs.

It is important to keep in mind that situations producing undesirable levels of stress for one individual may be the source of major satisfaction for another.

Causes of Stress

Stress can result any time individuals face a situation that requires a change in behavior or higher level of activity. *Anything that occurs which puts an individual off balance or increases the need to do something can produce stress.* Although different factors result in stress in different people, the following are typical causes of stress:

- *Physical factors* such as excessive heat, cold, noise, vibrations, air pollution, and light.
- *Interpersonal relations* with demanding or distressed individuals such as a dissatisfied customer, the employee who is angry about

disciplinary action, the individual who demands that something be done faster, or individuals who want others to solve their problems.

- *Organizational and job requirements* such as risk of physical injury, dull jobs, deadlines, extreme responsibility, making high-risk decisions, fear of losing a job, performance failure, and time pressures. Physical and interpersonal factors can also produce stress in organizations.

uncertainty can cause stress

Some individuals may experience pressure because they are *too* conscientious and work *too* hard. Individuals who are willing to impose demanding deadlines on themselves may experience the negative effects of stress. Situations that involve significant changes can create stressful conditions. Social, technological, and economic changes can produce high levels of stress for many people. When change or novelty leaves people uncertain and confused about what is going on, their stress increases.

emotionally induced stress

Stress can result from the way individuals emotionally respond to situations. In *emotionally induced stress*, the individual develops expectations that something undesirable (or even terrible) will happen. Although there are a number of ways emotionally induced stress can be classified, the following types are most common:

1. Emotional responses to *time pressures*. Individuals experience the pressure of deadlines. They may feel that "I must do something right now," being obsessed with "using" time, or try to make every minute count.

2. Emotional responses to *future events*. The individual experiences anxiety about what will happen in the future, anticipates the worst possible outcome of future events, and is fearful or worried about the future.

3. Emotional responses to *threatening situations*. When situations are perceived to be beyond one's control and there is the possibility of undesirable outcomes, stress can result. Threatening situations can involve past events that an individual feels guilty about.

4. Emotional responses in *interpersonal relations*. Dealing with unpleasant people can produce high levels of anxiety. Also, simply too much contact with other people can result in interaction overload. Figure 9.6 summarizes the factors contributing to stress.

Consequences of Stress

stress and various disorders

Stress has been reported to be a primary or contributing factor in numerous physical and psychological disorders. While individuals vary widely in their responses to stress, the following four effects are representative of consequences often associated with stressful conditions. It

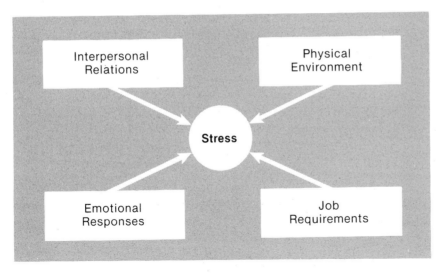

Figure 9.6 Factors contributing to stress.

should be kept in mind that causes other than stress can contribute to these conditions.

Physiological Effects of Stress The possible physical responses to stress include increased heart rate, high blood pressure, hot and cold spells, numbness, headaches, indigestion, skin disorders, physical fatigue, ulcers, strokes, and heart attacks.

Psychological Effects of Stress The psychological responses to stress can be a wide range of *feelings* which include anxiety, depression, aggression, fatigue, guilt, boredom, low self-esteem, alienation, loss of concentration, and feelings of inadequacy. The individual may become upset, nervous, jittery, high strung, or overly excited. As a result of stress individuals may make extensive use of defense mechanisms.

Behavioral Effects of Stress Included in the possible behaviors that may result from stress are the use of drugs and alcohol, overeating or undereating, nervous gesturing, pacing, emotional outbursts, restlessness, difficulty sleeping or too much sleep, aggression, and poor interpersonal relations. In extreme situations, stress can be a strong factor in suicide attempts.

Organizational Effects of Stress As a result of the behaviors of individuals experiencing high stress, organizations can be affected in a number of ways. These include absenteeism, lower productivity, interpersonal conflict, accident, turnover, job dissatisfaction and antagonism at work.

Individuals attempt to adjust and cope with stress through a wide variety of behaviors. It is important for individuals to develop reactions to stress that allow them to be productive and avoid the undesirable consequences of stress.

adjustment results in a wide variety of behaviors

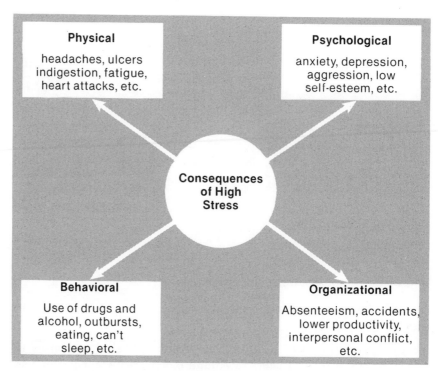

Figure 9.7 Consequences of high stress.

Figure 9.7 provides a graphic summary of the effects of severe stress on individuals and organizations.

Individual Actions to Reduce Stress

There are a number of approaches an individual can take to control stress. There is no one most effective approach. What works for one individual may not be effective for another. *A basic principle in any actions to reduce stress is that individuals must obtain and maintain control of their behavior.*

The following are three approaches that can form the basis for an effective strategy to control stress. They are summarized in Figure 9.8.

avoid pressure   1. *Avoid high pressure situations that produce unacceptable levels of stress.* For example, don't accept unnecessary additional responsibility. Don't volunteer to serve on committees. Don't go to the shopping mall when it is crowded. Don't make unnecessary trips in bad weather.

manage tension   2. *Manage situations to control the amount of stress and pressure.* Delegate some of the responsibility to someone else. Get the deadline extended. Obtain additional resources. Plan alternative courses of action in case the situation changes.

3. *React less intensely to situations.* Although it is easier said than done, a more relaxed response to pressure situations can produce significant reductions in stress. A technique that has been found useful is to ask yourself, "What is the worst thing that could happen?" and "Is this important enough to get upset about?" One manager put the following sign on his desk to help put situations in a realistic perspective.

control reactions

> I am not responsible
> for all the problems
> of the world

It is desirable for individuals to identify what is a reasonable level of stress and what is too much stress for them. In analyzing and controlling stress it may be useful to answer the following questions:

stress self-analysis

- How much stress can I handle?
- What kinds of stress do I have difficulty handling?
- What kinds of stress can I avoid by removing myself from situations?

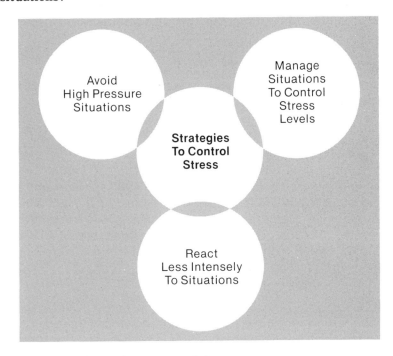

Figure 9.8 Strategies to control stress.

- What kinds of stress can I control by managing the situation?
- What situations should I respond to with less intensity?
- How can I maintain reasonable levels of stress while achieving my personal goals?

For controlled-stress living, individuals need continually to evaluate stress levels and control the total stress in their life by adapting to situations and maintaining a balance in their activities.

adapt to situations

Adapting means taking events in stride. Change those things you can, but accept the things you can't change. Make time to relax and get away from pressure situations. Adapt to situations by reducing the emotional intensity of responses.

balance activities

Balance means that need should be satisfied in a variety of different ways. To use an old saying, "variety is the spice of life." A balanced approach to life includes work and leisure, challenge and relaxation, solitude and socializing, exercise and rest.

controlled-stress living

Controlled-stress living means achieving goals and satisfying needs while enjoying life. Individuals who are living a controlled-stress life tend to exhibit the following behaviors.

- They express their emotions, desires, and feelings without giving explanations or apologies.
- They exert positive control over pressure situations and can say "no" without feeling guilty.
- They defend their personal rights and don't allow others to force unreasonable responsibilities on them. They protect their personal right to privacy.
- They have a sense of humor and participate in activities "just for fun."
- They have "escape routes" and are able to get away from problem situations and distressed people.

Sources of Job Stress

Although there are a variety of conditions that affect the overall stress level experienced by individuals, job pressures are a major source of the stress in day-to-day living. Since individuals may react differently to the same situation, *any job situation can produce stress*. A change in work methods can reduce stress for one employee and increase stress for another employee.

The following are job conditions that tend to produce stress in most people:

conditions producing job stress

1. *Quantitative job overload.* Although an individual can do the work, there is too much to do in the time available. Pressures can result from unrealistic deadlines. When the work load is too heavy,

there is overstimulation. The engineer who has the ability to design a new model but can't finish the design by the deadline is subject to stress from quantitative job overload.

2. *Qualitative job overload.* The individual lacks the ability to perform the required tasks. The job is "too challenging." Performance standards may be the source of job pressure when the individual cannot meet management's expectations. The engineer who lacks the specific training and ability to design a new model is subject to qualitative job overload.

3. *Underutilization of abilities.* The job is dull and boring, or the nature of the work does not require individuals to use their abilities. The engineer who must spend the majority of time doing routine office work and filling out forms may have stress from underutilization.

4. *Role ambiguity.* Lack of clear job objectives; the scope of responsibility is not understood. When individuals do not know what specific job performance is expected, they begin to experience stress. Role ambiguity can also result from not understanding what part a job plays in meeting organizational objectives. When individuals say, "I don't know what I'm supposed to be doing," they are indicating pressure from role ambiguity.

5. *Role conflict.* In this situation, stress is the result of conflicting job demands, expectations, and goals. To do a job both "faster" and "better" may not be possible. For example the production supervisor may want units produced *faster* while the quality control manager wants *better* units. Individuals caught between these two managers will experience the stress of role conflict. Who should they listen to? Role conflict can also involve conflicting expectations of an individual's family and the organization. The job demands more traveling, but the family wants the employee to spend more time at home.

6. *Undesirable physical working conditions.* Stress results from physical conditions such as noise, heat, cold, crowding, safety hazards, air pollution, vibration, motion, and uncomfortable spatial arrangements.

7. *Extreme responsibility.* Stress occurs when individuals have responsibilities that cannot be effectively managed. The stress may be heightened when individuals do not have adequate authority to carry out responsibilities.

8. *Destructive competition.* When the competition among individuals results in destructive actions, stress is increased. Some individuals may feel that if they can't get promoted they will make sure no one else does either. Job-related pressures intensify when people try to "look good" by making others "look bad."

9. *Changes.* A major source of stress involves frequent or significant changes that have a direct impact on an individual's job. The process of adjusting to the new elements of a job also produces pressure. In most changes there is an element of uncertainty and risk that contributes to stress. Change can be especially stressful if the person is afraid of losing a job.

stress carriers 10. *Contacts with distressed people.* The angry boss, the dissatisfied customer, or the obnoxious fellow worker can increase on-the-job stress. People's stress level is influenced by contact with individuals who are highly anxious, demanding, indecisive, depressed, or angry. These individuals have been referred to as "stress carriers."

The major job conditions that often produce stress are summarized in Figure 9.9.

Figure 9.9 Sources of job stress.

Controlling Job Stress

As part of a three-year study on managing job stress, Howard, Rechnitzer, and Cunningham[3] identified techniques that were used to cope with stress. Although there were individual differences in the use of these techniques, some interesting patterns of effective and ineffective methods were found, and are outlined in the insert section.

The best five techniques for coping with job tensions and stress were:

1. Build resistance by regular sleep, exercise, and good health habits.
2. Separate the work and nonwork life.
3. Engage in physical exercise.
4. Talk through problems with peers on the job.
5. Withdraw physically from high stress situations.

The worst techniques for coping with job tension and stress were:

1. Change to a different work activity.
2. Change the strategy of attack on work.
3. Work harder.
4. Talk through job problems with spouse.
5. Change to a nonwork activity.

Howard, Rechnitzer, and Cunningham concluded that "successful and unsuccessful coping with job tension seems to be characterized by the difference between working smarter and working harder." Individuals who effectively controlled stress were action oriented, took a preventive approach to stress, were aware of their capacities, and had a problem-solving orientation to factors causing stress.

work smarter

Minimizing Stress in Organizations

There are a number of things that managers can do to help minimize stress in organizations.[4] The effectiveness of any specific action will depend on the employees involved and the nature of the situation.

Managers can begin by helping employees analyze the sources of stress on their jobs. Understanding the factors that contribute to job tension is a necessary starting point to control the stress levels in organizations.

analyze sources of stress

Organizations can provide employees with information on stress management. Managers can work with individuals in developing approaches that they can use to control the sources of stress on their jobs. Some organizations have found it desirable to make stress management training available to their employees.

Managers can make sure they are available to *listen* to employees. When individuals experience high job stress, they often need a manager who will listen and understand. Managers should avoid trying to tell the employee what to do right away. There is often a temptation to "get the problem out of the way." Approaches need to be developed and adapted to the needs of the individual. Managers should *not* try to practice psychotherapy or psychiatry. They should deal only in areas where they are competent, which is usually work-oriented problem solving.

When confronted with employees who have severe psychological problems, it is usually best for the manager to try to help the individual obtain professional help.

Managers can analyze the conditions that exist in the organization to identify those that tend to produce job stress.

Actions to reduce stress must always be adapted to the organization and the individuals involved. The following are action-oriented questions a manager can ask to begin developing approaches to reduce major sources of stress.

1. *Quantitative job overload.* Can more resources be made available to reduce the load? Can better work methods be utilized? Can some of the work be done by someone else? Can more time be provided to accomplish the tasks?
2. *Qualitative job overload.* Can training be provided? Can some of the jobs be assigned to other individuals? Can the job be restructured so individuals will have the ability to perform effectively?
3. *Underutilization of abilities.* Can the nature of the job be expanded? Can individual assignments be changed to make better use of abilities? Could techniques of job enrichment be used?
4. *Role ambiguity.* Can clear job objectives be developed? Can specific performance criteria be developed? Can the scope of responsibility and authority be better defined?
5. *Role conflict.* Can a compatible set of job objectives be developed? Can methods be developed to resolve conflicts in demands and expectations from manager and employees? Can management structure jobs to minimize conflicts with off the job roles?
6. *Undesirable physical working conditions.* Can the physical sources of stress be reduced? Can employees be better protected from physical sources of stress? Can the spatial arrangements be modified to reduce stress?
7. *Extreme responsibility.* Can individuals be provided with resources that will help them carry out responsibilities? Do individuals need more or different types of authority? Can the level or type of responsibility be reduced?
8. *Destructive competition.* Can management redirect competition so it is productive? Can objectives and evaluation be reoriented to

reduce destructive competition? Can rewards be implemented for constructive competition?

9. *Changes*. Can people be informed before changes occur to reduce the impact? Can training help people adapt to changes? Can the uncertainty about the outcome of changes be reduced?

10. *Contacts with distressed people*. Can employees be trained to deal effectively with distressed people? Can the frequency of contact with distressed people be reduced? Are there distressed people who should be removed from the organizational environment?

Management can be more effective in reducing job tension by being aware of the causes and consequences of stress. Effective stress management can produce a more satisfying work environment and can increase productivity.

Quick Review

I. Motivational Conflict
   A. Many motives simultaneously affect an individual's behavior.
   B. An individual may not be aware of the motives leading to a specific behavior.
   C. When people have to choose between differing alternatives, conflict often occurs.
   D. The three basic types of conflict are:
      1. Approach-approach conflict
      2. Approach-avoidance conflict
      3. Avoidance-avoidance conflict
II. Frustration
   A. Frustration is the result of the inability to attain a goal due to a perceived barrier.
   B. Frustration is an individual condition and not a characteristic of the external environment.
   C. It is possible for frustration to arise either from real or imagined barriers.
   D. Frustration is always accompanied by tension.
III. Constructive Results of Frustration
   A. Increased effort can result from the focus on goal attainment to eliminate the cause of frustration.
   B. Creative approaches to problems can result from frustration through more thorough exploration of alternatives.
IV. Disruptive Effects of Frustration
   A. Frustration tension can lead to emotional reactions.
   B. There is a wide range of frustration tolerance among people.

C. Aggression is a common reaction to frustration and may be directed toward either objects or people.

D. Withdrawal is another common form of frustration reaction.

V. Defense Mechanisms

A. Defense mechanisms are psychological reactions to frustration that allow temporary relief from frustrating conditions.

B. Some common defense mechanisms include:

1. Rationalization—making excuses
2. Repression—motivated forgetting
3. Reaction-formulation—denial of desires
4. Projection—it's someone else's fault/problem
5. Identification—hero worship
6. Regression—childhood revisited.

C. Defense mechanisms are used at one time or another by nearly all people.

D. Managers should view people exhibiting defensive behavior as needing help.

VI. Stress Management

A. Everyone experiences stress as they cope with day-to-day problems.

B. Avoiding all stress would be undesirable because moderate levels of stress increase performance.

C. When individuals don't effectively manage stress undesirable or unproductive behavior occurs.

VII. Causes of Stress

A. Any situation requiring a change in behavior or a higher level of activity can produce stress.

B. Sources of stress include:

1. Physical factors
2. Interpersonal relations
3. Organizational and job requirements
4. Emotional responses to situations

VIII. Consequences of Stress

A. Stress can be a primary or contributing factor in numerous physical and psychological conditions.

B. Stress consequences can be grouped in four basic categories:
(1) physiological, (2) psychological, (3) behavioral, and (4) organizational.

IX. Individual Actions to Reduce Stress

A. Three approaches can form the basis for controlling stress:

1. Avoid high pressure situations that produce high stress.

2. Manage situations to control the level of stress.
3. React less intensely to situations.
B. Controlled-stress living requires adaptation and balance in activities.
X. Sources of Job Stress
A. Any job situation can produce stress.
B. Job conditions that reduce stress for one individual may increase stress for another.
C. Conditions that tend to produce job stress include: job overload, underutilization of abilities, role ambiguity, role conflicts, undesirable physical conditions, excessive responsibility, destructive competition, changes, and contacts with distressed people.
XI. Controlling Job Stress
A. Techniques that individuals have found to be effective include:
1. Build resistance by regular sleep, exercise, and good health habits.
2. Separate work and nonwork life.
3. Engage in physical exercise.
4. Talk through problems with peers on job.
5. Withdraw physically from high stress situations.
XII. Minimizing Stress in Organizations
A. Managers can help employees manage stress by:
1. Helping workers analyze the sources of job stress.
2. Providing information and training on how to control stress.
3. Being available to listen to employees and helping them deal with work-oriented problems.
4. Taking action to reduce and control the major sources of organizational and job stress.

Key Terms

Motivational conflict
Approach-approach conflict
Approach-avoidance conflict
Avoidance-avoidance conflict
Frustration
Aggression

Rationalization
Withdrawal
Repression
Defense mechanisms
Reaction formation projection
Stress management
Emotionally induced stress

Controlled-stress living
Adaptation
Balanced life
Job overload
Role ambiguity
Role conflict
Stress carriers

Discussion Questions

1. Give an example of approach-approach, approach-avoidance, and avoidance-avoidance conflict situations.
2. Can frustration be an aid to a manager? If so, how?
3. What constructive results can frustration have on an individual?
4. Describe an example of rationalization that you have observed individuals using.
5. Comment on the statement, "Behaviors can sometimes reflect the opposite motivation of what the behavior seems to be."
6. How could an employee who feels hostility toward the supervisor hide these feelings by using a defense mechanism?
7. Why do individuals use defense mechanisms?
8. What should a manager do when an employee becomes heavily dependent on the use of defense mechanisms to deal with frustration?
9. Describe the characteristics of a job that would tend to produce high levels of stress.
10. Develop an approach to control stress for a specific situation by using the strategies of avoiding pressure, managing the situation to control tension, and reacting less intensely.
11. Describe how you would apply the principles of *adaptation* and *balance* for controlled-stress living.
12. Using a job you have had or would like to have, identify possible sources of job stress and the actions you would take to control stress.

Case Incidents

"Sick Leave"

Ralph Scott supervises a group of eight social workers in a county social services department. The social workers, all highly trained professionals, are assigned welfare cases and are expected to work with little direct supervision. A social worker may be confronted with a wide range of difficult problems, including clients' family conflicts and their problems with relatives, landlords, businesses, and government agencies. In addition, workers may not be able to obtain enough funds for the people who need money. Client demands on social workers are heavy.

Jane Prentice is a very capable social worker but has fallen behind in her caseload reports because of her absences. She takes one or two days sick leave each month, usually on Friday or Monday.

The social service departmental policy states that a physician's statement is required after an absence of three working days, but Jane is never off that long. When Mr. Scott asks for an explanation of an absence, Jane always says that the stress of the job is the cause of the illness.

1. Should Mr. Scott accept Jane's explanation for the absences?
2. What should Mr. Scott do to deal with Jane's reported job stress?
3. What could Jane do to control the stress and get her reports completed?

The Continuing Argument

Pat Walker is the supervisor of the claims department for a life insurance company. During the past two months, two of the claims processors in the department have been continually interfering with each other's work. They do not provide each other with the information they need to complete claims reports and continually argue. Lately they have been sabotaging each other's work. Another employee reported to Pat Walker that one of the individuals knocked some completed forms off the other's desk, then wadded up the forms and said, "Oh, I'm so sorry. I'm sure it won't take you long to redo that work."

Pat Walker has been aware of the conflict between the two workers but has been hoping that by ignoring the problem it will go away.

1. Should Pat Walker continue to ignore the conflict in hopes that the individuals involved will solve the problem?
2. What alternative courses of action should Pat Walker consider to solve the problem of reduced effectiveness?
3. Can a course of action be developed that would lead to the employees involved accepting the responsibility for resolving the conflict?

Sensitive and Considerate

Linda Duncan is one of the most competent engineers in the planning department for a manufacturing company. She can always be counted on to make a maximum effort on any assignment. Linda is shy and very considerate of other people's feelings.

But her productivity is affected by the fact that if she feels someone has a heavy workload, she will not give them her work to do. Since her output depends on material being completed by technical writers, drafters, and typists, Linda is sometimes late in completing projects because she did not give others her work to complete. Everyone in the department recognizes her competence and productivity, but they also realize they can avoid doing her work since she is never demanding.

Conflict, Frustration, and Stress   255

Linda has never complained about the quality of work done for her. Even when typing or drafting are not up to department standards, she usually tells those doing the work "that it is all right."

1. What could be reasons for Linda's sensitive and considerate behavior?
2. Should Linda become aggressive in order to get her work done?
3. Should she be held responsible for seeing that department standards are met on the work done for her?
4. Should Linda be placed in a job where she is not dependent on other people to complete her work?

Exercise *Emotionally Induced Stress*

1. Identify and describe the last time *you* experienced each of the following types of emotional responses that induced stress.

2. For each of the situations you identify, describe what *you* could do to control stress. You should consider the basic approaches of (1) avoiding high pressure situations, (2) managing situations to control the amount of stress and (3) reacting less intensely to situations.

   •Emotional response to TIME PRESSURE

   situation:

   actions to control:

   •Emotional response to FUTURE EVENT

   situation:

   actions to control:

- Emotional response to THREATENING SITUATION

  situation:

  actions to control:

- Emotional response in INTERPERSONAL RELATIONS

  situation:

  actions to control:

Endnotes

1. Henry L. Sick, *Management and Organization*, 2nd ed. (Cincinnati: South-Western, 1973), p. 461.
2. For detailed reports of research on causes and effects of stress see: Michael T. Matteson and John M. Ivancevich, *Job Stress and Health* (New York: Free Press, 1982); John M. Ivancevich and Michael T. Matteson, *Stress and Work: A Managerial Perspective* (Glenview, Ill.: Scott, Foresman, and Company, 1980); and Leon J. Warshaw, *Managing Stress* (Reading, Mass.: Addison-Wesley, 1979).
3. John H. Howard, Peter A. Rechnitzer, and D. A. Cunningham, "Coping with a Job Tension—Effective and Ineffective Methods," *Public Personnel Management*, Sept.–Oct. 1975, pp. 317–326.
4. For additional approaches to deal with job stress see: Gary L. Cooper and Roy Payne, *Stress at Work* (New York: John Wiley & Sons, 1978); Rosalind Forbes, *Corporate Stress: How to Manage on the Job and Make It Work for You* (New York: Doubleday and Co., 1979); Alan A. McLean, *Work Stress* (Reading, Mass.: Addison-Wesley, 1979); and Arthur P. Brief, Randall S. Schuler, and Mary Van Sell, *Managing Job Stress* (Boston: Little, Brown and Co., 1981).

Working Together—Leaders and Groups

4

10 Leadership

Learning Objectives

After reading this chapter, you should be able to:

1. Discuss the importance of effective leadership for organizations.

2. Describe the major approaches used to analyze and explain leadership.

3. Explain the advantages and disadvantages of permissive, autocratic, and participative leadership styles.

4. Describe the five basic leadership styles used to analyze leadership with the managerial grid.

5. Discuss the contingency model of leadership efffectiveness.

6. Identify the dimensions of Fiedler's contingency theory.

7. Describe the path-goal theory of leadership.

8. Identify the basic elements in effective leadership.

Chapter Topics

Definition of Leadership

Theories of Leadership

Styles of Leadership Behavior

The Managerial Grid

Fiedler's Contingency Approach

Path-Goal Theory

Leadership Effectiveness

Preview and Self-Evaluation

Leadership is one of the most difficult concepts to define. Most of us are able to recognize leadership and many of us have been leaders. We know it involves influencing others in specific ways. We also know that some leaders are much stronger in their influence than others.

Leadership has been a subject of great interest for thousands of years. There have been many approaches to the study of leadership, ranging from the scrutiny of individual leaders to attempts to determine the traits that leaders have in common. The lives of outstanding leaders have been the subjects of countless papers and biographies. Scientists and nonscientists have attempted to identify the skills and abilities that have enabled outstanding leaders to produce significant effects on society.

The behavior of leaders seems to contain elements of magic and glamour. People are fascinated by the impact great leaders have had on society and how things might have been different if another person had been in the leadership role. The impact of effective leadership has been demonstrated in the history of every country and organization. Napoleon, Robert E. Lee, and George Patton are referred to in terms of their effects on military campaigns. The history of a country is often identified by the periods individuals served as leaders. It would be difficult to separate the history of any country or organization from the influence of its leaders. The business leadership of men like Henry Ford and Andrew Carnegie is legendary. It is generally agreed that an organization without effective leadership is in trouble.

In Chapter 10, we explore not only the meaning of leadership and its many uses but styles and applications of leadership as well. Before reading this chapter, try answering the following true-false questions. Take the test again after reading the chapter to see if your perceptions are the same.

Answer True or False

1. The process of leadership involves influencing individuals to work toward the achievement of organizational goals.   T   F

2. There is strong research evidence that leadership ability is inherited.   T   F

3. Many nonleaders possess most or all of the leadership traits that have been studied.   T   F

4. Organizations should limit the criteria for selecting leaders to specific traits and technical ability.   T   F

5. Leadership training should emphasize flexibility in behavior and ability in analyzing situations.   T   F

6. Leaders are effective because group members allow them to influence their behavior.   T   F

7. In most leadership situations in organizations the manager can be effective by leaving decisions entirely to a group of employees.   T   F

8. No leadership trait or ability has consistently been related to improved group performance regardless of the situation.   T   F

9. Due to the similarities among groups and among situations, leadership skills and abilities should always be applied in the same way.   T   F

10. The personal characteristics and personality of a leader are more important than determining which leadership style will fit the needs of a specific group.   T   F

ANSWERS: 1. T; 2. F; 3. T; 4. F; 5. T; 6. T; 7. F; 8. T; 9. F; 10. F

Definition of Leadership

When *leader* and *leadership* are used in everyday language, there is a great deal of difference in what is meant by the terms. There is no agreed-upon definition of what leadership is, and even less agreement on what it should be. The definitions of leadership range from short, general statements to long, detailed theories.

defining leadership

Leaders can be defined as those individuals who have the loyalty of others who are willing to follow them. No matter how leadership is defined, the essential ingredient in leadership is followers. It is the ability to obtain followers that makes a person a leader. Individuals who are perceived as providing methods to achieve objectives and satisfy personal needs tend to attract followers. Leadership and motivation of followers are interrelated. Leaders who do not facilitate satisfaction of the needs of followers are usually not leaders for long.

influence

One of the common elements in most definitions of leadership is *influence.* The process of leadership involves influencing individuals to work toward achieving organizational goals. Leadership is a relationship between people in which influence is unevenly distributed. The leader's influence may be the result of a legal agreement, consent of group members, delegation of authority by management, or possession and use of information.

In his definition of leadership, Ralph Stogdill states that *leadership is "a process of influencing the activities of an organized group in its tasks of goal setting and goal achievement."*[1] This definition can serve as a starting point for the analysis of leadership.

The concept of influence recognizes that individuals differ in the degree to which they are able to affect activities of a group. It requires interaction between leaders and followers to affect the behavior of group members and the group's activities.

Theories of Leadership

A number of theories of leadership have been developed in an attempt to explain why individuals become leaders and why some leaders are more effective than others. The first attempts concentrated on the individual characteristics of leaders. The basic approaches of studying leadership generally fall into three categories: (1) the "great man" theories, (2) the traits and abilities theories, and (3) behavioral interaction theories.

The "Great Man" Theory—"Leaders Are Born"

inherited characteristics

The earliest studies of leadership focused on the hereditary backgrounds of great men in an attempt to explain leadership on the basis of inherited characteristics. Some of these studies advanced conclusions that leadership, power, and influence were the result of inherited abilities. One writer even advocated that an adequate supply of superior leaders depends upon a high birth rate among the biologically superior classes.[2]

Those who believe the "great man" (or woman) theory assume that there are inherited characteristics that determine whether a person will be a leader. This theory is the simplest of all the approaches to leadership, and it is probably believed by more people in the world than any other leadership theory. For those who are not in positions of leadership, it may be satisfying to believe that they are not leaders because they were not born with leadership ability. The individual who is in a position of leadership may find the "great man" theory convenient because any failures or lack of effectiveness can be attributed to abilities that were not inherited.

An organization following the "great man" theory of leadership would concentrate on the selection of managers through the "great man" process. It would be concerned primarily with whether or not relatives of the potential managers had been successful leaders. The selection process might be heavily influenced by the assumption, "like parent, like child." When there is an assumption of inherited leadership ability, usually little effort is directed toward developing management programs or structuring management positions to fit individuals.

Most social scientists reject the "great man" approach to leadership, because it is an oversimplification and because research evidence does not support the position that leadership abilities are inherited.

The Traits and Abilities Approach to Leadership

As a natural extension of the "great man" theory, extensive research efforts have been devoted to discovering specific personal characteristics that distinguish leaders from nonleaders. Those who use the trait approach attempt to find out why leaders are successful by analyzing the personal characteristics of leaders.

The number of traits considered in leadership studies ranges from fewer than ten to more than twenty-five. With this wide difference in the number of traits investigated, it is very difficult to compare studies of leadership traits. Another difficulty results from the different methods used to measure the traits and the variety of definitions that are found for a given trait.

personal characteristics

An example of the problem of definition is illustrated by a study conducted by Perrin Stryker and reported in *Fortune*.[3] Seventy-five executives were asked to give definitions of various qualities of executives. The concept of "dependability" was defined by 147 different descriptive statements. From the 147 statements, a list of 25 different definitions for the trait was compiled. The definitions given for dependability included: behaves predictably, uses initiative, considers others, learns from mistakes, inspires confidence, and has good personal habits. This study points out that there is a great deal of difference in the way any given trait can be defined.

leadership traits   There is general agreement among those currently involved in research on leadership that the study of leadership traits has not been a very useful approach. One of the problems with application of the trait approach is that most of the traits that are associated with leadership are indications of patterns of behavior that are expected from an individual in such a position. One of the most critical analyses of the trait approach was made by Eugene Jennings, who stated, "Research has produced such a varied list of traits presumably to describe leadership that for all practical purposes, it describes nothing. Fifty years of study have failed to produce one personality trait or set of qualities that can be used to discriminate between leaders and nonleaders."[4] Many nonleaders possess most or all of the traits that have been studied, and most leaders do not have all of them. Traits are hard to define and identify, and the trait approach does not enable one to determine how much of a trait is needed to become an effective leader.

The failure of the trait approach to explain leadership may be primarily due to the complex interaction between the leader's behavior and the situation in which the leadership takes place. As Charles R. Milton pointed out, "The trait approach failed because it is the leadership situation—nature of the subordinates and the task—that determines what leader traits are essential for effective leadership. Such traits differ somewhat from situation to situation."[5]

five groups of leadership traits   Nevertheless, even with the limitations of trait studies in mind, there are five groups of traits which have been found to be associated with leadership effectiveness. In an analysis of over three thousand books and articles in the field, Stogdill found a relationship between leadership and the traits he labeled capacity, achievement, responsibility, participation, and status.[6] Stogdill's conclusions were supported by fifteen or more studies he reviewed in which the person in the leadership position possessed more of the trait than did the average member in the group. Each trait as defined by Stogdill involves a number of factors.

- *Capacity* was defined in terms of intelligence, mental alertness, verbal ability, originality, and judgment.

- *Achievement* referred to having made better grades, knowing how to get things done in a group, being able to present constructive ideas, and being successful in athletics.

- *Responsibility* was evaluated in terms of dependability, willingness to assume responsibility, initiative, persistence, self-confidence, and the desire to excel.

- *Participation* reflected a high activity level, sociability, cooperation, and adaptability.

- *Status* referred to social and economic position and popularity.

These leadership traits should not be surprising, since it is through participating in group activities and by demonstrating the ability to help the group achieve goals that individuals obtain leadership positions. To maintain a position of leadership requires participation and acceptance of responsibility for directing the activities of a group. The traits associated with leadership all involve relationships with the activities, characteristics, and objectives of the followers.

The Behavioral Approach to Leadership

Behavioral approaches to the analysis of leadership recognize the importance of the relationship among the leader, the followers, and the situation. With this approach, the most effective leadership style depends on the nature of the situation, the characteristics of the individuals in the group, and the leader's abilities.

situational approaches to leadership

Behavioral approaches include contingency theories and other situational approaches to leadership. Contingency theory is often referred to as the "it depends" approach to effective leadership. It assumes that there is no one best approach to leadership and stresses the influence of the total set of conditions in which the leader must function. Since the most effective leadership behavior varies with the situation, the leader must adapt his or her behavior to the situation or be able to modify the characteristics of the situation to be compatible with his or her leadership style.

The multidimensional approach to leadership is supported by studies conducted at Ohio State University by Stogdill and his associates.[7] Their study of 470 Navy officers who had forty-five different positions indicated that the effectiveness of their leadership was heavily influenced by situational factors such as the nature of the job, the organizational environment, and the characteristics of subordinates.

Additional studies have supported the position that the effectiveness of leadership depends upon (1) the leader's personality, needs, skills, abilities, attitudes, and values; (2) the subordinate's personality, needs, skills, abilities, attitudes, and values; and (3) situational factors, which include the characteristics of the group and the task, organizational policies and objectives, the physical environment, and external events that affect the situation.[8]

A person who is an effective leader in one situation may not be an effective leader in another. A person who can lead one group effectively may fail to lead another group with different characteristics and goals. An individual who is an effective company president might be unable to lead a church youth group or coach a little league baseball team effectively.

The most realistic approach to leadership takes into account the effect of the leader, the subordinates, and the situation. Figure 10.1 shows how these three factors are interrelated.

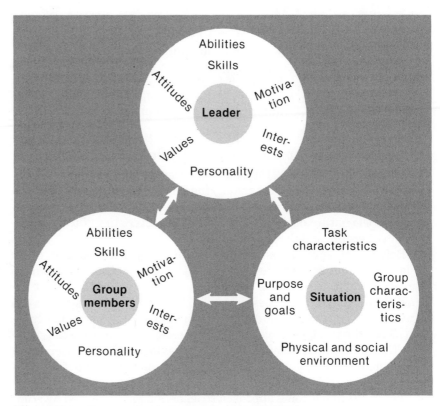

Figure 10.1 Factors that influence leadership effectiveness.

Styles of Leadership Behavior

three leadership styles
Three frequently discussed leadership styles are identified as permissive, autocratic, and participative. These three styles are seldom found in their pure form, because leaders vary in their behavior and the types can be considered as extremes. These leadership styles or behaviors focus on the approach the leader takes in attempting to influence the behaviors of individuals.

An individual in a leadership position does not have to choose to use the pure form of one of these three styles. These styles represent a range of behaviors that can be combined or used in differing degrees. Each of these styles of exerting influence has benefits and limitations. A leader may use variations of all three styles over a period of time. But most leaders tend to depend primarily on one style as their "normal" way of operating.

Permissive: Hands-Off Leadership

permissive leadership
A "pure" permissive leader would not often attempt to influence the members of the group. "Followers" would be encouraged to accomplish

Table 10.1 Summary of permissive leadership

STYLE CHARACTERISTICS

- Group members can make decisions independent of the leader.
- Leader does not attempt to control actions of group members.
- Group effectiveness depends on individual responsibility.
- The major influence on goals and procedures is desire of group members.
- Leader's role is to help individuals achieve personal goals.

POTENTIAL BENEFITS

- Working independently can be motivational for some people.
- May encourage suggestions, creativity, and innovations.
- Group is usually flexible and can adapt quickly to change.
- Open and direct communication with opportunity for self-expression.
- May increase the "quality of life" for some group members.

POTENTIAL DISADVANTAGES

- Can be a lack of coordination of group activities.
- Group objectives may be ignored, and individual objectives may dominate activities.
- There may be disruptive behavior because of a lack of control.
- Individuals may go their own ways, resulting in confusion.
- There may be very little cooperation.

the group tasks by using the methods they feel to be most desirable. Individuals would be allowed to devote their efforts to accomplishing individual objectives. Totally permissive leaders are rarely found, because in this style very little leadership is exerted. When a person with a permissive style holds a formal leadership position, the actual leader may be an assistant or someone who is an informal leader in the group.

A *permissive leader* depends on the group to establish its own objectives and solve problems as they arise. This approach can work effectively if group members are highly motivated to achieve group objectives and will assume responsibility for leadership functions. The leader's primary function may be making outside contacts for the group and obtaining information for group members. Since the leader does not provide direction and coordination, groups within an organization may perform in ways that are detrimental to the achievement of organizational objectives. The widespread use of permissive leadership in an organization can lead to confusion or even chaos. There are very few leadership situations in organizations in which the manager can leave decisions entirely to a group of employees. Table 10.1 presents a summary of permissive leadership.

Autocratic: Power-Oriented Behavior

The autocratic leader allows group members little or no voice in decisions. Subordinates are expected to follow instructions without any ar-   *autocratic leadership* guments. The effectiveness of employees is measured to a large degree by their compliance with the wishes of the leader. The *autocratic leader* depends on the formal power of the position and the ability to administer rewards and punishment. The leader makes the decisions and sets the goals for the group. Participation by group members in decision making is usually discouraged.

As with other management styles, there are few pure autocrats. Even the most autocratic leader is usually influenced somewhat by the attitudes and values of group members.

fear as a power base

Autocratic leaders frequently use fear as a power base. They tend to (1) distrust the people being led, (2) filter information given to the followers, (3) attempt to control and manipulate the motivations of the followers, and (4) attempt to control individual behavior. Most autocratic leaders have varying degrees of uncertainty about their own adequacy. Often, leaders attempt to camouflage the underlying fears which support the strategies of manipulation and control. The authoritarian leader usually assumes that the average person cannot be trusted.

The autocratic leader is continually challenged to create new rewards and gimmicks as old ones become ineffective. The person who is being "motivated" through extrinsic rewards tends to resist influence, either by withdrawing or acting aggressively. The punishment system may foster resistance, rebellion, resentment, cynicism, and a variety of other negative feelings. People who work under autocratic leaders learn to compete for rewards from the leader. Extrinsic rewards do not satisfy the needs for self-satisfaction and self-respect which are gained by achieving our personal goals as unique individuals. The techniques of autocratic leadership produce predictable results. Fear and distrust result in more fear and distrust. People who are distrustful tend to see untrustworthy behavior in others. If the relationship between a manager and a subordinate is basically one of distrust, almost any action on either's part is perceived by the other as untrustworthy. Table 10.2 presents a summary of autocratic leadership.

Participative Leadership

participative leadership

The *participative leader* shares authority and responsibility with members of the group. Leadership responsibilities are shared by involving group members in planning and decision making. This type of leadership allows group members to influence the decision-making process and the leader's behavior. Group members are treated with respect and their opinions are valuable inputs in decision making.

Participative leaders do not reject the responsibilities of leadership and attempt to be "just another member of the group." They are active leaders in making decisions, using the input of group members. They focus the activities of the group on achieving objectives and direct the

Table 10.2 Summary of autocratic leadership

STYLE CHARACTERISTICS

- Leader makes most decisions without consulting with group members.
- Leader controls group members by using rewards and discipline.
- Leader permits very little individual freedom of action.
- Leader tries to develop obedient and predictable behavior from group members.
- Group members are dependent on the leader to establish goals and plan activities.

POTENTIAL BENEFITS

- Can provide consistency in goals and procedures by leader making decisions.
- Decisions can be made very rapidly.
- Control can be centralized for orderly operations.
- Well-developed leadership skills can be applied directly to group activities.
- The leader can take direct control when there is a major problem or crisis.

POTENTIAL DISADVANTAGES

- May result in low motivation. It is difficult to develop motivation when the leader makes all decisions.
- Tends to reduce creativity.
- Group members may avoid responsibility for their performance.
- Misunderstandings may result from the one-way communication.
- It may be difficult to adapt to change.

flow of communication to provide group members with adequate information.

The participative leader assumes that individuals learn to evaluate their own abilities and can develop their basic potential. Subordinates are provided every opportunity to maximize self-evaluation and self-development. Individuals are allowed to assume responsibility for achieving objectives.

The participative leader tries to create a climate in which there is no need to impose external controls. Individuals who have participated in setting group objectives and have clearly stated their own goals tend to work to achieve those objectives without the leader having to exert control. Table 10.3 presents a summary of participative leadership.

Any leadership style has advantages and disadvantages, depending on the results desired by the leader. The permissive style may stimulate individual initiative and creativity but may also result in confusion and a lack of coordination. The autocratic style may produce order and obedience but produce few suggestions for improvement by group members. The participative style may result in coordination of activities and high motivation of group members, but the process of participation may result in compromise decisions that are not the most effective.

Table 10.3   Summary of participative leadership

STYLE CHARACTERISTICS

- Leader involves individuals in decision making and goal setting.
- Authority and responsibility are delegated to group members.
- To achieve group goals the leader coordinates involvement of group members.
- The leader uses two-way communication.
- Attitudes and feelings of group members are considered by the leader in making decisions.

POTENTIAL BENEFITS

- Participation can result in high motivation of group members.
- The knowlege and experience of group members can be used in decision making.
- Members may feel more committed to group goals.
- Individual abilities can be developed through participation.
- Group members may be better informed as a result of two-way communication.

POTENTIAL DISADVANTAGES

- Individuals may dominate the participation or make disruptive contributions.
- This approach can be very time consuming for the leader.
- Compromises can result in actions that are not the most effective.
- Conflict may be resolved by making the least offensive decision rather than the most effective.
- Situations can develop where responsibilities are not clear-cut.

The Managerial Grid

The *managerial grid* approach to analyzing leadership identifies five styles of leaders, based on their concern for people and production. The grid approach has been widely used in identifying leadership styles since its development by Robert Blake and Jane Mouton.[9] The grid is usually presented as a graph or chart indicating the manager's degree of concern or interest for people and production. The basic elements of grid representation are presented in Figure 10.2.

As the grid indicates, a leader can have both high concern for people and high concern for production. The five styles identified on the grid involve combinations of varying degrees of concern for people and production. The five basic styles are summarized in the following descriptions.

low concern for people and low concern for production

Impoverished Leadership   This style is very similar to the laissez-faire leader. The leader has low concern for people and low concern for production. Decisions of group members are accepted without question. The leader avoids taking sides and tries to avoid disagreeing with the opinions, attitudes, and ideas of others. This style involves trying to stay out of conflicts or remaining neutral when involved in conflicts. The leader tries to avoid responsibility and decision making by remaining neutral and not raising any controversial issues. Mistakes in task performance are ignored. The leader does just enough to get by.

Human Relations or Country Club Leadership   This kind of leader has high concern for people and low concern for production. There is high value for maintaining good interpersonal relations. The leader prefers to accept the opinions, attitudes, and ideas of group members and does not push for acceptance of personal positions. Every effort is made to avoid generating conflict. If conflict does occur, the leader attempts to soothe feelings and keep people together. The human relations leader is usually a very warm and friendly person. Interpersonal relations are considered all-important, and task accomplishment is of very minor interest. Task-related mistakes are glossed over with an attitude of "you'll do better next time." One of the leader's main objectives is for group members to be happy.

high concern for people and low concern for production

Task-Centered or Factors-of-Production Leadership   This type of leader has high concern for task accomplishment and low concern for people. The main concern is efficiency of operations and output. Human relations problems are viewed as interferences in getting jobs done. The leader places high value on making decisions that stick and wants group members to follow orders without raising questions. People are viewed solely in terms of their contribution to achieving task-related objectives. Tight controls of job behavior are usually developed and punishment systems are used to keep people in line. Creativity and

low concern for people and high concern for production

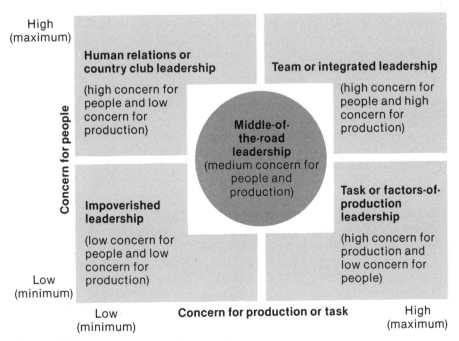

Figure 10.2   Managerial grid leadership styles.

suggestions are suppressed. The leader concentrates on direct control of group members to get tasks accomplished as efficiently as possible.

medium concern for people and medium concern for production

Middle-of-the-Road Leadership   This type of leader has medium concern for people and medium concern for production. An attempt is made to balance the necessity for task accomplishment and the morale of group members. In balancing the concern for people and production, the leader is not highly energetic or overenthusiastic about individual satisfaction or job accomplishment. The leader looks for decisions that are workable, rather than trying for "perfection." The leader's behavior is characterized by taking middle-of-the-road positions when there are competing demands for getting the job done and satisfying the individuals. When conflict arises, there is an attempt to be fair but firm and to obtain a compromise solution. There is a desire to maintain a good, steady job pace without creating conflict or dissatisfied individuals.

high concern for people and high concern for production

Team or Integrated Leadership   The team leadership style is the ideal. It involves high concern for people and high concern for production. The team leader concentrates on motivating and developing individuals while achieving the highest possible level of task accomplishment. High value is placed on obtaining sound creative decisions that result in understanding and agreement among group members. The leader has strong personal convictions but seeks out different ideas and opinions from group members. This style is characterized by a willingness to change as a result of objective analyses of problems and situations. When conflicts arise, the leader looks for the reasons and tries to eliminate underlying causes. There is a commitment to quality performance and effective interpersonal relations. When mistakes occur, the leader's approach is to help people learn from them. In relations with group members, the leader focuses on developing acceptance of responsibility and self-control.

The managerial grid approach to analyzing leadership styles has been found to be a useful method for identifying and classifying the extent of concern leaders have for people and production. The five primary styles that have been described are extremes or "pure types," and it would be rare to find a leader who consistently behaved according to one style. Most leaders vary their behavior in response to the nature of the situation. If the leader faces major problems in interpersonal relations in a group, he or she is likely to develop increased concern for people and move toward the human relations style. If the group is not accomplishing the tasks to maintain required levels of productivity, the leader will usually move toward the task style of leadership.

leader behavior varies in response to situations

Although the grid does provide a system of classifying styles, it does not provide an explanation of why a leader uses a particular style. Determining the way a leader adopts a specific style requires analysis of the total situation, including the leader's characteristics, the characteristics of the group members, the environment in which the group operates, the nature of the tasks, and other situational factors affecting the relationships between group and leader.

According to the theory behind the managerial grid, the style that should get the "best" results is the team style, with its high concern for both people and production. But the concept of one best style for all situations is not supported by research in leadership effectiveness. After reviewing the leadership studies, Lawrence Steinmetz and H. Ralph Todd concluded that "some leaders were very effective when they had low concern for people, yet others were very effective when they had low concern for production. Furthermore, still others were effective when they had low concern for both people and production."[10]

Fiedler's Contingency Approach

Extensive research by Fred Fiedler has resulted in the development of the "contingency model of leadership effectiveness."[11] In Fiedler's model, effective leadership requires that the leader's style match the demands of the situation. Leader effectiveness is defined in terms of group performance and how well the group accomplishes assigned functions. The effectiveness of the group depends upon the relationship between the leadership style and the group situation.

contingency model

Fiedler defines two basic styles of leadership. One style is "*task oriented*," in which the leader's major satisfaction comes from effective task performance. The other style is "*relationship oriented*" and focuses on having good interpersonal relations and achieving a position of personal acceptance.

Fiedler studied a wide variety of groups, including military units, boards of directors, manufacturing companies, church groups, student groups, and basketball teams. In these studies he found that three dimensions of the situation had a critical effect on the leader's effectiveness.

three dimensions of situations affect leader

1. *Leader-member relations*. This dimension refers to the degree of liking and trust between the leader and the group members. The most favorable condition for the leader exists when the group members are willing to follow him or her; the use of superior rank is not required to get the task accomplished. Fiedler regards this dimension as the most important from the leader's point of view, since the leader may not be able to control the "official" rank and power associated with his or her position.
2. *Task structure*. The task can be either very specifically defined so that it can be performed according to a standardized set of procedures, or it can be left unstructured and vague. When the task is specifically defined by a set of operating procedures, it is

difficult for an employee to question the leader's right to give instructions. Also, it is easier to control the quality of performance, and group members can be held responsible for performance according to the task definitions.

3. *Position power.* The amount of formal power the leader has because of the position is position power. It can be measured by the leader's authority to reward and punish group members. High position power would be indicated by having the authority to promote and demote, to decide pay rates, to hire and fire, and to determine work schedules. Most managers in business and industry have high position power. Leaders of voluntary groups usually have low position power.

These three dimensions are outlined in Table 10.4.

leadership effectiveness depends on situational factors

Fiedler's research supports the position that neither the task-oriented style nor the relationship-oriented style can be considered effective in themselves. The effectiveness of the leadership style depends of the three situational factors described above, that is, when the leader has good relations with the members, the task is highly structured, and

Table 10.4   Situation favorableness for the leader

	High Influence	Low Influence
Leader-member relations	Leader is trusted and liked by group members.	Leader is not trusted and is disliked by group members.
	Pleasant relations among members and with leader.	Tense and antagonistic relations among members and with leader.
	Cheerful and cooperative environment in the group.	Gloomy and uncooperative environment in the group.
Task structure	Job requirements clearly stated.	Job is unstructured and requirements are vague.
	Problems encountered can be solved by only one method.	There may several correct solutions to a problem.
	Only one correct solution to problem.	Correctness of decisions is a matter of opinion.
	Correctness of decisions can be objectively demonstrated.	Job can be accomplished by a variety of procedures.
Position power	Leader controls rewards and punishments of group members.	Group members control discipline and rewards.
	Leader establishes work rules and work schedules.	Individuals work independently of the leader.
	Leader has authority to hire, fire and raise salaries.	Leader's evaluation of performance has no impact on group members.

the position power is high. The situation is unfavorable when the leader has little support from the group, the task is vague and unstructured, and there is little position power. Using Fiedler's definition, the favorableness of the situation depends on the degree to which a given situation enables the leader to exert influence over a group.

Studies of the effectiveness of leadership styles indicate that the style most effective in one type of situation may be the least effective in another. The task-oriented leadership style was the most effective in situations where the leader had either very little or a great deal of influence. The leader who devoted time to interpersonal relations in the group was most effective in moderately favorable situations. In situations that were very favorable or very difficult, the task-oriented leader was the most effective. *effectiveness of leadership styles*

Implications of the Contingency Approach

Organizations should not limit the criteria for selecting leaders to individual traits or abilities. Specific traits and technical ability may be necessary, but they are only two of the factors that contribute to effective leadership. The effectiveness of a leader depends on a broad range of factors involving relations with group members and the nature of the situation.

The selection of leaders should focus on matching the attitudes, values, abilities, skills, and personality of the leader with the characteristics of the group members and the demands of the situation. If a change is necessary to improve leadership effectiveness, it is usually more desirable to change factors in the situation or to move the leader than to try to change his or her leadership styles.

Most leadership training programs attempt to develop or change patterns of behavior in the individual. This often means that the individual must make basic changes in leadership style and personality. Although it is possible to modify personality, the cost is very high and the rate of success is very low. Getting an individual to make basic changes in leadership style and personality to match a situation and the group members is not practical in many situations. Since there is no one best style of leadership, there is no one most effective approach to leadership training. Flexibility in behavior and ability in analyzing situations should be emphasized in leadership training. Leadership styles in an organization should vary with the requirements of the situations. Organizations should not attempt to require the same leadership style from all managers. *leadership training*

Improving leader effectiveness depends upon a match of (1) the leader's behaviors, (2) the group members, and (3) the situational factors. It is the interaction of the factors involved in the situation that control the leader's effectiveness in working with a group to accomplish objectives. *improving leadership*

Path-Goal Theory

The *path-goal theory* is a situational or contingency approach to leadership developed from the work of Martin G. Evans and Robert J. House.[12] The theory is termed path-goal because it concentrates on the leader's influence on (1) perceptions of work goals, (2) personal goals, and (3) paths (means) to attain goals.

leader effectiveness
According to the path-goal theory, leadership performance depends on how well the leader clarifies the path to desired rewards and makes rewards dependent on effective performance. Leader effectiveness depends on the ability to recognize strong unmet needs and help individuals satisfy these needs. For the leader to achieve organizational goals, it is necessary to develop paths for individuals so that both personal needs and work goals are fulfilled.

Path-goal theory suggests that a leader should behave differently with different individuals and in different situations. With this approach it is necessary for the leader to adapt his or her behavior to the characteristics of subordinates and the nature of the task situation.

Path-goal theory has resulted in the development of two important propositions:[13]

1. Leader behavior is acceptable and satisfying when subordinates perceive the behavior as an immediate source of satisfaction or as a way to obtain future satisfaction.
2. Leader behavior will be motivational when it makes satisfaction of subordinates' needs contingent on effective performance, and when it provides guidance, clarity of direction, and rewards necessary for effective performance.

individuals must see relationship between effort and rewards
Path-goal theory advises leaders to increase the number and kinds of rewards available to subordinates and to clarify the ways these rewards can be obtained. It is based on the expectancy theory of motivation which was discussed in Chapter 7. According to expectancy theory, the strength of motivation to perform work is a function of expectancies that effort will lead to desirable rewards. Path-goal theory deals with how leaders can affect motivation by increasing the availability and attractiveness of rewards and by strengthening expectations that these rewards can be earned. Individuals must be able to see the relationship between their efforts and the rewards for effective performance.

Leadership Styles

Path-goal theory differs from the contingency models that characterize leadership styles. The theory involves a higher degree of task orientation and relationship orientation, and a more complete set of leader behaviors. Four types of leader behavior studied are directive, support-ive, participative, and achievement oriented.

1. *Directive leadership*—lets subordinates know what is expected of them, provides guidelines, sets performance standards and controls behavior to obtain compliance.
2. *Supportive leadership*—shows concern for the welfare and personal need satisfaction of subordinates, concentrates on developing good interpersonal relations and cooperation.
3. *Participative leadership*—shares information and consults with subordinates, uses their ideas in making decisions, and is employee oriented.
4. *Achievement-oriented leadership*—sets challenging goals for subordinates, emphasizes excellence in performance, shows confidence that subordinates will assume responsibility and obtain challenging goals.

The leaders should use the style that will have the greatest positive effect on performance and achievement of organizational objectives.

Situational Factors

Two sets of situational factors are important in deciding on the most ef-fective leadership style: (1) the personal characteristics of subordinates and (2) characteristics of the work environment. All the possible effects of situational factors on the effectiveness of leader behavior have not yet been researched. The following are some examples of the interac-tion of situational factors and leader behavior.

leadership effectiveness requires adapting to the situation

Personal Characteristics of Subordinates

1. Supportive leadership is more effective with individuals who have a *high* need for affiliation.
2. Directive leadership is more effective with individuals who have a *high* need for security.
3. Participative leadership is more effective with individuals who have a *high* degree of self-confidence (who believe outcomes are a function of their own behavior).
4. Directive leadership is more effective with individuals who have a *low* degree of self-confidence (who believe outcomes are a function of chance or luck).
5. Supportive leadership is more effective with individuals with *high* social needs.
6. Directive leadership is more effective with individuals who have a *low* perceived ability to do the work.
7. Supportive leadership is more effective with individuals who have a *high* perceived ability to do the work.
8. Achievement-oriented leadership is more effective with individuals who have a *high* need for achievement.

individual needs

Characteristics of the Work Environment

task structure
1. Directive leadership is more effective for unstructured or ambiguous tasks.
2. Supportive leadership is more effective for boring tasks or simple tasks.
3. Supportive leadership is more effective when jobs involve stressful or frustrating tasks.
4. Participative and achievement-oriented leadership are more effective when jobs involve complex tasks.

It is easy to draw conclusions that oversimplify the complex relationships between leader behavior and situational factors. Managers should be careful to adapt the path-goal theory to the complexities of their situation. Because the theory has been introduced recently, there is a lack of supporting research in many areas. However, it is expected that the path-goal approach will make major contributions to the understanding of leadership effectiveness. Figure 10.3 summarizes the major elements in the theory.

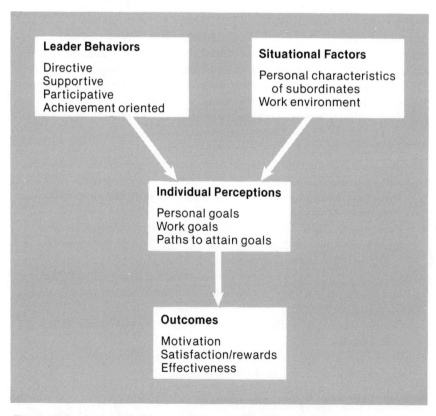

Figure 10.3 Key elements in path-goal leadership theory.

Leadership Effectiveness

As the research evidence indicates, attempts to explain leadership by analyzing only the traits and abilities of the leader or the style of leadership oversimplify the determinants of effective leadership.[14] No trait or ability has consistently been related to improved group performance regardless of the situation. Studies of leadership effectiveness provide no support for the conclusion that there is one style of leadership. Successful leadership involves the interaction of the leader, the group, and the situation. To be effective, the leader's behavior must meet the needs of the group and the demands of the particular situation (see Figure 10.4). There are always some similarities among groups and among situations, but there are also unique aspects that the leader must take into account.

leadership is often over-simplified

The way in which the leader's skills and abilities are applied must be adapted to the particular situation. Since the leader is trying to influence individuals, decisions must be made from analysis of individual characteristics of group members and not from research findings about other groups. The personal characteristics and personality of the leader are not as important as the ability to determine the leadership style that will fit the needs of a specific group.

leaders must adapt to the needs of the situation

Leadership requires continual effort; it is a full-time job. The effective leader does not wait to respond to problems or crisis situations. Leaders are effective because group members allow them to influence their behavior. The most effective leaders are able to generate cooperative and willing effort by group members in obtaining group goals.

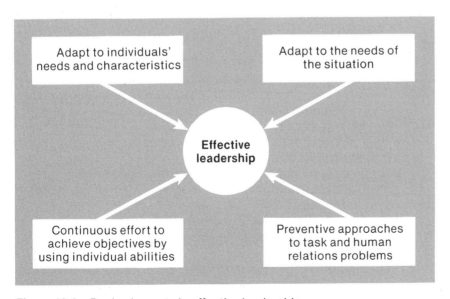

Figure 10.4 Basic elements in effective leadership.

Ten Guidelines for Managerial Leadership to Improve Productivity

1. *LEAD*
   Managers must be leaders who make judgments and take action.
2. *OBJECTIVES*
   Develop clear and measurable objectives that are challenging and attainable.
3. *PRIORITIES*
   Establish priorities and allocate resources according to these priorities.
4. *STANDARDS*
   Have specific and challenging performance standards with individual accountability.
5. *COMMUNICATE*
   Develop understanding and agreement; provide necessary, relevant and accurate information.
6. *FEEDBACK*
   Provide frequent and specific feedback on performance.
7. *CONTROL*
   Take corrective action when standards are not met, priorities are not observed, or objectives are not achieved.
8. *TRAIN*
   Provide training to develop individual abilities and effectively utilize human resources.
9. *ADAPT*
   Take a problem-solving approach and adapt to changing situations.
10. *REWARD PRODUCTIVITY*
    Provide meaningful rewards for high levels of performance.

Quick Review

I. Definition of Leadership
   A. There is no agreed-upon definition of leadership.
   B. The essential ingredient of leadership is that the leader have followers.
   C. An effective leader is one who attracts followers and can influence them toward the achievement of organizational goals.
   D. Stogdill defined leadership as "a process of influencing the activities of an organized group in its tasks of goal setting and goal achievement."

II. Theories of Leadership
   A. The "great man" theory assumes that leaders are born, not made. Heredity makes the leaders.
      1. Most social scientists reject the "great man" approach to leadership.
   B. The "traits and abilities" approach attempts to identify physical and psychological factors associated with leadership.
      1. The trait approach has not been very useful in explaining leadership behavior.
      2. Trait approaches fail to consider the entire leadership environment.
   C. Behavioral interaction approaches consider the interaction of the leader, the followers, and the situation.
III. Styles of Leadership Behavior
   A. Permissive leadership does not try to influence the behavior of members of the group. The permissive leader depends on the group to establish its own objectives.
   B. Autocratic leadership allows group members little or no voice in decisions.
   C. Participative leadership involves the sharing of authority and responsibility with group members.
   D. All leadership styles have both advantages and disadvantages.
IV. The Managerial Grid
   A. One way to analyze managerial behavior in terms of leadership is to use the managerial grid. The grid measures the leader's orientation toward both people and productivity.
   B. The managerial grid identifies five types of leader behavior:
      1. Impoverished leadership
      2. Human relations or country club leadership
      3. Task-centered or factors-of-production leadership
      4. Middle-of-the-road leadership
      5. Team or integrated leadership
V. Fiedler's Contingency Approach
   A. Fiedler's contingency model of leadership identifies the three dimensions of:
      1. Leader-member relations
      2. Task structure
      3. Position power
   B. According to Fiedler, the effectiveness of a given leadership style depends upon the degree of favorableness of the situation for the leader. In moderately favorable conditions, Fiedler found that

relationship-oriented styles worked best. In very
favorable and highly unfavorable conditions, task-
oriented styles were more effective.

    C. Leadership selection should focus on matching the
attitudes, values, abilities, and skills of the leader with
those of group members and the demands of the
situation.

VI. Path-Goal Theory

    A. Path-goal theory is a contingency approach that
concentrates on the leader's influence on:

        1. Perceptions of work goals

        2. Personal goals

        3. Paths (means) to attain goals

    B. Two important propositions of goal-path theory are:

        1. Leader behavior is acceptable and satisfying when it
is seen as a source of satisfaction.

        2. Leader behavior is motivational when it makes need
satisfaction dependent on effective performance.

VII. Leadership Effectiveness

    A. Leadership effectiveness depends on the
interrelationships involved in a specific situation with a
specific group.

    B. The basic elements in effective leadership are:

        1. To adapt to the needs and characteristics of
individuals.

        2. To take a preventive approach to task and human
relations problems.

        3. To adapt to the needs of the situation.

        4. To devote continuous effort toward achieving
objectives through the abilities of individuals.

Key Terms

Leader	Participative	Situation
Leadership	leadership	favorableness
Great man theory	Managerial grid	Path-goal theory
Traits & abilities	Fiedler's contingency	Directive leadership
approach	model	Achievement-oriented
Situational approach to	Leader-member	leadership
leadership	relations	Supportive leadership
Permissive leadership	Task structure	Participative
Autocratic leadership	Position power	leadership

Discussion Questions

1. Why do some people choose to be leaders and others choose to be followers?
2. Do some people have unique abilities for leadership?
3. Describe how group characteristics can be determinants of leadership effectiveness.
4. Describe the potential benefits and potential disadvantages of permissive, autocratic, and participative leadership.
5. How should leadership styles vary as the characteristics of situations differ?
6. Why would a task-oriented leader tend to perform more effectively in some situations?
7. Using the managerial grid styles, could there be situations in which any one of the five styles would be the most effective?
8. What would be the most effective leadership style in each of the following situations?
   a. the intensive-care unit of a hospital.
   b. a "great books" discussion group.
   c. an automotive production assembly line.
   d. the English Department in a university.
   e. a group of design engineers in an aircraft manufacturing company.
   f. a group of sales clerks in a discount department store.
   g. a road maintenance crew for a city government.

Case Incidents

Resistance to Change

Randy Hammer is a recent college graduate who has been hired to supervise the computer data processing functions of a savings and loan company. To provide the required services in the most efficient manner, he feels it is necessary to change some of the operational procedures. Randy has also proposed to acquire a newer computer to keep up with the "state of the art" in computer data processing.

Frank Armstrong has worked in the data processing section longer than any other employee and is the senior programmer. He does not have a college degree and worked his way up by learning programming on his own. Frank has stubbornly resisted any changes Randy proposes and will institute new procedures only after repeated direct orders. Frank tells other employees that he knows the systems better than anyone else. Another employee told

Randy he overheard Frank say that "no young college punk can possibly know what is going on unless he has worked in the field over five years." When Randy tries to discuss changes with Frank, he argues that what has worked since 1980 should not be changed.

1. What are possible reasons for Frank resisting Randy's efforts to improve the computer data processing?
2. What could Randy Hammer do to be a more effective leader and obtain Frank's cooperation?
3. Is a new "young" manager always likely to have difficulty being an effective leader with "older" employees?

The Boss's Favorite

Martha Collins is the director of finance and accounting for a city in the midwest. The city manager of the town of 30,000 appears to be very partial toward Cindy Kern, one of the accounting clerks who work for Ms. Collins. It has reached the point where the city manager provides special favors for Cindy, such as a special city parking permit. The permit allows her to park in the lot closest to the city office building, although the lot is reserved for the city council and distinguished visitors. The other employees in the finance and accounting section have begun to complain to Ms. Collins about the situation. It is obvious that the employees' unhappiness about the situation is affecting their work.

1. Is it possible that the partial treatment is "imagined" by the employees?
2. If you were Martha Collins, how would you go about finding out the "nature" of the relationship between Cindy and the city manager and the extent of the favoritism?
3. What course of action should Martha Collins take to reduce the employee dissatisfaction and restore effective working relations?

The Real Leader

Richard Gill was recently hired as the supervisor of an automotive parts warehouse. One of the first things Richard has observed is that the employees depend heavily on Tom Vale for information and advice. Tom has been with the company longer than any of the other employees and is respected because he was a local war hero. The employees look to Tom for advice on how to do their jobs, and they ask him what rules they should and should not be concerned about. They talk with Tom during lunch and at coffee breaks to obtain information about what is happening in the warehouse in relation to work rules, raises, layoffs, and job changes.

Richard feels he is losing any ability to provide leadership, because the employees are becoming more and more dependent on Tom.

1. Should Richard Gill be concerned about the employees' dependence on Tom for advice and information?
2. Why do the employees rely on Tom for advice and information?
3. Has Tom become the real leader in the warehouse?
4. What are the possible long-term effects if this situation continues?
5. What courses of action should Richard Gill take?

Exercise   *Leaders You Have Known*

In developing your leadership skills, it is helpful to identify the behaviors of leaders you have observed. Evaluating the effective and ineffective behaviors of people in positions of authority can increase your awareness of how different approaches contribute to leader effectiveness.

From your experience in groups and organizations, think of the "best" (most effective) leader you have known and the "worst" (least effective) leader you have known. Identify the behaviors for each leader that you felt indicated effective and ineffective leadership.

THE BEST LEADER I HAVE OBSERVED
Effective Leadership Behaviors

_____

_____

_____

_____

Ineffective Leadership Behaviors

_____

_____

_____

_____

THE WORST LEADER I HAVE OBSERVED
Effective Leadership Behaviors

_____

_____

_____

_____

_____

Ineffective Leadership Behaviors

_____

_____

_____

_____

_____

WHAT WERE THE MOST IMPORTANT DIFFERENCES IN THE BEHAVIORS OF THE "BEST" AND "WORST" LEADER YOU HAVE DESCRIBED?

_____

_____

_____

_____

_____

Endnotes

1. Ralph M. Stogdill, "Leadership, Membership, and Organizations," *Psychological Bulletin*, January 1950, p. 4.
2. A. E. Wiggam, "The Biology of Leadership," in *Business Leadership*, by H. C. Metcalf (New York: Ditman, 1931).

3. Perrin Stryker, "On the Meaning of Executive Qualities," *Fortune*, June 1958, p. 189.
4. Eugene E. Jennings, "The Anatomy of Leadership," *Management of Personnel Quarterly*, Autumn 1961, p. 2.
5. Charles R. Milton, *Human Behavior in Organizations: Three Levels of Behavior* (Englewood Cliffs, N.J.: Prentice-Hall, 1981), p. 296.
6. Ralph M. Stogdill, *Handbook of Leadership* (New York: Free Press, 1974), pp. 63–64.
7. Ralph M. Stogdill, C. L. Shartle, and associates, *Patterns of Administrative Performance,* Bureau of Business Research, The Ohio State University (Columbus, Ohio, 1956), sec. IU.
8. James L. Gibson, John M. Ivancevich, and James H. Donnelly, Jr., *Organizations*, 4th ed. (Plano, Texas: Business Publications, 1982), pp. 252–82.
9. Robert R. Blake and Jane S. Mouton, *The Managerial Grid* (Houston: Gulf Publishing Co., 1964), and Robert R. Blake and Jane S. Mouton, *The New Managerial Grid* (Houston: Gulf Publishing Co., 1978).
10. Lawrence L. Steinmetz and H. Ralph Todd, *First-Line Management: Approaching Supervision Effectively,* rev. ed. (Dallas: Business Publication, 1979), pp. 165–66.
11. Fred H. Fiedler, *A Theory of Leadership Effectiveness* (New York: McGraw-Hill, 1967), and Fred E. Fiedler and Martin M. Chemers, *Leadership and Effective Management* (Glenview, Ill.: Scott, Foresman and Company, 1974). For interpretations of contingency models see "Leadership Symposium" *Organizational Dynamics*, Winter 1976, pp. 2–43.
12. M. G. Evans, "The Effects of Supervisory Behavior on the Path-Goal Relationship," *Organizational Behavior and Human Performance,* May 1970, pp. 278–98; and R. J. House, "A Path-Goal Theory of Leader Effectiveness," *Administrative Science Quarterly,* September 1971, pp. 321–32. Research support for path-goal theory is reported in Charles N. Green, "Questions of Causation in the Path-Goal Theory of Leadership," *Academy of Management Journal*, March 1979, pp. 21–41, and Chester A. Schriesheim and Angelo DeNisi, "Task Dimensions as Moderators of the Effects of Instrumental Behavior: A Path-Goal Approach," *Academy of Management Proceedings,* 1979, pp. 103–6.
13. Robert J. House and Terrence Mitchell, "Path-Goal Theory of Leadership," *Journal of Contemporary Business,* Autumn 1975, p. 84.
14. For a detailed report of leadership research see Gary A. Yukl, *Leadership in Organizations*, (Englewood Cliffs, N.J.: Prentice-Hall, 1981), and Bernard M. Bass, *Stogdills' Handbook of Leadership: A Survey of Theory and Research*, rev. ed. (New York: Free Press, 1981).

11 Group Behavior

Learning Objectives

After reading this chapter, you should be able to:

1. Discuss the importance of group behavior in organizations.

2. Describe the properties of groups.

3. Explain how group norms influence behavior in groups.

4. State how role relationships affect behavior of individuals in groups.

5. Discuss how status develops and affects group processes.

6. Identify conditions that increase and decrease group cohesiveness.

7. Explain how groups apply pressure to members to obtain conformity with norms.

8. Discuss how individuals respond to and are affected by group pressure.

9. List guides for working effectively with groups.

Chapter Topics

Preview and Self-Evaluation

History is crowded with instances of individual achievement. Most meaningful work, however, is not accomplished by individuals working alone but by people working together to achieve common goals. In work organizations, people may be placed in formal, structured relationships with specific areas of authority and responsibility. There are also the ever-present informal relationships derived from friendship, physical proximity, common interest, common assignments, or similar values. All organizations include both formal and informal groups. Sometimes strong, informal ties weld the formal organization into a cohesive force. Other times, groups within larger groups, frequently known as cliques, can be divisive and counter-productive. Groups, with their own internal norms, role conflicts, and status relationships, are the subject of Chapter 11.

Before reading this chapter try answering these true-false questions to test your perceptions. Check the questions again after reading the chapter. You may find a few surprises.

Answer True or False

1. Most of the behaviors of individuals are influenced
   by the groups to which they belong.　　　　　　　　T　　F

2. For most people, individual success depends on the ability to work effectively in groups.　　T　F

3. Individuals may behave very differently when in groups than when they are outside the group.　　T　F

4. Executives of large organizations find that their most important leadership roles depend on their ability to work in small groups.　　T　F

5. If a student group places a high value on academic achievement, its members usually make higher grades than they would have if they did not belong to the group.　　T　F

6. Cases have occurred in which individuals were fined or suspended from a union for working at speeds above the normal standard provided in a contract with an employer.　　T　F

7. Much of an individual's learning involves determining the appropriate behavior in different group situations.　　T　F

8. Groups are usually more attractive to members when there is internal competition than when relationships are cooperative.　　T　F

9. When a group shares a common fate as a result of external attack, the group usually becomes less attractive to members.　　T　F

10. When a group member's output is above or below what is expected by the group, pressure is usually applied to "bring the person into line."　　T　F

ANSWERS: 1. T; 2. T; 3. T; 4. T; 5. T; 6. T; 7. T; 8. F; 9. F; 10. T

Groups

An understanding of group processes is important in dealing with human behavior in an organization. Since we are all involved in groups, understanding group processes is also important in functioning effectively as individuals. All organizations involve interrelationships among groups within the organization and with groups in other organizations.

Individuals seldom, if ever, behave without being influenced by the groups they belong to. Most people spend the majority of their lives involved with family groups, social groups, professional groups, recreational groups, civic groups, and work groups among others. For most people, individual success depends on the ability to function effectively within groups. The group interpersonal relationships that develop are extremely complex and are never completely understood.

Most people belong to several groups. Groups have a major effect on individual behavior while the individual is interacting in the group. This effect carries over when the individual is outside the group. But individuals may behave differently when they are involved in group activities than when they are functioning on their own. To increase the complexity of the relationship between individual behavior and groups, it has been observed that the same individual may change behavior patterns when involved in different groups. Most people probably underestimate the degree to which their behavior is affected by the groups they belong to.[1]

The chance for individuals to assume leadership roles is much greater in small-group situations. Very few individuals will ever have the chance to be top-level managers or executives of large organizations. But most people will assume a variety of leadership positions in different types of small groups during their life. Even those individuals who become executives of large organizations find that their critical leadership roles depend on their ability to work in small groups. An organization involves a number of small groups that are linked together to achieve organizational objectives.

Definition of a Group

group defined

A *group* can be defined as two or more individuals working together to achieve a common goal. Any definition of a group process necessarily involves face-to-face interaction and communication among individuals as a basic component. As individuals interact to achieve goals, it is inevitable that status relationships develop—a necessary element in any group situation.

Possibly the most discussed characteristic of groups are their norms and values. Every group develops sets of values and norms that regulate the behavior of individual members in areas important to the group process.

Distinction Between Togetherness Situations and Group Processes

togetherness situations

Togetherness situations are temporary associations in which individuals interact. There are no prolonged, stable status and role relationships among the individuals. No sets of values or norms extend beyond the particular situation. In togetherness situations, the nature of the immediate task or problems is the only effect on the behavior of the individuals involved.

Group situations exist when individuals participate as members of a group structure. There are specific status relationships indicating each member's authority and responsibility within the group. There are role relationships which define the areas of activity that are appropriate for each member of the group. And there is a set of shared norms defining the acceptable behaviors in the process of achieving objectives that involve the group.

group situations

It is possible for togetherness situations to result in the development of a group. For this to occur, the individuals must interact over a period of time and develop shared objectives. There are obvious degrees of relationship among individuals, ranging from the casual meeting of strangers to the highly structured interaction of close-knit groups.

Groups do not suddenly exist with a set of well-defined relationships among members. Groups develop well-defined sets of relationships as their members communicate and achieve objectives (see Figure 11.1). The most important relationships revolve around the development of status, roles, and norms. These relationships develop and stabilize as a group defines its objectives and develops methods of rewarding and punishing group members for their behaviors.

groups develop as members communicate

Group Norms

Group norms are the values that group members hold concerning acceptable behaviors in specific situations. The group norms are the

norms and values

—Reward Systems—   —Status—   —Structures—   —Norms—

—Roles—   —Tasks—   —Values—   —Objectives—

Figure 11.1 Properties of groups.

"ideal" behaviors expected of group members. The norms specify what individuals should do, not necessarily how they actually behave. Norms apply only to those situations that are most important to the group; they do not cover all possible behaviors in every situation.

norms provide guides for behavior

Norms are one of the most significant products of the interaction among individuals working together to achieve common objectives. As norms develop, they specify the expected behavior in performing the tasks the group is involved in and the expected behavior in interpersonal relations. They cover people, physical objects, and situations. Norms also include the value judgments of the group, what is "good and bad" and "right and wrong."[2]

One example of an employee group norm is the belief that "we should not help new employees learn their jobs because that is management's responsibility." Another group norm might be to take every production problem to the boss, but to settle interpersonal problems within the group. The norms form guidelines and the individuals decide on the specific behavior that falls within the guidelines.

The norms of a group usually provide guides for three general types of behavior: the things you *should not do*, the things you *should do*, and the things you *may do*.

Examples of "should not" norms include: You should not swear in the group. You should not criticize group members outside the group. You should not have long hair. You should not wear a tie.

Examples of "should" norms include: You should take your coffee break with the other group members. You should tell group members about any proposed changes in work rules. You should lend tools to group members.

Examples of "may do" norms include: You may help group members when they have personal problems, but you are not expected to. You may make suggestions to management on how to improve production, but you are not expected to.

norms direct behavior

Most groups will develop sets of norms that they find useful in "directing" the behavior of individuals toward achieving the objectives of the group. These norms may become very powerful in standardizing the behavior of group members. Individuals who do not behave in accordance with the norms are usually subjected to group pressure to force their behavior within the acceptable range of the norm.

Group norms seldom specify just one way of behaving. They usually designate a range of acceptable (or at least tolerable) behaviors, which may vary a great deal from group to group. The "permissiveness" of the group usually depends on the importance of the situation and the position of the individual in the group's hierarchy. Norms which do not involve important group issues usually allow for wide variations in behavior. Matters which are of critical concern may involve norms where the acceptable range of behavior is very narrow. The most critical norms of behavior usually involve the identity and reputation of the group, the achievement of major group goals, and the continued existence of the group.

The development of group norms is influenced by three basic factors: (1) the nature of the environment in which the group functions, (2) the characteristics of the individuals in the group, and (3) the group goals and tasks required to achieve the goals (see Figure 11.2).

factors influencing norms

Obtaining conformity to group norms is important if the group is to function effectively and maintain the commitment of its members. A group establishes itself and develops its identity by members conforming to group norms. Groups are often referred to by the characteristics reflected by their norms. A university department may be characterized by a high level of faculty publication and research, effective teaching and concern for students, or faculty service to the community.

conformity

By enforcing norms, groups protect themselves from outside threats and maintain the commitment of their members to group goals. The attitudes and behaviors of individuals are modified by the norms of the groups they belong to, and it is often difficult to separate individual goals from those of the group. A student who joins a group that emphasizes campus activities will probably achieve prominence in extracurricular activities. If the group places a high value on academic achievement, its members will usually make higher grades than they would have otherwise.

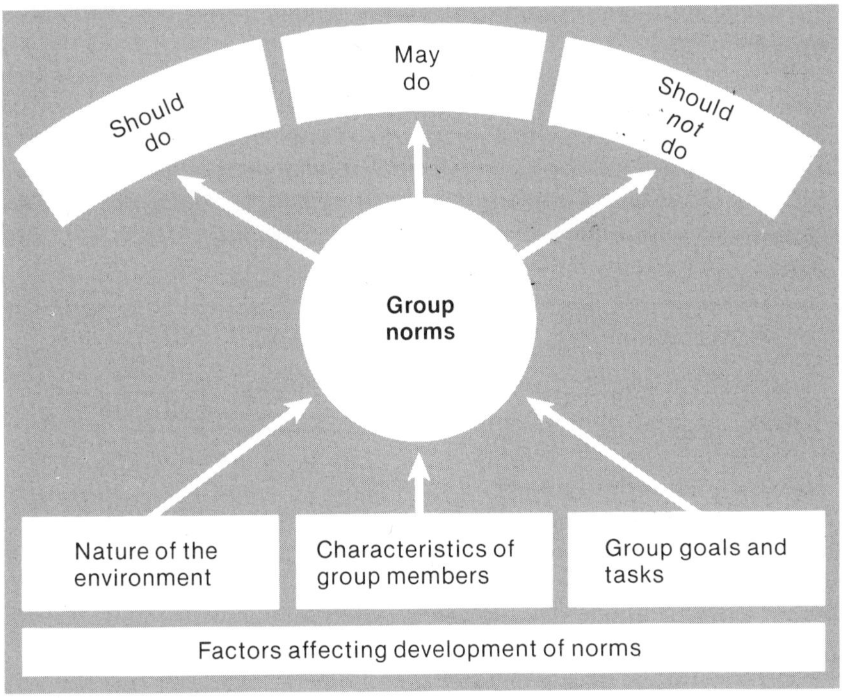

Figure 11.2 Group norms are established by the group and affect the behavior in the group.

The norms of work groups can have a powerful effect on productivity. Individual levels of work are almost always affected by group norms and the pressures to conform to them. Those who work above the norm in industry are usually referred to as rate-busters and are often subjected to severe group pressure to reduce output. There have been situations in which union members were charged by fellow workers with "working too hard." Cases have occurred in which individuals were fined or suspended from a union for working at speeds above a normal standard provided in a contract with an employer.[3] Norms may be established by a work group as a means of achieving job security goals, avoiding extra work, and obtaining better working conditions or other benefits.

The Comfortable Pace

At Zadandma Clothing Company, a major women's sportswear manufacturing firm in Fair Oaks, California, workers are paid by both piece and hourly rates. No worker earns less than $3.50 per hour. Standards for different sewing tasks allow operators to earn much more if they produce more than the established standard. Nearly all Zadandma workers earn $4.63 per hour. Workers who, because of higher production than that of most other employees, earn more, are often totally ostracized by the rest of the group. One worker, whose average earnings are $7.38 per hour, said when asked, "I don't have a damn friend here. They hate me and harass me because of my pay. I just work harder than those lazy bums." Newcomers to Zadandma are warned by fellow employees not to work too hard. Slower workers are frequently helped to "keep up." Very few workers actually achieve their full capacity. The norm is a comfortable pace slightly above standard.

Roles

Roles are the behaviors expected of those in particular positions in a group. In formal organizations there are usually job or position descriptions that define behavioral expectations. In most group situations, role expectations are developed by the group members. In many situations, the most important role expectations are never written. They develop as a result of experience on the job.

All members of a group develop a definition of the role they feel they are expected to assume and the roles that other members of the group should assume. The development of these role expectations involves the perceptions, attitudes, and feelings of the individuals toward other group members and toward the objectives of the group. Much of an individual's learning involves determining the "appropriate" or "accepted" role behavior in different group situations. In a family role, expectations affect the behavior patterns of the wife, husband, and children. Although role definitions vary from family to family, there are often common elements in the role expectations of a wife or husband. The role of the husband may involve responsibility for maintenance of family cars, mowing the grass, driving on family trips, painting the house, and so forth, while the wife may be responsible for the care of the children, fixing meals, washing clothes, cleaning the house, and so forth. As with any role definition, these roles imply the existence of related positions. The position of the husband implies the position of the wife. The relationship between husband and wife is a role relationship from which other roles may arise. The wife may be a daughter-in-law, a mother, and the family purchasing agent. Multiple roles are shown in Figure 11.3.

multiple roles

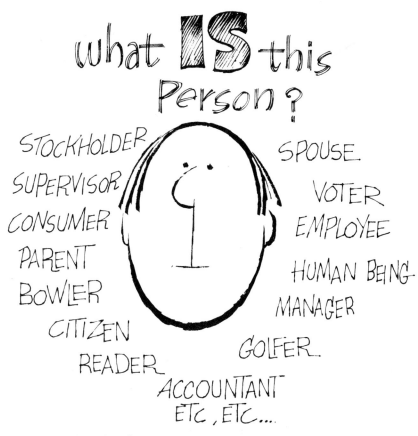

Figure 11.3 Multiple roles.

role relationships   The structure of a group involves the pattern of role relationships within the group. In a business, there may be complex role relationships among managers, technicians, staff advisors, secretaries, and a variety of specialists. In an organization, individuals are influenced by sets of role expectations which are part of the formal organizational requirements. These expectations also affect their role relations with superiors, subordinates, fellow employees, and individuals in a wide variety of positions.[4]

Individuals in organizations are involved in carrying out a number of roles in meeting organizational responsibilities. The individual's formal role responsibilities include relating to others in the organization's chain of command, the authority associated with a position, the specific functions required by a position, the formal status in the organization, and the decision-making responsibility.

role responsibilities   The structure of roles in a formal group is designed to help accomplish group responsibilities. These responsibilities are translated into role responsibilities for group members. The roles may be initially structured without any consideration for specific individuals. It is assumed that those who have the ability and desire to perform according to the role definition will fill the position. As any group functions, the roles change as a result of the abilities and desires of the individuals in the positions. The role expectations of individuals are usually modified when the manager of the group is changed. A new manager may expect different role behaviors and may use different methods to reach group objectives. When role expectations change, the individuals involved must adjust their behavior if the group is to function effectively.[5]

Role Conflict

role conflict   *Role conflict* occurs when an individual is faced with role expectations that are incompatible. For example, if role expectations of the family are that a "parent" should spend time with the children in the evening and company role expectations are for "salespersons" to spend the evenings entertaining clients, a role conflict could result. Conflicts between family and career roles can take a number of forms, as shown in Figure 11.4.

To obtain acceptance as a member of an informal group of employees, an individual may be required to violate the role expectations of the formal organization. For example, workers may have to engage in a work slowdown to place pressure on the organization to meet employee demands for pay increases or other changes. Conflicts between union and management are obvious examples of situations that can produce role conflict for employees.

Role conflict can have its origin in any of the forces that influence role expectations: the formal organization's role expectations, the informal or work group role expectations, and the individual's role expectations. Role conflict will occur more frequently in situations where inconsistent role expectations are rigidly enforced by the groups involved. The effect of a role conflict on an individual depends on his or her ability to ignore some of the conflicting role expectations or "play" the expected role while interacting with a group.

The plant manager's expectation for the production supervisor may be to increase output by reducing quality, while the informal work group expects to produce the highest quality product, reflecting their professional pride. In this situation there is a conflict in role expectations involving the formal organization and the informal work group.

The production supervisor could face conflicting role expectations from individuals in different positions within the formal organization. Quality-control managers may expect the quality of the final product

Figure 11.4   Role conflict.

to improve by closer inspection and reworking items that do not meet high quality standards. The accounting department may expect the production costs to be reduced by not enforcing the quality standards.

conflict with individual value systems

An employee may face a conflict between management's job expectations and individual value systems. For example, a secretary is expected to "fake" expenses so the bosses can receive payment for expenditures that, according to policies of the organization, are not supposed to be paid. If the secretary's role expectation is to be totally honest, then a role conflict can result.

who is supposed to do what?

A role conflict may also result when the individual's definition of appropriate job responsibilities differs from the manager's. A manager assumes the role of the secretary includes cleaning the conference room after meetings, and the secretary assumes that cleaning is part of the janitor's role. A role conflict occurs because of the confusion over who's supposed to do what.

The specific behavior of an individual in a role conflict situation will depend on the individual's values and the perceived rewards and punishments associated with the expected role behaviors. If an individual is forced to make a choice between conflicting role behaviors, the choice will usually be made on the basis of maximizing rewards and minimizing the chance for punishment. If informal work group membership is valued and the reward system of the formal organization is seen as weak or more remote than the reward system of the work group, the individual will usually behave in ways to meet the role expectation of the work group.

Status

Status refers to an individual's relative position or rank in a group. Basic to the concept of status is the comparison of group members in terms of their value to the group. The evaluation of a person's rank is usually based on the extent to which the individual is able to influence the achievement of group objectives and meet the needs of group members.

formal and informal status

Status is often classified as either formal or informal. *Formal status* is the "official" rank of an individual, as designated by an organization. The position of vice-president indicates a formal status designation by the organization. *Informal status* refers to the social position or rank of an individual as a result of the evaluation of others in a group. A group of employees may look for advice and leadership from an individual who has no formal management position but has been accorded informal status by the group.

Both formal and informal status have an impact on the behavior of individuals in an organization. The actions of individuals and groups are affected by the desire for status. In many cases, status considerations are significant factors in attracting individuals to join groups and organizations. Individuals tend to be attracted to groups perceived as having high status and to avoid groups with low status. An individual may accept a job with lower pay in an organization that has high status. Some individuals are much more concerned with achieving status than with the amount of pay they receive.

Status is important in many groups because it defines the rights and privileges that an individual has. The effect of status is reflected in the frequently heard statement, "Rank has its privileges." Usually, the privileges of status are a result of the position occupied by the individual in a social structure. The privileges cannot be obtained through more or harder work.

status defines rights and privileges

Group Cohesiveness

Cohesiveness refers to the amount of unity in the group and the degree to which members are pulling in the same direction. The cohesiveness of a group results from the attraction of the group for its members. Attraction depends on the need satisfaction that results from membership. Individuals join groups to satisfy needs; if the group's ability to satisfy individual needs decreases, the attractiveness of the group will decrease.

Group cohesiveness is reflected in the attitudes and actions of the members. The following factors are often used as cohesiveness indicators: loyalty to the group, defense of the group, responsibility for group activities, identification with the group, acceptance of group decisions, conformity to group norms, and agreement with group goals (see Figure 11.5).

indicators of cohesiveness

In order to contribute to group activities and conform to group norms, the individual may be required to change personal objectives or methods of satisfying needs. As a result, members frequently develop goals that are consistent with essential group activities.

Changes occur in society that affect the role of groups in satisfying individual needs. During times of high unemployment, individuals may join groups that they feel will help maintain employment. For example, an employee might join a union. An individual who has "lost status" in the community may be attracted to a group because of its prestige. Employees may desire to belong to a group including managers because they feel that it would give them higher status.

Association with the members of the group may be a major factor in group attraction. An individual may join the group to satisfy social needs for belonging and friendship. If the individuals in the group are primarily satisfying social needs, the other goals and activities of the group may be unimportant. The cohesiveness of some groups can be attributed to the desire of group members to be with each other.

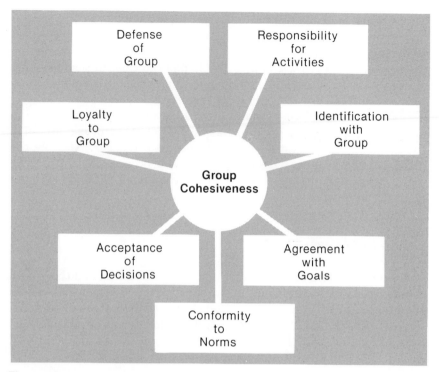

Figure 11.5 Indicators of group cohesiveness.

Groups may be attractive because they help in attaining goals that are outside the group itself. In this type of situation, the individual's needs are not satisfied by the achievement of the group's goals. For example, a manager may join the country club because the prestige of membership may help in obtaining a promotion. The manager's promotion is not a goal of the country club, but the manager sees value in membership because it helps meet needs outside the group.

satisfying member needs The cohesiveness of a group is a function of the contribution the group makes in satisfying the needs of its members. The nature of a group's activities varies, depending on the sources of attraction for the group members. When the primary attraction is satisfaction of social needs, the activities will focus on interpersonal relations. The attractiveness of a professional group may depend on satisfaction of needs for achievement and recognition, and its activities will be oriented toward the professional development of members. The attractiveness of a work group may be more strongly affected by the employee's ability to perform and the recognition for achievement than by the number of friends made.

Different ways in which cohesiveness is produced result in different patterns of influence and communication. When cohesiveness is based on personal attraction, the group members may focus on influencing each other through long discussions and conversations. When

Chapter 11

cohesiveness is based on effective task performance, discussions may be short and directly related to completing the task quickly and effectively, with influence based on achieving effective performance. When attraction is based on the prestige or status resulting from belonging to the group, the group members may concentrate on their own actions and be very cautious about trying to influence each other so as not to risk their status. Under conditions of minimum cohesiveness, the group members may behave independently of each other and with little consideration for others in the group.

Conditions Increasing Group Cohesiveness

Although there is no absolute formula for increasing the cohesiveness of a group, the following conditions usually result in the attractiveness of the group increasing:

increasing cohesiveness

1. The group becomes more attractive for individuals who gain prestige or status within the group.
2. Cohesiveness is higher when group members are in cooperative relationships than when there is internal competition.
3. When group members can fulfill more needs through participating in the group, the attraction of the group increases.
4. An increase in the prestige or status of the group in an organization or in the community usually results in increased attraction for group members.
5. When the group is attacked from the outside, the cohesiveness usually increases as the members deal with the external threat. When the group shares a common fate as a result of external attack, the reaction is usually to focus the group's resources on protecting the group. The response to an outside threat is reflected in the statement, "United we stand, divided we fall."

To increase the attractiveness of a group, it is necessary to make the group better serve the needs of the group members. A group will be more attractive the more it satisfies the needs for recognition and achievement, the more cooperative the relationships, the freer the communication, and the greater the security provided for members.

Conditions Decreasing Cohesiveness

Although the behavior of groups is complex and difficult to predict accurately, the following conditions usually result in the cohesiveness of the group decreasing:

decreasing cohesiveness

1. When interpersonal conflict results from members' disagreements over ways to achieve group goals or solve group problems, the attractiveness of the group will decrease. The greater the interpersonal conflict, the greater the decrease.

Members of highly cohesive groups may often have disagreements, but they try to settle them quickly.

2. If participation in the group results in unpleasant experiences for an individual, the attractiveness of the group will decrease. When group activities result in embarrassment for an individual, the individual's attraction to the group is usually reduced.
3. If membership places limits on the individuals' participation in other activities or groups outside the group, cohesiveness may be lowered.
4. If conditions exist in the group which prevent or restrict effective communication, cohesiveness will decrease. Reduced communication may result if some members are too dominating or if some members are unpleasant or obnoxious in their communication behavior.
5. The cohesiveness may be reduced if group members feel the activities involve too great a personal risk. The risks could be physical danger or psychological threats. Risk could involve the group engaging in activities which individuals feel may be illegal or immoral. Risk could also involve group actions in an organization that the individual feels might result in getting disciplined or fired.
6. If the evaluation of the group by outsiders who are respected becomes negative, this can result in the group becoming unattractive to its members.

In general, the attractiveness of the group will decrease if the needs it has been satisfying for the individual can be better satisfied by other means or if the needs which led to the individual's involvement in the group have been reduced. The suitability of a particular group in satisfying an individual's needs may change drastically over time.

Results of Cohesiveness

results of cohesiveness

Commitment to Group Goals Members who are highly attracted to a group tend to assume more responsibility for the achievement of objectives. In highly cohesive groups, members tend to have a high level of participation, remain in the group longer, and work longer and harder to achieve group goals.[6]

Interpersonal Influence Highly cohesive groups are able to more effectively influence the behavior of group members. Members are more willing to attempt to influence others in the group, and individuals are more willing to listen to others in the group. In highly cohesive groups, there is usually greater acceptance of the opinions of others and more willingness to change attitudes to be consistent with other group members.

Similarity of Values and Standards Where there is strong member attraction to the group, there is usually close agreement on group stan-

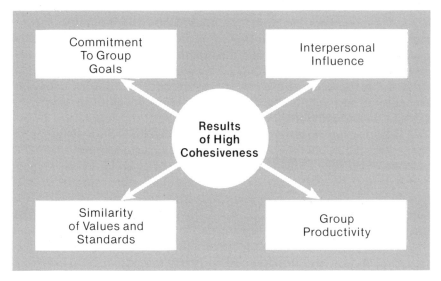

Figure 11.6   Results of high group cohesiveness.

dards. Members work to protect the group's standards by exerting pressure on individuals who do not conform. In highly cohesive groups, members who do not adopt the group's values and standards are usually "expelled" from the group. The greater the cohesiveness of the group, the more the group will expect and enforce compliance with group standards.

Group Productivity   Highly cohesive groups usually have very specific expectations of how much each member should contribute to group productivity. The more cohesive a group, the more it will try to insure that there is conformity with group norms for production. A cohesive group will make every effort to have members increase output if it is lower than expected, and pressure will be applied to members who are seen as producing "too much." *high cohesive groups regulate productivity*

A highly cohesive group will regulate productivity so it conforms to group norms. As a result, the greater the group cohesiveness, the higher the achievement of organizational objectives if the group supports the organization and the lower the achievement if the group objects to organizational goals. Within an organization, a highly cohesive group that opposes management can be very effective in reducing output and preventing the achievement of organizational objectives. Figure 11.6 illustrates the results of strong group cohesiveness.

Group Pressure

In order to obtain conformity with norms, groups exert pressure on members. At the most basic level, they reward members who behave in accordance with group norms and work to achieve group objectives. *conformity is rewarded by the group*

Group Behavior   307

When members fail to conform to norms and do not contribute to achieving objectives, the group provides some form of punishment. In most organizations, individuals become members of work groups composed of individuals who work on the same project, in the same department, or in the same area.

Most work groups have specific norms relating to work behavior, including norms regulating the quantity and quality of productivity expected from individuals. When individual output is above or below that expected by the group, pressure is usually applied by the group to "bring the individual into line."

One of the best-known studies of the effect of group norms on productivity was conducted in the early 1930s at Western Electric's Hawthorne plant near Chicago.[7] The study was conducted under the assumption that with an incentive pay system employees would try to maximize their pay, even though group pressure would be exerted on individuals to conform to an "acceptable" level of output. The pay system was set up so the individual's hourly pay rate was revised every six months based on individual productivity levels. There was also the possibility of a bonus based on the output of the department. Under the system, employees' total pay was affected by changes in individual output and changes in the output of the total group. A group could increase the total earnings of individuals by increasing the total output of the group. It was assumed that employees' economic interests would result in motivation to maximize output.

The study found that there were group norms concerning an appropriate day's output. It was considered to be an acceptable output when an employee wired two units a day. Usually, most of the work was done in the morning, and work slowed down when employees were sure they could finish two units.

results of group pressure The group norms resulted in individuals who produced "too much" being referred to as rate-busters. Individuals who produced "too little" were called chiselers. Anyone who said anything negative about a fellow employee to management was called a squealer.

As in all groups, the work group developed methods for the enforcement of norms. It had been assumed that the incentive system would result in group pressure being exerted on the slower employees, but the strongest pressure was actually exerted on the highest producers. Pressure applied to the individuals producing more than the norm included calling them names like Speed King and Slave, and "binging" them, which involved a blow to the upper arm.

steps in applying group pressure When members of a group do not conform to its norms, the first step in applying group pressure is usually to describe the expected behavior. This description is usually accompanied by the reasons the behavior is necessary for group members. If the individual does not begin behaving within the group norms, members usually try forceful persuasion, which may include threats of some form of punishment. If the individual can withstand the group persuasion for long enough, the

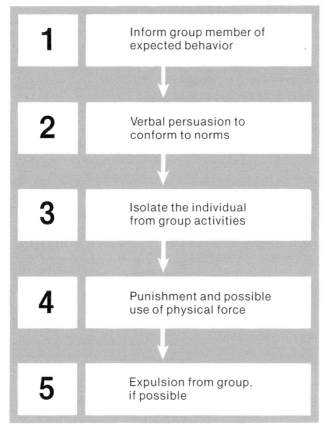

1	Inform group member of expected behavior
2	Verbal persuasion to conform to norms
3	Isolate the individual from group activities
4	Punishment and possible use of physical force
5	Expulsion from group, if possible

Figure 11.7 Steps in applying group pressure to obtain conformity with norms.

group will usually isolate the individual from interaction with the group. If isolation fails, the group may harass the individual with verbal statements or use some form of physical violence. At this point, the individual may withdraw from the group to avoid pressure, or the individual may be forced out of the group. The individual is no longer a part of the group, and the group members may act as if the individual did not exist. Figure 11.7 presents the steps in applying group pressure.

Responses to Group Pressure

When subjected to group pressure, some individuals resist conforming to the norms. The extent of the resistance will usually depend on the value the individual places on membership and the amount of pressure exerted by the group. An initial resistance to group pressure may take the form of attempting to get the group to change the norm or to have the group make an exception to the norm. Unless the individual has

exceptions to the norms

Group Behavior   309

abilities or resources that are very valuable to the group, it is unlikely that an exception will be made. If a group is playing baseball and the owner of the only bat wants to get four strikes, the group might allow it in order to be able to continue to use the bat. But the next time they play, more than one person will probably bring a bat. It is not unusual for fraternities to allow individuals who are star athletes or campus leaders to deviate from the group norms.

If the individual is unsuccessful in obtaining an exception to the norm, he or she usually conforms. When behavior required by the norm is very objectionable, the individual may remain in the group and continue to endure the pressure.

withdrawing to avoid group pressure
When it is no longer "worth it" to endure the pressure, the individual will withdraw from the group by physically leaving or by psychologically isolating himself or herself from the group. In a work group situation, physically leaving may not be possible without quitting. It is not uncommon for individuals to try to transfer in an organization or look for another job to avoid the pressure of conforming to work group norms.

When an individual becomes isolated from groups within the organization, the manager should be concerned about the reasons that led to the isolation. It is important for the manager to know whether the individual was isolated by the group or if the individual withdrew from it. The manager should also be aware of the group pressures being exerted on group members. The manager may need to take action if the pressures are excessive, become detrimental to the welfare of individuals, or prevent the achievement of organizational objectives.[8]

Implications for Managers

coordination of group efforts
Effective managers must develop productive working relationships with groups. Achievement of organizational objectives requires effective coordination of group efforts. Unless groups within an organization integrate group goals with organizational goals, conflict will result. Management must continually work to develop harmony among and within groups in the organization. The integration of group and organizational goals is often a difficult task.

In order to develop effective working relations with groups, the manager must consider the motivational impact of the group on its members, the involvement of individuals in group decision-making processes, and methods of maintaining effective communication with the group.

If the actions of the manager threaten satisfaction of individual needs, the result may be defensive action by the group. If the group develops a defensive position, the manager's actions may unwittingly encourage the development of group norms and goals that conflict with organizational goals.

If group norms and goals support productivity for the organization, the manager should encourage strong group loyalties. When the group is supportive of organizational objectives, the manager should help the group increase cohesiveness. This can be done by rewarding the group, providing status to individuals because of their group membership, providing resources for the group, or delegating responsibility to the group.

The manager should develop effective working relationships with the informal group leaders. It is not uncommon for managers to consider informal leaders as troublemakers. But, because these leaders usually represent the group's norms and goals, the manager should communicate with them and respect their positions. Effective managers obtain advice and assistance from informal leaders in achieving organizational goals.

informal group leaders

The manager should use every opportunity to illustrate how groups fit into the organization and how they contribute to the success of the organization. He should recognize the contributions that groups make to the organization. He should reinforce individual pride in group membership and group achievement. The manager should support group efforts to increase their effectiveness in contributing to organizational goals and member need satisfaction.

Since much of the behavior of individuals is influenced by the groups they belong to, effective management requires continual attention to group processes.

Guides for Working with Groups

1. Participation in groups is a basic source of social need satisfaction for employees.
2. Informal groups try to protect their members and provide security. They will try to protect members from perceived threats from management.
3. Groups develop communication systems to provide information that members want. If management does not provide the information employees want, the informal group will try to obtain it.
4. Both formal and informal groups obtain status and prestige within an organization. Groups may use their status and prestige as a power base to influence others in the organization.
5. Groups develop and enforce norms for the behavior of members. The group norms may be supportive of management or may work against management objectives.
6. The more cohesive a group is, the more control it has over the behavior of its members. The highly cohesive group can produce high achievement of organizational goals. However, it can work just as

effectively against organizational objectives when the group opposes management.

7. Both formal and informal groups within an organization establish roles that affect the activities and responsibilities of members. Accepting role responsibilities in an informal group may require that an individual violate the role expectations of management.

Quick Review

I. Groups
   A. An understanding of group processes is important in dealing with human behavior in organizations.
   B. The chance for leadership is greater in small groups.
   C. People underestimate the degree to which their behavior is affected by the groups they belong to.

II. Definition of a Group
   A. A group can be defined as two or more people working together to achieve a common goal.
   B. An important element in group situations is the relationships individuals have with each other, including status relationships.
   C. There is a clear distinction between togetherness situations and group processes.
      1. In togetherness situations, there are no stabilized status and role relationships that continue for prolonged periods of time.
      2. It is possible for togetherness situations to result in the development of a group.

III. Group Norms
   A. Group norms are the values that group members hold concerning the way members should behave in specific situations.
   B. Norms establish the expected behavior regarding people, physical objects, and situations.
   C. Norms include judgments of things members should, should not, or may do.
   D. Group norm development is influenced by:
      1. The nature of the group's environment.
      2. The characteristics of the individuals in the group.
      3. The group goals and the tasks required to achieve the goals.
   E. Group norms encourage and enforce conformity.

IV. Roles
   A. Roles refer to the behavior expected of a particular position in a group.

1. All members of the group develop roles and assume expected role behavior.
        2. Role relationships are affected by group structure.
    B. Role conflict occurs when role expectations are incompatible.
  V. Status
    A. Status is either the formal or informal position of the person in a group.
    B. Status defines individual rights and privileges.
 VI. Group Cohesiveness
    A. Cohesiveness refers to the degree of group unity that exists.
        1. Cohesiveness is a function of the contributions the group makes to satisfy the needs of its members.
        2. Conditions increasing cohesiveness include:
            a. Increase of prestige or status.
            b. Cooperative relationships.
            c. Participation.
            d. Community or organizational recognition.
            e. A threat from outside forces.
        3. Conditions decreasing cohesiveness include:
            a. Interpersonal conflict.
            b. Unpleasant personal experiences in the group.
            c. Limitation of individual participation.
            d. Restriction of effective communication.
            e. High personal risk resulting from group membership.
            f. Negative evaluation by outsiders.
    B. Cohesiveness can result in both positive and negative organizational behavior.
VII. Group Pressure
    A. Groups exert direct and indirect social pressure to insure conformity.
    B. Group pressure to conform to group norms may depress as well as enhance individual performance.
VIII. Implications for Managers
    A. Managers must develop productive working relationships with groups.
    B. The following factors should be kept in mind by managers:
        1. Participation in groups is a basic source of social need satisfaction.
        2. Informal groups provide security from threats.
        3. Groups develop communication systems.
        4. Both formal and informal groups obtain status and prestige.
        5. Groups develop and enforce norms.

6. Highly cohesive groups exert strong controls over members.
7. Formal and informal groups establish role behavior.

Key Terms

Groups	Roles	Formal status
Togetherness situations	Role expectations	Informal status
	Role relationships	Cohesiveness
Norms	Role conflict	Group pressure
Conformity	Status	

Discussion Questions

1. How do groups affect the behavior of individuals?
2. Why do groups that are not a part of the formal organizational structure develop within organizations?
3. What kinds of effects can group norms have on productivity in an organization?
4. How do the role expectations of an individual affect his or her behavior?
5. What are examples of role conflict that may be faced by a student?
6. Why would individuals want to have high status in an "informal" group?
7. What conditions would tend to increase the cohesiveness of a group?
8. How do highly cohesive groups differ from groups with little cohesion?
9. How do groups apply pressure to group members to conform to norms?
10. What can an individual do to resist group pressure?

Case Incidents

The Friendly Supervisor

Bob Gomez manages the customer relations department of a public utility company. The department is responsible for replying to customer requests for information and to customer complaints. There are seven typists in the department who handle the correspondence to customers dictated by the staff.

Mr. Gomez recently promoted Barbara Thompson to office supervisor. Barbara had been a typist in the department for ten years. She was considered the fastest and most accurate typist who had ever worked for Mr. Gomez. Barbara had the best attendance record in the department, and Mr. Gomez considered her his most dependable employee. She was very well liked by all the typists, and they considered her to be a good personal friend.

As a supervisor Barbara does a good job of handing out work assignments, but she does little else to supervise the typists. She does not like to criticize the typists and does not enforce office rules. No matter what a typist does Barbara will not take any disciplinary action. She makes no attempt to check the work of the typists for compliance with quality standards or to see that work is completed on time. In fact, she spends most of her time typing to reduce the work load of the other typists.

Mr. Gomez has been receiving an increasing number of complaints from the department staff about the poor quality of the typing and about the slow turnaround time for work. He has also received complaints about the typists taking excessively long coffee breaks and spending time on personal phone calls.

When Mr. Gomez talked to the typists, they told him that Barbara frequently invites them to her house for dinner or to play bridge. It appears to Mr. Gomez that the typists all like Barbara as a friend, but they are becoming concerned about her lack of supervision.

Mr. Gomez mentioned to Barbara that she should focus her effort on improving the work of the typists. She replied, "These women are my friends, and I don't feel right about cracking down on them."

1. Can an individual effectively manage a group and be a close personal friend with group members?
2. What should Mr. Gomez do to ensure that the work of the typists will improve.?
3. Should Barbara Thompson have been promoted to office supervisor?
4. If you were Barbara, what would you do? Would you quit the supervisor's job? Would you no longer be friends with the typists?

Life in the Office: The Letter from Nancy

Dear Professor Campbell:
Several things have happened at my job that make me remember some of the ideas I learned in management classes. I guess I never really thought that any of those things would come to pass in my life. The pressures from my peers and those about me have begun to

mount. It so happens that my immediate supervisor and his boss were gone Friday to the groundbreaking for a new store. After they left all the women in my office decided to call it a day, and it was only 3:30. There was some work which needed to be done before the weekend, so that was what I was working on. One of the supervisors in another section came by and asked me why I was working now that the others had left. After I told him, he said that I should know that he had nothing to do with getting me a raise. I said I knew that, and that wasn't why I was still working.

When another secretary noticed that I was working, she started in on me: "You are going to make everyone look bad if you keep on working when the supervisor is gone." There are also subtle hints that are given to me. I am being excluded from most of the conversations in the office. The others in the office manage to avoid me at lunch, so I don't eat with the "group" anymore.

I don't have much in common with them anyway. They all sit around at lunch and crochet or knit and talk about whoever happens to be absent that day. I told my feelings about the "group" to one of the girls and it immediately got out. So as far as I'm concerned, the "lunch bunch" can sit and mold. Besides all that, I guess our goals are different. Their goals are babies and afghans. They don't want to improve their minds beyond *Woman's Day.*

The men in the office have molds to put all women into, of course—those sex-retaries don't help the image any.

I really don't know how long this job will last. I have a feeling I might get fired.

Anyway, I guess it would be easy to fit in around here. Just close your senses up. Sometimes I think I'm one of those fire-breathing dragons stomping around, stirring up a little dust. But I would rather do that than mold. So far this job has been a real "observing" experience. Interesting from that standpoint.

One more thing to rant and rave about and I'll get off the subject. If *one* more supervisor swats me on the tail, he's going to have one hell of a mad chickie on his hands. I think I'll swat him back and see how he likes that.

See you someday.
Nancy

1. What group norms is Nancy violating in her behavior?
2. What forms of group pressure are being used to get Nancy to conform to the norms?
3. What courses of action do you think the group will take toward Nancy in the future?
4. What action, if any, should management take in this situation?
5. What advice would you give Nancy to help her deal with this situation?

Engineering Improvement Address

A manufacturer of farm equipment conducted a management improvement survey (attitude survey) to determine employee dissatisfactions and areas where management policies and procedures could be improved. After the results were tabulated, the employees in each department elected representatives to meet with management and develop specific recommendations for improvement. At the beginning of the meeting in the engineering department, the employees handed the following "address" to the manager and walked out.

Engineering Improvement Address

One decade and nine years ago our corporation brought forth on this department, a new system conceived in management and dedicated to the proposition to control all workers under it. Now we are engaged in a great improvement survey testing whether that system, or any system so conceived and so dedicated can be right for the employees. We are met on another meeting ground of that survey. We have come to discuss a portion of that policy to find a solution so that the department might function in harmony. It is altogether fitting and proper that we should do this. But in a larger sense we cannot communicate, we cannot coordinate, we cannot invent and be rewarded under this system. The loyal engineers who struggle here are confused by it far above our poor power to use or understand. The corporation will little note nor long remember what we say here, but it can never forget the products that were engineered here. It is for us the uninformed, rather, to be controlled by this system as those who worked here before us so nobly did. It is rather for us to be here dedicated to the great communication problem remaining before us that from these neglected employees we give increased attention to the ideas which they gave to aid the design of the products. That we here highly resolve that these innovations shall not have been given in vain. That this system, under management, shall have a new birth of communication and that recognition of the achievements by the employees for the corporation shall not perish under the system.

---

1. Why did the employees write the Engineering Improvement Address and give it to management?
2. How strong is the informal organization in the engineering department?
3. What are the most important points that the employees are trying to get across to management?
4. Should disciplinary action be taken against the employees who wrote the Address?
5. What should management do in this situation?

Exercise   *Expected Behaviors in Groups*

Expected behaviors (norms) may be verbally communicated (in writing or orally), or may be left to individuals to "figure out."

Answer the following questions from your experience as a group member. Use a specific group you are (or were) an active member of and whose membership is (or was) important to you.

1. What were three behaviors expected by the group that were communicated to you verbally (either orally or in writing).

   _____

   _____

   _____

2. What were three behaviors expected by the group that you had to discover on your own?

   _____

   _____

   _____

   How did you determine the expected behaviors that were not communicated verbally?

   _____

   _____

3. Which expected behaviors (norms) were the most important to the group; those communicated verbally or those you had to "figure out"?

   _____

   _____

4. How did you participate in the communication of expected behaviors to group members?

   _____

   _____

5. What happened to group members who violated group norms by not behaving as the group expected?

   _____

   _____

   _____

6. Did you ever violate group norms by not behaving as the group expected? What happened?

_____

_____

_____

(You should find it interesting to compare your answers with those of other students.)

Endnotes

1. For a review of the study of group behavior see Alvin Zander, "The Study of Group Behavior During Four Decades," *The Journal of Applied Behavioral Science*, 15, No. 3, 1979, pp. 272–82, and Alvin Zander, "The Psychology of Group Processes," *Annual Review of Psychology*, 1979, pp. 417–51.
2. For additional discussion of group norms see Richard M. Steers, *Introduction to Organizational Behavior* (Santa Monica, Calif.: Goodyear, 1981), and Marvin E. Shaw, *Group Dynamics: The Psychology of Small Group Behavior*, 2nd ed. (New York: McGraw-Hill, 1976).
3. *The Wall Street Journal*, 10 November 1961, p. 2.
4. For relevant studies see J. Jackson, *Norms and Roles Studies in Systematic Psychology* (New York: Holt, Rinehart and Winston, 1976); R. S. Schuler, "Role Perceptions, Satisfaction, and Performance: A Partial Reconciliation," *Journal of Applied Psychology*, December 1975, pp. 683–87; and C. E. Schneier and P. W. Beatty, "The Influence of Role Prescriptions on the Performance Appraisal Process," *Academy of Management Journal*, March 1978, pp. 129–34.
5. For an excellent discussion of roles see L. Roos and F. Starke, "Roles in Organizations," in *Handbook of Organizational Design*, W. Starbuck and P. Nystrom, eds. (Oxford, England: Oxford University Press, 1980).
6. For additional research see P. Cartwright and A. Zander, *Group Dynamics: Research and Theory* (New York: Harper & Row, 1968), and K. L. Dion, "Cohesiveness as a Determinant of Ingroup-Outgroup Bias," *Journal of Personality and Social Psychology*, 28, 1973, pp. 163–71.
7. Committee on Work in Industry, National Research Council, *Fatigue of Workers: Its Relation to Industrial Production* (New York: Van Nostrand Reinhold, 1941), pp. 77–86. Also see Henry A. Landsberger, *Hawthorne Revisited* (Ithaca: Cornell University, NY State School of Labor Relations, 1968), and "Hawthorne Revisited: The Legend and the Legacy," *Organizational Dynamics*, Winter 1975, pp. 66–80.
8. Relation of personal goals to group goals is discussed in Alvin Zander, Thomas Natsoulas, and Edwin J. Thomas, "Personal Goals and the Group's Goals for the Member," in *Group Development*, Leland P. Bradford, ed (La Jolla, Calif.: University Associates, 1978).

12 Group Performance and Productivity

Learning Objectives

After reading this chapter, you should be able to:

1. Discuss the conditions that make groups potentially more productive than individuals working alone.

2. State the factors that contribute to the productivity of a group.

3. Explain how task factors affect group productivity.

4. Describe how interpersonal relations affect the achievement of group objectives.

5. Identify sources of interpersonal conflict and approaches to reduce conflict.

6. Describe the characteristics of highly productive groups.

7. Discuss how effective group leaders behave.

Chapter Topics

No Magic in Groups

Groups and Individual Productivity

Group Productivity

Task Factors Affecting Productivity

Interpersonal Relations and Productivity

Effective Group Leadership

Preview and Self-Evaluation

People are the basic ingredient of any organization. By the very nature of organizations, tasks are accomplished through the coordinated efforts of people working together in job-related groups. Groups may either be formally designated or may develop spontaneously on an informal basis. A primary characteristic of groups is the dependency of members on one another to accomplish group goals. Cooperative, coordinated groups are one of the most powerful tools available to management. They can, and often do, accomplish more than the most highly motivated individual working independently of others. There is, unfortunately, a tendency to forget that groups are made of individuals with differing values, needs, attitudes, and abilities. True organizational effectiveness depends on the manager's understanding of both groups and individuals in groups.

In this chapter, groups and forces affecting individuals in groups are discussed. Factors that encourage productivity as well as those that decrease productivity are examined. Before reading this chapter, take the true-false quiz to test your perceptions. Then after reading the chapter, check the questions again to see if your perceptions are the same.

Answer True or False

1. A group should not deal with problems that could be better solved on an individual level.   T   F

2. Groups should be used to take the place of individual initiative in solving problems.   T   F

3. Groups have the potential for increasing individual initiative and individual productivity.   T   F

4. According to the research on group versus individual productivity, groups are always superior to individuals working alone.   T   F

5. The desire to satisfy social needs always acts as an incentive for increased productivity in groups.   T   F

6. The lack of specific group goals usually has little effect on group members' performance.   T   F

7. Group members usually understand task problems much better than interpersonal problems.   T   F

8. When individuals look to high-status group members for all rewards, cooperation in the group increases.   T   F

9. Status symbols motivate people to work for more status symbols.   T   F

10. The achievement of group objectives depends on individual performance but not on how well group members can work together.   T   F

ANSWERS: 1. T; 2. F; 3. T; 4. F; 5. F; 6. F; 7. T; 8. F; 9. T; 10. F.

No Magic in Groups

Much of the success of any organization depends on how effectively individuals work in groups. The basis of productivity is often the collective, cooperative effort of groups. If they are managed effectively, groups can reach levels of productivity that exceed what individuals can accomplish working by themselves.

Although groups are often highly productive, they are not automatically effective because people are together. Forming a group will not necessarily solve problems or increase output, although some people seem to attribute superior virtues to togetherness. In some organizations the response to problems is, "Let's form a group."

The *"do-it-in-a-group" disease* plagues many companies. Every organization is a potential victim, and the destruction of individual effort can result. "Do-it-in-a-group" is not a new disease. Organizations in all fields and of all sizes are constantly forming new groups. Anyone who refuses to affiliate with all the appropriate groups can become an object of curiosity, if not suspicion.

What is the basic cause of "do-it-in-a-group?" Can it be stamped out or controlled? It should not be destroyed, because in some cases the pool of intelligence, or ignorance, as the case may be, aids in the solution of problems and contributes to the understanding of the people involved. The group also has certain psychological values for the participants and especially for the leader who can reaffirm a status position in the group. There may be some who need the psychological security provided by groups. There may also be a need to let people know where they stand on a variety of group-supported issues.

A group can only serve a useful function when it is well organized and concerned with a problem that can best be solved on the level of group interaction. A group should not deal with problems that could be better solved on an individual level. Groups cannot and should not take the place of individual initiative.

Organizations which are group conscious and suffer from "do-it-in-a-group" should ask the following questions:

1. Are the groups composed of people who are willing to do nothing individually, but as a group can meet and decide that nothing can be done?
2. Are the groups popular because the individuals are afraid to go out on a limb?
3. Do the groups engage in transferring problems from one graveyard to another?
4. Are the groups a storehouse of knowledge because the individuals bring so much knowledge in and take so little out?
5. Are the groups considered useful in proportion to the time they consume rather than their capacity for productivity?

Groups and Individual Productivity

Our discussion of groups has emphasized the great differences among groups as well as among individuals in groups. The *productivity* of a given group is often hard to predict because of these differences. Under certain conditions one group may be successful while another may fail. It is difficult to make accurate generalizations about group productivity.

Groups have the potential to destroy individual responsibility and creativity, and at the same time increase individual initiative and productivity. Many researchers have compared the productivity of individuals working alone with the productivity of individuals working together in a group. When research on group versus individual productivity is analyzed, one cannot conclude that groups are superior to individuals working alone. The productivity of a group is only *potentially* greater than the productivity of individuals working alone. To achieve its potential a group must use its resources effectively and motivate members to achieve group goals.[1] Furthermore, the influence of members on each other in decision making should result in "better" decisions.

1. *Groups have potentially greater resources.* A group is not necessarily more productive than individuals working alone. There are no group characteristics, which in and of themselves, make it productive. Group situations can result in very low levels of productivity. A group has potentially greater resources than individuals operating alone for two basic reasons:

    a. In groups, division of labor is possible. Effective *division of labor* involves individuals doing jobs they are best prepared to do. Individuals can specialize, each performing the job for which he or she has the highest aptitude and training.

    b. In group situations, *duplication of effort* is also possible. If part of the group is not meeting required schedules, employees can help each other. If a production line slows down, one way to speed it up is to move additional people from another production line. The basic concept of duplication of effort is that when something "catches fire," everybody goes to put out the fire. In a group, people can be shifted to the area where they are the most needed. However, duplication of effort can become an excuse for not solving basic problems in an organization. It is possible to keep shifting people rather than deal with the basic problems. Duplication of effort often turns into wasted effort when too many people are assigned to a job.

2. *Social motives in groups influence individual performance.* Motivational effects occur as a result of social motives evoked in a group. Primary social motives include esteem, affection, and recognition. Social motives can act as an incentive for increased production, or they can satisfy social needs without contact with other people. Satisfaction of affection or friendship needs requires interaction with others. In a close-knit or cohesive work group, an individual may also obtain both status and recognition from the group.

    A group can be productive from the individual's point of view and be unproductive in terms of achieving organizational

group productivity depends on effective resource utilization

division of labor

duplication of effort

social motives affect productivity

objectives. Members of a work group may get together and say, "We're tired of busting a gut, and we're all going to slow down!" The individual who doesn't slow down is "going to get it from the group." The group may withhold status, affection, or recognition from those who refuse to restrict productivity. Cohesive groups can be highly effective in achieving their own objectives when they slow down or, conversely, choose to increase productivity.

Management's problem is to make group objectives consistent with the objectives of the organization. This is often a difficult task. The objectives do not have to be identical, but must lead to the same end result.

groups can perform error-correcting function

3. *Decisions in groups can be better because of social influences.* A potential advantage of groups is social influence for better decisions. Groups involved in decision making usually demand supporting evidence. If a procedure is to be changed, individuals in the group will want evidence to support the desirability of the change. A group can perform an *error-correcting function* by insisting that decisions are consistent with the objectives of the organizations. A group may also use the experience of members to prevent the repetition of mistakes. If group members are committed to the achievement of organizational objectives, it usually exerts a positive influence on decision making. Figure 12.1 illustrates the potential for group productivity.[2]

Group Productivity

group productivity can exceed that of individuals working alone

The *productivity of a group* depends on the resources available to it and its ability to use those resources to achieve group objectives. By effectively using the available resources, the group's productivity may exceed that of the individuals working alone. The way group members relate to one another and to the task can result either in effective coordination to achieve objectives or in wasted effort.

Two major factors that contribute to the productivitiy of a group are (1) individual effectiveness in accomplishing tasks and (2) interpersonal relations of group members.

Contributions that are made to the total group productivity by individuals working alone vary with the nature of the task and the organization of the group. It is possible that many of the outputs of groups can be produced by individuals working alone. It is also possible for

group bonus effect

groups to produce outputs that are better than those the best group member can produce alone and which are not the result of a simple addition of individual member productivity. A *group bonus effect* occurs when the group is able to achieve objectives which could not have been achieved by an individual working alone or by a combination of individual efforts. Group bonus effect is achieved through cooperation, inter-

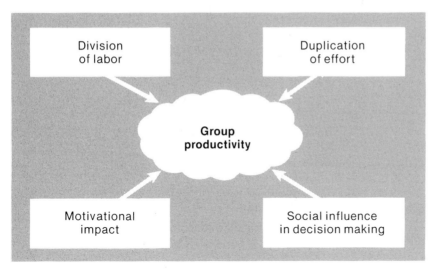

Figure 12.1 Potential for group productivity.

dependent effort, division of labor, and the motivational influences of the group.

As illustrated in Figure 12.2, the productivity of a group depends on individual task performance and the effectiveness of group members working together. A group has tasks to be accomplished in order to achieve group objectives. The employees in the group must be able to develop interpersonal relationships that facilitate productivity.

Task Factors Affecting Productivity

Individual responses to task accomplishment depend on the *motivation* to do the task, the *ability* to perform the task, and the *support* received. Obstacles or problems that create difficulties for individuals in trying to accomplish tasks can be grouped into three areas: (1) lack of task structure, including vague objectives; (2) lack of adequate resources (either physical or human) to support task accomplishment; and (3) lack of skill or training to accomplish the task.[3]

motivation, ability, and support affect task performance

Structure and Objectives

Although it may appear desirable to have unstructured groups with virtually unlimited freedom in performing tasks, the resulting productivity is usually very low. Without specific objectives, group members have only a vague idea of what accomplishments are expected. As the old saying goes, "If you don't know where you are going, there is no way to get there."

Some people may be initially attracted to an unstructured group atmosphere, but they become dissatisfied when they realize that there are no goals to be reached. The lack of specific goals usually results in confused and frustrated group members.

structure and objectives are necessary

An example of an unstructured situation can occur in a college course. How would students react if the instructor announced to a class, "We will just play it by ear in this course and decide as we go along what will be covered and how it will be covered. At the end of the course, a grading procedure will be determined. The course will be unstructured, with no course outline and no specified testing procedures."

The same situation can occur in an organization. If work groups do not have specific goals, people are uncertain about the way in which they are going to be evaluated. They question whether their jobs are going to exist over a period of time. Groups are more productive when there are specific and measurable objectives that are understood by

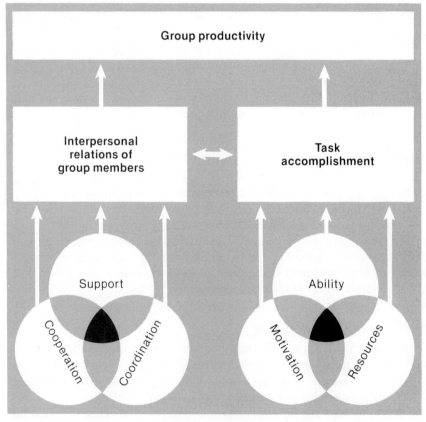

Figure 12.2 Factors affecting group productivity.

group members. The objectives are most meaningful to people when they are tied to individual evaluations and reward systems.

When the structure of a task is clear and specific, productivity is higher. To determine if tasks are specific, individuals have been asked what they are expected to do to contribute to group productivity. Responses like "I am supposed to do a good job" or "I am supposed to work hard" may indicate ambiguous tasks. When people are uncertain of roles in performing group tasks, productivity usually suffers.

factors needed for effective structure

Two factors are needed for effective structure: (1) specific and measurable group objectives and (2) a definition of specific tasks that are necessary to accomplish objectives.

Goal Setting at Tenneco

Setting goals for any company is no easy matter. The problems are compounded when that company is a multi-industry firm employing approximately 82,000 people and operating eight major industries. One such firm, Tenneco, based in Houston, Texas, has developed a unique approach to the problem of goal setting.

The system emphasizes that personal development goals should receive equal weight with quantitative, organizational goals. Measurements used to evaluate progress should look at both development and organizational objectives.

The program was designed by a task force comprised of representatives from all of Tenneco's companies. The task force stressed that the program would depend on continual communication between managers and employees to develop good measures of performance, taking into account the unique characteristics of each job and each worker. It was hoped that the program would help prepare more employees for promotion, since workers set their own achievement goals.

The task force also emphasized the following four conditions to help the program succeed: (1) management support at all levels, (2) minimum of procedure and paperwork, (3) training for managers in how to implement the program, and (4) continual communication and feedback among participants.

When the companies began to implement the program, Tenneco took five key steps to make sure the goal-setting technique got off to the best possible start.

1. Management determined if the employees and the organization were suited for this particular program.
2. They prepared employees for goal setting through training, communication, and action plans.
3. They emphasized the characteristics of goals that should be understood.

4. They conducted reviews to modify the goals.
5. They performed final reviews to check on goals, modifications, and accomplishments.[4]

Support Resources

A group must use physical and human resources to achieve objectives. Physical resources include space, equipment, and supplies. Human resources include the people directly involved in performing the tasks to achieve objectives and the support personnel.

When the level of support is reduced, one effect may be to reduce the level of individual motivation. Where the quality of support resources is low, the message communicated to group members may be that the task performance expectation is for low-quality work. As an employee of a machine shop put it, "When you give me junky equipment to work on, you're telling me you want a junky job done." The way resources are allocated is a key element in the nonverbal communication on any job.

An interesting experiment was performed with highly trained machinists. New machinery was rigged so half of the machinery would periodically break down. (This was done by electronically rigging the equipment to stop operating on a random basis.) The machinists that worked on the equipment that broke down periodically were provided with a recreation room equipped with all kinds of facilities. When the equipment broke down, they were allowed to go to the recreation room and still receive full pay. The equipment was down one-fourth of each day. Half of the machinists worked on equipment that was well maintained and operated approximately eight hours each day. Which group had the highest productivity per hour when the machines were operating?

The machinists that worked the full eight hours a day on the machines that were well maintained had the highest productivity per hour. The group that had approximately two hours off each day to go play in the recreation room had the lowest productivity per hour. The eight-hour-a-day people had the highest productivity in terms of both quality and quantity. When people are provided with low-quality support facilities and equipment, the quality and quantity of task accomplishment will be below the individual's ability to achieve.

support personnel
In most groups, the ability to achieve objectives in a group situation is dependent to a large extent on support personnel. An engineer may need the support of technical writers, draftsmen, and test personnel. When cost reductions are necessary, it is the draftsman rather than the engineer who is cut from the work force first. Why the draftsman?

It is usually based on the assumption that people with the lowest qualifications are the easist to replace. When the lowest qualified support personnel are cut, it is necessary for highly qualified technical and professional people to do support jobs.

Some organizations try to save money by not hiring adequate numbers of support personnel. Such organizations often become overstaffed with highly trained and highly paid technical and professional workers. When they lack support personnel, the technical and professional employees spend valuable time doing support tasks. They are often inefficient and dissatisfied in performing support jobs. They become frustrated, and motivation effectiveness drops.

Organizations have been criticized for not using enough support personnel, even in medicine. Doctors may be doing tasks that could be done by nurses. Nurses may be doing tasks that could be done by orderlies. Doctors may also be doing tasks that could be done by accounting support personnel. Nurses may find themselves doing tasks that could be done by administrative assistants.

both professional and support staff are necessary

Organizations need both professional staff and support staff to develop effective work groups. Resources must be appropriately allocated to ensure that the concept of division of labor is used effectively.

Skill and Training

The prerequisite for motivating employees is that they have the ability to accomplish an assigned task. If a letter is to be typed, the employee assigned the task of typing must know how to type before he or she can be motivated. If an employee lacks the skill and training to perform an assignment adequately, he or she cannot be motivated.

you cannot motivate someone unless they have the ability to accomplish the task

Individuals are often placed in jobs without adequate evaluation of their ability to perform the required tasks. It is usually assumed, often incorrectly, they will be trained once they get on the job. Individuals are also promoted without adequate training to positions that differ significantly from the jobs they previously held. A skilled machinist who does an outstanding job may be promoted to a supervisory position without training or analysis of his or her skills or readiness for supervision. Often, promotions take place on the assumption that the individual will learn on the job. This usually results in low effectiveness from first-line supervisors who are promoted from line positions without being given adequate management training.

There should always be an evaluation of an individual's ability to perform the tasks required in a position. The best salesperson in an organization may not have the abilities needed to be an effective sales manager. The tasks involved in sales and the tasks involved in sales management are not the same. An individual would not be expected to be able to play the piano just because he or she is a good basketball

to be an effective supervisor requires more than having been a good employee

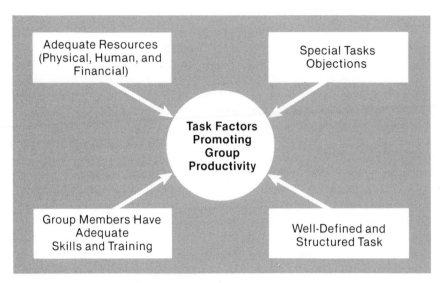

Figure 12.3 Task factors that facilitate group productivity.

player. By the same reasoning, it should not be assumed that just because a person is skilled in the technical aspect of a job, he or she is able to manage effectively. Task factors promoting group productivity are presented in Figure 12.3.

Interpersonal Relations and Productivity

cooperative effort necessary for group productivity

The achievement of group objectives depends not only on individual task performance but also on how well group members can work together. In any group the effort of individuals must be coordinated.

Developing interpersonal relations which produce cooperative effort is difficult in any group. Members must devote time which could be spent on accomplishing tasks to interacting with others. The coordination and cooperation resulting from interpersonal relations must balance the time consumed in developing and maintaining them. An employee working alone can direct his or her efforts solely to accomplishing a task. When working with others, however, it is necessary to deal with interpersonal relations.

Group members usually *understand task problems* much better than *interpersonal conflict*. Yet, effectively dealing with interpersonal problems can contribute to productivity as much as solving task problems. In many groups, interpersonal conflicts are the major obstacles to achieving group objectives.

These conflicts arise from a wide range of factors, including conflicts in attitudes, individualistic motivation, and status differences.[5]

Differences in Attitudes and Values

When people are in groups, there are nearly always differences in attitudes and values. These differences provide the potential for interpersonal conflicts. When conflicts arise and individuals spend time arguing with each other, it detracts from efforts to achieve group objectives.

One approach that can minimize attitude conflicts is to control group membership. A group can be composed of members with similar backgrounds and attitudes. When people agree with each other, the possibility of conflicts is usually lessened. If groups are composed of similar individuals, however, they lack the variety of inputs necessary for creative problem solving.

minimizing conflicts

When attitude conflicts arise, management can handle the problem by requiring that both parties assume responsibility for developing methods to resolve their conflicts and work together cooperatively. To do this, management must first develop a climate in which each individual feels responsible for supporting efforts leading to cooperative work relations.

A manager must be concerned about the effect of interpersonal conflict on group productivity, but should not try to get people to agree for agreement's sake. Group members must be able to have attitude differences and still work effectively with each other. At the most basic level, it should be a responsibility of each group member not to interfere with anyone else's work.

Off-the-job conflicts often influence job performance. A conflict arose between two engineers when they coached opposing little-league football teams. One of the engineers accused the other of coaching his team to play rough and dirty. As a result of the outside conflict, they began interfering with each other's work. They did not provide each other with information needed to complete engineering designs and continually argued about how to coach a little-league football team. It reached a point where they sabotaged each other's effectiveness by withholding test data or providing inaccurate test results.

off-the-job-conflicts can affect job productivity

At first the manager ignored the conflict, hoping it would go away. But when it was apparent that the conflict was not subsiding, he decided to place the responsibility for solving the problem on the engineers. The manager met with them and made it clear that whatever their personal differences, the reduction in productivity must be stopped. He gave the engineers a room to meet in and assigned them responsibility for determining how they were going to eliminate the conflict. He pointed out that if they could not solve the problem, he would have to take action, which could include termination.

managers should avoid "getting in the middle" of employee conflict

The manager was amazed at how quickly the engineers developed a plan to cooperate. The manager did not have to get "in the middle" of an employee conflict. Managers can deal with conflict by placing responsibility with employees.[6]

Individualistic Motivation

When rewards are based on individual productivity and working with others in a group is *not* rewarded, there is usually high *individualistic motivation.* Situations that promote individualistic motivation are characterized by people *not* being rewarded for cooperation or coordination. As a result, cooperation is reduced, and people concentrate only on their own productivity. When cooperation is necessary to achieve group objectives, the conditions do not exist that are necessary to obtain the desired cooperation.

high individualistic motivation reduces cooperation

If rewards are provided that promote high individualistic motivation, it is more productive to have people working independently than interdependently. To achieve group productivity, individuals must be rewarded for cooperating with and supporting the efforts of other group members.

rewards for group achievement

Benefits can be structured so individuals are rewarded for their total contribution to group productivity. Some organizations provide rewards to groups for achievement of group objectives. A technique that some organizations use is to allocate bonuses to work groups for high group productivity. In some cases, the work group is given the opportunity to divide the bonus among members in any way it wants, as long as there is unanimous agreement among the members on the allocations. For group allocation of rewards to work effectively, there needs to be a provision that if the group cannot come to a unanimous agreement, management will decide on the allocations to group members. When the choice is whether the group will agree on how to allocate the bonus or have management decide, it is apparent that group members almost always agree to a group-developed allocation method.

In order to reduce individualistic motivation, it is necessary to reward efforts that support group productivity. Benefits that are usually available include pay raises, promotions, recognition, and job assignments.

Status and Status Symbols

Status affects the interpersonal relations of every member of a group. The privileges often associated with status are used to provide "extra" rewards. A leader may use status to achieve control over group members. Since all groups have members with differing degrees of status, it is a factor that must be dealt with if group objectives are to be achieved.

When people's awareness of status positions is heightened by status symbols, the effect is to increase social distance and reduce interaction. As interaction is reduced, the ability to coordinate is reduced.

High-status individuals in a group have increased power, prestige, and ability to influence group members. High-status differentials often undermine the competition for respect among the group members. Instead of competing for respect with other group members, individuals compete for respect from the high-status individual. Where there are very strong status positions, cooperation among group members is reduced, and individuals compete for the rewards that the leader has the power to provide. When individuals look to high-status members to provide rewards, they usually do not help each other correct errors or improve performance.

The effect of status and status symbols became dramatically clear in one manufacturing firm. Parts designs were sent from the engineering department to the tool shop, which made the tools required to produce the parts. The company had specified that the engineers would certify the drawings by placing their approval stamp on them. The use of this stamp, which was the engineers' "status symbol," made the people in the tool shop more aware of the engineers' status. Before this procedure was required, workers in the tool shop would notify engineering of any suspected errors in a drawing. After awareness of the engineers' status was heightened, the people in the tool shop decided they were supposed to say nothing if they thought there was an error. In one instance they were to make couplings to connect parts they had previously made the tools for. Even though the workers determined that the couplings were the wrong size, they made the tools and sent them to production. Ten thousand parts were made that did not fit and had to be scrapped. Such incidents can happen when errors are known but not corrected because of a heightened emphasis on status. *status symbols can have undesirable effects*

Problems resulting from status cannot be completely eliminated, but they can be reduced. In the situation cited above, the people in the tool shop were irritated by the emphasis on status symbols. Status symbols that create social distance include a bigger name on the door, a key to the executive washroom, the ability to eat in the executive dining room, and a reserved parking space. What do status symbols motivate people to do? They motivate people to work for more status symbols. A system that places a high value on status symbols will motivate people to seek status symbols rather than to be more productive.

Avoiding Interpersonal Relations Problems

One of the most common reasons for interpersonal relations problems is that managers avoid dealing with conflicts. When employees do not get along with each other, a manager may ignore the problem and hope it will go away. Interpersonal relations problems usually adversely affect productivity, and they seldom work themselves out. Employees involved usually find the situation uncomfortable, and the manager who avoids the problem is not accepting the responsibilities of managing. *people problems don't go away because they are ignored*

One reason managers avoid dealing with interpersonal conflict is that they find the situation uncomfortable. If managers are uncertain about their ability to handle interpersonal relations, they will probably be reluctant to deal with the problems employees have with one another.

Figure 12.4 presents a summary of interpersonal conflicts and methods of dealing with them. Most managers can identify interpersonal relations problems and determine approaches to solve them. However, in most areas of human activity, people do not practice what they know. Students usually know how to make better grades in a course, but often fail to do it. Although most managers know how to manage more effectively, they often avoid dealing with interpersonal relations problems.[7]

One of the most honest answers to the question, "Why don't you manage as effectively as you know how?" came from the manager who replied, "Because I don't want to." When asked why he didn't want to, the manager answered, "I would rather spend my time and effort doing more enjoyable things."

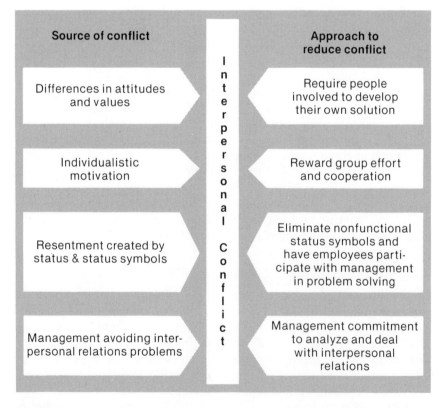

Figure 12.4 Sources of interpersonal conflict and approaches to reduce conflict.

If is difficult to determine methods to bridge the gap between knowing how to manage and putting that knowledge into practice.

Important interpersonal relations factors that promote group productivity are presented in Figure 12.5.

Characteristics Frequently Observed in Productive Groups[8]

- Group members accept leadership responsibilities.
- Relationships among group members are relaxed and cooperative.
- Members express loyalty to the group and support group activities.
- There is mutual confidence in the ability of group members.
- Group members trust each other.
- There is understanding of and agreement with group goals.
- A supportive atmosphere exists where group members help each other to succeed.
- Members communicate openly and directly with each other.
- Group members understand and accept the norms and values of the group.
- Members of the group help each other to develop their full potential.
- The group sets challenging goals.
- There is a strong team spirit.

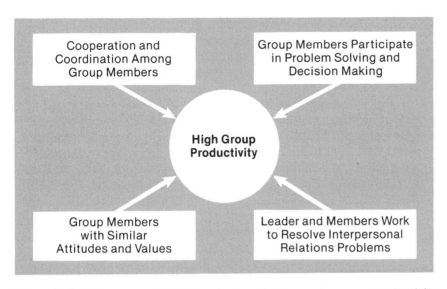

Figure 12.5 Interpersonal relations factors that promote group productivity.

Effective Group Leadership

The research on *group leadership* has produced a variety of findings that contribute to our understanding of leadership effectiveness in groups. Hundreds of research projects have been conducted to identify the behaviors of effective group leaders.[9] The research strongly supports the necessity for group leaders to adapt their behavior to the specific situation and the group members. With the caution to adapt leadership behavior, the following are generalizations from the research studies on group leadership that can be applied in most situations.

- There are NO universal traits of leaders, but some leadership behaviors do contribute to group effectiveness in most situations.

   For example: Unlike ineffective leaders, effective leaders let group members know what is expected of them, inform group members of changes, explain reasons for decisions, and get members' reactions before going ahead with changes.
- Leadership effectiveness depends upon group members perceiving the leader as competent and fair.

   These perceived qualities are not independent but affect each other. It is not a question of whether the leader is "really" competent and fair but whether group members *believe* the leader is competent and fair. A leader's competence is judged in large part by whether the leader can distinguish between effective and ineffective performance. The leader's fairness is usually evaluated on the basis of how the leader distributes rewards and punishments in relation to individual needs and the performance of group members.
- For a leader to be effective, group members must perceive the leader's behavior as consistent and predictable.

   If the leader's behavior is predictable and consistent, the group can generally function without unnecessary disturbances. There is more certainty in the group and ongoing activities will be smoother.
- The leader's *actions* are the primary form of communication to indicate the behaviors desired of group members.

   It is by actions that the leader indicates priorities and the activities that are most important. Effective leaders communicate through their *behaviors* as a way of securing commitment to joint action and achievement of group goals. Leaders who can translate information into action are more effective than leaders who depend on talking and writing to communicate with group members.
- There are situations where group leadership is most effectively exercised by "keeping hands off."

   Effective leadership requires giving group members the opportunity to develop and grow. Restraint is one of the hardest things for most leaders to practice. There is often a strong temptation to overlead—to "do something" as an exercise of authority and leadership.

- Autocratic leadership is necessary and effective in some situations.

    Although participative leadership can be effective with most groups, it is not effective in all situations. In a crisis situation an autocratic style is usually effective. Crisis creates conditions that call for prompt and decisive action. An autocratic style may be more effective in cases when the group leader has the information and ability to make high-quality decisions and group members are willing to accept the leader's judgment.

- Effective group leaders develop a "sense of what might occur" and plan for possible future events.

    Leadership effectiveness requires that plans are developed for contingencies. These plans may not be needed, but developing alternatives contribute to effectiveness by providing options for the group and identifying possible pitfalls.

- Effectiveness as a group leader depends on having ability to exert social influence.

    Skills in social influence include developing peer relationships, carrying out negotiations, motivating group members, resolving conflicts, and disseminating information. Without the ability to influence the behavior of group members, a leader has no hope of being effective.

Suggestions for Developing Effective Group Leadership

These guidelines indicate leader behaviors that usually have a positive effect on group productivity. Although these behaviors are not equally applicable in all group situations, they are frequently exhibited by effective group leaders.

- Make a genuine effort to understand group members as individuals.
- Try to match individuals to the group activities for which they are best suited.
- Involve group members in decisions that affect them.
- Develop high standards and high expectations for performance.
- Encourage and support individual efforts to improve performance.
- Listen to suggestions, answer questions, and discuss problems.
- Provide individuals with frequent feedback on performance.
- Recognize and give credit for outstanding performance.
- Make a special effort to help individuals who have low performance.
- Maintain two-way communication and accept feedback from group members.

- Avoid trying to impose personal attitudes and values on group members.
- Make decisions as fast as possible.
- Develop priorities and time limits for group activities.
- Anticipate problems whenever possible and take preventive action.
- Accept responsibility for your decisions and their consequences.
- Avoid "putting individuals down."
- Explain reasons for decisions.
- "Get the facts" before criticizing.
- Show respect for individuals and for their ideas and feelings.

Quick Review

    I. No Magic in Groups
       A. The basis for productivity in most organizations is the collective, cooperative effort that takes place in groups.
       B. To test whether or not a group will be effective, the following questions should be asked:
          1. Is the group made up of nondeciders who feel that nothing can be done?
          2. Does the group provide a security blanket?
          3. Does the group transfer problems from one place to another?
          4. Do the group members fail to use pooled knowledge?
          5. Is the group judged by time in meetings rather than productivity?
    II. Groups and Individual Productivity
       A. Individual differences make prediction of group effectiveness uncertain.
       B. Groups can both destroy and increase individual initiative.
       C. The productivity of a group is potentially greater than the productivity of individuals.
          1. Groups have potentially greater resources. Both division of labor and duplication of effort are possible.
          2. Social motives in groups influence individual performance.
          3. Decision in groups can be better because of social influences.

III. Group Productivity
  A. The productivity of a group depends on the availability of resources and the ability of the group to use those resources.
  B. A group bonus effect occurs when groups achieve more than an equivalent number of individuals can achieve working alone.
IV. Task Factors Affecting Productivity
  A. Task factors affecting productivity include:
    1. Task structure and objectives
    2. Adequate resources
    3. Skill and training
  B. Structured groups with clear objectives are more effective than unstructured groups with vague objectives.
  C. An organization must have support resources that allow groups and individual specialists to concentrate fully on their primary tasks.
  D. Skill and training is mandatory for both group and individual effectiveness.
V. Interpersonal Relations and Productivity
  A. The basic organizational unit is the individual, whether working in a group (interdependent) or functioning independently.
  B. Interpersonal relations have a direct effect on cooperation, coordination, and productivity.
    1. Conflict in groups may arise because of differences in attitudes and values. One solution to conflict is to require that the people involved develop their own solutions.
    2. Individualistic motivation destroys group effectiveness. Rewards should support group rather than individual activity.
    3. Status and status symbols often create psychological distance and resentment.
    4. The poorest course of action for managers to take is to avoid interpersonal relations problems.
VI. Effective Group Leadership
  A. No universal leadership traits have been identified, but some leader behaviors are effective in most situations.
  B. Where group members perceive the leader as competent and fair, the leader is more effective.
  C. Consistent and predictable behavior by the group leader contributes to effectiveness.

D. Leaders indicate desired behaviors by their actions.
E. Effective leadership requires giving group members the opportunity to develop and grow.
F. In some situations, autocratic leadership is necessary and effective.
G. Effective leaders develop contingency plans.
H. To be effective, a group leader must be able to exert social influence.

Key Terms

"Do-it-in-a-group" disease

Group productivity

Division of labor

Duplication of effort

Social motives

Error-correcting function

Group bonus effect

Group productivity

Group objectives

Support resources

Interpersonal conflict

Individualistic motivation

Group leadership

Discussion Questions

1. What are some examples of using groups to do tasks or solve problems that could be better dealt with by individual effort?
2. Why is the productivity of a group *potentially* greater than the productivity of individuals working alone?
3. Describe a specific example of the use of division of labor.
4. How can the motivational impact of a work group adversely affect the achievement of organizational objectives?
5. Describe a situation where the output of a group could be better than the best group member could have produced alone and which could not have resulted from simply adding the productivity of individual members.
6. How can task structure affect group productivity?
7. What effect can the lack of support resources have on the motivation of members of a group?
8. Why would a manager avoid dealing with interpersonal conflict?
9. List all the methods you can think of for reducing conflicts that could result from differences in attitudes and values.
10. What action can management take to reduce individualistic motivation?

11. Give an example of a conflict in a group that resulted from status differences.

12. What can be done to bridge the gap between knowing management concepts and putting them into practice?

Case Incidents

Who Is in Control?

About six months ago Wanda Benson was hired as supervisor of the employee benefits section in a city government personnel department. The benefits section handles employee health insurance, life insurance, retirement benefits, educational benefits, and worker compensation claims.

Six employees have worked together in the section for the past five years. They have become a very close-knit cohesive group, and they cooperate well with other city employees. The benefits section has established an excellent reputation, and there have been few complaints about how they handle employee benefits. One employee, Sharon Hill, has become the informal leader of the section, and the other employees look to her for advice and assistance.

Since Ms. Benson became supervisor, she has had great difficulty getting employees to follow her orders. During a training session on new procedures for processing health insurance claims, Sharon Hill interrupted the meeting and told the other employees that Ms. Benson did not understand the new procedures. Later, when Sharon had the employees to her house for dinner, she advised them not to follow Ms. Benson's instructions because her information was incorrect. As a result, the employees agreed to ignore the new procedures Ms. Benson had described.

The next day Bill Evans, an employee in the benefits section, went to the city personnel manager and complained that Ms. Benson could not control the operation of the section. He suggested to the personnel manager that Ms. Benson should be removed as supervisor and that the employees wanted Sharon Hill to become the supervisor of the benefits section.

After a meeting with the personnel manager, Ms. Benson told a colleague, "I've lost the respect of the personnel manager, and I can't control the employees in my section. Maybe I am not cut out to be a supervisor."

1. If you were the city personnel manager, what action would you take? Why?

2. How could Ms. Benson prevent this situation from developing?
3. Should Ms. Benson discipline Sharon Hill? If so, how?
4. What are alternative courses of action Ms. Benson could take to gain the confidence of the employees? Which course of action should she try first and why?

Mr. Inconsiderate

Nick Baca is the manager of the research and development department of a toy manufacturing company. The most productive and creative designer in the department is Bill Dixon. Bill is very demanding and inconsiderate of other employees. He expects his work to be done immediately, even if it means other people's work must wait. Bill frequently demands that people work overtime on his projects. Everyone in the department recognizes that Bill is extremely productive and creative, but they also resent his high-handed manner.

Representatives from the drafting department have approached Mr. Baca with an ultimatum. They stated, "Bill Dixon's work is no longer going to receive special treatment or be done ahead of other people's work without your specific approval. We want Bill's work to go through the manager first, and he is not to set foot in the drafting room."

1. What do you feel are the reasons for the inconsiderate behavior of Bill Dixon?
2. If Nick Baca does not take any action, what do you think the other employees will do?
3. Do you think Bill Dixon's behavior can be changed? If so, how?
4. What action should Nick Baca take to reduce the conflict and maintain the productivity of the department?

Fatherly Advice

Ann Steel is the manager of the personal loans department for a bank located in a large southwestern city. As a result of a suggestion from the bank president, Ann hired George Casper as a loan officer. George had previously been vice-president of a bank in a small southern town and moved to the southwest for his health.

From his first day on the job, George gave unrequested and unwanted advice to the other employees in the department. He would look through the loan applications on the desks of other loan officers and provide advice on their dispositions. When his advice was rejected, he would comment, "People just don't respect their elders anymore."

George did not limit his advice to "how to run the bank"; he also attempted to be a personal advisor to employees. He made suggestions on the clothing people should wear, where they should go out to eat, who their friends should be, and on every aspect of their personal life. Employees tried to avoid George whenever they could and alerted others to his approach with, "Look out, here comes Father George."

It was obvious that George interfered with other people's work. Employees began mentioning to Ann that if they received any more fatherly advice from George, they were "going to hit him in the mouth."

1. Why is George Casper's behavior creating conflict?
2. If management takes no action, what will be the reaction of the other employees?
3. What action could Ms. Steel take to solve the interpersonal conflict in the department?

Exercise *Group Productivity*

If you were the supervisor of a work group, how would you manage the following situations to maximize productivity? Describe the specific actions you would take in each situation.

1. You are supervisor of the appliance section in a department store. Two of your best employees, Dave and Gary, get into an argument over who should work the late shifts on Friday night. You discover they have been trading work assignments without your approval. Dave now feels Gary is being unfair; Gary won't trade with him so Dave can go to a concert on Friday night. Dave has said that if Gary doesn't trade, he will never help him again.
2. You supervise a machine shop where the old equipment frequently breaks down. The machinists have told you that they are *not* going to try to produce high quality parts unless the company gets some new equipment. Your boss has told you that new equipment cannot be purchased until the quality of parts improves so the company can get additional orders.
3. You supervise nine typists who are responsible for typing correspondence to customers. The typists have formed two cliques hostile toward each other. You have discovered that the reason for their hostility is that they support different candidates in the local school board election. What would you do?

4. You supervise a group of seven insurance salespersons who all consistently exceed their sales goals. During the last year, one salesperson, Jennifer, outproduced all the others and received an award from the company as the top seller of the year. Now the other salespeople are interfering with her work by not taking phone messages for her and by discouraging potential customers from talking with her. It looks as if they are doing everything possible to prevent Jennifer from making sales. What would you do?

Endnotes

1. For analysis of group productivity see Dennis W. Organ and W. Clay Hammer, *Organizational Behavior: An Applied Psychological Approach*, rev. ed. (Plano, Tex.: Business Publications, 1982), Chapter 13, and James H. Davis, *Group Performance* (Reading, Mass: Addison-Wesley, 1969).
2. Techniques for group decision making are presented in Don F. Seaman, *Working Effectively with Task-Oriented Groups* (New York: McGraw-Hill, 1981).
3. For research studies see Alvin Zander, *Groups at Work* (San Francisco: Jossey-Bass, 1979), and Rensis Likert, "The Nature of Highly Effective Groups," in *Readings in Organizational Behavior,* Jerry L. Gray and Frederick A. Starke, eds. (Columbus, Ohio: Charles E. Merrill Publishing Co., 1977).
4. For additional information see John M. Ivancevich, J. Timothy McMahon, J. William Streidle, and Andrew D. Szilaggi, Jr., "Goal Setting: The Tenneco Approach to Personnel Development and Management Effectiveness," *Organizational Dynamics*, Winter 1978, pp. 58–80.
5. Sara Kiesler, *Interpersonal Processes in Groups and Organizations* (Arlington Heights, Ill.: AHM Publishing 1978).
6. For additional approaches to managing conflict see S. P. Robbins, "Conflict Management and Conflict Resolutions Are Not Synonymous Terms," in *The Dynamics of Organizational Theory: Gaining a Macro Perspective,* J. F. Veiga and J. N. Yanouzas, eds. (St. Paul, Minn.: West Publishing Co., 1979) pp. 359–70; Richard B. Robinson, "Conflict Management: Individual Preference and Effectiveness," *Proceedings of the Academy of Management* (1978); and Charles R. Milton, *Human Behavior in Organizations: Three Levels of Behavior* (Englewood Cliffs, N.J.: Prentice-Hall, 1981), Chapter 14.
7. For research on different methods see Ivan D. Steiner, *Group Processes and Productivity* (New York: Academic Press, 1972), and Ernest Stech and Sharon E. Ratliffe, *Working in Groups,* (Skokie, Ill.: National Textbook Company, 1976).

8. For in-depth analysis see P. B. Smith, *Groups Within Organizations* (New York: Harper & Row, 1973), and Linda N. Jewell and H. Joseph Reitz, *Group Effectiveness in Organizations* (Glenview, Ill.: Scott, Foresman and Company, 1981).

9. See Rodney W. Napier and Matti K. Gershenfield, *Groups: Theory and Experience*, 2d ed. (Boston: Houghton Mifflin, 1981), Chapter 5, and Marvin E. Shaw, *Group Dynamics*, 3d ed. (New York: McGraw-Hill, 1981).

Beliefs and Realities

5

13 Management Beliefs About Human Behavior

Learning Objectives

After reading this chapter, you should be able to:

1. Describe how assumptions and beliefs about human behavior affect managers' actions.

2. Explain the operation of the self-fulfilling prophecy.

3. Discuss how the expectations of others affect an individual's behavior.

4. Describe how an individual's high expectations for another person can increase that person's performance.

5. Identify the Theory X and Theory Y assumptions about behavior.

6. Explain how managers' beliefs about behavior affect organizational communication.

7. Analyze the impact of management beliefs on overall organizational performance.

Chapter Topics

Preview and Self-Evaluation

Henry Ford is reputed to have stated that "the average employee wants a job that doesn't require hard work . . . most of all he wants a job that doesn't require him to think." Ford's management philosophy, and the attitudes of his employees, was based on his assumptions concerning people. Ford was not alone in his beliefs. Many managers, then and now, believe that people want to be highly paid for little effort. Research shows that employees tend to act the way managers assume they will act. If a manager assumes employees will be lazy and irresponsible, they will tend to behave exactly as expected. Some managers who, on the other hand, treat employees as if they are eager to work and are seeking responsibility find that their employees are neither lazy nor irresponsible. In Chapter 13 managerial assumptions about behavior and the effects of these assumptions are discussed. Since we like our beliefs to be supported and confirmed, we may behave to make things happen the way we believe they should happen. It is possible that an individual's successes and failures are the result of believing that he or she would succeed or fail. People like to prove themselves right. People may even behave in ways that are not in their best interest in order to support their beliefs about behavior.

The following true false questions should stimulate your thinking about the material in this chapter. Take the test before reading the material, then come back to the questions and answer them again. See if your perceptions have changed.

Answer True or False

1. An individual's behavior is often strongly influenced by the expectations of others.   T   F

2. Many of an individual's beliefs are inherited from his or her parents.   T   F

3. It is possible for individuals to fail or succeed primarily because they *believe* they will fail or succeed.   T   F

4. If managers communicate high standards for individuals, then people will tend to expect more of themselves.   T   F

5. People try to live up to the expectations of individuals important to them, even if those expectations are negative.   T   F

6. There will always be higher productivity if all employees take their break at the same time every morning.   T   F

7. Highly standardized jobs and close supervision make the best use of people's abilities.   T   F

8. When employees are involved in decision making on their jobs, communication and understanding in the work place improve.   T   F

9. Most people must be coerced and threatened before they will do an adequate job.   T   F

10. If managers carefully limit and control the amount of information given to employees, they can increase productivity.   T   F

ANSWERS: 1. T; 2. F; 3. T; 4. T; 5. T; 6. F; 7. F; 8. T; 9. F; 10. F.

Management Beliefs About Human Behavior

Everyone has beliefs about the nature of human behavior. As a result of these beliefs, people develop ways of interacting with others. Beliefs about behavior include the attitudes, assumptions, and values we have about why people work and how to get people to accomplish organizational objectives.

actions are based on beliefs about behavior

Managers base their actions on what they believe about the behavior of employees. Based on these beliefs, managers develop strategies to obtain both personal and organizational objectives, and devise rewards or penalties for employees.

Our beliefs are learned as we interact with our environment. Beliefs that have resulted in the satisfaction of needs are reinforced and maintained. Beliefs learned in organizations are perceived as being consistent, logical, and valid because of the "evidence of experience." We retain the beliefs that help us to develop and maintain a satisfying view of the world.

differences in beliefs result in different methods of dealing with people

Since people have different experiences in interpersonal relations, their beliefs concerning what people want differ. These belief differences lead to different ways of interacting. If a person believes that people are basically dishonest and will take advantage of others, his or her communications will be characterized by suspicion and distrust. A person who believes that people are basically helpful and constructive will relate to people with trust and confidence. Each person's behavior is derived from a set of beliefs which form a philosophy of dealing with people.

Figure 13.1 illustrates the ways a manager's beliefs affect the managerial practices used to achieve productivity. Managerial beliefs about behavior are the bases for developing principles and concepts of effective management. Management practices and procedures are designed to implement principles and concepts. Employee behavior is affected by management actions that implement the practices and procedures. The behavior of employees provides the "evidence" that management may use to evaluate the validity of their beliefs.

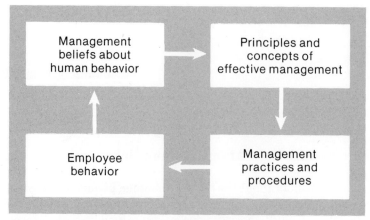

Figure 13.1   The effects of management beliefs.

The Self-Fulfilling Prophecy

The beliefs a person holds often result in actions that lead to further support for the belief. A student, for example, who believes that he is not smart enough to pass a course does not waste time studying. He fails the course and concludes that his belief was correct. This process of "making" a belief come true is referred to as the *self-fulfilling prophecy.* People are often able to make things happen that they believe will happen; they may fail or succeed primarily because they believe they will fail or succeed.

"making" a belief come true

A person's perceptions play a major role in the self-fulfilling prophecy. If an individual believes that a party is going to be dull, it is almost certain that, regardless of what actually happens, the party will be perceived as dull. Perhaps it is; or perhaps the party goer will do everything possible to see that it is. Individuals make prophecies and then ensure that they are fulfilled.

One reason people develop self-fulfilling prophecies is that they obtain satisfaction from "proving" their belief correct. The person who seems to do everything possible to get people to respond negatively may be convinced that other people dislike her. Her behavior encourages people's dislike and confirms the original belief. It may be more satisfying for the individual to support a belief than to be liked.

self-fulfilling prophecies

The operation of the self-fulfilling prophecy takes place in the following four-step sequence:

1. Something is believed to be true.
2. Behavior is based on the belief.
3. Outcomes result from the behavior.
4. Interpretation of the outcomes is perceived to verify the belief.

Placebo Effect

People also tend to behave in ways that are consistent not only with their own expectations but with the expectations of others. This is especially true when the expectation comes from an individual who is perceived to be highly competent and authoritative.

In medicine the effect of a patient's expectations has been recognized by physicians for a long time. The patient's trust and belief in the physician can affect the outcome of a treatment. Doctors have been able to use *placebos,* such as sugar pills or a water injection, to relieve symptoms reported by patients. The success of placebos is often cited as an example of the effects of expectations. If a patient expects the pill to reduce the pain, the pain may "go away."

In an experimental study of patients hospitalized with peptic ulcers, 70 percent had "excellent results lasting over a period of one year" when given injections of distilled water and told that it was a new medicine that would cure their ulcers.[1]

Placebos can produce an effect based on the patient's confidence in the physician and the patient's expectations that the treatment will produce desired results. Placebos have been effective in cases involving a variety of illnesses from cancer to the common cold. An example of the physiological effects of placebos to heal tissue is in the treatment of warts. Painting warts with a bright colored dye and telling patients the wart will be gone by the time the color wears off is as effective as any other wart removal treatment, including surgery.[2]

The reports of the effect of placebos should not lead one to conclude that most people are hypochondriacs or that most illnesses are simply "in the person's head." These studies do provide evidence that the belief in the physician's competence and expectations about results are important factors in healing.

If managers communicate high expectations for individuals, then people will tend to expect more of themselves. Conditions can be created that foster challenging goals and high performance. Most people want to fulfill the expectations of those in positions of authority and responsibility.

Sweeney's Miracle: The Power of Expectations

The case of "Sweeney's miracle" is a dramatic example of expectations influencing performance. James Sweeney was a professor of industrial management and director of the Biomedical Computer Center at Tulane University in the 1960s. Sweeney managed employees whose jobs ranged from maintenance to computer programming. "Sweeney's miracle" involved his expectation that he could train a poorly educated black hospital janitor to be a competent computer operator. He convinced a janitor, George Johnson, to spend his afternoons learning about computers. Because of Sweeney's strong belief, George Johnson's life was profoundly changed.

George was making good progress in learning about computer operations when a university official informed Sweeney that an IQ test had to be passed before operators were allowed in the computer center. George took the test and did not pass. The results were interpreted as an indication that he would not be able to learn computer operations. Sweeney believed otherwise. He had full confidence in his ability to teach and George's ability to learn, and he persuaded the administration to let George continue. Sweeney assured them that George would develop full proficiency as a computer operator. In time, George Johnson became so proficient an operator that he was put in charge of training new employees.[3]

Chapter 13

Expectations and Performance

The way managers interact with employees is affected by what the managers expect of them. If a manager has high performance expectations, employee performance is likely to be excellent. If the manager's expectations are low, performance is likely to be low. Employee performance tends to increase or decrease to meet management's expectations.

An early observation of the effects of expectations on performance involved training machine operators. In 1890, the U.S. Census Bureau began using Hollerith tabulating machines, which required clerks to punch data on cards. The inventor of the machine considered the work very demanding and expected a trained operator could punch about 550 cards a day. After training, the operators produced at the expected rate of 550 cards per day. Some operators began to exceed the expected rate but were discouraged from doing so by their supervisor.

management expectations

To handle an increased requirement for input data, a new group of 200 operators were hired. The new group knew nothing about the machine or the expected output rates. After they were trained, the new operators were not provided with an expectation about performance standards. They were encouraged to punch as many cards as they could each day. The new operators were soon producing 1,400 to 2,100 cards a day without being exhausted.

When limiting expectations are removed and the highest possible productivity is encouraged, performance usually improves. It is important for managers to develop high expectations and avoid developing self-fulfilling prophecies for lower than possible performance.

low expectations can limit productivity

Supervisors' Expectations

Recent studies have repeatedly demonstrated the impact of expectations on performance. An example of the self-fulfilling prophecy occurred when supervisors were told some new employees scored very high on a preemployment exam and that others scored very low.[4]

In fact, what the supervisors were told about employee test scores had no relationship to the actual scores the workers had made on the test. The production records of the employees were evaluated after several months on the job. The analysis indicated that for employees identified as scoring high on the exam, their productivity was significantly higher than the employee average. The productivity of employees identified as scoring low on the exam was lower than average. An analysis of the employee's actual test scores revealed that there was no relationship between individual productivity and the preemployment test score. The results of this study have been interpreted as indicating that a self-fulfilling prophecy resulted from the supervisor's expectations.

J. Sterling Livingston reported how district managers' expectations largely determined the performance of insurance agents.[5] A district manager for an insurance company put the highest producing agents together under the most capable assistant manager in the district. The district manager told this group of "high performers" that they were expected to produce two-thirds of the total sales made in the district the year before. The manager's expectations were realized. The high performers achieved high sales and boosted district performance about 40 percent. The manager's expectations for low producing agents were also realized. The group composed of low producers actually had a decline in sales level.

people try to live up to expectations

The conclusions drawn from this situation were that when people are treated by their managers as super producers, they try to live up to that expectation and do what super producers are expected to do. When people are treated by their managers as low producers, the negative expectation also becomes a self-fulfilling prophecy.

Developing Expectations in Others

The effect of expectations on behavior does not occur by magic. For expectations to have a positive impact on behavior requires more than wishing or thinking positively. How people are treated by others who are important to them, such as friends, family, co-workers, and managers, is a powerful influence on their behavior. As people interact with these individuals, expectations about their behavior are communicated. People will try to fulfill these expectations, whether they are positive or negative. If persons who are important communicate high and realistic performance expectations, individuals will usually set high goals for themselves. If low expectations are communicated, low performance goals may be accepted.

as people interact, expectations are communicated

Developing high performance expectations in others requires actions as well as words. The way people are treated can strongly indicate expectations about their behavior. What a person is asked to do and not asked to do indicates expectations about the person's skills and abilities.

high expectations can be developed

The following are actions that can aid in the development of high performance expectations in others.

- Reinforce and support high performance goals when they are expressed by the individual.
- Be positive in your nonverbal communication, including tone of voice, gestures, and eye contact.
- Develop a positive atmosphere in interpersonal relations by indicating you believe the individual can achieve challenging goals.
- Be a supportive resource to help solve problems and achieve goals. Treat the individual as a "winner."

- When you are in a position of authority, show high expectations by delegating authority and responsibility. Make challenging assignments.
- Provide information that will be helpful to the individual. Time spent explaining can strongly communicate high expectations.
- Listen with interest when the individual discusses performance and goals. Behavior that shows interest and concern communicates expectations for achievement.

Effects of Management Beliefs

A belief about human behavior may be reinforced as a result of a manager's acting as if it were true. If a manager believes that people dislike work and will avoid it, and people respond as shown in Figure 13.2, a principle of closely controlled employee behavior is adopted. The principle is implemented by designing highly standardized jobs with close supervision. Employees respond to the standardization and close supervision with resentment and a lack of interest. The employees' negative reactions reinforce the manager's belief that people dislike work. When the manager's belief is confirmed he or she increases the control procedures, which usually will result in increased negative employee behavior.

Each individual's beliefs about management are unique. There can be as many different belief systems as there are people. But beliefs about the nature of work behavior tend to conform to general patterns. Manager's beliefs tend to be similar because they have similar backgrounds and experience.

individual belief systems are unique

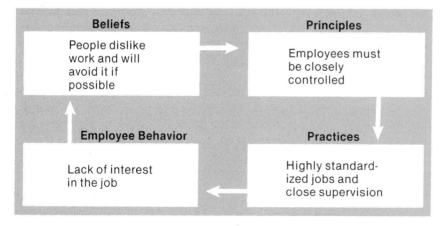

Figure 13.2 Effects of the management belief that "people dislike work."

Theory X and Theory Y

Most discussions of management beliefs and their effects describe two extreme positions. By looking at the two extremes it is possible to see the range of belief differences that can occur. The potential danger in discussing extremes is that it may be concluded that only two alternatives exist. It should be kept in mind that the actual beliefs of most managers fall somewhere between the extremes.

Theory X and Theory Y

The following discussion of two extremes uses the framework developed by Douglas McGregor.[6] He referred to the extremes or boundaries by identifying sets of beliefs as *Theory X* and *Theory Y*. McGregor used the labels X and Y to avoid value-laden terms that could evoke emotional responses.

Behavioral scientists have developed concepts of human behavior that challenge some traditional management concepts. McGregor applied behavioral science findings to develop the concepts of Theory Y. Theory Y has been given many names, including "participative management," "team management," "nonstructured management," and "enlightened management." This theory of management, regardless of its specific title, is based upon a set of beliefs about human behavior in which people are seen as having positive attitudes toward work.

We will briefly outline both the Theory X and Theory Y beliefs concerning human behavior, describe the principles of management that grow out of these beliefs, and illustrate the effects that changing beliefs about human behavior can have upon organizational effectiveness.

Impact on Organizations

Although the controversies over theories of management and beliefs about human behavior are interesting, the primary concern of managers is the impact of these theories on the operations of their organizations. Management's area of interest and responsibility covers areas within the organization and its environment. Since specific management acts reflect beliefs about human behavior, management principles used in an organization cannot be isolated from the total impact of the organization on employees.

Assumptions Underlying Management Actions

Theory X beliefs

The actions of management are based upon its expectations of results, which are in turn based upon beliefs about human behavior. Although individuals vary in their beliefs about others, McGregor formulated what he considered to be the extremes along a spectrum of potential beliefs. Theory X beliefs about human behavior form one end of this spectrum. They include the following:

1. Most people dislike work and will avoid it if they can.
    Management believes that it must have a system *forcing* workers to perform satisfactorily.

2. Most people lack ambition, dislike responsibility, and prefer to be led. Management believes that it must assume responsibility for the worker's performance and behavior.
3. Most people must be controlled and threatened with punishment before they do a good job. Management believes that it must have a system of punishment to successfully alter behavior.
4. Most people are inherently self-centered and are indifferent to organizational goals. Management believes that policies are necessary which attempt to force workers into behavioral molds to meet organizational demands.
5. Most people are gullible, easy to fool, and not very bright. Management believes that the threat of punishment is necessary to produce productive behaviors.
6. Most people are inherently resistant to change. Management believes that individuals will not change their behavior unless forced to do so.

Figure 13.3 illustrates the Theory X view of human behavior.

The other end of the spectrum is occupied by Theory Y. It is based upon the following assumptions about human behavior: *Theory Y beliefs*

1. The average person does not inherently dislike work. Work may be a source of satisfaction. Management believes that indviduals are productive when the job satisfies their motivation.
2. The average person learns not only to accept but also to seek responsibility. Management believes that individuals can be responsible for their behavior.

Figure 13.3   A Theory X view of the nature of human behavior.

Management Beliefs About Human Behavior   361

3. External control and threats of punishment are not the only means to get people to do an adequate job. Management believes that negative behavior on the part of management usually elicits negative behavior from employees.
4. Commitment to work objectives is a function of the rewards associated with their achievement. Management believes that individuals are committed to work objectives when the completion of those objectives satisfies individual motives.
5. The intellectual ability of the average person is only partially used. The capacity for solving problems is widely distributed. Management believes that individuals are capable of performing their tasks without being led by the hand.
6. People resist being forced to change. Management believes that individuals accept change when the primary pressures for change are self-imposed.

Figure 13.4. illustrates the Theory Y view of human behavior.

How Assumptions Affect Management Actions

Theory X management principles

Beliefs about human behavior, in themselves, do not bring about managerial action. Management's actions are only derived from the beliefs.

The assumptions about human behavior which result in Theory X actions have led to the following management principles:

1. Work behavior should be controlled by breaking down jobs into specialized elements.
2. There should be established norms of production.

Figure 13.4   A Theory Y view of the nature of human behavior.

3. Equipment should be designed so that the worker's pace is more or less controlled.
4. Incentive wage payment systems should be used to reward the superior workers and penalize the laggards.
5. Accounting and budgetary controls should be used to make sure that subordinate managers do not deviate from established standards.
6. The amount of information and responsibility given to subordinates should be carefully limited and controlled.
7. The boss can never really trust subordinates.

Under Theory Y beliefs, expectations result in emphasizing the following management concepts:

1. Mutual responsibility and shared objectives should be emphasized.
2. There should be a recognition of the interdependence of people in organizations.
3. High standards of performance should be expected. A minimum of external control should be supplemented by self-imposing controls and a high degree of self-direction.
4. Discussion at all levels should be encouraged in order to obtain cooperation.
5. Company objectives and subobjectives should be communicated to all employees.
6. Organizational authority should be widely delegated and organizational structure decentralized.

Results of the Application of Management Theories

The consequences of Theory X management have plagued businesses and organizations almost since their beginnings. There are many possible results of the application of Theory X management:

possible results of applying Theory X

1. When rule makers are not available, lower management is afraid to make exceptions, even when the underlying purpose of the rule (cost saving, etc.) might be achieved. Thus, lower management avoids making a decision.

   Example: A supervisor does not approve overtime, even though it would result in a job being completed at a lower cost, because of a rule that overtime should be used only in "exceptional" situations.
2. Routine action supports the system of rules rather than the underlying management objectives which the system was set up to attain.

   Example: Employees always take their coffee break from 10:00 to 10:15 in the morning because of a "rule" on the time for coffee breaks, even though there may be situations in which it would be more productive to take a break when it fits a natural break in completing a job.

3. There can be little sense of achievement, which is one of the key factors in job satisfaction for the subordinates.

   Example: Highly standardized jobs and close supervision leave little room for people to use their abilities to the fullest.

4. Management by rules stifles the initiative of subordinates and reduces the possibility of innovations which might increase productivity.

   Example: Concentrating on following numerous rules may mean people are unable to make decisions about their job performance or look for ways to increase productivity.

possible results of applying Theory Y

Some of the possible results of application of Theory Y are:

1. Lower management focuses on achievement of organizational objectives. Employees are accountable for achieving objectives, and exceptions to rules are made to support increased productivity.

2. Routine actions by employees support management objectives.

3. A sense of achievement, which increases motivation, can be developed by employee involvement in on-the-job decisions.

4. Increased productivity results from initiative and development of innovations.

Effect of Management Beliefs on Organizational Communication

One of the areas in which beliefs are most clearly reflected is in organizational communication. The communication behaviors of managers are usually a good indication of their beliefs about the nature of human behavior.

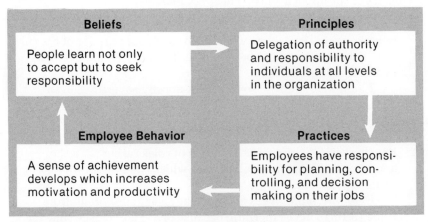

Figure 13.5 Effects of the management belief that "people seek responsibility."

Theory X Approach When management holds Theory X beliefs, the information flow is primarily downward. The downward communication focuses on job-related information and announcements of management decisions. Because communication is usually limited to information that is felt to be absolutely necessary for job performance, the grapevine actively functions to provide information employees are not getting from management. Communication between employees and management is cautious, and marked by distrust. Upward communication usually makes heavy use of the grapevine, since formal channels are not receptive to information from lower levels. Often, "spy systems" develop in which employees secretly report information about operations and other employees to managers. Decisions may be based on partial or inaccurate information, because decision making is concentrated at the top of the organization. Upward communication is very limited.

Theory X communication

Theory Y Approach The manager who has Theory Y beliefs about behavior will usually develop communication systems where information freely flows up, down, and across the organization. Management encourages upward communication by listening to employees and showing interest in their problems. Employee involvement in decision making increases communication and understanding. Open and honest communication takes place. Since decision making is based on information from all levels of the organization, the accuracy and quality of decisions are improved. The Theory Y orientation makes it possible to develop confidence and trust in organizational communication.

Theory Y communication

Effect of Management Style on Overall Performance

In conjunction with the concern about increasing effective management of organizations, behavioral scientists have explored the contributions of individuals necessary for an organization to survive and thrive. In general terms, the individuals must exhibit at least three patterns of behavior if an organization is to function effectively in the long run.[7] We can compare how well Theory X and Theory Y styles fulfill these conditions.

1. *Individuals must join and stay within the system or organization.*
   —Under Theory X it is assumed that individuals will be forced by monetary considerations to join and remain in the organization. However, with competition among organizations for employees, an individual need not join or remain with an organization for purely economic reasons.
   —Under Theory Y the primary motivation for joining and staying within the organization is the satisfaction of individual needs on the job. It is assumed that people's motivation involves more than monetary rewards.

joining and staying with an organization

2. *The individuals in the organization must display dependable behavior in the performance of the roles as defined by the organization. The desired behavior must meet or exceed both quantitative and qualitative objectives of performance.*

—Although performance is a main concern of Theory X management, it attempts to attain this goal indirectly by concentrating on the rules for performance rather than upon the performance itself. Management may attempt to elicit the desired behaviors by using threats of punishment.

—Theory Y management attempts to construct the work situation so effective performance depends upon employees being able to satisfy individual motives.

innovative
behavior

3. *The individuals within the organization must exhibit innovative behavior if the organization is to survive a changing environment. This innovative behavior is required under the assumption that no organization's initial structure is perfect or all-inclusive.*

—Theory X management usually stifles innovative behavior through punishment of behavior not specified by organizational rules.

—Theory Y management not only recognizes the need for innovative behavior but attempts to cultivate it at all levels of the organization.

People Are Complex and Variable

no one best theory
of management

No one set of beliefs is valid for all people or all situations. Since all people are not alike, there is no one best theory of management. People must be managed as they actually are, not as we would like them to be.

Beliefs about human nature are often over generalized. When characteristics of behavior are applied to everyone, the unique character of each individual is ignored. Each individual has a number of needs that motivate behavior at any one time. The importance of individual needs is subject to change depending on the situation. The motivation to perform a job is affected by more than one need, and there are usually a number of methods available to the individual for achieving goals.

An individual may respond positively to a number of different managerial approaches. It is not possible to develop one set of management principles that will work with all individuals in all situations. An individual who responds positively to Theory Y management in one situation may respond equally positively to Theory X management in a different situation. There are times when employees want management to tell them in no uncertain terms what to do and how to do it.

behavior may
vary as a result of
organizational
characteristics

The nature of an individual's behavior may vary as a result of organizational characteristics and management expectations. The self-fulfilling prophecy effect can result in individuals adapting their behavior to meet the conditions existing in the organization. The characteristics exhibited by employees in adapting to an organization are affected by the type of economic rewards, the methods available to satisfy social needs, and the opportunities for achievement.

Beliefs about human behavior are often not useful because they are oversimplifications and overgeneralizations. Managers should be able to recognize the qualities that make each employee different. Flexibility is essential to meet the demands of different situations and to make use of employees' unique abilities.

Quick Review

   I. Management Beliefs about Human Nature
      A. People develop ways of interacting with others as a result of their beliefs about human nature.
      B. Managers base their actions on beliefs about the behavior of employees.
      C. Management beliefs determine managerial principles and concepts from which practices and procedures are derived that influence employee behavior. Employee behavior, in turn, reinforces management beliefs.
  II. The Self-Fulfilling Prophecy
      A. The beliefs a person holds often result in actions that lead to further support for the belief. People often make things happen that they expect or believe will happen.
      B. Self-fulfilling prophecies are characterized by the following steps:
          1. Something is believed to be true.
          2. Behavior is based on the belief.
          3. Outcomes result from the behavior.
          4. Interpretation of the outcomes is perceived to verify the belief.
      C. People tend to live up or down to the expectations of others. These expectations can have a "placebo" effect on a person's behavior.
 III. Expectations and Performance
      A. Employee performance is strongly influenced by managers' expectations.
      B. When managers have high expectations, employees will also expect more of themselves.
      C. High performance expectations can be communicated by actions as well as words.
      D. Managers can develop high performance expectations in others by:
          1. Reinforcing and supporting an individual's own expectations.
          2. Being positive in nonverbal communication.

3. Indicating through positive interpersonal relations that the individual can achieve the goals set.
4. Acting as a supportive resource.
5. Delegating authority and responsibility.
6. Providing information.
7. Listening to the individual discuss performance and goals.

IV. Effects of Management Beliefs
   A. A manager can reinforce a belief about human nature by acting as if that belief were true.
   B. Negative beliefs about human nature tend to produce highly controlling management policies and procedures.
   C. Beliefs about the nature of work behavior tend to conform to general patterns.

V. Theory X and Theory Y
   A. Theory X beliefs include:
      1. Most people dislike work.
      2. They lack ambition.
      3. They must be controlled.
      4. They are self-centered.
      5. They are not very bright.
      6. They resist change.
   B. Theory Y beliefs include:
      1. The average person does not inherently dislike work.
      2. The average person can learn to seek responsibility.
      3. External controls are not the only means to get people to work.
      4. Commitment to objectives is a function of rewards.
      5. The intelligence of most employees is only partially used.
      6. People resist being forced to change.
   C. Each set of assumptions affects management actions in different ways. Theory X relies on external controls; Theory Y relies on self-control, leadership, and responsibility.
   D. Theory X is punishment oriented; Theory Y is reward oriented.
   E. Theory X communication is from the top down and fosters suspicion and mistrust. Theory Y communication is free-flowing among all levels and fosters openness and trust.
   F. Individuals must exhibit three patterns of behavior if an organization is to function effectively.
      1. People must join and remain within a system.
      2. They must meet certain standards of behavior and performance in their assigned roles.

3. They must demonstrate innovative behavior to help the organization adapt to change.

VI. People Are Complex and Variable
   A. No one set of beliefs is valid for all people in all situations.
   B. Beliefs about human nature are often overgeneralized and oversimplified.
   C. Individuals may respond positively to a number of managerial approaches.
   D. Flexibility is essential to meet the demands of different situations and to make use of unique abilities of employees.

Key Terms

Self-fulfilling   Expectations and   Theory Y
   prophecy   performance
Placebo effect   Theory X

Discussion Questions

1. Give an example of how a manager's beliefs about human nature can affect managerial practices.
2. Describe how a self-fulfilling prophecy operates.
3. Give an example of a situation you have observed in which someone has developed a self-fulfilling prophecy.
4. Describe a placebo and give an example of its effects in healing.
5. Give an example of how a manager's expectations for a new employee can help or hinder that employee's productivity.
6. How can managers develop high performance expectations in employees?
7. Describe the Theory X and Theory Y beliefs about human nature.
8. Comment on the statement, "It would be very rare for a person to develop to his or her fullest potential under Theory X."
9. Why would Theory X beliefs result in management carefully limiting and controlling the amount of information and responsibility given to subordinates?
10. What management actions could help employees develop a sense of achievement that would increase motivation?
11. Discuss the main reasons why beliefs about human behavior are often not useful.

Case Incidents

Too Much Control?

JoAnn Good has recently been promoted from quality control inspector to supervisor of the quality control department. Bill Scott, her boss, informed her that he is receiving complaints from production that quality control is sending back items marked "defective" that are perfectly sound. Mr. Scott has asked JoAnn to see what can be done about improving the work of the department.

JoAnn learned from the former supervisor that most of the inspection errors have been traced to Tom Austin, one of three final inspectors. Since JoAnn wanted to check things out for herself, she assigned another inspector to check the work of all three final inspectors.

As soon as the inspectors heard of the new procedure, the other two final inspectors went to JoAnn and protested having their work checked. They said their work had always been accurate, and everyone knew that Tom Austin was the problem. They also stated that if this new procedure was implemented, they would go to Mr. Scott with their complaint. They believe JoAnn is wasting money on unnecessary inspections rather than taking action to correct Tom's errors.

1. What are JoAnn Good's assumptions about human behavior?
2. Could JoAnn's actions be creating a "self-fulfilling prophecy"? If so, how?
3. What courses of action would you recommend JoAnn consider taking?

The President's Method of Improving Management

William Davis is president of Davis Finance and Credit Corporation. He is committed to continuing management education and frequently attends management development seminars at universities in the area.

The most recent seminars that Mr. Davis attended were on philosophies of management. The seminars emphasized the work of Douglas McGregor and his Theory X and Theory Y concepts. The material presented in the seminars convinced Mr. Davis that his company would be more effective if Theory Y management was practiced by all his managers.

To implement Theory Y he bought copies of McGregor's *The Human Side of Enterprise* and sent a copy to each manager in the company with the following memo:

TO:　　All Managers/Davis Finance and Credit Corporation
FROM:　　William Davis, President
SUBJECT:　Management Practices.

I have recently become convinced that we must begin practicing Theory Y management. Accompanying this memo is a copy of *The Human Side of Enterprise*, which explains how to practice Theory Y management. I expect each of you to read this book over the weekend and begin implementing the management practices next week.

Note that we are committed to Theory Y. You should realize that managers who do not implement Theory Y practices will find it difficult to remain with this organization.

1.　Are the president's actions consistent with the assumptions and practices associated with Theory Y?
2.　What reactions do you feel the managers will have to President Davis's memo?
3.　What other courses of action could the president take to implement Theory Y?

The Overtime Decision

In a natural gas company, an order was issued by the president prohibiting supervisors from authorizing overtime under any conditions. A repairman was working on one of the company's gas pipelines that had developed a leak and had to be shut down. While the line was being repaired, gas had to be supplied by rerouting it through another distribution system, which increased the company's cost.

About an hour before quitting time, the repairman realized that the job could not be finished during regular working hours. He asked the supervisor whether he should work overtime to finish the repair. He estimated that it would require two hours. The supervisor telephoned the maintenance manager, since he did not want to make a decision on an exception to the overtime order. The maintenance manager did not want to make a decision either, so he telephoned the construction manager, who told him to use his own discretion. The "decision" was transmitted down the line to the supervisor, who was told to use his discretion.

1.　What are the reasons for and against the supervisor approving the overtime?
2.　What decision do you think the supervisor made and why?
3.　What was the president's objective in prohibiting superviors from authorizing overtime.
4.　What assumptions do you think the president had about employees and human behavior?

Exercise   *What Are the Manager's Beliefs About Behavior?*

For each of the following descriptions of management behavior, indicate what beliefs you think the manager has about employees.

Description of the manager's behavior	What beliefs do you think the manager has about employee behavior?
1. The manager has designed specialized jobs so employees would not need much training and they could be tightly controlled. The manager has established productivity standards for each job; the names of employees who do not meet the standard are posted on a bulletin board each day.	
2. The manager expects high levels of performance, but uses a minimum of external control. Performance goals are determined by having discussions with employees.	
3. The manager establishes rigid controls on expenditures to make sure employees try to cut costs. Even small expenditures for office supplies must be approved by the manager. The responsibility delegated to employees is severely limited so they do not have an opportunity to take advantage of the organization.	
4. The manager uses discussion with employees to develop cooperation. Organizational objectives are communicated to all employees. Authority and responsibility is widely delegated. The manager explains the reasons for decisions to employees.	

Endnotes

1. Jefferson Fish, *Therapy: A Practical Guide to Social Influence in Psychotherapy* (San Francisco: Jossey-Bass, 1973).
2. Ibid.
3. Cited in Robert Rosenthal and Lenore Jacobsen, *Pygmalion in the Classroom* (New York: Holt, Rinehart and Winston, 1968).
4. C. S. Raben and R. J. Klimoski, "The Effects of the Experimentation Upon Task Performance as Moderated by Levels of Self-Esteem," *Journal of Vocational Behavior* 3, 1973, pp. 475–83.
5. J. Sterling Livingston, "Pygmalion in Management," *Harvard Business Review*, July–August 1969, pp. 81–89.
6. Douglas McGregor, *The Human Side of Enterprise* (New York: McGraw-Hill, 1960).
7. Daniel Katz and Robert L. Kahn, *The Social Psychology of Organizations*, rev. ed. (New York: John Wiley & Sons, 1978).

14 Status, Power, and Politics

Learning Objectives

After reading this chapter, you should be able to:

1. Understand some of the ways power and status are acquired.
2. Identify how status symbols and power are linked.
3. Discuss the meaning of distributive justice, status congruence, and status compression.
4. Understand the differences between power and authority.
5. List the dangers and value of psychological contracts.
6. Describe the functions and nature of organizational politics.
7. Discuss the expectations of employees regarding the use of influence and authority.

Chapter Topics

Status, Power, and Politics

Status—Meaning and Symbols

Power

Politics

Realities of Organizational Life

Expectations, Status, and Power

Preview and Self-Evaluation

A common practice of many large corporations is to locate highest level management offices on the top floors (sometimes an expensive restaurant or penthouse is located at the very top of the building). Lower-level corporate managers, marketing and financial specialists, sales and promotion experts, clerical support, and service organizations are located on successively lower floors. With a reasonable degree of accuracy, the power of individual departments or managers can be estimated by knowing the floor on which they are located and the number of floors between their offices and those of top management. While this widely used arrangement of symbolic power is not true of all corporations, it is, in reality, a display of power and status. Those who are at the top have the power. In a sense the buildings and the level of their occupants are a type of living organizational chart. Getting to the top really means getting to the "top."

To test your knowledge of status and power, answer the following questions. After you've read the chapter, try answering them again.

Answer True or False

1. Power is measured by the amount of influence one person has over another.   T   F

2. Status is either positive or negative.   T   F

3. Power and authority are, in reality, the same.   T   F

4. The status-power game can become more important than organizational goals.   T   F

5. Psychological distance means the boss is unfriendly.   T   F

6. Employees expect their managers to act like managers.   T   F

7. When power is concentrated in one person or group, it makes others less dependent on that person or group.   T   F

8. People assign status to others.   T   F

9. Most people do not like to associate with power or high status.   T   F

10. Power is basically unnecessary to most aspects of organizational life.   T   F

ANSWERS: 1. T; 2. F; 3. F; 4. T; 5. F; 6. T; 7. F; 8. T; 9. F; 10. F.

Status, Power, and Politics

Early in life most of us realize that some people exert more influence over people and events than do others. Those who are stronger, smarter, more determined, more daring, more attractive, and sometimes more objective judges of behavior are able to get others to do what they want. While some of the ways an individual influences others may be negative, such as threats of punishment or embarrassment, they are frequently positive. For example, a manager may encourage employees to work toward advancement or show them how to do a specific job easier and better. We measure power by the amount of influence a person has in his or her relationships with other individuals or groups. People who consider themselves powerless are those who feel they have little or no influence. By the same reasoning, people who "get things their way" most of the time have considerable power.

perception of power

In addition to our perceptions of power, we frequently assign a greater worth or rank to some people than we do others. Ask who has the higher status in our society, a used car salesperson or a prominent scientist, and nearly everyone will rank the scientist much higher. While power is acquired and in some cases granted to people, status is assigned by individuals to other individuals. In general, *status is a method we use to compare one person to another.* We assign special status to people we regard highly or whom we believe deserve special respect or consideration. Those we deem less worthy to society or the

assigning status

group to which they belong are assigned low status. Status is based almost entirely on our perceptions of personal or social worth. It is neither positive nor negative. It is, however, descriptive of a person's rank compared to others.

politics   Power, on the other hand, is often accumulated, not through personal characteristics, but by persuasion, association with powerful people, manipulation of people and events, and by becoming a part of special in-groups. Techniques used to accumulate and wield power are known as *politics*. Like power itself, politics may be either positive or negative. Politics and power are realities of any modern organization; people need to be accepted into informal communication and influence groups. These "in-groups" are relatively easy to recognize. They are generally comprised of people who are seen as either having power or being closely associated with power. To gain their friendship or acceptance, or because of similar interests, others outside these support networks keep members informed of changes, potential key decision outcomes, and organizational gossip. Good organization politicians know who to ask for information, how to time their actions, and methods of influencing those to whom they report as well as those who report to them.

Status—Meaning and Symbols

selective and   When we believe another person has something more or greater than
general status   we do, we are assigning status. Status may be either selective or general. *General status* is the perceived rank of a person when compared to others. *Selective status* refers to a comparison of a single attribute with ours. If someone can consistently win at chess, while we lose, that person has greater status as a chess player. The machinist who is consistently assigned work that requires extreme care, close tolerances, and complete accuracy may not be paid more than other workers in the same classification but will be seen as having greater status. A typist who, because of speed and knowledge, receives requests to do the most important reports is also conferred a higher degree of respect or status by other typists.

Other types of status are determined by the position a person holds in an organization. Presidents have greater status than vice-presidents; secretaries have greater status than file clerks; maintenance mechanics have greater status than custodians.

Status Symbols

To a large extent, status is dependent on the symbols that identify the comparative position of a person with those of others. High status in work organizations is often recognized by the size and furnishings of an office, by parking privileges, by the kind of clothes a person wears, by job title, and by the many other things or conditions we use to compare ourselves with others.

In our society, we expect those who have the greatest authority and responsibility in our organizations to receive the greatest rewards in symbols. The belief that those who do more should have more is called *distributive justice*. In recognition of this principle, seniority is often given some status through longer vacations, selection of job assignments, and personal recognition by upper levels of management. Promotions, presumably based on competence and potential, are usually recognized with higher pay, larger offices, and other symbols.[1] Table 14.1 compares the executive offices at one large company.

distributive justice

Closely related to the principal of distributive justice is the expectation that certain symbols are associated with position. A first-line supervisor promoted to a management department head position may expect to be given a private office, clerical assistance, a telephone, and other symbols associated with promotion. New managers not given the symbols they expect will see themselves as having lower status than other managers at an equal organizational level. Nonmanagement employees also perceive and judge position by the symbols associated with status. Yet at times symbols can be inappropriate because they

status congruence

Table 14.1 Status indicators in the executive offices of Ohio Bell

Indicators	President's office	Vice-presidential offices
Room size	Huge	About ½ size of president's office
Floor	Parquet wood and oriental rug	Wall-to-wall carpeting
Windows	Two window walls with direct view of Lake Erie	One window wall with angled view of Lake Erie
Chair	High back to rest neck; padded	Padded and comfortable
Desk	Huge and decorative and luxurious	Smaller, but nice
Fixtures	Button to open and close drapes, plus rheostat to control lighting level	Pull rope to open and close drapes, plus switch to turn lights off and on
Furniture	Luxurious; many pieces plus liquor cabinet	Nice, fewer pieces; no liquor cabinet
Bathroom	Shower; sink with cabinet, large mirror, toilet; decorative wall covering	Sink, toilet; painted walls
Entrance	Huge and decorative entry; door at end of hall	Smaller and plainer; door along side of hall

Source: Don Hellriegel and John W. Slocum, Jr., *Organizational Behavior: Contingency Views* (St. Paul: West Publishing Co., 1976), p. 346.

are too lavish for the assignment. A newly promoted manager with a private secretary, carpeted office, and expensive office furniture may have an inflated feeling of staus compared to others at similar levels. Symbols associated with status must be appropriate for the position. This is known as *status congruence*. Congruence, as used here, means that the expected symbols and the position must match.

Battle of the Badges

At one large, West Coast defense plant, what began as a simple means of identifying various employees nearly turned into a full-scale class struggle. The trouble began when employees in the plant were given color-coded ID badges for easy identification.

Blue-bordered badges signified nonmanagement personnel, assigned to specific areas, who required only minimal security clearance.

Green-bordered badges were worn by administrative specialists, technical personnel, first- and second-level managers, and employees such as mail clerks and time keepers who needed to move from one department to another.

Mid- and upper-level administrative assistants and security people wore red badges. Red-badged personnel were listed in a separate section of the company phone book.

Although green-badged employees often earned less money than blue-badged employees, the green badges clearly signified higher status in the organization. Green-badged employees in turn deferred to red badges, although authority levels between the two colors were often similar.

Over a period of time, a clearly defined caste system developed along badge-color lines, and employee relations were marked by friction and resentment. At one point, the dominant union in the company made abolishing the badge colors a contract issue. Recognizing the potential harm that could occur if the situation continued, top management ordered all badge design differences eliminated. Almost immediately, relations among all levels of employees improved.

---

status compression

There are many examples of a trend against obvious status symbols. Movement toward *status compression*, the deliberate avoidance of discriminatory status symbols, is very strong. At some colleges, professors who are given managerial assignments are seen merely as having a new type of work with no greater status than that of their former classroom work. Many companies have eliminated private offices and personal secretaries except for the very top levels of management. Perhaps most significant is that perceptions of status symbols have changed. As employees become more affluent, they can and do acquire many of the external status symbols that at one time only upper-level management could afford. Luxury automobiles, boats, recreational vehicles, and similar symbols external to the job are increasingly losing their value as indicators of position.

Status perception, however, still remains. One of the more interesting ways status is assigned is by job titles. Since 1925, pollsters have asked thousands of people to identify occupations that are high prestige and those with lower prestige. There has been remarkably little variation in perceived status for almost sixty years. Scientist, physicians, engineers, clergymen, and college professors are consistently in the higher ranked occupational categories. Bartenders, automobile salespeople, taxi drivers, and janitors are among those consistently receiving low status ranking. Recent information published by both the Gallup Poll and Louis Harris and Associate organizations, two of the best known survey organizations in the United States, demonstrates the high degree of consistency in the ways occupational status is perceived. Their results vary little from data published during the past five decades. Figure 14.1 shows the relationship between occupation and prestige (status) reported by Louis Harris and Associates and published in the *American Educator*.

status perceptions and job titles

Power

Like status, power is part of our everyday language and can be recognized easily by most people. But the concept is difficult to define precisely. *Authority* is related to power and in many cases is an important power tool. People with authority have the right to act, decide, direct, change, approve, or the right to do none of these. While it is obvious that power and authority are linked, they are not the same. Authority stems from the rights that go with a task and are delegated by higher authority. In work organizations, authority is granted by ownership, boards of directors, or top management.

power and authority

Power, on the other hand, is the influence an individual has in dealing with other individuals or groups. Two managers with similar authority may have different degrees of power. One may be more persuasive, more credible, and better able to get things done than the other. While either may have the authority to implement new budget procedures or work schedules, one may seem to get people to accept the changes far more quickly and with less objection than the other.

power

Power is based on the two-way concept of influencing others and being influenced. We have only as much power as others will allow us to have. If, as an example, a manager can recommend promotions, discipline, change another person's assignment, or decide whether an em-

power based on two-way concept of influence

ployee may continue working, then that manager has a great deal of potential influence, through the use of authority, over others. Whether or not an employee responds depends on the amount of power the manager is perceived as really having.

In some cases, appearing to be powerful is just as important as being powerful. As an experiment, one of the authors of this text demonstrated power to a colleague in an amusing but effective way.

Helen's class was designed for educators who were upgrading their skills in school administration. Students were primarily high school and grade school principals, vice principals, master

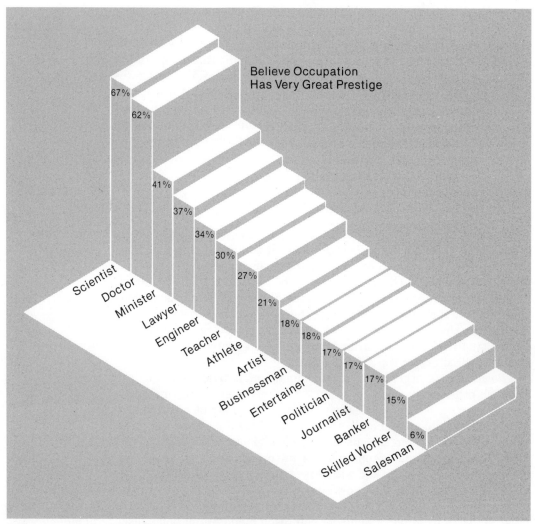

Believe Occupation
Has Very Great Prestige

Scientist 67%
Doctor 62%
Minister 41%
Lawyer 37%
Engineer 34%
Teacher 30%
Athlete 27%
Artist 21%
Businessman 18%
Entertainer 18%
Politician 17%
Journalist 17%
Banker 17%
Skilled Worker 15%
Salesman 6%

Source: Survey by Louis Harris and Associates, October 8–16, 1977.

Figure 14.1 Prestige: How occupations rate.

Chapter 14

teachers, and a few college professors. It was taught in the
summer and everyone including Helen was usually very casually
dressed. One morning after Helen's class had been in session for
approximately twenty minutes, I walked briskly into the room
(dressed in a suit and tie) said to Helen in a rather curt tone, "I'm
sorry but I must interrupt." Without a smile, I continued, "Will
everyone please rise." Every person in the room stood. "Will you
now walk outside in an orderly fashion and remain together." My
orders were carried out perfectly without question. It wasn't until
Helen told her students that they were part of an experiment in
perceived power and authority that they realized that I had
neither.

Sources of Power

In his delightful text *Eupsychian Management*, A. H. Maslow alluded
to "baboon power" and "chimpanzee power."[2] Baboons exert power by
threats, screams, display of claws and teeth, and bullying of weaker
members of their groups. Chimpanzees, on the other hand, influence
members of their groups by showing the way to food supplies, playing
with younger group members, and encouraging participation in nearly
all activities. While primate psychologists may not totally agree with
Maslow's analogy, managers often revert to either the baboon or chimpanzee styles to influence others in their organization.

"baboon" and "chimpanzee" power

Power and dependency are closely linked. Threats, approval, desire
to be liked, fear of disapproval or embarrassment, and the need to
achieve goals all make us dependent on others to some extent. Dependence means we assign power to others. Many managers, unfortunately, recognize the dependency of nonmanagement employees, and use it
to strengthen their power. To a large extent the more we depend on others to decide, plan, and direct our lives, the more power we allow them
to have. Personal power is related to the influence we have on others
and the degree they depend on us.

power and dependency

It is virtually impossible to classify all types of power. A criminal
with a knife or a gun has a certain type of negative power. Money is frequently associated with power. Ancient Greeks wrote about the grant-
ing or withholding of sexual favors as sources of personal power. Several years ago, J. P. R. French and B. H. Raven developed classifications
of power that have become a part of the language of organizational uses
of power:[3]

1. *Legitimate power* is derived from a perons's position in an
   organization, job assignment, or recognized leadership functions.
   It is the kind of power accepted as a normal, justifiable, and
   necessary component of communication between members of an
   organization. In many instances legitimate power is associated
   with level of authority and is an expected, undisputed part of work
   relationships.

power based on a person's position

power based on ability to punish

2. *Coercive power* has its sources in the ability to threaten, punish, or alter another person's self-esteem or job status. Unfortunately, legitimate power is often used coercively when coercion is neither desirable nor necessary. Coercive power can result from perceptions that a peer has damaging or embarrassing information as well as from the more direct threats that come from higher authority. While it is entirely negative, and its use often breeds counteraction in the form of slower and less effective performance, many managers, for lack of real leadership skills, substitute coercion as their primary tool for direction and control.

power based on ability to reward

3. *Reward power* is somewhat similar to coercive power, but emphasizes the ability to approve action, influence promotions, or assign more desirable tasks. B.F. Skinner, in many of his writings dealing with operant conditioning and reinforcement of desirable behavior, points out that reward power is a very useful tool in promoting change. Employees will repeat desirable actions if they feel that either tangible or intangible rewards will be received as a result of their efforts. They will tend not to repeat actions that result in neither reward nor punishment, and will deliberately avoid those that are associated with punishment.

power based on behavior models

4. *Referent power* is demonstrated when an individual serves as a model for the behavior of others. When employees refer to their manager in quoting work rules or assignments, when they arrive at work at the same time or before the manager does, when they copy the manager's style of work or even dress, then the manager is using referent power. The manager's attitude, goals, and approach to problems serve as reference points and are adopted by others.

   A second type of referent power is based on who we know or associate with either within the organization or in some cases outside the organization. Employees who know influential people on a personal or social basis may be seen by others as having influence, which may or may not be true. This type of referent power may be developed to strengthen personal security, obtain higher priorities from service organizations, or to bolster feelings of self-esteem.

power based on knowledge or skill

5. *Expert power* is derived from knowledge or skill. An employee with specialized statistical knowledge may be courted by those who need his or her assistance in solving problems. Employees who can perform specific tasks faster and more accurately than others are often given special attention.

Managers use all these types of power defined by French and Raven but are not limited to them. Over long periods of time, expert power and referent power seem to be most important. However, expert power is difficult to maintain in many cases since expertise is a comparative term. An expert is only an expert as long as he or she is seen as knowing more or being able to solve problems and make decisions better than others.[4]

There are other sources of power somewhat more difficult to recognize but equally as real as those just reviewed. When an employee is promoted to a managerial position, a psychological distance often develops between the person and his or her former co-workers. *Psychological distance* refers to the recognition that those in positions of authority must have greater influence and a broader organizational perspective than those in positions of less authority.

Psychological distance is a necessary component of any manager's life. Employees expect their managers to be objective, to treat employees equally, to evaluate performance fairly, and to avoid any preferential treatment of other employees. To do all this, managers must remove themselves to some degree from the employee's frame of reference and see situations not only in individual terms but in terms of the consequences for the organization as a whole.

However, psychological distance extended too far may alienate employees. They may feel the manager is aloof, lacks personal sensitivity, or cannot understand their problems.

As a result, effective managers have the difficult task of being with their employees yet at the same time remaining apart from them. These managers realize that psychological distance is an essential factor in effective work relations.

It is undeniable that power also stems from personal characteristics. Appearance can be a source of power. Other personal qualities, such as conviction, persuasiveness, personal credibility based on past actions, and willingness to accept responsibility, assume authority, and take recognizable risks, are all sources of power. One news reporter said his primary source of power was his "go-to-hell fund." He had systematically saved the equivalent of a year's salary. If he felt threatened or coerced, he could tell his boss to go to hell and not feel he was depriving himself or his family while searching for another job. He reported that the power he felt from having such a fund was reflected in his independent thinking and frequent promotions.

With all its negative connotations, power is a fundamentally necessary component of organizations. Someone must finalize and implement decisions, analyze and correct, set and measure goals, and direct courses of action. Power, when strongly centered in one person or in relatively few people in an organization, ultimately develops dependency relationships. As citizens depend on governmental agencies to solve a variety of problems, so do employees depend on those with recognized power for decisions, information, and support. If power is diffused or spread throughout the organization, then there tends to be less dependency, greater self-reliance, and often less control. Basic organizational patterns, climates, and structures develop from the top-level management view of appropriate power relationships. When no one knows where the power in an organization is located, confusion inevitably results. While ensuring order and control, power that is too highly centralized can lead to excessive dependency, slow reaction to change, and inefficient use of resources.

Politics

political games In organizations, the acquisition and use of power can become a kind of political gamesmanship. Employees sometimes can gain a type of referent power by flattering an egotistical manager and by providing special services or favors. In many organizations, politics as well as ability help determine promotions, salary increases, and favorable job assignments. Politics involve not only the way power is developed but also its uses. Recognition of what the boss likes and dislikes is a key to successful political action.

> In a medium-sized city bank in Madison, Wisconsin, a newly hired management trainee carefully noted that the bank manager wore a well-tailored, fur-collared overcoat, hat, and conservative suits and ties. The young trainee spent most of his initial pay checks buying a wardrobe similar to but not as expensive as the top manager's. One day, after he had worn his new clothes for a couple of weeks, he was called into the manager's office for discussions. "Somehow," the manager told the trainee, "you seem to stand out among all the trainees. I'd like you to consider an assignment as my administrative assistant." Today as vice-president of his original bank, with many branches throughout the area, the former management trainee credits his first promotion to the politics of dressing like the boss.

Politics are not only based on creating psychological allies, as is done through flattery, special favors, or alliances with people who represent power, but they have also spawned a variety of political games.

mutual support can be a beneficial result of political power Some politics are blatantly malicious. But political gamesmanship can be beneficial as well as destructive. In order to successfully promote a point of view or influence the outcome of a decision, a manager will often diligently advance his or her point of view to other managers who can either individually or as a group influence the final action. Agreement by two or more people to mutually support the actions of each other is another common and often beneficial political behavior.

An effective as well as positive political action is the open display of competence, confidence, dedication, and willingness to accept appropriate responsibility. Managers and nonmanagement employees who do their homework, are well prepared for meetings, and who complete significant assignments on schedule or well ahead of time are seen as being more capable. An equally impressive action is the admission of limitations in specialized areas and recognition of the most competent person for the task. Open support of a decision known to be different from one's personal preference, when selectively applied, is still another effective and frequently positive political move.

Dirty Tricks in the Corporate Boardroom

Bill, a manager in a California aerospace company, had suffered the humiliation of having his ideas ridiculed by a colleague, Greg, during a weekly executive meeting. To make matters worse, the joint division chief had witnessed the entire spectacle. Bill carefully thought out a plan of retaliation that would strike at Greg's credibility and prestige.

After the next executive meeting, Bill issued a memorandum outlining specific recommendations to strengthen the company's financial position. Implementation of the plan would be directed by Greg.

Copies of the memo were sent to the division chief and all other members of the executive meeting except one—Greg. His copy was delivered just after he left for the meeting. When the executive session convened, everyone knew about the new plan except the man most responsible for implementing it. Greg protested that he had not seen the memo but was at a loss to explain why everyone else had their copy. The more he tried to prove his innocence, the worse he looked.

Bill had the satisfaction of watching while the division chief criticized Greg's carelessness and lack of organization. He felt sure that next time Greg would think twice before ridiculing someone in front of the executive board.

Realities of Organizational Life

Employees expect their managers to act like managers, to have the symbols of management, and to be able to influence the organization upwards, horizontally, and downward. The perceived degree of influence a manager has with other managers strongly influences employee willingness to accept the legitimate positional power of those who direct their activities. By the same token, managers have similar perceptions and expectations of themselves and others.

Status and power are esteemed not only by the status holder but also by those with whom he or she is associated. Most of us enjoy meet-

*most people like
to associate with
power*

ing and knowing people of influence. We not only like being associated with power, but we also value the recognition that often comes with such association. While not all people are status seekers or power grabbers, many are.

Weak, insecure managers often bolster their power needs by selecting and employing weak, equally insecure employees. These managers see themselves as superior to their employees and relatively more powerful. Successful managers use a different approach. They select and train people for promotion. It is desirable, they feel, to have employees who want their boss's jobs. Such managers know that they are judged not only by their own ability, but also by the competency of those in their work unit.

Status, power, and politics are all important components of most human interactions, especially at work. The ideal of absolute equality may never be achieved as long as people assign status, recognize power, and use the political actions of negotiation, compromise, private agreements, and gamesmanship to achieve their personal organizational goals. Political warfare exemplified by power struggles is readily apparent throughout the organization and ultimately affects both individual and group effectiveness. It is easy for the status-power game to become more important than the accomplishment of organizational goals.

*misuse of power
can result in
managerial failure*

Misuse of power is often a major contributor to managerial failure. Employees have little respect for indecisive, fearful managers. They also react negatively to those who are arrogant and overbearing, and who treat employees as inferiors. Effective managers demonstrate strength based on willingness to accept leadership responsibilities that center on supportive relationships. In their organizational roles, supportive managers use their influence both upward and horizontally, as well as downward.

Management Power Styles

primitive power

There are many ways of looking at power styles used by managers. Some managers utilize a negative power style defined by David McClelland as primitive power. Primitive power is the use of threats, coercion, and force to influence the behavior of others. Because they are able to affect the pay, status, work assignments, and the security of those who report to them, managers who rely on primitive (negative) power may either directly or by implication use threat and coercion as tools in enforcing employee conformity and job performance. Fear of the retribution of such managers may result in cautious, rule-oriented, highly impersonal employee behavior. Such managers may also use selective rewards to achieve similar results. Conformity and obedience are rewarded while other behavior is punished. It is the traditional "carrot and stick" approach to organizational control.[5]

Unlike negative power, positive power is not used as a compensation for weakness or as a demonstration of dominance for the sake of ego satisfaction. Managers who use power positively are concerned with defining goals more clearly, developing involvement and enthusiasm for accomplishing work objectives, and building a supportive relationship between themselves and employees. They tend to be analytical rather than critical, corrective rather than punishing, and see themselves as developers of people.

positive power

Although there is no single model of the way managers use power that adequately describes all manager power styles, it is relatively easy in most organizations to observe the relationship between influence and attitudes. High influence managers with negative or neutral feelings toward employees will tend to use threatening, coercive styles. Low influence managers with negative attitudes will be suspicious, fearful, withdrawn, and indecisive in the absence of a policy, rule, or written order. High influence managers with positive attitudes rely on coaching skills, encouragement, delegation, and high but realistic expectations to achieve work goals. Low influence managers with positive attitudes spend time developing strong friendships, providing personal services, and working toward a "happy climate." They tend to be less concerned about job necessities than being personally liked by their employees. Table 14.2 shows this relationship.

relationship of influence and attitudes

It should be noted that while the power styles shown in Table 14.2 are based on behavior that may vary a great deal in intensity, managers

Table 14.2 Manager power styles

Degree of Influence	Negative	Positive
High Influence	Decisive Blames others Egocentric Critical Authoritarian Reluctant to delegate Motivated by dominance and power	Decisive Analytical Team oriented Delegates as much as feasible Wants success for others as well as self Sees self as developer of people Motivated by personal and team achievement
Low Influence	Indecisive Rule oriented Suspicious Fearful Critical Does not deviate from rules Motivated by need for survival	Indecisive Friendly People oriented Supportive Criticizes self Accepts blame Service directed Motivated by need for approval, friendship, and acceptance

tend to adopt a primary style. Although conditions may alter their behavior dramatically, they will generally return to the style they have
used in the past.

Expectations, Status, and Power

status, influence,
and power in
organizations

We have developed many expectations about the nature, benefits, and
liabilities of possessing status and power. Status, for example, may be
associated with job title, money, or perceptions of social worth to a
community. We expect those to whom status is given to use their standing for the benefit of others or the representation of a set of ideals. Influence is often directly associated with status. Applicants for employment frequently list ministers, teachers, or well-known community
leaders as references even though the references may know little about
the applicant's past job performance or capabilities.

There is a strong relationship between status and referent power. A
reality of organizational life is that employees prefer association with
managers who demonstrate the power to effect change, to influence upward and downward in their organizations, and who are skilled in the
art of strengthening their position through being able to recognize and
use effective politics. The degree of influence a manager has in the organization will affect the willingness of employees to accept the manager's leadership. The status and power of managers are also important
for those who work with them. Recognition is often received as a result
of "who you know." Associations with powerful individuals give some
people a feeling of power.

influence tends to
decline over time

There are two additional points that need to be recognized in viewing power relationships. Over a period of time, the degree of direct influence a person has over another person or group tends to decline.
While this is not always true, a degree of accommodation occurs during
association with high influence people either in a positive or negative
sense. They begin to seem less fearful, less powerful, and more human.
Such changes in the power balance are easily recognized and may
strengthen real working relationships.

influences
affected by
situation

A second factor is that situations strongly affect the degree of influence a person has or is allowed. In dealing with nonmanagement employees, a manager may be very dominant and have considerable influence. In a staff meeting with other managers of equal or higher rank,
the same manager may have no more than equal influence with that of
other managers and in some cases have considerably less.

Status, power, and politics are important elements in the interpersonal relationships in organizations. People will always recognize power and assign status. Political actions and gamesmanship will probably
always be an important aspect of achieving personal and organization-

al goals. Managers must constantly guard against power-status struggles becoming more important than the achievement of organizational objectives.

Quick Review

I. Status, Power, and Politics
  A. Many people react negatively to the realities of status, power, and politics.
  B. Status is related to rank; power, to influence; and politics, to methods used to acquire status and power.

II. Status—Meaning and Symbols
  A. When we believe another person has more or is greater than we are, we assign status to them. Status is position compared to others.
  B. Status may be either selective or general.
  C. Status symbols are the objects, titles, furnishings, etc. surrounding people that determine our perception of their position.
  D. Distributive justice is the belief that those who do more should have more.
  E. Status congruence refers to the appropriateness of the symbols for the position.
  F. Status compression is the deliberate avoidance of discriminatory status symbols.

III. Power
  A. The degree of influence exerted is a measure of power.
  B. Power and authority are not the same. Authority is conferred by a task and a higher authority.
  C. "Baboon power" is based on threats. "Chimpanzee power" is based on encouragement and helpfulness.
  D. Power has many sources. Some are:
    1. Legitimate power
    2. Coercive power
    3. Reward power
    4. Referent power
    5. Expert power
  E. Psychological distance is a necessary component of effective manager-employee relations.
  F. Power also stems from personal characteristics.
  G. Power, when strongly centered, results in dependency.

IV. Politics
  A. The acquisition and use of power can become a kind of political gamesmanship.

B. In many organizations, politics as well as ability help people get ahead.

C. Political gameplaying can be beneficial or malicious, either gaining others' support or destroying their influence.

V. Realities of Organizational Life

A. Employees expect their managers to act like managers.

B. Status and power are esteemed not only by the status holder but also by the person's associates.

C. It is easy for the status-power game to become more important than the accomplishment of organizational goals.

D. Some managers use primitive power based on fear and coercion.

E. Other managers use power to define goals, build morale, and motivate and support workers.

F. It is relatively easy in an organization to observe the relationship between influence and attitudes.

VI. Expectations, Status, and Power

A. We expect status and power to be closely linked.

B. People prefer working for managers who are perceived as having status and influence.

C. Over time, a person's influence, good or bad, tends to decline.

D. The degree of influence a person possesses is strongly affected by the situation.

Key Terms

Power	Status compression	Psychological
Authority	Legitimate power	distance
Status	Coercive power	Politics
Politics	Reward power	Primitive power
Status symbols	Referent power	Power styles
Status perception	Expert power	

Discussion Questions

1. Who is the single most powerful world figure today? Why?
2. In what ways are status and power related?
3. Distributive justice seems prevalent in nearly all societies. Why do you think distributive justice exists?

4. Why, in survey data, do scientists, doctors, and college professors, consistently rank higher in status than salespeople, bartenders, and automobile mechanics?
5. Physically attractive people seem to have greater influence than physically unattractive people if other attributes such as intellect, training, and socio-economic status are approximately equal. How can this phenomena be explained?

Case Incidents

The Power of the Right Attitude

"Your approach to customers should be as customer service specialists rather than salespeople," said Grace Mitchell to her five district managers. As marketing manager for Topcop Electronic Office Systems Company, Grace had been largely responsible for much of the company's recent growth in a highly competitive market. "All of our salespeople not only must look and act like professionals, but they must see themselves as experts in helping customers solve office problems with Topcop equipment. They've got to learn to analyze problems and fit the right equipment to the right job. If the problem can be solved without new equipment, fine. In the long run, we'll have the customer's trust."

As the meeting ended, Leron Wilson, who headed the large southwestern district remarked to Diane Stone, eastern district manager, "Grace knows her stuff. If we could get all our salespeople to have the same attitude she has, we'd have it made." "I agree," returned Diane, "she's one of the few people that I've worked for that I really admire. She looks at long-range results before the immediate bottom line."

1. What kinds of power did Grace use to get the support of her management staff?
2. If salespeople emphasized products instead of service, what action would you predict Grace would take.
3. How can she get her staff to reflect the same attitude she has?

Getting to the Top

"One of the things you'll have to do," Laura advised Duane, "is to learn to look and talk like a manager. The first thing people notice is your speech and your appearance. You've also got to learn to write clearly." Duane knew he was a good worker and that he had a knack for taking charge when others were floundering with problems. Faced with his first opportunity for promotion, he was surprised and disturbed by Laura's emphasis on things other than work itself.

Laura told Duane that studies show those people with good social and communication skills, and who "look the part," tend to move toward the top faster than those who concentrate on work alone. She mentioned that some management consultants and analysts feel that, frequently, less qualified but socially skilled people are advanced over those who are better equipped in knowledge, experience, and actual managerial skills.

1. How should Duane react to Laura's advice?
2. Do you believe that social and communication skills can outweigh job abilitiy in promotional situations? Why?
3. Is it either necessary or good that a person create a personal image that gives a feeling of power and status? Explain your response.

Who's the Boss?

Steve Davis supervises a company printing shop that prints all the labels and instructional materials for the products the company produces. The operations manager, who is Steve's boss, frequently visits the print shop and suggests methods and procedures to the employees that differ from the instructions Steve has given them. The boss's suggestions do sometimes increase production, but the employees wonder who their real boss is.

1. What are possible reasons for the behavior of the operations manager?
2. What would be possible consequences if Steve Davis tells the operations manager *not* to give any advice to employees in the printing shop?
3. What actions should Steve Davis take to eliminate the problem of employees wondering who their real boss is?

Exercise   *Power and Status*

1. With other class members, develop a role-playing situation or experiment to demonstrate power.
2. Working with three or four other students, list as many job titles as possible in fifteen minutes. Exchange your list with that of other groups. Arrange the list received by your group in order highest to lowest status. Compare rankings of each group. Are there any common rankings?
3. Devise a demonstration of organizational politics aimed at increasing power.
4. Role play a high influence negative manager dealing with a low influence negative manager. How does each react?

Endnotes

1. David Lawless, *Organizational Behavior* (Englewood Cliffs: Prentice-Hall, 1979), p. 386.
2. A. H. Maslow, *Eupsychian Management* (Homewood, Ill.: Irwin-Dorsey, Inc., 1965).
3. John R. P. French, Jr. and Bertram Raven, "The Bases of Social Power," In Dowin Cartwright and Alvin Znder (eds.) *Group Dynamics* 3d ed. New York: Harper and Row, 1968, pp. 259–69.
4. Fred Luthans, *Organizational Behavior*, 3d ed.(New York: McGraw-Hill, 1981), pp. 393–95.
5. David McClelland, "The Two Faces of Power," *Journal of International Affairs*, January 1970, p. 36.

15

Managerial Effectiveness and Performance Improvement

Learning Objectives

After reading this chapter, you should be able to:

1. Describe the organizational and managerial characteristics that improve performance and productivity.

2. Identify the effects and characteristics of an organizational climate that is goal oriented.

3. Design a system for goal setting that will improve individual performance and aid in achieving organizational objectives.

4. Describe organizational practices that promote innovation and creativity.

5. List guidelines for the effective administration of discipline.

6. Discuss conditions necessary for developing effective delegation.

7. Explain how a supervisor can improve performance and productivity.

Chapter Topics

Managerial Effectiveness and Performance Improvement

Goal Orientation

A System for Goal Setting

Innovation and Creativity

Constructive Discipline

Delegation and Responsibility

Effective Supervision

Preview and Self-Evaluation

Effective organizational action must, by its very nature, be goal directed. A shoe manufacturing plant must manufacture shoes. An insurance company must sell insurance. Lumber companies must cut and process wood products. Colleges must provide instruction. Successful achievement of organizational objectives is dependent on the effectiveness of managerial ability to define and translate goals into employee action. The entire thrust of modern organizational behavior theory is directed not toward employee satisfaction or happiness but toward achievement of both organizational and personal goals.

Two prerequisites for reaching goals are: (1) managers must be able to define where they want to go and (2) they must know how to get there. In Chapter 15 we discuss the necessary ingredients required for defining goals and realizing their achievement.

Before reading this chapter, try answering the following true-false questions. Then, after reading the chapter, check the questions again to see if your perceptions are the same.

Answer True or False

1. In an organization where the boss makes all the decisions, individuals have little incentive or opportunity to contribute to organizational effectiveness.

   (T) F

2. There are quick procedures available to managers that will create the necessary conditions for long-term employee motivation.

   T (F)

3. For the welfare of both the individual and the organization, a person should not be allowed to remain in a position where he or she cannot achieve positive accomplishments.

   (T) F

4. To increase creativity an organization should hire a variety of personality types and avoid hiring people only like those in the organization.

   (T) F

5. Discipline is necessary as a form of control only for a small number of individuals.

   T (F) X

6. Delegation is a necessary part of any manager's job.

   (T) F

7. One of the most effective ways to create pride in job performance is to involve individuals in decision making.

   (T) F

8. The supervisor who sees the job as "bossing" people around finds people do not respond with their best effort.

   (T) F

9. Supervisors should criticize employees in front of others so the criticism will have the greatest possible impact.

   T (F)

10. Effective supervisors keep orders to a minimum and encourage individuals to ask questions.

    (T) F

ANSWERS: 1. T; 2. F; 3. T; 4. T; 5. T; 6. T; 7. T; 8. T; 9. F; 10. T.

Managerial Effectiveness and Performance Improvement

individuals seek meaningful work

Management has been facing an increasing number of problems in achieving productivity. Many of these problems arise because individuals have left old anchorages, no longer follow old cultural patterns, and have developed greater desires for achievement and self-fulfillment. Most individuals find that they have a greater number of alternatives to choose from, and there are greater possibilities to satisfy needs for achievement, growth, recognition, and responsibility. Many individuals no longer find it desirable to look to authoritative standards as guides. Individuals are seeking meaningful work under conditions where management's power is based on competence and not status in the organizational structure.

There is no shortage of programs to motivate employees. But managers continue to ask, "How do I get employees to achieve organizational goals?" In response to their question we find articles, books, speeches, and training programs in ever-increasing numbers. Many of the current materials on motivation are collections of gimmicks and procedures designed to produce quick and easy results.

Unfortunately, there are no easy gimmicks or quick procedures that produce the conditions necessary for long-term individual motivation in organizations. In order to obtain organizational effectiveness and human productivity, systems must be developed and maintained that will maximize the potential of individuals. Effective management for motivation and productivity should have at least the following five characteristics:

1. Goal orientation
2. Innovation and creativity
3. Constructive discipline
4. Delegation of responsibility
5. Effective supervision

Goal Orientation

climate that lacks a goal orientation

The managerial climate that promotes human effectiveness in an organization has a *goal orientation*. It is through goal attainment that individuals satisfy needs for achievement, growth, recognition, and responsibility. When the organizational climate lacks goal orientation, individuals tend to seek security and protect themselves from the system. Where there are no specific goals, individuals may function in blind obedience to orders from superiors. Employees may not look for better ways to accomplish objectives but may look only for better ways to satisfy their bosses. In an organization where the boss calls the shots, the individual is provided with little incentive or opportunity to contribute to increased effectiveness of the organization. "Automatic conformity or obedient jumping through hoops, is little better than a pattern for 'serving time' on the job."[1]

Employees usually characterize such organizations as having arbitrary and unchallenging goals, confusing and restrictive administrative systems (red tape), and interpersonal conflict. These conditions lead to feelings of individual failure and often result in management disapproval and punishment, which in turn produce feelings of guilt, frustration, and apathy. The individual's defenses take the forms of cynicism, hostility, and efforts to obtain need satisfaction from sources unrelated to organizational goals. This behavior further aggravates human relationships, and the unproductive conditions are reinforced (see Figure 15.1).

Goal-oriented individuals see job goals as a meaningful part of broader organizational objectives and as a way of achieving personal goals. With goal-oriented management, individuals receive constructive feedback and satisfaction directly from the work itself and the achievement of goals. Knowledge of the job enables the individual to intitiate self-corrective action and to grow with accomplishments.

goal-oriented climate

Goal orientation is supported by management actions that develop meaningful goals, supportive and helpful management systems, and interpersonal respect and trust. These conditions maximize the indi-

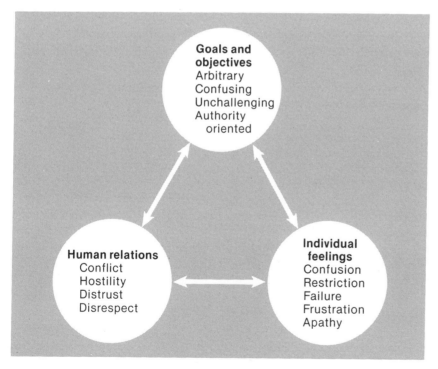

Figure 15.1 Climate that lacks goal orientation.

vidual's opportunity to achieve goals and earn approval and reward. The resulting motivation favorably affects the individual's perception of the job and encourages the individual to reach out for greater achievements. Conditions that develop a positive outlook reinforce interpersonal respect and support a process of individual achievement and goal attainment (see Figure 15.2).

Organizational Goal Setting Systems

characteristics of goal setting which leads to achievement

Goal setting which leads to achievement has the following characteristics: (1) individuals are involved in the process of setting organizational and specific work goals, (2) individuals are able to relate personal goals to organizational goals, (3) the organization has supportive and helpful systems for setting and achieving goals, and (4) individuals are able to respond favorably to organizational goals and make a commitment to the organization.

Systematic goal setting can help organizations and individuals within organizations evaluate individual performance and potential. A goal setting system can aid management in measuring the success of other organizational systems and procedures.

An effective goal setting system should improve on the informal goal setting which occurs naturally in an organization. A formal sys-

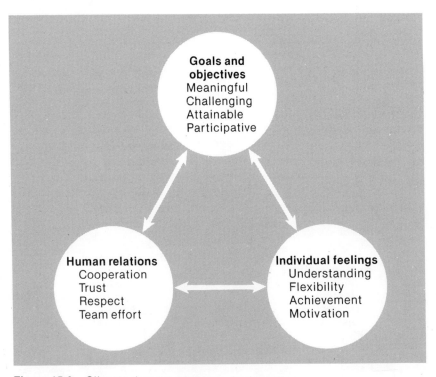

Figure 15.2   Climate that promotes goal orientation.

tem can develop a more realistic basis upon which individuals can build expectations about their jobs, their organization, and themselves. Formal goal setting systems can establish a foundation upon which a continuous goal setting process can be built.

If a goal setting system is to be successful in helping an organization meet its objectives, it must be based upon employee involvement and must facilitate the growth and development of individuals. Additionally, a goal setting system cannot succeed unless the organization is willing to evaluate its programs and systems on the basis of human effectiveness and productivity, rather than on the basis of organizational structure, such as degree of control, proper status differential, and so forth.

employee involvement in goal setting promotes growth and development

There are two commonly used methods of implementing a goal setting system:

The first method is to start at the top of the organization and then proceed down successive levels. This method has the advantage of emphasizing the relationship of organization-wide objectives to those set at lower levels. It allows people to experience first as subordinates a technique they will later employ as superiors. Implementation from the top down tends to minimize any problems that might arise because managers employ practices their bosses do not understand or sanction.

methods of implementing goal setting

A second way to implement the system is to install it in one segment of the organization—a branch, plant, or department. This can have the advantage of allowing some "learning through experience" before the program is extended to other segments of the organization. It also allows for comparisons between units using the system and those not yet involved.

The first step in implementing any managerial system is to decide that it is worth total commitment. A willingness to "give it a try" is not enough. A goal setting program costs an organization time and effort. If it is to be successful, it requires a continuing commitment by those involved. A commitment to meet together an hour or so a week is not enough.

Those involved must construct a goal setting program that will suit the organization and that they are willing to maintain.

The following description of a goal-setting program is a suggested one. It is not a universal "right way" and should not be considered as such.

A System for Goal Setting

Position Description In the first step, the individual employee discusses his or her job description with the manager, and areas of responsibility are defined. The *results* the individual is responsible for attaining are specified.

Individual Goals   The second step is to obtain agreement of the manager on the duties required of the position. The employee should then prepare a list of goals that represent reasonable performance in each of the areas of responsibility. The employee *plans* activities so they support the overall goals of the unit and organization.

individuals must know the goals of the organization

In establishing performance goals, the individual must know the goals of the organization and the goals of the particular organizational unit. Every organization imposes some limits on individual activities, and these limits must be communicated to the individual by management. An individual can establish reasonable and obtainable goals only when the overall goals of the organization and the goals of the unit are known.

Agree upon Goals and Establish Evaluation Procedures   In the third step, the employee and the manager mutually agree on the employee's goals. This step is the most difficult and the most complicated in the goal setting procedure. For one thing, the moment the manager asks an employee to raise or lower a goal the individual has set, the goal then becomes the manager's, not the employee's.

agreement on goals requires discussion

The manager should act in the role of questioner, advisor, counselor, trainer, developer, and even "warner." The manager should not play the role of God or judge!

The manager and the employee jointly establish the standards, or the checkpoints, to be used by both parties during and at the end of the evaluation period to determine the employee's success in attaining objectives. Examples of such checkpoints are due dates; sales, financial and cost figures; statistical data; and comparisons.

judgment is always necessary in evaluating performance

Evaluation of Performance   In the fourth step, the *results* of a person's performance are evaluated. Either the individual has attained goals, exceeded goals, or failed to attain goals. The attainment of or failure to attain a goal is not of significance in *itself*. The most important consideration is, What has the person *accomplished?* Obviously, a person who establishes extremely high goals and then almost attains them has accomplished more than the person who establishes low goals and then exceeds them. Judgment must be used in evaluating performance. The manager's responsibility is to eliminate undesirable performance and to reward positive achievements appropriately.

a person should not remain in a position where he or she cannot achieve positive accomplishments

Undesirable performance is a warning signal that something *must* be done. The employee may need additional training or development. Maybe the individual needs additional support resources or new equipment. The individual could be "misplaced" in the current position. After the manager has exhausted all means of help and guidance and the individual continues to show undesirable performance, the manager must take action to transfer the individual to a position in which he or she can achieve positive accomplishments. For the individual's welfare and for the effectiveness of the organization, a person should not be continued in a position in which positive accomplishments cannot be achieved. On the other hand, the manager should appropriately reward individuals who have achieved positive accomplishments.

In these procedures, no mention has been made of personality traits. The psychological causes of an individual's activities are not explored; the individual is not put on a couch and psychoanalyzed. Instead, a person is judged on the basis of *results and accomplishments*. If an individual has serious (not imagined) personality deficiencies, this will inevitably result in undesirable performance. The manager, by eliminating undesirable performance, will probably eliminate the negative impact of personality problems. The task of identifying and solving serious personality problems should be left to the professional.

Advantages of Goal Setting Systems

The primary advantages of goal setting systems are as follows:

- Individuals know in advance the basis for evaluation.
- The manager and employee both understand the responsibilities of the position.
- A goal setting system should strengthen the manager-employee relationship, because it does not require the manager to be an arbitrary judge.

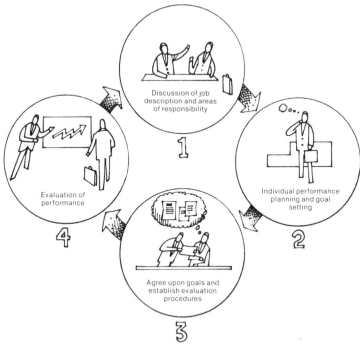

Figure 15.3 A system of goal setting.

- The system can be self-correcting, helping people set goals that are both challenging and attainable.
- Goal setting helps in identifying training needs.
- The system helps the manager gain a better understanding of employee problems.
- Goal setting treats as a total process a person's ability to identify organizational problems, develop ways of attacking them, translate ideas into action, and carry plans through to results.

Innovation and Creativity

The organization that achieves long-term effectiveness and maximum development must place a premium on *innovation and creativity*. The effective manager realizes that it is more productive to seek better things to do (effectiveness) rather than to do more efficiently the things already being done.

creativity requires challenging objectives

A climate for innovation and creativity cannot be created by gimmicks. Promoting creativity requires challenging objectives and individuals who feel their work is important. In the past, management has often assumed that individuals could be divided into two classes–creative and noncreative. Most individuals in organizations were placed in the noncreative category and originality was not expected from them. Today, it is generally agreed that creative potential is not restricted to a small group, but exists to some degree in almost all individuals.

> The capacities of the average human being for creativity, for growth, for collaboration, for productivity (in the full sense of the term) are far greater than we have recognized . . . it is possible that the next half century will bring the most dramatic social changes in human history.[2]

An organization that has an environment for creativity makes use of creative potential of individuals throughout the organization. The characteristics of the organization reflect the personalities of many employees, at all levels, rather than a few at the top. Creativity and innovation are found in all activities and functions of the organization, including hiring practices, development of objectives, compensation, design of organizational structures, and so on.

B. F. Goodrich's Creativity Training

Can you *teach* creativity? The top management at B. F. Goodrich think so. They have developed two courses on creativity, one for supervisors and middle managers, and one for senior management.

The overall objective of the program is to get managers to accept creative thinking as a natural part of daily management rather than an exotic, separate "technology." The two courses each last two and a half days; managers are trained to overcome personal and organizational obstacles to creativity and become more receptive to new or unusual ideas.

The course for middle managers and supervisors concentrates on intra- and interpersonal aspects of creativity. Managers learn how to free their minds to be more creative and open to fresh ideas. They examine how personal relationships can inhibit or encourage creative thinking. Finally, they discuss ways of responding to original ideas and overcoming fears of criticism or ridicule in presenting or receiving new ideas.

The course for senior managers puts greater emphasis on the organizational aspects of creativity and on developing a climate that nurtures and develops creative ideas.

B. F. Goodrich feels that by training management to be more flexible, receptive, and creative, the company can foster creativity throughout the organization without the need to train every employee.[3]

Personnel Practices

To provide an environment for innovation and creativity, the organization should hire a variety of personality types and avoid hiring only people like those already in the organization. Individuals should be hired who have proven their abilities to create and innovate in other organizations. Nonspecialists should be assigned to planning and problem-solving groups. The selection and promotion of individuals should be made only on merit.

hire a variety of personality types

Communication

Open channels of communication should be developed and maintained so there is fluid communication. Individuals should be encouraged to communicate with sources outside the organization, such as professional groups. One way to promote open communication is to form "idea" groups that are responsible for obtaining and evaluating suggestions for improving productivity and the achievement of organizational objectives.

maintain open channels of communication

Planning

Maximum flexibility should be maintained in long-range planning so that creativity and innovation are not hindered by "fixed" plans that are difficult to change. In the planning process there should be an attitude of "give everything a chance." There should be broad participation by individuals in all levels in the organization as plans are developed.

use broad participation in planning

Management Practices and Policies

*creativity
requires creative
managers*

Ideas should be evaluated on their merits and should not be affected by the status of the originator. Top-level management should not develop a close-minded commitment to present policies and procedures. Management must do more than attempt to "follow the leader," whether the leader is another organization or an individual. If an organization is to develop a favorable climate for innovation and creativity, it must have creative managers.

*supervising for
creativity*

The AC Sparkplug Division of General Motors recognized the importance of management's influence on innovation and creativity and constructed a program entitled "Supervising for Creativity." The program focused on three areas:

1. *The Supervisor-Employee Relationship.* The supervisor should strive to build an atmosphere which encourages new ideas and changes. Supervisors should design positive approaches to stimulate and encourage creativity in each individual. Supervisors should give recognition for all new ideas and commendation when deserved.

2. *Active Support of Creativity.* The supervisor should actively support the creativity of individuals. Supervisors should maintain effective communications with their own and other departments. A definite or formal procedure should be established for the fair and consistent consideration of all ideas conceived in the department.

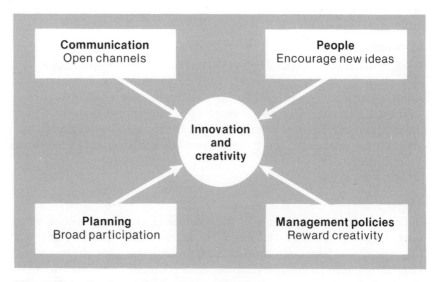

Figure 15.4 Factors contributing to the development of innovation and creativity.

3. *The Highly Creative Person.* The supervisor should permit the creative individuals to work in an atmosphere where they can easily try out their ideas. The creative individual should be provided with an environment conducive to study and work. The assignment of work to the creative individual should be done very carefully.[4]

In any program to develop innovation and creativity, the managers must understand the creative process and must be creative themselves, not only in technical areas, but also in organizational influence and management practices.

"Innovation begins with example. When management acts in an innovative way, and managers at every level show appreciation for good ideas you have a climate that attracts and nourishes creative people, and you will always have innovation."[5]

Harry J. Gary
Chairman, President and CEO
United Technologies

Constructive Discipline

To be effective, discipline should focus on learning and improvement. Poor disciplinary practices can result in resentment and hostility and cause individuals to develop methods to protect themselves from management. *Constructive discipline* can help to develop a feeling of mutual respect among the individuals in the organization.

discipline should focus on learning

Objectives of Discipline

The primary objective of discipline should be to develop effective individual and organizational performance. Discipline is necessary as a form of control only for a very small number of individuals. If the organization has a large number of individuals who can be controlled only by disciplinary measures, it should closely examine its selection and retention practices. In some situations, discipline is necessary for the protection of the rights of individuals and the organization.

Constructive discipline should always be results oriented. Discipline should not be used "to get even." When management attempts to "get even" with employees, the result is usually a decrease in productivity and action by employees to "get even" with management.

Approaches to Discipline

The most desirable and most effective discipline is self-discipline. No organization has sufficient resources to control and police the behavior of individuals in the organization. Through delegation of responsibility and support from management, individuals can improve their effectiveness through self-discipline. Unless individuals are given responsibility, management should not expect them to behave with a high degree of self-discipline. Where group teamwork exists, management can usually count on group discipline to supplement self-discipline.

Management can avoid many of the problems involved in disciplinary action if rules are seen as reasonable and justified. Individuals will usually observe rules when they understand why they are necessary. Rules should be periodically reviewed; and if they cannot be positively justified, they should be discontinued. The procedures the organization uses for discipline should be developed with broad participation from representatives of the individuals who are subject to discipline. Managers should never lose sight of the fact that discipline problems usually are the result of ineffective management.

An Example of Constructive Discipline

The following case involves the discipline of production workers in a large Douglas fir plywood mill.[6] The management became aware that unsatisfactory work performance and disciplinary matters were being handled in an undesirable manner. The company had developed an informal method for dealing with these situations:

1. The supervisor would either ignore or casually mention initial and minor infringements of rules.
2. Repeated infractions, depending upon the issue involved, usually resulted in discharge, demotion, or suspension of pay.
3. This arrangement had two general consequences. First, there was a general conflict between the management and the union as a result of the union's ability either to lessen the punishment or nullify any effects that it might have by providing a monetary cushion for suspended workers. Second, the discipline system was costly to the company in terms of:
    a. the training costs to replace demoted or discharged workers.
    b. the costs of multiple temporary job movements when workers were suspended.
    c. the costs in management time involved in grievance meetings.
4. Usually the procedure produced further incidents, because workers returning from suspension attempted to save face with their fellow workers by repeating previous actions and by producing the feeling among the workers that the union would protect them in almost any grievance situation.

Faced with this situation, the management set out to reexamine the firm's discipline policies and to take remedial action where possible. It was first recognized that discipline problems usually did not occur without warning. The management next considered that the problem might be one of enforcement and that a formal system of written warning slips should be established. It was recognized, however, that this would not, to any great degree, affect the costs mentioned above. The managers then reviewed their basic assumptions about human behavior and the effects of punishment. They concluded from their experiences and from the experiences of others that punishment in itself does not change behavior. They also concluded that although many motivational factors are involved, the major motivation for satisfactory performance and disciplined behavior is respect for the authority behind the rules (the organization) and respect for oneself. The company therefore decided to adopt the following policy for developing and enforcing disciplined behavior: *discipline problems can occur without warning*

1. The company will no longer apply disciplinary demotions, suspensions, or other forms of punishment.
2. When unsatisfactory work performance or lack of discipline occurs, the following steps are followed:

   Step 1: The supervisor will casually remind the worker what is expected of him or her (on the job site).

   Step 2: If another incident arises within four to six weeks, the worker is again casually reminded (on the job) of his or her responsibilities. The supervisor also speaks privately to the worker in an attempt to explain the purpose for the particular rule, to listen for a reasonable excuse, to ascertain whether the incident was unintentional, and to express the hope that the worker can conform to the expected behavior.

   Step 3: If the situation repeats itself within six weeks, step 2 is repeated in the presence of the supervisor's boss. This step is then confirmed with a letter to the worker's home.

   Step 4: If within six weeks of step 3 the incident is again repeated, the worker is called off the job and sent home for the remainder of the day (with pay) and is instructed to decide whether he or she wishes to comply with the expected behavior. The worker is also told that another occurrence within a reasonable time period will result in termination.

3. If another incident does occur within a reasonable amount ot time, the worker is immediately terminated.
4. In extreme cases of several incidents in a short period of time, steps 2 and 3 may be skipped. In cases of criminal behavior or in-plant fighting, termination is immediate.

The value of these actions lies in their results. During the first seven months of operation of the plan, two workers were terminated for fighting (before the plan could be announced); three workers progressed through step 4 (two returned to quit, and one had no further incidents); several workers proceeded to step 3 and afterwards remained out of trouble; and the conflict between the supervisors and the union was eliminated. As a consequence of these improvements, the company saved both time and money and improved the worker productivity in the firm.

The Hot-Stove Rule

Effective discipline involves learning through experience. What has been referred to as the "hot-stove rule" illustrates four basic concepts of effective discipline.[7] This rule draws the analogy between touching a hot stove, and the application of discipline. When an individual touches a hot stove the discipline (and learning) is immediate, consistent, impersonal, and usually with some warning. The most effective disciplinary process provides advance warning of the consequences of behaviors that are considered undesirable. If these behaviors occur, the consequences are immediate, consistent, and impersonal. When an individual touches a hot stove there is no question of cause and effect. The burn is the result of a behavior and not because of any characteristics of the individual. The discipline is a result of an act and not directed against the person. The stove is not "out to get" anyone; everyone who touches it gets burned.

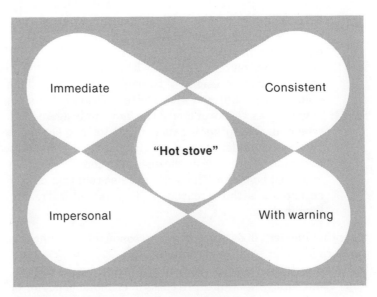

Figure 15.5   The hot-stove rule of discipline.

Chapter 15

General Guidelines for Administering Discipline

All managers use some form of disciplinary procedure. When implementing any disciplinary procedures to correct undesirable behavior, the following commonly accepted guides should be considered:

guides for discipline

1. The discipline is for the undesirable behavior and not directed against the person.
2. Disciplinary action should take place in private.
3. Discipline should be handled in a constructive manner.
4. Disciplinary action should be the responsibility of the immediate supervisor.
5. Disciplinary action should promptly follow the undesirable behavior.
6. Discipline for similar undesirable behaviors should be consistent.
7. After a disciplinary action, the supervisor should help the employee to perform successfully on the job.

Delegation and Responsibility

Part of any manager's job is to get things done through people. This requires delegation of authority and responsibility to achieve organizational objectives. Many managers attempt to perform too much of the job themselves. In doing so, they fail to maximize the use of their own time and the abilities of individuals who work for them

Delegation makes possible more effective performance, because it can place the responsibility for decisions closest to the problems. Individuals most directly involved in an operation are usually the best equipped to solve the problems that occur at their level. There is often a tendency to delegate responsibility one level above the point at which the action is occurring.

decisions made by individuals closest to the problems can increase effectiveness

Delegation can be motivational when individuals have the authority and responsibility to use their judgment in decision making on their jobs. One of the most effective ways to create pride in job performance is to involve individuals in decision making. Individuals become more involved in their jobs and more committed to quality results.

If an organization is to develop individuals capable of advancing in the organization, it is necessary to give them chances to exercise authority and responsibility. One of the most effective ways to develop employees is to ensure that they learn to exercise authority and accept responsibility through delegation.

Advantages of Delegation

- Manager can't handle everything.
- Decisions by people closest to the problems.

- Pride in results from one's own judgment.
- Feeling of involvement.
- Development of employees.
- Effective use of individual abilities.

areas of authority and responsibility must be understood before delegating

Delegation may not be effective, however, when there is a lack of agreement between superior and subordinate on specific areas of authority and responsibility. The subordinate may not understand specifically what is necessary to assume authority and responsibility. In order to delegate effectively, managers must clearly understand their own responsibilities and authority. If they cannot clearly define them, managers will not know what responsibilities or authority can be delegated most effectively. These and other reasons for the failure of delegation are shown in Figure 15.6.

Goal Orientation

If delegation is to work effectively throughout an organization, there must be a goal orientation. Individuals should understand the relation-

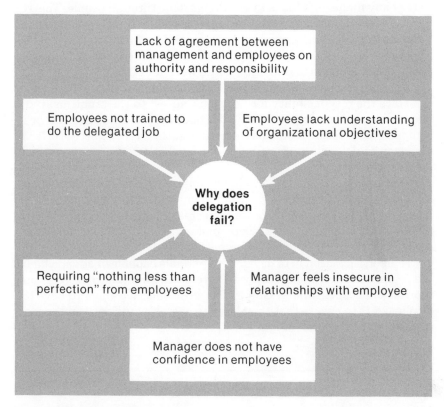

Figure 15.6 Why delegation fails.

ship of their job to the overall objectives of the organization. When delegation is supported by programs of individual and organizational goal setting, it becomes easier to delegate effectively, because individuals understand how their jobs contribute to the overall operation of the organization. Individuals' roles in achieving organizational objectives should be defined by management and employees who must work together to arrive at the results to be achieved. Results should be periodically reviewed, and there should be specific time periods set for accomplishing objectives.

Delegation Involves Risk Taking

A manager does not always know that subordinates will be able to achieve the desired results. If the manager is unwilling to take risks, he or she usually will not delegate effectively but will attempt to perform too much of the job. When a manager is unwilling to take risks by allowing individuals to make decisions, the chance for individual development and motivation is reduced.

Delegation can become ineffective when individuals perceive the manager as requiring "nothing less than perfection." Under these conditions, individuals will seldom accept responsibility, because they will be unable to live up to the manager's expectations. For delegation to be effective the entire process must occur in a supportive environment where managers seek to help individuals correct their mistakes rather than punish them when mistakes occur. The process of delegation must be a part of the total learning process for individuals.

effective delegation requires a supportive environment

Managers Must Develop Secure Relationships with Employees

When a manager has insecure relationships with individuals, he or she will usually be extremely hesitant to delegate. One reason for insecure relationships is that the manager has no real confidence in the workers. When they realize that the manager feels this way, they usually are reluctant to accept responsibility. In personal relationships, it is necessary for managers to see that individuals understand what is expected of them. To develop an effective understanding with their employees, they must establish a climate of open communication. Individuals should feel free to ask questions and clarify their own positions in terms of their authority and responsibility.

In order for delegation to contribute to maximum motivation, it must provide challenges related to the job. Often, individuals are delegated responsibilities only for the undersirable tasks that the manager does not want to perform. Where delegation works most effectively, individuals are challenged through the delegation of responsibility to make job-related decisions. Workers will be challenged when they are responsible for planning and controlling activities related to thier jobs.

delegation should provide challenges

Focus on Results and Goal Attainment

Delegation works most effectively when individuals are responsible for results and not for specific steps to be performed. When individuals are responsible for the results in a goal-oriented environment, they will tend to accept responsibility naturally. To encourage this tendency, management must reward those who are effective in achieving results. Management must allow individuals as much latitude as possible in the methods they use to get jobs done. When the focus is on results and goal attainment, there is less need for specific operating procedures; and specific rules can be held to a minimum. When individuals are rewarded for achievement of results, they usually seek out additional responsibility.

fix the problem, not the blame

If delegation is to contribute to the attainment of organizational goals, managers must guard against responding to problems by looking for someone to blame. Problems must be analyzed to determine why they occurred and how management can help individuals avoid encountering the same problem in the future. Management must concentrate on developing effective performance by supporting individual development. This can be done effectively when there is an attitude of helping rather than an attitude of controlling or blaming.

Figure 15.7 shows the various ways management can help create a climate for effective delegation.

The delegator's role in an organization requires that the manager develop "the will to manage." A manager with the will to manage gets satisfaction from leading and supporting individuals in the achievement of organizational goals. The manager must enjoy the success of employees.

Effective Supervision

always room for improvement

The supervision of employees is a constant challenge. There is always room for improving performance. *Supervison* involves both the utilization of resources and getting work done through the efforts of other people. *Effective supervision* depends both on the individual effort of the supervisor and the productivity that employees achieve. Satisfaction from supervising should be derived from the accomplishments of others.

Effective supervision involves much more than giving orders and administering discipline. The supervisor who sees the job as "bossing" people around finds that people do not respond with their best effort. Most employees expect their supervisor to assume a number of roles, including those of leader, advisor, and consultant. In these roles the supervisor is responsible for both rewarding and disciplining employees. Providing opportunities for individual need satisfaction through the achievement of organizational objectives is the basis for effective supervision.

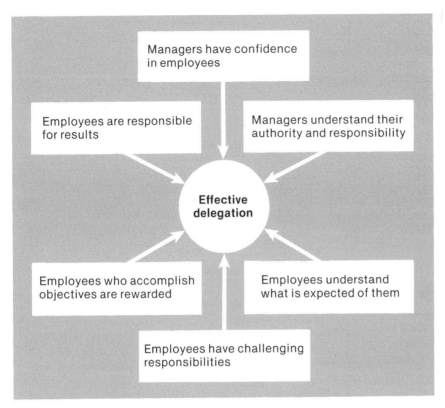

Figure 15.7   Conditions for developing effective delegation.

The effective supervisor sees the job as an obligation to create a climate of support by being open and receptive to people's ideas. In supporting employees it is important to share information and delegate responsibilites. *receptive to people's ideas*

The effective supervisor:

1. Tries to raise the motivation levels of employees by helping them develop self-confidence and self-esteem.
2. Takes an active interest in employees and tries to understand their problems.
3. Treats people as individuals, recognizing the worth of each individual.
4. Allows individuals the opportunity to accept responsibility for achieving job objectives.

Effective supervisors recognize employee needs for responsibility, recognition, and growth. They develop methods that provide opportunities for satisfaction of these needs. Effective supervisors supply information and advice to employees when necessary, but they generally *emphasize personal responsibility* avoid "looking over an employee's shoulder." They emphasize personal responsibility and accountability while providing a climate of freedom for work accomplishment.

The role of the supervisor should involve trying to draw out and develop the best of each employee and to direct behavior toward achieving both employee and organizational objectives. To do this the supervisor must earn the respect and cooperative support of employees.

Leadership

The effective leader does not hold the opinion that employees only want "a fair day's pay for a fair day's work." For a few employees this may be true, but many other needs usually exist in a work situation.

The effective supervisor's leadership style usually involves:

1. Delegation of as much decision-making authority as the employee can effectively handle.
2. Trust in the judgment of employees to try to make the best decision.
3. Obtaining input from employees on decisions that will affect them.
4. Listening to what employees have to say on issues that concern them.

The general *pattern* of leadership is more important than any one action or behavior by a supervisor. Being *consistent* in all areas of leadership helps improve productivity.

Rules It is important that employees know why each rule exists, and how rules will be enforced. Rules should be specific and cover only areas over which the organization has legitimate authority. If a supervisor cannot justify a rule to employees, he or she should bring the matter to the attention of the next higher level of management for clarification and interpretation.

avoid favoritism   *Fairness* Favoritism should be avoided. However, people are different and may require different treatment in special cases.

When an employee has violated an organizational rule the following procedure should be used:

1. Approach the individual about it in *private*.
2. *Explain* what was wrong and why it was wrong.
3. Allow the individual to explain his or her version. *Listen* attentively.
4. Do *not* become emotional.
5. Give the employee an opportunity to suggest solutions.
6. If justified, follow through with the predetermined discipline for such cases.

7. Try to create an atmosphere of learning and improvement rather than one of punishment and judgment.

focus on learning and improvement

Criticism   It is far better to criticize an employee in private than in front of others. Private criticism allows the person criticized to maintain respect in his or her peer group. Criticism should be stated in matter-of-fact, unemotional tones. It should be presented in terms of job performance rather than personality characteristics. The employee should have an opportunity to explain his or her view of the situation.

criticize in private

Giving Orders   Often employees learn more about their jobs if orders are kept to a minimum. Effective supervisors encourage individuals to ask questions. Questions allow the supervisor to display true interest in helping employees do a better job.

encourage questions

Leadership effectiveness, in addition to requiring patience, tolerance, and consistency, is determined by one's skill in developing a personal view of employee behavior. This means that supervisors need to:

1. Recognize the feelings and attitudes that they bring to a situation.
2. Have an accurate evaluation of their own experiences.
3. Develop an ability to understand what others mean by their actions and words.
4. Strive to learn communications skills.

Therefore, an effective supervisor is continually working to:

1. Be available when needed.
2. Develop open and natural employee contracts.
3. Be consistent in behavior and avoid favoritism.
4. Praise when people do a good job.
5. Delegate authority where possible.
6. Be tolerant and avoid placing blame on others.
7. Adjust to the needs of the situation at hand.
8. Let individuals know how they are doing.

Handling Mistakes   Honest mistakes by individuals must be handled carefully. Snap judgments, criticism, or punishment may achieve a temporary solution, but it won't be long before affected employees will be seeking ways to avoid new responsibilities. In the end an employee may learn only how to avoid being caught and to push the blame on to others.

However, employee mistakes should not be ignored. When they occur, the supervisor should:

don't ignore mistakes

1. Call the mistakes to the employee's attention.
2. Explain the proper action and provide correct information.
3. Find out what the problem was from the employee's point of view.
4. Encourage the employee to learn and improve from mistakes.
5. Avoid embarrassing the employee in front of others.

have employees make decisions

Decision Making   Some supervisors look upon their job as the center of all decision making in their area of authority. The supervisor may think that failing to make each and every decision possible is shirking from management duties. Yet effective supervisors find that it is often more effective to let employees handle work-related decisions whenever possible.

There are a number of reasons for delegating the authority to make job-related decisions to employees:

1. It increases the individual's interest in the job and feelings of importance. People will begin to feel "in" on the organization's objectives and will be much more likely to carry out decisions they make.
2. It puts the decision making closer to the level where the needed information is available.
3. It contributes to individual development and helps prepare people for managerial duties in the future.
4. It motivates individuals to find out more about their own job as well as goals of the organization.
5. The quality of decisions made may be better.

conditions for participation in decision making

When involving employees in decision making, the following conditions should be met:

1. Allow ample time for participation by employees *before* action is required.
2. Participants must have the abilities, knowledge, and experience needed to make job-related decisions.
3. Participants must communicate with each other and with their supervisor.
4. Employees should not feel threatened if they participate or if they decide not to participate.

Participation in decision making allows employees to satisfy their needs for achievement, responsibility, and growth. One of the main benefits is to increase individuals' sense of responsibility and self-respect.

Delegation of Responsibility

Delegation of responsibility provides individuals the opportunity to achieve, accept responsibility, and earn recognition. Delegation is a way to give individuals broader areas of responsibility than they would otherwise have, including more influence on planning, organizing, and controlling their job activities.

To delegate effectively:

1. Provide individuals with specific objectives and make certain there is agreement on what is to be accomplished.
2. Help individuals set goals for their jobs—*don't* set goals for them.
3. As far as possible, allow individuals to develop methods of achieving goals but be available for counseling and support.

Delegation is a way to support the worth and importance of the individual. It frees the supervisor for other work and allows time for planning and coordinating, so the supervisor does not become lost in daily operational details.

Communication

No single supervisory skill is more important in improving performance and productivity than the ability to *communicate*. It is important for supervisors to be receptive to the complaints and suggestions of employees as well as to provide information.

be receptive to suggestions

Communication is most effective when it leads to *mutual influence* between supervisor and employees. It should be a two-way street, with ideas, information, and suggestions flowing freely between supervisor and employees. Each should be willing to listen and learn from the other.

listen to learn from others

The following are suggestions for effective communication:

1. Keep an open mind.
2. Don't enter into a dialogue with the attitude that you are always absolutely right.
3. Do more listening than talking and encourage suggestions.
4. Try to increase face-to-face communication with employees.
5. Be sensitive to the world of the employees. Try to understand the needs of employees.
6. Use direct and simple language. Don't try to impress people with a fancy vocabulary.
7. Be sensitive to the proper *time* to talk with an individual. When an individual is under great stress, obviously depressed, busy, distracted, or overly tired, wait until the situation is more suitable for a discussion.
8. When listening, be alert to unspoken or unintended meanings in what is said.

A good portion of a supervisor's communication should be in the form of feedback to employees about where they stand and how they are doing. Supervisors should inform employees about changes that will affect them.

effective communication requires trust and respect

Effective communication is based upon mutual trust and respect. Employees must feel that they can have the supervisor's attention when it is needed. They must also feel that what is said to their supervisor in confidence will remain in confidence. An effective supervisor never underestimates the value of open lines of communication.

Positive Reinforcement

people behave in ways that satisfy their needs

All the supervisory behaviors discussed have one thing in common: desired employee behaviors must be reinforced. *Positive reinforcement* is necessary, because employees perform in ways that are most satisfying to them. By providing reinforcement it is possible for performance to be improved.

A supervisor should be concerned with rewards such as responsibility, recognition, growth, and opportunity for achievement. Some of these can be provided by the supervisor (recognition, responsibility) and some must be "earned" by the employee (growth, achievement).

To use rewards effectively to stimulate better performance, a few essential factors need to be considered:

1. The desired performance level must first be *specified* and clearly *understood.*
2. Rewards must be *appropriate* to the performance and the individual.
3. Rewards should follow *as soon as possible* after the desired behavior has occurred.

It is important to note that effective supervision is in itself a positive reinforcement. The more supervisors build employees' positive self-image, the more they will be willing to support efforts to reach organizational objectives.

The factors contributing to effective supervision are summarized in Figure 15.8.

Quick Review

I. Managerial Effectiveness and Performance Improvement
   A. Management has been facing an increasing number of problems in attempting to motivate employees.
   B. Many individuals no longer find it desirable to look to authoritative standards as guides.
   C. There are no easy gimmicks that produce conditions for long-term motivation.

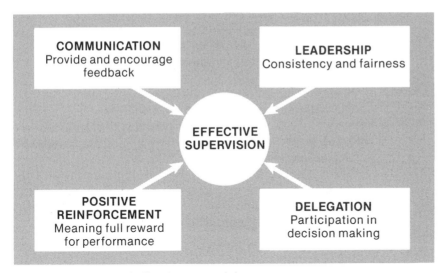

Figure 15.8   Basis of effective supervision.

II. Goal Orientation
   A. In an authority-oriented climate, individuals are provided with little incentive to increase effectiveness.
   B. Goal-oriented employees see job goals as a meaningful part of organizational objectives and as a means for achieving personal goals.
   C. Goal orientation is supported by a management that depends on meaningful goals and supportive systems with respect and trust.
   D. Goal setting can encourage achievement through:
      1. Individual involvement in goal setting.
      2. Individuals being able to relate personal goals to organizational goals.
      3. Organizations with supportive systems for goal attainment.
      4. Individual commitment to the organization.
   E. Two methods of implementing goal setting systems include:
      1. Starting at the top and then proceeding to other segments of the organization.
      2. Starting with a selected branch, department, or division.
III. A System for Goal Setting
   A. Agreement between employee and supervisor on the individual's job description, responsibilities, and results to be achieved.
   B. Performance planning and setting of individual goals.

C. Agreement of employee and superior on goals, standards, and checkpoints.
D. Evaluation of results by both employee and immediate supervisor. Judgment is based on accomplishments.
IV. Innovation and Creativity
A. Innovation and creativity are necessary for an organization to achieve long-term effectiveness.
B. An environment for creativity makes use of people's creative potential at all levels and in all activities of the organization.
C. Factors often contributing to the development of innovation and creativity are channels of communication, encouragement of new ideas, broad participation in planning, and management rewards for creativity.
V. Constructive Discipline
A. The objective of discipline should be to develop more effective performance.
B. The most desirable and effective discipline is self-discipline.
C. Effective discipline involves learning through experience.
D. Disciplinary action should be directed against the act, done in private, handled constructively, and administered fairly and consistently.
VI. Delegation and Responsibility
A. Delegation makes it possible for more effective performance.
B. Delegation can provide motivation when individuals have the authority and responsibility to use their judgments in decision making.
C. For delegation to work effectively, it must be goal oriented.
D. Delegation involves managerial risk.
E. Managers must develop secure relationships with subordinates.
F. Effective delegation focuses on results and goal attainment.
VII. Effective Supervision
A. Supervisors are responsible for both rewarding and disciplining employees.
B. Effective supervisors share information and delegate responsibility.

C. Leadership style should be characterized by consistency and fairness.
D. It is most effective to have employees make work-related decisions whenever possible.
E. Effective communication is based on mutual trust and respect.

Key Terms

Goal orientation
Goal setting systems
Innovation and
   creativity
Constructive
   discipline

Hot-stove rule
Delegation
Supervision
Organizational
   climate

Mutual influence
Effective
   supervision
Positive
   reinforcement

Discussion Questions

1. Discuss the characteristics and effects of a goal-oriented organizational climate.
2. Why would an organizational climate in which goals are seen as arbitrary, confusing, unchallenging, and authority oriented develop individual feelings of failure, frustration, and apathy in employees?
3. Under what conditions is goal setting by employees most likely to lead to high levels of achievement?
4. Discuss two methods of implementing a goal-setting system in an organization.
5. What are the advantages of a goal-setting system?
6. What action can management take to develop innovation and creativity in an organization?
7. How can constructive discipline be developed in an organization?
8. Why is it necessary for a manager to develop secure relationships with subordinates for delegation to be effective?
9. Describe the characteristics of a manager you have observed who was an effective delegator.
10. What are the characteristics of an effective supervisor's leadership style?
11. To use rewards effectively, what factors should a supervisor keep in mind?

Case Incidents

Turnover

Luis Gonzalez is the director of the finance division of a county government. Luis has two managers who work for him, and they each supervise twelve employees. The finance division handles all the accounting for the county government, including accounts payable, accounts receivable, payrolls, and budgets. The jobs in the department require extremely accurate work, because errors can substantially increase the costs involved in county government, result in adverse publicity, and create negative reactions from the public. Although the daily work of employees is highly repetitive and monotonous the workers seldom make errors because they double check each other's work.

The county manager and county commissioners feel finance is the most efficient department in the county governemnt but are concerned about the department's high turnover rate. The county commissioners believe that the turnover rate reflects the general problem of recruiting and retaining qualified employees for the government. The county manager has decided that the situation warrants hiring an outside consultant to analyze the city government's personnel problems.

The consultant began with the finance department. Part of his efforts included administering an attitude survey, which was completed by all the employees in the department. The results indicated that generally the workers were pleased with the physical working conditions, with their supervisor, and with all the managers in the county government.

But the employees expressed three areas of major dissatisfaction: (1) the pay was low, (2) the work was monotonous, and (3) there was almost no opportunity for advancement.

The results of the attitude survey were given to Luis as part of a problem-solving report for the county manager.

1. Should Mr. Gonzalez obtain more information before preparing his report? If so, what information should he obtain?
2. What are factors that may be contributing to the problems of recruiting and retaining employees?
3. What are approaches that Mr. Gonzalez could recommend to solve the recruiting and retention problems?

The Secretary

Mr. David Owens is the new regional marketing manager for Scientific Products, Incorporated. He is thirty-six years old, and considered by top-level management as one of the most effective sales managers in the company. He is often consulted by the vice-president for marketing on major marketing decisions, and it is rumored he is being groomed for a vice-presidential position.

On assuming this new regional marketing manager position, Mr. Owens found that he had a very effective sales force composed of highly motivated and extremely competent salespeople. It appeared that his major problem in the regional office revolved around the secretary, Judy Campbell. The salespeople began making frequent comments about the problems they were having with the secretary. He heard statements like, "I hate to come in the regional office because I get insulting remarks from the secretary." "I have never seen a secretary who complained so much about her work." "You should do something about the secretary, she thinks she runs the company." "The secretary challenges every statement I make. I am getting damn tired of it." "There is too much back talk from the secretary."

Mr. Owens tried to respond neutrally to the comments from the salespeople and to evaluate the work of the secretary objectively. Judy had been in the position for four years and had come well recommended from her previous job. But Mr. Owens began to notice other problems related to her performance. There was little resemblance between the letters and sales memos he dictated and what was typed. When he pointed this out to the secretary, she usually commented that she had captured the intent and tried to write them in the most effective way.

He had difficulty finding material that should have been in the office files. On several occasions when he had asked Judy to locate materials, she began going through the papers on his desk, to look for the information.

Judy also was responsible for supervising four clerk typists who worked in the office. It appeared at times that they did not have work assigned or were working on items of low priority when higher priority work was not being done.

Mr. Owens reached the conclusion that the secretary was trying to do a good job as she saw it, but that she defined the job very differently than he or the salespeople did. After thinking the situation over, Mr. Owens decided that he would attempt to correct matters by pointing out to Judy areas where he thought her behavior should be changed. He pursued this strategy for two weeks. He let Judy know when she made statements that irritated the salespeople and when work was not being performed as he felt it should be. The result of this strategy was that he received prolonged arguments from Judy as to why the salespeople were wrong and why work wasn't getting done.

1. If you were Mr. Owens, what specific course of action would you take to correct the situation?

Managerial Effectiveness and Performance Improvement

2. What communiction would you have with Judy Campbell in terms of the content of the communication and the method of communication?
3. What guidelines should a manager follow in attempting to change or discipline the behavior of an employee like Judy?

Early Retirement Program

In a midwestern manufacturing plant, rumors began to circulate about possible reductions in the work force. There were numerous articles in the local newspaper about a decline in the demand for the company's products. One morning the following memo was posted on every bulletin board, and there was a copy on every desk and at every work station.

TO: All Personnel
SUBJECT: Early Retirement Program

As a result of automation, as well as a declining work load, management, must, of necessity, take steps to reduce our work force. A reduction in staff plan has been developed which appears to be the most equitable under the circumstances.

Under the plan, older employees will be placed on early retirement, thus permitting the retention of those employees who represent the future of the company.

Therefore, a program to phase out older personnel by the end of the current fiscal year via early retirement will be placed into effect immediately. The program shall be known as RAPE(Retire Aged Personnel Early).

Employees who are RAPE'd will be given opportunity to seek other jobs within the company, provided that, while they are being RAPE'd, they request a review of their employment status before actual retirement takes place. This phase of the operation is called SCREW (A Study of Capabilities of Retired Early Workers).

All employees who have been RAPE'd and SCREW'd may then apply for a final review. This will be called SHAFT (Study Of Higher Authority Following Termination).

Program policy dictates that employees may be RAPE'd once SCREW'd twice, but may get the SHAFT as many times as the company deems appropriate.

Management discovered that the memo was printed in the plant printing shop without authorization. Three individuals were identified who had a part in running off the memo. The method used to gain access to the printing shop was not determined, and other employees who were involved in running and distributing the memo could not be identified.

1. Why did the employees distribute the memo?
2. What reply, if any, should management take to the employees about the memo?
3. Should the employees involved in printing and distributing the memo be disciplined?
4. What guidelines should management follow in dealing with a reduction in the work force?

The Perfectionist

Dale Hill is the manager of a machine shop that makes specialized tools and parts for aircraft manufacturers. The employees are highly trained and experienced machinists. Mr. Hill recently promoted Terry West to be a supervisor. Terry has been with the company for fifteen years and was an outstanding machinist.

After two weeks of Terry West's supervision, the employees working for him requested a meeting with Mr. Hill. They stated that Mr. West was making it impossible for them to get their work done. He was characterized as a nitpicker and perfectionist.

Comments by the machinists included the following: "Terry is rejecting finished parts that meet specifications if he feels they are not perfect." "The only right way is *his* way." "The supervisor's job has gone to his head. " "He wants everything cleaned up twenty times a day—he must think this is a hospital." "Terry may be perfect but we aren't." "He stands over us like we didn't know how to do our job." "He's got to realize that there is more than one way to skin a cat." "If you don't do a job exactly the way he would have done it, then you're wrong." "If he keeps telling me about his high standards, I'm going to get some earplugs."

1. If you were Dale Hill, how would you determine whether or not the employee complaints are justified?
2. Should Terry West have been promoted to supervisor because he was an outstanding machinist?
3. What should Mr. Hill do to help Terry West improve his supervision?

Exercise *Productivity Problems*

The following are typical problems many supervisors encounter. For each situation indicate the action you think the supervisor should take and the results you would expect.

Problem	Recommended Action	Expected Results
Mary is absent an average of one day a week. She thinks it should be O.K., because she doesn't get paid when she's not here.		
John messes up his work area. He thinks the clean-up man needs more work.		
Alice takes breaks that are too long. She thinks a few minutes doesn't make any difference.		
Jack is usually 15 to 20 minutes late for work. He says it doesn't matter, because if he gets behind he takes shorter breaks.		
Todd reduces productivity by spending too much time talking with employees. He says it is desirable because it increases morale.		
Ann pushes her work onto other employees. She thinks others are getting out of doing work.		

Endnotes

1. M. Scott Myers, "Conditions for Manager Motivation," *Harvard Business Review*, January–Februry 1966, p. 66.
2. Douglas M. McGregor, *The Professional Manager* (New York: McGraw-Hill,1967), p. 244.
3. From *Management Review,* March 1980, pp. 29–30.

4. Walter J. Friess, "A Case History on Creativity in Industry," in *Creativity: An Examination of the Creative Process*, ed. Paul Smith (New York: Hastings House, 1959), p. 192.
5. From a speech by Harry J. Gary, quoted in *Business Week,* 27 July 1981, p. 89.
6. John Huberman, "Discipline Without Punishment," *Harvard Business Review*, July–August 1964, pp. 62–68; and John Huberman, "Discipline Without Punishment Lives," *Harvard Business Review,* July–August 1975, pp. 6–8.
7. George Strauss and Leondard R. Sayles, *Personnel: The Human Problems of Management*, 3d ed. (Englewood Cliffs, N.J.: Prentice-Hall, 1972), pp. 267–68.

Values and Responsibilities 6

16 Managing Change

Learning Objectives

After reading this chapter, you should be able to:

1.   Describe the major characteristics of change.

2.   Identify three major types of change affecting organizations.

3.   Understand why managers must recognize, plan, and direct change.

4.   Explain the various management techniques used to introduce organizational change.

5.   Discuss quality of worklife as a major new trend influencing many organizations.

6.   Describe the characteristics and use of quality circles, tiger teams, and ringi in the work place.

7.   Explain how innovation and creativity are related to planned change.

8.   Understand how change is an inevitable part of life.

Chapter Topics

Preview and Self-Evaluation

One of our classes in organizational behavior met in a room with chalkboards at each end and along the full length of one side. The room was a rather long rectangle that seated approximately seventy students. A door opened into the building's main hallway near each end of the room. Because of nearly identical door and chalkboard arrangements at each end, the classroom had no clearly identifiable front or rear other than the placement of the instructor's table and the direction student desk-chairs faced. As a class experiment, exploring the effect change has on behavior, students reversed the student desk-chair direction and moved the instructor's table and chair to the opposite end of the room. To a stranger, the new arrangement would seem perfectly normal. Several of us waited in the hall to observe the effect of the reversed seating arrangement on the following class. Without saying a word to each other, the first five students of the next class who entered the room checked the room number as soon as they spotted the rearrangement to be sure they were in the right place. When a few more students arrived, they began, without discussion, reversing all seventy student desk-chairs and quickly moved the instructor's table and chair to their original positions.

Although the new arrangement really made no difference from an instructional point of view, it was clear that the students were disturbed and confused by the simple reversal of seating.

From our observations and interviews with the students who found their classroom "backwards," we gathered some interesting information:

1. Unplanned or unexpected change is strongly resisted by some people. One student reported, "It was like being forced to sleep on the wrong side of the bed." Most students interviewed said the new arrangement made them feel uncomfortable.
2. People are affected differently by change. Two students reported they liked the new arrangement better and one said, "I didn't notice any difference."
3. When asked why they voluntarily restored the room to its former arrangement, the most frequent response was, "It wasn't right. The chairs were in the wrong direction."

While our classroom experiment dealt with only one kind of change, managers of modern organizations find dealing with the many types of changes they face almost daily one of their most important functions.

In Chapter 16, the effect of change on organizations and management's role in planning and introducing change are discussed. Some of the basic questions relating to change are contained in the true-false test. As in previous chapters, responding to the questions will help you evaluate your own knowledge. How many can you answer before reading further?

Answer True or False

1. Although technology changes, most jobs remain the same and require the same skills. T F

2. Change affects some parts of our jobs but not others. T F

3. In a very real sense, the management of organizations is the prevention of change. T F

4. Information processing and distribution has been an area of modest change in recent years. T F

5. Social change is the most difficult for management to predict and control.　　T　　F

6. Many changes are relatively routine and cause few management problems.　　T　　F

7. People actually seek change and rarely resist it.　　T　　F

8. Quality of worklife is a worldwide change movement.　　T　　F

9. At the present time Japan is the only country using quality circles.　　T　　F

10. Change for change's sake is neither desirable nor meaningful.　　T　　F

ANSWERS: 1. F; 2. F; 3. F; 4. F; 5. T; 6. T; 7. F; 8. T; 9. F; 10. T

Change: Invasion of the Future

One of the most common questions well-meaning adults ask children is, "What are you going to be when you grow up?" It is, by its nature, virtually unanswerable. Although there are some jobs whose titles remain relatively unchanged, most of today's jobs did not exist when the people performing them were children. Even in those jobs that have the same titles, the actual work, in most cases, has been significantly altered. We live in a world where robotics, computers with the potential for artificial intelligence, biotechnology that allows us to direct evolution, automated offices, and a flood of new approaches to improving the quality of worklife are everyday events. It is easy to forget that with every accepted technological development there are changes in required job skills that are difficult to predict. We know only that everything changes; it is an undeniable fact of our existence.

everything changes　　Change affects every part of our lives but is most easily recognized in the work place.

> One of the first major newspapers to convert to modern computerized type setting, automatic presses, and automated insert additions was the *Miami Herald*. Modernization eliminated numerous traditional skills such as linotype and stereotype operators. It also created new jobs in computer programming, key data entry, and computerized equipment maintenance. To make the changes, management at the Miami newspaper developed innovative approaches that have served as models for other newspapers. Displaced employees were retrained for new jobs, older employees were given advanced retirement benefits,

and all employees were indoctrinated into changes resulting from the newer technologies of producing daily news. Through careful planning, management had successfully managed a major change that directly affected each of its employees.

In a very real sense, management of organizations is the management of change. Familiar clichés like, "It's the same old thing," "Nothing has really changed," "You're the same as you always were," are simply not true. Change is constantly occurring in all people and all things. Rather than let change occur as a natural consequence of the passage of time, knowledgeable managers work toward creating conditions that help control and direct events to ensure the growth and ultimate survival of their organizations. Failure to recognize change can be disastrous not only to a specific business but to an entire industry!

change and the automotive industry

Since 1970, Japan has rapidly gained an increasingly large share of the world automobile market for a number of reasons. According to James E. Harbour, one of the automobile industry's top consultants, U.S. automakers have failed to recognize changes in public tastes including appreciation for both quality and economy.[1] Unions have failed to recognize the impact of both wages and work practices on operating costs.

Although recent union concessions and a spirit of employee-management concern which is new to the industry may help, the road to recovery will be difficult. A major reason for the Japanese cost advantage is productivity as well as wages. An average Japanese car is assembled in 14 worker hours compared to 33 hours for the average U.S. car. Greater use of robotics, improved production techniques, and the efficient use of labor all contribute to the lower rate. While U.S. managers know the old techniques no longer work, change will be expensive, time-consuming, and painful. A great many of the needed approaches to improvement are under way at General Motors, Chrysler, Ford, and American Motors. Hopefully, these strategies will be successful.

new occupations

The invasion of the future is seen most dramatically in the rise of information-related activities. It is estimated that in 1982 almost 55 percent of the work force was engaged in the business of "generating, producing, handling, storing, transmitting, or regurgitating knowledge and information," according to Joseph F. Coates, one of the country's leading research specialists on the future.[2] Dr. Coates also points out that there will be new occupations in the fields of energy, materials, and genetics that will alter the qualifications required of the work force at a steadily increasing pace.

the older work force

In 1980, the largest population age group was 20 to 24 years with both the 15 to 19 and 25 to 29 age groups only slightly smaller. By the year 2000, the 35 to 39 age group will be the largest with the 40 to 44 and 45 to 49 age groups close behind. One interpretation of such data is that the major work force is steadily becoming older. As a result, society in the year 2000 will reflect the values, attitudes, and beliefs of a group older than those of the mid-1980s. Work organizations will be comprised primarily of employees who will be, on the whole, the oldest work force in terms of average age ever seen in the United States.

Rapid growth in new technologies coupled with changing lifestyles, age groups, economic and political forces, as well as the way society views itself all create a clouded view of the future.

Characteristics of Change

rate, direction, and diffusion of change

There are a number of special characteristics of change that most people recognize from personal experience. For a variety of reasons, primarily habit or routine, these qualities or special features of change are frequently ignored. At least three are of vital importance to all people in work organizations and especially to managers. The first of these is *rate* of change or the speed with which change takes place. Another significant aspect is the *direction* of change. A third characteristic involves the *diffusion* of change far beyond its point of origin.

Rate of Change

the rate of change may increase in the future

During the lifetime of most living adults, more technological and social change has occurred than in the entire previous history of humanity. There is a considerable body of evidence indicating that changes will continue at a possibly even greater pace than in the past. Change, however, does not occur at the same rate for all things or sets of conditions. With the development of the small electronic calculator and its ultimate reduction in price, the slide rule, which as late as 1974 was the primary calculating tool of students and professionals in engineering and science, has become virtually obsolete. On the other hand, the common graphite-tipped wooden pencil has changed very little since around 1658, except for the addition of erasers in the early 1700s. More subtle changes in our society have also taken place at different rates and in more complex ways.

Nearly all organizations are affected by rate change. Rapid change affecting a large segment of an organization can create a great deal more difficulty than step-by-step, carefully controlled rates of change. In addition to rates of change, managers are faced with the more unpredictable direction of change.

Direction of Change

Direction of change is the term used to define the way present conditions will alter future events.

Beginning in the early 1930s and extending through the mid-1950s, many people felt that the small airplane, or at least some type of personal flying vehicle, would become a commonly accepted part of nearly everyone's lives. High school students were encouraged to take courses in aviation technology; books and newspaper articles hailed the coming of the air age. Aviation did change rapidly, with a tremendous impact on public transportation, but not in the predicted direction. Private aircraft as a percentage of total transportation has changed very little while commercial air transportation has grown into an essential industry.

Direction of change as well as rate of change can cause significant problems for organizations. Some change in direction is reasonably predictable. During the past ten years, there has been a steady acceleration of unionization of federal, state, county, and municipal employees. We can predict that this change from nonaffiliated to unionized public employees will continue for some time. Other directions of change are not as easy to forecast. When the laser system of producing amplified pure light was announced in 1960, few people imagined the many directions of change it would bring. Lasers are used to determine the precise location of a football when there is doubt about whether a first down has been made, to treat certain eye disorders, to serve as part of some computer memory systems, and to drill percise holes in steel. These represent only a small number of the activities laser technology has changed. Figure 16.1 shows the varying rates and direction of change in three other areas.

can you predict the changes that will result from laser technology?

In work organizations, managers are constantly concerned with the direction of the marketplace. Will the public buy more synthetic

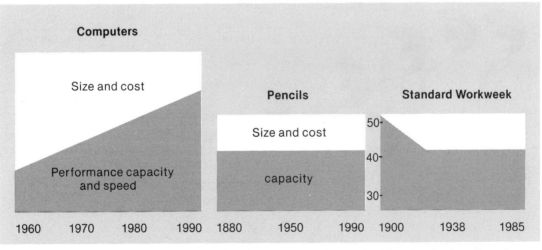

Computers have greatly increased in performance, memory capacity, and speed of response. Their cost and physical size (per operation) has been greatly reduced.

Uninflated costs, size, and capacity of ordinary graphite lead pencils have changed very little in the past 100 years.

The standard workweek declined steadily until 1938. At that time the 40-hour workweek became, by law, a national standard and has not significantly changed since.

Figure 16.1 Comparison of rates of change.

clothing than natural fiber clothing this year? What will be the requirements of new governmental regulations? Will unions ask for more benefits or shorter hours? What new technological shifts will affect the organization? Will environmental concerns outweigh production demands? All these questions demonstrate a concern for the direction of change. The need to predict the course of change accurately is as vital as forecasting how rapidly it will occur.

Diffusion of Change

One change frequently causes other changes. The term *diffusion* means to spread out. In most cases, change is diffused over a wider area than anticipated.

"domino effect"

Diffusion of change is frequently called the "domino effect" (see Figure 16.2). An amusing television or state presentation (and a frequent pastime of some children) involves setting up hundreds of dominoes so that when the first one is pushed over, it sets up a chain reaction that runs until they all eventually tumble. If dominoes are arranged in complex patterns, we can witness their fall in several different directions.

In work organizations, we frequently see diffusion. A change of weather in California that results in smaller tomato crops may in turn cause price increases in catsup and tomato paste sold in New York,

Figure 16.2 The domino effect.

layoffs at food processing plants, loss of sales by suppliers to food processors, local decreases in business activities because of lower plant payrolls, increased numbers of people receiving unemployment compensation, and either increased taxes or a rising federal debt to offset the added costs.

> At the Cordoban Chemical Company, employees accrue seniority both in their jobs and in the plant. In the event of a reduction in the work force due to lack of work, senior employees may displace employees with less seniority in lower job classifications for which the senior employees qualify. In a recent layoff due to automation of test equipment, highly skilled test technicians "bumped" process inspectors who in turn bumped processors. Affected processors displaced loaders and packers with still less seniority. The loaders and packers, in some cases, bumped custodians who displaced, in a few instances, cafeteria dishwashers. A layoff in the test area resulted in a dishwasher hunting for a new job!

the diffusion of change throughout an organization

Managers must constantly recognize the diffusion of change throughout an organization. A change in procurement procedures may result in changes in several other departments, such as accounting, receiving, inspection, and material control. It is virtually impossible to change any part of an organization or the way it operates without affecting to some degree all of its other parts.

Coming Together

Rate of change, direction of change, and diffusion are all important concepts and usually affect organizations at the same time.

Change and the Ripple Effect

For nearly fifty years, the General Electric manufacturing plant in Ontario, California, had been one of the primary producers of electric irons in the country. Then in the spring 1982, economic conditions forced General Electric to close the plant. The action had an immediate impact on the 850 employees laid off; and over the following days and weeks, that impact rippled outward, affecting an ever-widening circle of workers and businesses.

First hit were the service shops and establishments in Ontario. Since the 850 General Electric workers no longer had money to spend, the town's economy began to slow down. As a result, 1,200 workers in grocery stores, banks, barber shops, and many other establishments were also laid off. Next to feel the pinch were parts manufacturers and suppliers who could no longer sell their products to the GE plant. They were soon letting some of their workers go as well.

Yet the story in parts of Mexico and Indonesia was quite different. After closing its Ontario plant, General Electric opened new facilities in these two countries to manufacture plastic rather than metal household products.

One change—and rapid, multidirectional, diffuse effects.[3]

Although the General Electric case seems extreme, it is an all too common example of the widespread effects of only a moderate change. A dock workers' strike in New Orleans may affect wheat prices in Montana if the strike prevents shipping to overseas markets. A simple change in the interpretation of tax laws may affect millions of taxpayers.

Change may occur slowly, rapidly, or at any rate. It may be helpful or harmful, or more likely, helpful to some and harmful to others. Either way, it cannot be stopped, only managed or altered.

Types of Change

In addition to the characteristics of change (rate, direction, and diffusion), there are many types of change that affect organizations. All require careful management attention. Each type of change can occur at different rates, can travel in many directions, and can diffuse throughout not only an organization but a whole society. While it is impossible to list all of the types of changes that organizations are concerned with, we can classify some important types of change into three major categories. *Technological changes* that involve new equipment, materials, or facilities are the easiest to identify. A second type of change more difficult for management to deal with includes the shifts in attitudes, values, and beliefs known as social change. The third category we call *internal change* includes the changes that effect day-to-day work activities and are directly under management's control. Changes in job assignments, organizational structure, personnel practices, procedures, equipment, and facilities (apart from technological shifts) are grouped in the third category. These three types of change are shown in Figure 16.3.

Managers aware of change forces must plan effective ways of introducing new concepts, ideas, and courses of action. Changes within the work force also influence managerial change strategies.

Technological Change

change can require new skills and eliminate the usefulness of old skills

Whenever we find a new or better method for doing things, it frequently involves what has become known as *technological change*. In some areas of work, technological change is far more noticeable than other kinds of change. Computer-terminal cash registers and the widespread use of registers with electronic price reading devices have changed the entire retail industry. Inventory data, departmental efficiency, clerical errors, and market planning data are available to management on an immediate request basis. Banks have moved to install more electronic tellers, electronic records management, and electronic transfer of funds. New skills are required and old ones no longer needed. Computerized production control and automated manufacturing using so-called smart machines have changed the meaning of mass production. Medical centers throughout the world rely to a large extent on automatic analyses of examination data to help in diagnosing patients' illnesses. While, in many cases, machines are performing repetitive operations considered boring to most employees, technology is also reducing the challenge of other jobs.

Introduction of new technology into the work place is nearly always seen as threat by the employees affected. Although some job displacement can occur, introduction of technological change is most often accompanied by a shift in employee assignments and skills rather than absolute reductions in the work force. It is true that mechanization has drastically reduced the number of people in certain industries such as agriculture, but increased production has created more jobs in food processing, distribution, sales, and allied service industries.

In a desperate move, an owner of a small plant that processed local fruit into jelly and jam asked for a management consultant's help in reducing costs. A major expense item was the handling of

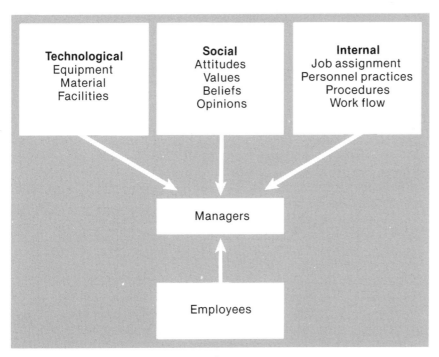

Figure 16.3 Organizational change forces.

bulk sugar shipped by rail in hundred-pound sacks to a nearby warehouse and then by truck to the plant, where the sacks were stored and emptied as needed into cooking vessels. The consultant suggested installation of a tank to hold liquid sugar that could be automatically metered during the cooking process. The entire sugar handling problem, along with its workers, was eliminated. Improved efficiency, however, ultimately resulted in expansion of the plant and an increase of additional personnel in other activities such as marketing, purchasing, shipping, and distribution.

In a world whose population will double during the next twenty-five years, with a corresponding doubling of needs (and doubling of impoverished as well as affluent people), survival will depend on increased efficiency, not only in work methods but in technology. Choosing appropriate technology, training employees, and promoting acceptance of new job requirements will continue to be a major challenge to managers of work organizations.

The Computer Age Gap

As New York computer executive Charles Lecht laments, "If you were born before 1965, you're going to be out of it." Lecht is referring to the explosion in micro- and minicomputer use that has hit the 1980s. Even now, conventional typewriters, file cabinet storage, and familiar office procedures are rapidly disappearing as companies convert to the "electronic office." Small computers are becoming more powerful, memory units more compact, and printers more sophisticated. Soon every field of work and knowledge will find ways to employ these versatile machines.

Surprisingly, children adapt to computer usage much faster and with more imagination than their parents. Steven Jobs, co-founder of Apple Computer, Inc., observes, "Those kids [today's gradeschoolers] know more about the new software than I do." Steven was only 27 in 1982—hardly an oldtimer.

Perhaps the change is best reflected by the ten-year-old who stated, "When I grow up, it's going to be the Computer Age. It won't affect parents. They're out of the Computer Age. They had their own age."[4]

Social Change

social changes can result in changes in employee demands

Managers have little chance of controlling the *social change* that influences their organizations. Social change occurs when a large segment of the general population adopts a different set of values. Major social changes can be the result of economic shifts, threats of war, alteration in personal values, resource shortages, or any number of factors that directly or indirectly change or threaten individual and group lifestyles. In its direct effect on management, social change is most evident in attitudes toward authority, increasing demands for work that is personally rewarding, introduction of women into the work force, enforcement of equal economic opportunity, legislative requirements, and the compression of pay differentials between skill levels. Astute managers carefully note changes in social climate and adjust to their requirements rather than resist their almost overwhelming force.

Social change also affects employees in clearly discernible ways. Younger employees often exhibit different value systems than older employees, which results in mutual misunderstanding and, frequently, open dissension. Many younger employees do not show what older workers feel is proper "respect." The younger employees also have expectations that differ from those of their work organizations and their unions. They willingly revolt against the traditional values of both in demanding faster promotion, less control, and greater personal freedom. Managers report that the "new employee" is less frightened of authority and less subservient than more traditional employees. Younger employees' potential may prove to be a primary asset to management in the long run. They are forcing managers to reexamine their own beliefs and methods of dealing with employees. Bradford Boyd, in his excellent *Management Minded Supervision*, points out that, ultimately, work is controlled by employees, not managers.[5] Whether work is accomplished is the choice of the employee, not the manager. Increasingly, employees realize this.

change forces managers to reexamine their beliefs

In the much read book, *Work in America*, published by the Department of Health and Human Services, a study by researchers from the University of Michigan emphasizes a long-term social change recognized by management theorists for many years. In rating job characteristics such as security, safety, pay, adequate help and assistance, seeing the results of one's work, and other similar items, interesting work was chosen as the most important job consideration by more of the 1,053 employees sampled than any other factor rated. Although it is not a new need, many workers increasingly seek interesting work that is relevant to their lives. A major challenge facing management now and in the future is the necessity as well as the desirability for providing work that allows personal psychological growth opportunities as well as pay.

interesting work

There is evidence that Americans adjust very rapidly to social change. Prior to 1964, many colleges and universities, particularly southern states, had no blacks participating in sports programs. By 1974, an all-white student body or athletic program was considered an oddity. Before 1972, women assigned to field engineering positions by utility companies were virtually nonexistent. Today, in contrast, women are in nearly all utility company classifications, including the previously male-dominated field engineering positions. The same changes,

rapid adjustment to social change

noticeable at first but now so common that they are unnoticed, are true for nearly all fields and levels of work. Problems do arise, however, from sometimes unexpected sources. When women patrol officers began working as partners with male officers, one city police chief reported that, while he had few problems with the new officers, the wives of male employees were constantly checking and accusing his department of encouraging "homewrecking." After a few months, complaints subsided and women patrol officers were fully accepted by both fellow workers and the community at large.

wage compression   Although it is essentially an economic problem, wage compression also marks a major social change. Truck drivers often earn more than dock managers; school custodians may be paid nearly as much as school principals and considerably more than beginning teachers; workers in a warehouse often earn as much and frequently more money than the office manager for the facility. Differences between money paid for necessary work requiring little skill and work requiring long periods of specialized training have steadily been compressed. Trained personnel are often resentful, and management may feel it is paying too much for too little. On the other hand, workers performing the low-skilled tasks resent what they feel are the unfair attitudes of skilled employees. The disappearance of financial elitism in the work force has in many cases become a reality.

Management's success in dealing with social change hinges on sensitivity to rapidly changing values, recognition of forces that bring such changes, and flexibility in adjusting policy and organizational style rather than resisting such changes. Effective communication, planned participation, improved job design, and careful implementation of policies are all necessary.

Internal Change

Within all work organizations, changes are constantly taking place. Those based on management decisions and unrelated to technology or social change are called *internal changes*. Many changes are relatively routine and cause few management problems. Others are far more difficult and require careful attention. The impact of change is determined by how much it disturbs what employees perceive as a balanced, non-threatening situation. Change in job assignment in some organizations, where people are usually assigned one particular set of tasks, can be very threatening and cause a great deal of unrest. In organizations that regularly rotate employees through a variety of assignments, job shifts may seem perfectly normal and routine.

change often results in a shift in power   Changes in organization structure, such as combining departments or creating new functions, are frequently difficult for both managers and nonmanagement employees. Changes imply a shift in power—someone new will be in charge. As long as organizational changes in structure are nonthreatening to those affected, there is little resistance. A perceived loss of status or position of influence can be disrupting to those affected.

No change in an organization other than complete closure affects employees and management as traumatically as a major reduction in work force.

Long before it was generally recognized by other employees, the project manager of a large chemical producer's "Environmental Equipment Development" program learned that new approaches by a competitive firm would eventually cause his project, the equipment manufacture, to be abandoned. In subsequent discussions with higher-level management it was confirmed that all people associated with environmental equipment development would have to be terminated if they couldn't be placed in other segments of the organization. To meet current obligations, the project manager was told he would have to keep his work force of twenty-three specialists working at close to peak efficiency for sixty days and then lay them off in a period of two weeks.

The project manager knew that his department would learn of the impending reduction in force. As he saw it, his alternatives were (1) try to hide the real impact of the layoff until work on hand was nearly complete, (2) tell selected personnel that they would be affected, (3) let his section managers break the news as the rumors became widely known, or (4) call all of his department to a meeting and explain what he foresaw for the forthcoming period. He chose to follow the last alternative and openly explained the situation. He also let workers know that he was working with the personnel department to help relocate as many people as possible and was personally contacting other firms who might need the special skills possessed by his employees. Contrary to his worst expectations, and those of his immediate superior, morale actually increased and work was accomplished on time. One of his section heads explained, "We knew it was coming, but somehow hearing it from you made it seem not quite as bad and not your fault."

While openness and honesty are not always cure-alls, they are effective starting places in planning organizational change of any kind.

openness and honesty are necessary for effective change

As we observed earlier, it is nearly impossible to list all of the kinds of changes that occur as a result of managerial action within an organization. The degree of success a manager has in implementing changes is dependent on careful assessment of how employees will react to the change and to the ultimate goals planned. Effective managers of change use a variety of techniques to assure smooth transitions from old to newer and more effective ways of accomplishing work.

Managing Change

In a very real sense, managers accomplish work not only through the efforts of others, but also through planning, organizing, implementing, and controlling change. They must recognize the human processes involved in change and know how to use a variety of techniques in introducing it. Management of change begins with the recognition that change is needed. Asking the right questions is a good place to start planning for change. What needs to be done to accomplish work easier or more efficiently? Why are we doing this the way we are? How can we improve what we're doing? Planned changes begin not only with identifying needed change, but also with the recognition that people are going to be affected. Success or failure may depend on their reactions.

Reactions to Change

Nearly sixty years ago, William Issac Thomas, a sociologist well known at the time, identified what he felt were the four basic personality forces or "wishes" of people:

personality forces

1. The wish for new experiences.
2. The wish for security.
3. The wish for recognition.
4. The wish for response.

Although modern behavioral science has long since abandoned Thomas's view of personal needs, his viewpoint is useful in looking at reactions to change.

many people seek new experiences

Many people, as Thomas predicted, do seem to seek new experiences. Studies of limited-scope, repetitive jobs, such as stacking boxes all day long, counting forms, filing reports, checking bottles for cracks and dirt, sorting grocery coupons, or any other "dull" jobs, consistently show high rates of turnover, absenteeism, or other symptoms of dissatisfaction. In such cases, employees usually seek and welcome change. When change is not initiated by management, employees will frequently create their own by disrupting work, staging an accident, or in some cases, developing a resentment toward management. There is a growing body of evidence that employees who are provided a variety of activities with minimum successive repetition of the same task show a greater degree of job satisfaction. This observed need for new experiences can be a valuable clue to managers responsible for designing jobs.

However, when change is perceived as a potential or possible threat, it is frequently resisted according to Thomas's theory. With the exception of those who constantly seek risks as a way of obtaining recognition, self-esteem, or self-fulfillment, most people are somewhat dubious of change that can be a threat to their status, influence, pay, or job.

In planning for change, then, managers are faced with two seemingly conflicting types of human behavior: the need for change and the resistance to change, both acting simultaneously.

the need for change and the resistance to change

When it became obvious that it had outgrown its present facilities, management of the Gulf-Western Telephone Company decided to move to a new, more modern, and larger facility. When the announcement was made, virtually every manager was deluged with complaints. "The new facility is too far away." "Parking is no good at the new place." "The new building is in a strange neighborhood." The complaints went on and on.

To help ease the disruption caused by the impending move, employees were taken in groups by their immediate supervisor and his or her department manager on a guided tour of the new facility. All employees were shown exactly where their desk or work station would be located, where they would park, the new cafeteria, and given a tour of neighboring shopping centers. Prior to the move, a map of the new facility provided to each employee showed their new office and even desk location by number. Complaints were dramatically reduced. When the actual move was made, there was little turnover in personnel or loss of efficiency.

Some resistance to change may be based on a logical analysis of its probable effects. If a change is seen as making work more difficult or less efficient, resistance will frequently be apparent. A great deal of resistance to change, however, is emotional and is the result of fear of failure, loss of security, or lack of understanding of possible benefits. Over a period of time, managers have developed ways of alleviating both types of resistance, as shown in Figure 16.4.

reducing resistance to change

1. Encouraging participation in planning and implementing change by the people directly affected is a useful method of minimizing resistance. A north-central railway company placed a large piece of plywood on the wall of the employee lunchroom with a simple sign asking, "How should the shop be remodeled?" After some hesitation, small models of carefully labeled machines and equipment began appearing on the board. At the end of a two-month period, the shop superintendent announced that a study had been made of the employees' shop layout and that it had been accepted by management. The new shop is still a source of pride to the employees who helped in its planning.

   Participation in developing procedures, improving work methods, and setting goals has also been effective. In introducing change through participation, however, management must carefully avoid any suggestion of manipulation, condescending attitudes, unfounded criticism of employee efforts, and failure to explain lack of management action. Once destroyed by improper

Values and Responsibilities   451

or inept handling of decisions based on employee participation, management credibility is usually lost forever.

2. Change in many cases can be introduced in small increments. Gradual, step-by-step changes allow adjustment over an extended period of time. An example of this technique is the introduction of metric measurement in the United States. In work organizations, new equipment or methods are frequently added in gradual steps.

3. If properly administered, education and training that demonstrate the personal as well as organizational benefits of the planned change can often alter resistance to change. Care must be taken to explain both disadvantages as well as overriding advantages when education for change is undertaken.

While many techniques of introducing change are available, a cardinal rule in all is to carefully plan, expect some resistance, and realize that most people will adapt to positive change with positive attitudes. Unless definite benefits can be seen, however, by the people most affected, change introduction can be a very bumpy road.

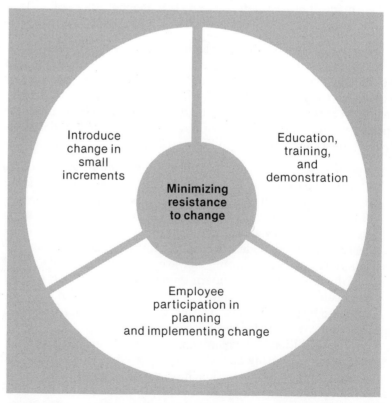

Figure 16.4 Approaches to reducing resistance to change.

Organizational Change Techniques

While most deliberate change centers on a specific problem area, it is sometimes desirable to alter the basic way an entire organization functions. Nearly all such changes come from the recognition that interpersonal relations, attitudes, or fundamental ways of managing and operating need improvement.

Some of the more popular change techniques include management by objectives, organizational development, survey feedback, behavior modification, transactional analysis, and contingency approaches. Frequently, two or more methods are used simultaneously. A brief description of these approaches to change will show how they differ.

Management by Objectives

Approximately twenty years ago Dr. Peter Drucker, a highly respected management writer, consultant, and university professor, stated that the only way management performance can be objectively evaluated is by results. If a manager commits himself or herself to achieving specific, clearly defined, measureable objectives within a definite time period, then performance can be measured in terms of what was or was not achieved. Drucker's philosophy, although not a new or revolutionary concept, served as a basis for the development of what is now popularly called *management by objectives (MBO)*. In its simplest terms, MBO is a systematic approach to setting organizational goals and determining how well they have been attained.

MBO

Although most careful management planning includes some elements of the MBO process, the system has some unique features:

1. MBO ideally involves everyone in an organization. Each person defines in clear, unambiguous terms what he or she intends to achieve in a given period of time, how he or she will achieve the intended goals, and when each of the separate goals will be attained. These personal objectives are then discussed with the person's immediate supervisor or manager. A consensus between manager and subordinate is reached regarding the measureability and appropriateness of individual goals. The consensus discussion also takes into account whether the goals truly represent the scope of the employee's assigned area of responsibility. After the goals and plan of action are agreed to by both the manager and the subordinate, a goal review timetable is also set.

   well-defined goals

2. Periodically, as determined by the review timetable, progress toward goal achievement is discussed in additional manager and employee interviews. During such discussions the employee reports to the manager on progress and problems in reaching the previously set goals. One of the MBO's strongest points is its

   review progress toward goals

value in shifting responsibility for the attainment of job objectives from the manager to the employee.

mutually supportive goals

3. For employees in managerial positions, the process is very similar. Each manager defines goals, timetables, and plans of action which are discussed with and refined in meetings with the next higher level of management. As in the case of nonmanagement employees, periodic reviews are also arranged. Managerial goals include not only personal goals but departmental or divisional goals as well. At the very highest executive levels in the organization, top management sets overall objectives for the total organization as well as personal goals. Top-management goals are frequently reviewed by special committees or boards. Since goals are discussed fully at each level in the organization, they are mutually supportive. By mutually supportive, we mean that the employee's goals support those of his or her department and manager. Each manager's goals support those of higher-level management as well as the overall organizational objectives. Conference sessions that include other managers are used to coordinate departmental and divisional goals. Such goals are also submitted to top management for review.

MBO requires training

For an MBO system to work effectively, it must become the guiding philosophy of an organization. Some organizations have tried MBO and discontinued its use. A primary difficulty is that MBO can, if not carefully planned and directed, become a massive paperwork system of elaborate records and reports. It is also dependent on the careful training about its use throughout the organization and the enthusiastic backing of top management. Some managers feel that MBO puts a great deal of pressure on individuals to set and meet goals and that the danger of too many "easy" objectives is always possible. Perhaps its greatest strength, however, is its concentration on results rather than subjective evaluation of performance.

personal objectives plan

To better understand MBO in action, let us examine Table 16.1, the "Personal Objectives Plan" of Sherry Gunderson, an accounting technician who works for Howell Office Supply Company.

The actions marked with a double asterisk (**) are special problem-solving activities. On the date Sherry and her immediate manager have previously agreed upon, they will meet to again review objectives and progress toward their accomplishment. In circumstances beyond Sherry's control, such as a change in procedures or actions by another department, objectives may be altered and completion dates changed. This type of MBO procedure allows Sherry, as well as her manager, to evaluate job performance in terms of actual accomplishments. While Sherry's goals are short-range, objectives that take longer periods of time may be used equally well.

advantages of MBO

Although, as mentioned earlier, MBO requires considerable effort and a great deal of coordination to work properly, its advantages are

Table 16.1 Personal objectives plan of Sherry Gunderson

Job objectives	Objective action	Completion date
Classifying procurement documents	Decrease classification errors to less than 2% from present 3%	June 1
Verification of document completeness	O.K.—No action required	
Posting procurement actions	Have all posting complete within 24 hours of issue	June 1
Completing procurement document daily report	Develop simpler report format for management review**	Aug. 15
Maintaining procurement document files	O.K.—No action required	
Providing accounting procurement data to data processing	Develop summary data form for easier interpretation	Aug. 15
Collecting procurement data for market analysis	Submit data to marketing department no later than 10 a.m. daily.	Immediately

usually greater than the problems it creates. Organizational change is brought about through the systematic encouragement of careful planning, and commitment to both individual and organizational goals, and the evaluation of performance in terms of tangible achievements. Because of its focus on individual responsibility in accomplishing work, MBO can be one of management's strongest motivational tools, especially in types of job assignments where employees control their own work pace. Where productivity is determined largely by machine or conveyor speed and in highly routine activities, the system is likely to have less value.

MBO fails when the system is used as a threat or when the setting of objectives becomes so routine they are meaningless. MBO also fails when the system of recording and evaluating objectives is so burdensome and complex that both management and employees rebel. The steps in MBO are summarized in Figure 16.5.

Organizational Development

Organizational development, usually known simply as OD, is a popular term that describes many long-range approaches to changing the basic ways an organization operates. It can incorporate a wide variety of training and personal development of systems for improvement. While a precise definition of OD is difficult, certain characteristics are common to many OD programs:

1. OD is concerned with the effectiveness of the total organization rather than concentrated retraining of managers or installation of management development programs.
2. OD is planned. A specific set of actions are designed to improve the climate, health, and effectiveness of an organization.
3. OD is not a specific technique but is instead a systematic approach to redirect the energies of people in organizations to more effective behavior.
4. OD tries to help answer the fundamental management questions, Where are we now? Where do we want to be? and How do we get there?

Organizations that have OD programs frequently use outside consultants who have the necessary expertise, objectivity, and analytical ability to evaluate organizational operations. The consultant is recognized as being outside the normal political forces of the organization and can effectively act as a primary force or agent of change. It is high-

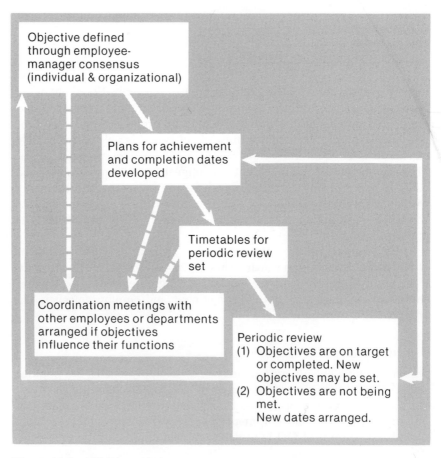

Figure 16.5 MBO in action.

ly likely, as time passes, that OD will become a more clearly defined method of organizational analysis and change with increasing influence on management thinking.

Survey Feedback

As a method for changing behavior in organizations, the *survey feedback* system has had considerable success. Developed by the Survey Research Center at the University of Michigan, the survey feedback system includes a questionnaire used to gather information about an organization. The data is then given to the managers of the organization with interpretations usually provided by an outside consultant. After discussion of the survey information in meetings between managers and their subordinates, employees are encouraged to participate in planning corrective actions for problems revealed by the questionnaire. Areas covered by the questionnaires include a wide range of organizational functions. As in the use of many other change techniques, a consultant may be involved in helping to develop and interpret data. The consultant also assists managers, beginning with the top and working through each level, in their meetings with their subordinates and in the planning of actions to correct problems that have been defined. Survey feedback methods have the inherent weakness, if not carefully used, of creating defensive behavior on the part of many managers and polarizing differing points of view.

Behavior Modification

Growing largely out of the work of the well-known psychologist B. F. Skinner, behavior modification as an organizational change method is relatively new. From a theoretical point of view, it is relatively easy to understand, but it is sometimes difficult to implement.

Over thirty years ago, Skinner and other behaviorist psychologists developed well-documented studies of the effectiveness of respondent conditioning and the principle of reinforcement. *Respondent conditioning* involves rewarding desired behavior and not rewarding undesirable behavior. If we want to train a dog to respond to a whistle, we can whistle and show the dog a reward such as a dog biscuit. When the animal approaches out of curiosity or comes to get its reward (i.e., the biscuit) we also give it a friendly pat and say "good dog!" or some other appropriate warm-sounding phrase. After a few trials, the dog will come when we whistle whether we have a biscuit or not. It will respond to the reward of expected praise or affection rather than food. As long as it can expect a reward of some kind, the animal will continue to come to us when we whistle. The dog has been conditioned. Its behavior has been modified to our desires. Its continued response is strengthened by the expectancy of a reward for correct performance.

During his early studies, Skinner found that animals, if properly rewarded, can be trained to do a variety of fairly complex tasks. Repeated

respondent conditioning

rewards are call *reinforcements*. Skinner found that for effective reinforcement, a carefully planned schedule must be followed. Constant re-
reinforcements   wards, too closely spaced, are not as effective as those timed to meet
the animal's need. A plate full of corn left in a pigeon's training box is
not as effective as the reward of a few grains of corn for pecking the correct lever. Rewards must also be properly timed. The most effective rewards are those that immediately follow the desired behavior.

extinction   Skinner also found that positive rewards, such as praise or food, are
generally more effective than negative reinforcement, such as punishment. When neither rewards nor punishment is present, a condition of
no reinforcement, then *extinction* occurs. Extinction refers to the loss
of a behavior. A tape recording of our whistle with no pat, praise, or biscuit will soon result in our dog's ignoring whistles altogether. Further
studies by Skinner and others demonstrated that respondent conditioning also works with people. Human behavior can be shaped or
modified by rewards and punishments using similar techniques to
those used with animals.

Behavior modification, as respondent conditioning is popularly
called, has some intriguing possibilities for management application.
One of the best documented examples of the potential of behavior
modification in industry is its application at the Emery Air Freight
Company in Los Angeles.[6] At Emery Air Freight, supervisors were
carefully and thoroughly trained to praise work correctly performed by
employees, such as keeping records of activities, improving delivery
times, or responding to telephone requests for information. In one department, employees were required to package goods for shipment by
air. The size and shape of packages used was critical. Skinner had each
employee record the size and type of box used on a checklist sheet each
time an item was packaged. The checklist gave the employee immediate reinforcement that his or her performance was correct. At carefully
planned interviews, supervisors reviewed the checklists and made favorable comments about the employee's accuracy to further reinforce
the desired behavior. A 90-percent reduction of packaging errors was
attained almost immediately after the system was installed. Similar
types of reinforcement procedures (i.e., checklists for immediate feedback, coupled with praise) were designed for other types of activities.
The results were beyond the expectations of Emery's management.
Several hundred thousand dollars in actual savings were realized the
first year of the program. Over two million dollars were saved during
its first three years.

characteristics of   Successful reinforcement in work situations is dependent, then, on
successful   two factors: (1) immediate feedback in the form of clearly identifiable
reinforcement   evidence of correct behavior and (2) the expectancy of rewards (or in
some cases, the avoidance of punishment). As we noted earlier, behav-
ior modification techniques are not new but their application in work
organizations has been limited because of lack of trained specialists to
sell and develop behavior modification programs. The terms *respon-*

dent conditioning and *behavior modification* also create images of manipulation, brainwashing, and "big brotherism" to some people. It is likely that skilled consultants will eventually create a less frightening terminology and behavior modification will become a more widely applied organizational change force than it is today.

It should be noted that behavior modification has been widely used in special education programs and correctional institutions, although its full potential in work organizations is yet to be realized. Unlike many other change techniques, behavior modification concentrates on specific operational problem areas rather than the total organization.

Quality of Worklife

Many of the techniques used to encourage and direct change in organizations are proven, valid, and workable approaches to moving organizations in desired directions. It is unfortunate that gullible managers often listen to consultants who are both ignorant and incorrect in their methods. Many managers also fall into the trap of accepting untested popular psychology theories that are potentially harmful. Because they are busy and often seeking expert help, they may become victims of incompetent advisors.

"popular" approaches often wrong

A move that shows definite promise and, to a large extent, avoids the pitfalls of false prophets is known as *quality of worklife* or QWL. QWL is not based on a definite theory, technique, or system, but is primarily concerned with building a climate of mutual respect between management and employees. Although not new in its approaches, QWL is a worldwide movement that seems to be finding its greatest resistance in the United States where many managers see it as another way of pampering already spoiled employees.

While no specific system has been clearly defined, the QWL movement seems to have certain underlying principles that encourage shared responsibility, increased individual responsibility and authority, and a greater consultative relationship between managers and employees. Status differences are diminished and the concepts of shared partnership is encouraged not only between managers and employees but between employees and employees as well as among managers of various departments. Companies such as Westinghouse, Kodak, AT&T, General Motors, Martin Marietta, General Foods, Weyerhauser, and others have found that less concern with control and increased attention to positive work relationships, job design, and shared decision making pay off.

shared partnership

Table 16.2 outlines some of the key ingredients of the QWL movement.

Perhaps most seriously, the QWL movement challenges traditional authority and accountability relationships, as well as traditional adversarial union-management relationships. It is difficult for both employees and managers, long accustomed to task-oriented authoritarian values, to change to an essentially people-oriented, task-achievement type

union-management challenge

Table 16.2 General Quality of Worklife Principles

1. Jobs are designed to optimize job depth. Employees, when feasible, are given control over essential task decisions and are responsible for its achievement.
2. Whenever possible, "natural work teams" are formed where each member is an essential ingredient of a productive effort. At Volvo in Sweden, employees work as a team of ten to twelve people to assemble an entire automobile rather than individually installing a single component on an assembly line. Other companies have adopted similar methods.
3. Management teams work as problem solving and goal development groups to achieve more functional organizational formats and improved work flow. Organization functions are considered more important than individual departments.
4. Decisions affecting employees, their work, new products, procedures, or policy changes are discussed with employees. Decisions are not implemented until total employee input has been received. Decisions are evaluated in terms of both employee and management recommendations. Management avoids the "we know everything" type of control that is frequently counterproductive.
5. Most importantly, a climate of partnership between managers and employees is encouraged rather than the all too frequent adversarial relationships.
6. Managers become resource persons, evaluators of performance, and developers of people rather than controllers of people.

of thinking. Some employees, undoubtedly, may find working for managers who accept total responsibility, make all essential decisions, and are highly directive but benevolent easier to work for than those who encourage personal responsibility, team effort, and decisions by employees. The extent to which the QWL movement becomes an accepted reality rather than a lip-service philosophy remains to be seen through the 1980s and 1990s. At best, it promises that cooperation between management and employees can yield better products and services at lower costs with greater personal satisfaction. At worst, it can be another popular notion that neither management nor employees can accept.

Theory Z   It should be noted that the "Theory Z" concepts popularized by William Ouchi are based on QWL concepts.[7] Ouchi's approach incorporates the principles outlined in Table 16.2 as well as those of quality control circles or, more popularly, quality circles discussed next.

Quality Circles, Tiger Teams, and Ringi

A technique gaining increasing popularity is the use of "quality circles" to improve quaililty and morale. *Quality circles* are small groups of employees who meet on a regular basis, usually one hour per week, to identify and solve both quality and production problems. Members volunteer problems, prioritize needs, devise actions and make direrct recommendations to management. Companies such as Ford, Chrysler, Lockheed, Northrop, General Motors, Westinghouse, and a number of other organizations have reported good results. However, there has been some union resistance to quality circles; and, in some cases, employees have felt they were being asked to assume too many of management's responsibilities. Some managers have also objected to this approach, since they regard decision making and problem identification as traditional management functions.

While not a complete system, quality circles promise to be a useful tool in increasing employee involvement in both problem identification, solution decision, and action implementation. At this point, their long-range effectiveness is untested. How long employee interest can be maintained in quality circle efforts may be a major concern in the future. At worst, quality circles represent an effort to increase employee involvement; at best, they may represent a significant step toward new management-employee relationships.

One variation of the quality circle is known as "tiger teams." *Tiger teams* are made up of employees and managers who work together to solve a specific problem, devise a plan for implementation of solutions, and implement the plan. There are no status differences between tiger team members, and the group's leader may be either management or nonmanagement. Basically, the tiger team approach is aimed at concentrating the efforts of an organization's best qualified people, management and nonmanagement, on a specific problem. Members of the team work outside the organization's regular chain of command and are responsive only to top management until their objectives are completed and the team disbanded. Like other techniques, "tiger teams" have the advantage of intense involvement of employees and managers in solving common problems. They also remove the employees and managers from regular assignments and can disrupt routine work.

tiger teams

Ringi is a Japanese word that describes a decision-making process involving all levels of management but not employees.[8] Ideas are discussed, argued, and examined by all managers before a decision is made. When an apparent consensus has been reached, the decision is written on a form and routed to each manager for approval, which they indicate by placing their manager's seal or personal stamp on the form. If a seal or stamp is placed upside down or on its side, the manager has reservations about the matter and in some instances disagrees with the decision. In such cases, the discussions start again, the decision is amended, or the disapproving manager is convinced that it is a correct action and finally grants approval.

ringi

Ringi decisions must be unanimously approved, which means they are extraordinarily time-consuming by United States organizational standards. Even Japanese firms reserve ringi for major decisions and handle routine operational problems in much the same way as in American organizations. Ringi has both obvious advantages and disadvantages. Decisions are generally carefully formulated, totally accepted and supported; they can, however, consume considerable time and energy.

Innovation and Creativity

Planned change offers several tangible benefits. Improved processes, increased employee satisfaction and effectiveness, and better understanding of personal roles are just a few that are readily recognized. Additional benefits can also occur when employees at all levels are encouraged to develop new approaches or an entirely new process to accomplish their work. Managers who consistently fail to make use of the creative intelligence of their employees are not only discouraging the use of a valuable human asset, but are also preventing their organizations from reaching full potential.

While a number of organizations give lip service to the encouragement and development of new ideas, workable programs are, unfortunately, rare. Because they fail to listen or respond, or because they see concepts developed by subordinates as personal threats, some managers, either directly or indirectly, discourage innovation and creativity.

suggestion plans Suggestion plans that offer monetary rewards for cost-saving or work improvement concepts are widely used to encourage innovative or creative ideas. While some suggestion plans work fairly well, others become so bogged down in evaluation proceedings that a year or longer can pass before an employee's ideas are either accepted or rejected. In a few organizations, employees' suggestions are responded to promptly with a preliminary reward or explanation of why the suggestion cannot be used. Those given preliminary acceptance are evaluated further. Finally, a percentage of the suggestion's cost savings or an explanation of why it cannot be used is given the employee.

In small manufacturing organizations, plans that encourage cost-saving ideas and benefit the entire work force are relatively common. Ideas that are incorporated into regular work activities result in added pay for everyone in the organization.

From time to time, managers will ask employees to submit ideas for improvement. Only when such requests are sincere and not manipulative tricks to give employees a false sense of participation are they successful. Employees' ideas for improvement or new ways of performing must be responded to as promptly as possible with an explanation of why they can or cannot be used. Failure to do so eventually results in a lack of new concepts and limited performance improvement.

Problems and Promises

change for Change is an inevitable fact of existence. In its many forms, it affects
change's sake is people in organizations constantly. Managers of organizations are also
not desirable managers of change. Recognizing that change is taking place and determining its probable direction and speed and the extent of its diffusion are vital management functions. Only by learning to observe, un-

derstand, predict, plan, implement, control, and evaluate change can a manager be truly effective. When problems are recognized and traditional or habitual solutions fail, change is necessary. Change for change's sake, however, is neither desirable nor meaningful.

While deliberate, well-planned change is frequently desirable in nearly every aspect of organizational life, our thinking and psychological makeup often prevent us from realizing that change is needed. We feel comfortable with the familiar, and seldom feel the need to seek new or better ways of getting things done. The feeling of doing things right can also be one of our worst enemies, particularly in the world of work.

Quick Review

  I. Change: Invasion of the Future
    A. Change affects every part of our lives.
    B. Jobs and organizations are changing more rapidly than ever before.
  II. Characteristics of Change
    A. Rate of change is the speed with which change takes place.
    B. Direction of change defines the way present conditions alter future events.
    C. Diffusion of change is the way one change frequently causes other changes.
    D. Rate, direction, and diffusion of change usually affect management at the same time.
  III. Types of Change
    A. Technological changes involving new equipment, material, or facilities are the easiest changes to identify.
    B. Social change occurs when a large segment of the population adopts a different set of values.
    C. Internal changes are those changes based on management decisions rather than technology or social change.
  IV. Managing Change
    A. Management of change begins with the recognition that change is needed.
    B. When change is perceived as a threat, it is resisted.
    C. While some resistance to change is logical, much is emotional.
    D. Management can minimize resistance to change by:
      1. Introducing change in small increments.
      2. Educating and training employees and demonstrating the new equipment or procedures.

3. Enabling employees to help plan and implement the change.
V. Organizational Change Techniques
  A. Management by objectives (MBO) concentrates on results that can be objectively evaluated. MBO ideally involves everyone in the organization.
  B. Managers and employees set well-defined goals, review progress toward those goals, and evaluate their achievement.
  C. Organizational development (OD) uses many techniques in changing the basic ways an organization operates. It is concerned with change in the total organization.
  D. Survey feedback is a system of initiating change based on questionnaire and discussion data.
  E. Behavior modification creates change by rewarding and reinforcing the desired behavior.
  F. Quality of worklife (QWL) is a major organizational change movement primarily concerned with building a climate of mutual respect between management and employees.
  G. Quality circles, tiger teams, and ringi are techniques used to implement QWL.
VI. Innovation and Creativity
  A. Managers who fail to use their employees' creative intelligence are frequently failing their organizations.
  B. Some managers discourage innovation and creativity.
  C. A key to encouraging innovation and creativity is a quick, appropriate response.
VII. Problems and Promises
  A. Change affects people in organizations constantly. Management must try to forecast and manage change.
  B. Deliberate, well-planned change is desirable, but often our old habits prevent us from realizing changes are needed.

Key Terms

Rate of change
Direction of change
Diffusion of change
Technological change
Social change
Internal change
Change resistance

Management by
  objectives
Organizational
  development
Change recognition
Behavior modification
Quality of worklife

Theory "Z"
Quality circles
Tiger teams
Ringi
Innovation
Survey feedback

Discussion Questions

1. Why do employees frequently resist changes implemented by managers new to their organization?
2. The United Farm Workers Union has objected very strongly to the development of new agricultural labor saving equipment by university agricultural engineering departments. Why?
3. Increased utilization of computer technology in the office and in factories switching to robotic manufacturing is rapidly taking place. How will this affect the general work force?
4. Why is the United States lagging behind most countries in growth of productivity?
5. What has caused the quality circle movement to receive such widespread publicity?

Case Incidents

One Step Forward, Two Steps Back?

In early 1982, Charles Spruce purchased a CPU (central processing unit) for use in establishing a word-processing unit at the Municipal Utility District (MUD) headquarters. The CPU was a master computer that serviced thirty-two separate typing-processing stations. All correspondence, reports, and forms had formerly been completed by clerical personnel working with conventional electric typewriters.

When news of the purchase became known, a wave of uncertainty swept through the MUD facility. Clerks were afraid of losing their jobs; managers were concerned with loss of control; and many managers and administrative staff were distrustful of computers in general.

As MUD's operations manager, Charles was surprised at the workers' apparent resistance in converting to modern office technology. He had previously discussed the processing equipment and its advantages at a staff meeting of top management. The president and MUD's three senior vice presidents had endorsed his ideas. Now the whole organization seemed to be in an uproar.

1. What did Charles fail to do in implementing change?
2. How will the change be diffused in the organization?
3. What are likely to be the long range effects of the change?

It Could Be Worse and Probably Will Be

"You've got a tough assignment," said Laura Crosley, looking directly at Stan. He was being promoted and placed in charge of a section responsible for classifying, coding, and filing fingerprint records for the state department of criminal justice. "In the group you'll be supervising, one employee is an active agitator who manages to keep from getting fired because he knows the system so well. Three others follow his lead and are constantly finding things to complain about, while the other four try to stay out of trouble and do their jobs." Laura handed the employees' personnel folders to Stan for review. "The main thing," she continued, "is that you change the sloppy way work is being done in the section and improve performance."

Stan, after a moment's hesitation, asked, "What was their former supervisor like?" "Well," replied Laura, "Jane had semiretired on the job. She was more interested in not rocking the boat than in getting things done. As I said before, it's a tough assignment." Stan slowly smiled, "It could be worse, only half the crew are troublemakers. It's better than having to change the whole crew."

As Stan left Laura's office, he thought of a number of alternatives.

1. What should Stan do when he first takes over Jane's old section?
2. Identify some of the changes he has to bring about, in order of importance.
3. How should he handle the chief troublemaker?
4. What should he do to increase the quality and quantity of the section's work?

The Suggestion for Change

Lou Blake is the supervisor of a production line manufacturing camp trailers. Part of the manufacturing process includes the installation of a water supply system that is currently constructed of copper tubing. After a great deal of investigation and testing, Nancy Park determined that the copper tubing could be replaced by a new type of plastic tubing that would cost less than one-third as much as copper tubing and would be much easier to install. Nancy's tests indicated that the plastic tubing would hold up better than the copper with much less chance of the connections leaking. Nancy suggested this change to Lou, who then sold the idea to top management. Lou never told them that it was Nancy's suggestion. Lou received all the credit for the improved product and, as a result, received a cash bonus for the suggestion and a salary increase.

1. What effect will Lou Blake's action have on the willingness of other employees to make suggestions that will improve the product or cut costs?
2. What action should Nancy Park take to receive credit for her suggestion?

3. How should Lou Blake have handled the suggestion from Nancy Park?

Exercise   *Changes in the Work Place*

1. List major changes that have occurred at work places of students in your class. Determine each type of change: technical, social, or internal.
2. What jobs can members of your class identify that did not exist twenty-five years ago but are commonplace now?
3. Poll students in your class to determine why manufacturing in the United States has declined and service occupations have increased.
4. What major social changes are taking place now as seen by members of your class?

Endnotes

1. Andrew C. Brown, "The Man Who Warns Detroit 'This Is War,' " *Fortune*, 8 February 1982, p. 38.
2. Joseph F. Coates, "The Changing Nature of Work," *VocEd.*, January/February 1982, pp. 27–29.
3. Based on CBS program "60 Minutes," 7 March 1982.
4. Based on Fredric Golden "Here Come the Microkids," *Time,* 3 May 1982, pp. 50–56.
5. Bradford Boyd, *Management Minded Supervision,* 4th ed. (New York: McGraw-Hill, 1980).
6. CPM Films, "Behavior Modification," 1975, narrated by B. F. Skinner and Emery Air Freight Company officials.
7. William Ouchi, *Theory Z* (New York: Ballentine Books, 1980).
8. Jean Johnston, "Ringi," *Management World*, May 1981.

17 People, Unions, and Organizations

Learning Objectives

After reading this chapter, you should be able to:

1. Outline a brief history and the likely future of labor unions in the United States.
2. Understand why employees are motivated to form unions.
3. Explain the meaning of bilateral and unilateral relations.
4. Define key labor relations terms.
5. Describe major labor-management relations and collective bargaining issues.
6. Understand representation, due process, arbitration, and jurisdiction.
7. Describe the grievance procedures used to settle employee complaints.

Chapter Topics

Preview and Self-Evaluation

Near the end of Chapter 1, we pointed out that some organizations are *executive* in their work climate and others are *associative.* Austin Gerber, the originator of the executive-associative view, believes that unions are far more likely to develop in executive organizations than in associative ones. Executive organizations tend to stress control, vestment of authority at the top, minimal decision making by employees, adherence to rules, and impersonal treatment. Employees have little or no influence on policy, work rules, schedules, or anything else beyond the narrow responsibility of their immediate tasks.

Associative organizations, on the other hand, tend to encourage employee participation, personal responsibility, achievement on both an individual and group level, and a collaborative effort on the part of management and employees to achieve the organization's goals. Unions, according to Gerber, almost never occur in associative organizations. If his observations are correct, we can safely assume that management and its resulting organizational style, are the chief causes for employees banding together.

Before reading further, take the true-false quiz to test your knowledge of unions. Take the quiz again when you have finished the chapter. How many of your perceptions were correct?

Answer True or False

1. Unions are gaining membership as a percent of the total work force.   T   F

2. Unions are, from a historical point of view, recently developed organizations in the United States.   T   F

3. Traditionally, there has been an adversarial relationship between labor and management.   T   F

4. Unions are concerned with pay and benefits but little else that benefits employees.   T   F

5. Equal opportunity law has prevented seniority from protecting all employees.   T   F

6. Very few new kinds of work are seen for the future between now and the year 2000.   T   F

7. An employee with a grievance is represented by the union except in cases involving arbitration by an independent third party.   T   F

8. It is highly probable that traditional authoritarian management approaches will continue to increase in dealings with unions.   T   F

9. Jobs are protected, to some extent, by the type of union and the job classifications of its members.   T   F

10. Union-management relations are not likely to change during the next ten years.   T   F

ANSWERS: 1. F; 2. F; 3. T; 4. F; 5. F; 6. F; 7. F; 8. F; 9. T; 10. F.

Why People Form Unions

Unions have been in existence for at least one hundred years before the United States developed from the thirteen original colonies. Cordwainers (shoemakers), printers, and tailors formed isolated unions to   *early union history* improve work hours and increase pay. Early unions were all made up of employees in skilled trades. They did, however, have several characteristics still true of union organizations today. Perhaps most importantly, they were comprised of employees who felt that collectively they could deal with management more effectively than they could as individuals. *union goals* They had as their primary goals better wages, hours, and conditions of work. Like their modern counterparts, the early unions wanted guarantees from management that agreements would be honored.

The United States work force numbers about 110,000,000 people, some of whom are unemployed but still eligible for work. Of these, slightly more than 20,000,000 belong to labor unions. Simple arithmetic reveals that for each person in the work force who is a union member, *union* five employees are not. Although they are clearly a minority of all *membership* workers, unions exert a powerful influence on the national economy, on the way organizations are run, and on local, regional, and national politics. Whether admired or detested, unions are a reality of life that affects everyone. Table 17.1 lists the largest unions in the United States today.

In some instances the only way employees feel they can influence management is through the collective power of unionism. By joining together, they are able to obtain concessions from management that would be much more difficult to achieve as individuals. At the core of all union activities is the concept that unified groups of employees have greater influence than individuals in dealing with management.

Support Your Local "Operating Engineers"?

Red Bluff, California, city police learned that law enforcement officers in other parts of the state were receiving their uniforms and "safety equipment" (guns, bullets, and the like) free from their cities or counties. In Red Bluff, police had to buy their own equipment and uniforms.

The obvious inequity became a major point of dissatisfaction. When the officers petitioned Red Bluff city council for a change in policy, they were repeatedly turned down. The police felt their only recourse was to form a union.

To obtain help in their organizing efforts, they contacted a number of unions for advice and assistance. After some hesitation, they decided against forming their own local and instead joined the Union of Operating Engineers, whose membership was primarily heavy equipment operators. Nevertheless, as "operating engineers," the police were able to negotiate a written contract with the city that provided an allowance for purchasing uniforms and safety equipment![1]

Table 17.1 The 23 largest unions in the United States

Employee Group	Membership
Teamsters	2,000,000
Automobile Workers	1,800,000
Steel Workers	1,400,000
Electrical Workers (IBEW)	1,000,000
Machinists	943,280
Carpenters	820,000
Retail Clerks	650,876
Laborers	650,000
State, County, and Municipal	648,160
Service Employees	648,000
American Federation of Teachers	550,000
Meat Cutters	525,000
Communication Workers	498,743
Hotel and Restaurant	451,989
Operating Engineers	421,395
Ladies' Garment Workers	340,936
Clothing Workers	510,000
Paper Workers	324,000
Government (AFGE) Workers	300,000
Musicians	300,000
Mine Workers	250,000
Painters	192,700
Electrical Workers (IUE)	165,000

Source: World Almanac, 1981. New York: Newspaper Enterprise Association, Inc. pp. 135–36.

Unilateral and Bilateral Relations

Traditionally, at least in the belief of many people, there has been an adversarial relationship between management and employees. In most companies, managers make the rules and employees follow them. This one-sided rule making is known as a *unilateral relationship.* As long as employees feel the rules are consistent and fair, and are applied with judgment and some degree of flexibility, they generally accept them. Effective managers will usually make an effort to avoid dissension between themselves and employees. A stable work force is an essential asset in most organizations.

unilateral relations

Realistically, however, differences between managers and employees are almost inevitable. Managers are concerned with organizational goals such as productivity, quality, costs, schedules, implementation of plans, determination of new goals, and effectiveness of the work force. Employees frequently value personal needs such as pay, benefits, fair treatment, proper work assignments, opportunity to develop and advance, and personal security. Although the two points of view are not necessarily opposed to each other, they can easily serve as a basis for major differences in the ways organizational priorities are viewed. Employees who feel that management is not interested in employee needs and values show their resentment. Management also resents any prob-

People, Unions, and Organizations

473

lems caused by the work force in terms of productivity, quality, excessive costs, or schedules. When each side views the other as violating their own needs and organizational expectations, conflicts arise that are difficult to heal.

To gain some influence over management rule making, protect threatened security, increase financial benefits, ensure fairness, and control their job destiny to some degree, employees will form unions to deal as a group with management. When managers and employees jointly arrive at a set of personnel rules affecting wage, hours, and conditions of work, the rules are written and signed by both parties. Joint *bilateral relations*   rule making by management and employees establishes *bilateral relations*.

In those organizations with bilateral relations, neither side may change the rules without the consent, through negotiation, of the other. *negotiation*   *Negotiation* is the process that organized employee groups use to reach agreements. Any time people talk to each other and mutually agree on a course of action satisfactory to both, some negotiation takes place. *quid pro quo*   An important principle called *quid pro quo* forms the basis for negotiation. *Quid pro quo* literally means "something for something." Each of the negotiating parties, in this case management and organized employees, gives and receives through the negotiation process.

To gain an in-depth understanding of collective bargaining relationships, a great deal of study and experience is usually necessary. Some key terms associated with union-management relations are helpful in grasping the basics of this complex subject.

Language of Labor Relations

Over a period of many years, managers and union employees have developed a set of terms to describe their relationship and the rules that are negotiated. While we are not concerned with the entire vocabulary of labor relations, some terms are essential:

Appropriate unit is defined as employees with common interests and/or similar jobs who join together in a unit. All technicians, for example, may be an appropriate unit, while all clerical personnel in the same company may be another appropriate unit. Once a union is formed, the appropriate unit name is usually dropped, and it is known only as the unit or bargaining unit.

Bargaining and negotiating are essentially the same process of give and take to reach agreement. The terms are used interchangeably. *Collective bargaining* is a somewhat broader term that includes all of the relationships between management and unionized employees.

Contract or agreement is the written result of negotiations. In its basic form, it is a set of personnel rules that both employees and managers must follow. A contract, sometimes called an agreement, is a legal document and binds both parties to its contents.

Federation is an association of affiliated Locals and Internationals. The single federation in existence today is the AFL-CIO (American Federation of Labor-Congress of Industrial Organizations). Its primary purpose is to influence national politics and national policy related to work, employment, and other social goals.

Grievance. A written employee complaint. It is processed by a steward or employee representative through a negotiated step-by-step grievance procedure.

International is a group of similar locals that have joined together to exert political influence at a local level, determine common policy, and provide a service organization for member locals. The International Association of Machinists and Aerospace Workers, United Automobile Workers; Teamsters, Warehousemen, and Chauffers; United Steel Workers; and Ladies' Garment Workers Union are all examples of Internationals.

Local is the basic organizational unit of union members. It is like a troop in scouting organizations or a chapter in a social or philanthropic organization.

Management rights defines management's personnel rights such as the right to hire, terminate, lay off, promote, transfer, assign work, discipline, train, etc.

Recognition. Under current law, management must recognize a union formed by more than 50 percent of the employees, usually by election process, as the sole bargaining agent for employees. The union is the representative of all employees in the appropriate unit whether those employees have become union members or abstained from union membership.

Representation means that on all personnel matters including pay, benefits, discipline, promotion within union classifications, seniority, overtime, transfers, discharge and any other personnel matter, employees will be represented by the union. A *steward* or employee representative speaks for the union on behalf of the employee and is charged with protecting the employee and ensuring that management does not violate negotiated rules.

Shop is the place union members work. A shop may be an insurance company, hospital, factory, school, department store, farm, or any other place of work.

Unions are, in the simplest terms, groups of employees recognized by management as legitimate partners in the rule-making process. *Bargaining unit* is a term frequently used to define the union at a particular location.

Union security. Rules that are negotiated, preserve the union, and ensure its perpetuation and maintenance are known as union security. Such rules include *checkoff* that makes union dues automatically deductible from an employee's check and defines the type of shop as either an *open shop* with voluntary union membership, an *agency shop* where all employees pay an amount equivalent to dues regardless of membership in a union, or a *union shop* where membership is automatic after thirty days of employment, and other related union clauses.

Issues in Collective Bargaining

articles in collective bargaining

There are many issues in collective bargaining. Most contracts will include at least twenty to thirty articles, each dealing with a separate issue or set of issues. In addition to those dealing with work rules (schedules, amount of work, break times, smoking regulations, etc.), pay for time worked, pay for time not worked (vacations, holidays, breaks, personal time off), seniority, grievance procedures, benefits, and overtime distribution, there are numerous other issues important to employees.

meeting employee needs

One of the most difficult issues to address is employees' desire to work in a system that meets their needs for fairness, equity, opportunity, and responsive management. As robots replace many traditional manufacturing jobs and electronics changes the nature of the office, employee relations in both unionized and nonunionized environments become crucial.[2] Douglas Fraser, President of the United Automobile Workers International Union, has been, like many other progressive union officials, a leader in defining the future course of union-management relations. He views the future as one that must include greater job security, improved productivity based on technological advances, greater worker participation in corporate decision making, and rededi-

need for greater cooperation

cation to quality. Many managers are restating Fraser's views in their own words. Significantly, there is some indication that union-management relations are cautiously moving toward a more cooperative stance. In a widely syndicated newspaper article, Fraser summed up what he believes the survival of America may depend on, at least in part:

> The key to the future depends greatly on whether there can be a broader move toward shared responsibility between unions and corporations—a shared responsibility that involves greater decision-making power and job security for workers.
>
> Those of us who want to see more economic and social justice in America must be willing to take risks and try new approaches . . . As we attempt to develop more progressive labor-management relations, we won't forget that those who insist on making cooperation impossible make confrontation inevitable.[3]

Individuals and Unions

Individual union members are sometimes torn between loyalty to their union and its goals and the realization that survival of their organizations is directly tied to their own personal survival. While they may successfully develop a dual loyalty to both their union and their work place, at times these two organizations may have divergent goals.

dual loyalties

Managers, especially first-line supervisors who work directly with the labor force, also face problems in dealing with union employees. Their ability to direct the work force, discipline, schedule and assign work, promote, give performance evaluations, establish general rules of conduct, and make decisions regarding job content (what an employee can and cannot do) is often limited by the labor contract.

limitations on management

There are two prevalent views of administration of union-management contracts. One view is that the contract is a legal document and must be followed to the letter. In some work places "do it by the contract" is a standard phrase. Another view holds that the contract is a set of guidelines for both management and employees and that the "spirit" of the agreement is as important as its literal language. Under this view some flexibility in interpreting provisions is allowed by both management and employee representatives, especially when special circumstances are involved. Management and union representatives attempt to use the contract as a positive tool for improving relations rather than as a means of policing each other's actions.

letter and spirit of contract

Special Problems in Union-Management Relations

Seniority is a time-honored principle in union-management relations and is frequently found in modified form as part of the general policies of nonunion organizations. In its simplest form, *seniority* is usually defined as the length of service a person has with a company in a specific job classification. Its primary purpose is to assure employees that in the event of reductions in the work force, those with greatest seniority will be laid off last. The principle of seniority can also cover benefits such as promotional opportunities, job assignments, shift preference, work location, amount of vacation, retirement benefits, choice of vacation schedules, and opportunity to transfer. Employees with greater length of service have several advantages over newer employees.

seniority

However, seniority can cause problems in organizations with affirmative action plans designed to increase opportunities for women and minorities in jobs from which they were previously excluded. Seniority systems can frustrate the aims of these plans by protecting long-term seniority employees, frequently white males, to a greater degree than workers employed as part of an affirmative action effort. In the event of a reduction in force due to economic recession, loss of contracts, or other reasons, less senior employees are laid off first. Employees hired under affirmative acion programs are likely to be among the less senior and are most vulnerable to layoffs.

seniority and affirmative action

In a famous court case in 1977 (*International Brotherhood of Teamsters* v. *United States*, 431 U.S. 324) a ruling was made that if a seniority system was established without the purpose of discriminating, the seniority provisions of such contracts were not an unlawful employment practice, even if the system has some discriminatory consequences.[4] In effect, the Supreme Court said that traditional seniority systems based on a simple length of service provision were satisfactory provided other personnel practices were not discriminatory.

Several attempts have been made to find alternative seniority systems, but few have actually been put into practice. One approach is the *dual seniority* establishment of dual seniority. *Dual seniority* is the establishment of two seniority lists. On one list, employees with an excess of a predetermined number of years, for example five, would be listed by job classification in order of seniority. On another list, employees who were part of a program designed to meet affirmative action goals with less than five years experience would be listed in order of length of service. If a reduction in force occurred, the same percent of workers from each list would be affected. When a work force reduction of 5 percent occurred, 5 percent of the employees from each list would be laid off. A substantial number of employees hired as part of equal economic opportunity goals would retain their jobs. Even this system has drawbacks. Unions usually insist that recalls from layoffs be by order of seniority. In such cases, the most senior employees from the "regular" employee list would be recalled first.

A related problem is associated with the rule of reasonable accommodation. *Reasonable accommodation* means that organizations will *reasonable* try to arrange special schedules or conditions of work regardless of *accommodation* union rules if the situation requires it. A person who will not work Saturdays or evenings because of religious prohibitions may be provided a special assignment to accommodate his or her beliefs. Inevitably such treatment is seen by other employees as discriminatory and preferential. Management is frequently caught in the dilemma of trying to decide between the need to comply with the principle of reasonable accommodation and the equal need of maintaining both the spirit and letter of a written union contract.

One of the most critical issues faced by management, especially supervisors of employees who perform the organization's day-to-day activities, is treatment of employees after a strike. Strikes are costly, difficult experiences for both employees and managers. Resentment on *after the strike* both sides can build during the strike period. Effective managers know that rebuilding normal, friendly relationships after a strike has been settled is much wiser than attempting to make employees feel guilty for their actions.

Personal Security and Representation

In addition to its bargaining for pay, benefits, favorable work rules, and a system of formalized employee-management relations, unions also in-*employee security* sure employee security in several ways. We have already mentioned seniority provisions that protect employees and afford workers numerous other benefits based on their length of service. Two other important protections are also offered by union-management agreements: jurisdiction and grievance procedures.

Jurisdiction is, in its simplest form, the protection of a worker's job through union membership in a given craft. For example, electricians, carpenters, machinists, clerks, and automobile assemblers usually belong to different unions. Because different types of work are associated with a particular union, only that union's members are allowed to perform the work. For instance, only members of the electrician's union can repair electrical switches; carpenters, and only carpenters, may install doors; clerks, and only clerks, may file. Members of a union may perform only that work covered in the job descriptions of its members.

Not only is there union jurisdiction, but members of the same union may be protected equally as well by their job descriptions. Storekeepers in a factory take inventory and report shortages in items. They also issue parts and material and maintain appropriate records. Production control specialists who need to know the availability of materials and supplies in order to plan production runs may not count or record supplies. To do so would be a violation of the storekeepers' job rights. Jurisdiction and rights conveyed by job descriptions assure employees a degree of job protection. Management's flexibility in assigning work is restricted to specific specialized job descriptions. The familiar, "and other duties as assigned," job description phrase is usually not valid in union-management relations.

jurisdiction

How to "Keep on Truckin' "

The job of truck driver got a new twist at one United Grocers store in Houston, Texas. Normally, produce orders are filled by warehouse workers who stack the needed items on fork lift carriers, drive them to the loading stations, and load the produce into waiting trucks.

However, local Teamster Union drivers were able to negotiate a contract forbidding anyone other than a Teamster member to set foot in the trucks. At the present time, groceries are left stacked on the docks at the truck's rear entrance. The truck driver hand loads the boxes, drives to his destination, and then unloads the produce. The process is time-consuming and costly but ensures that only Teamster drivers are allowed to do "truck work."

Perhaps the most important protection offered through union membership other than seniority, is the right to due process. Unlike seniority, due process applies to all employees regardless of length of service. *Due process* is the guaranteed right to a fair hearing in the event of an action against an employee by management or the belief that management has acted improperly in its treatment of an employee. To

due process

ensure that due process is properly administered, nearly all labor-management agreements contain a grievance procedure.

Grievance Procedures

Grievances are formal written complaints requiring management action. Most people complain about something at work at one time or another. When the complaint becomes serious enough to discuss with management, it may become a grievance.

grievances

Some grievances are based on facts. A wrong has been done or believed to have been done. In most cases, there is also a more subtle reason. An employee who is dissatisfied but unable to correct the dissatisfaction may look for a grievance cause to vent his or her anger.

> Susan Snell normally would dump dirty ash trays in the waste basket, pick up scattered paper, and generally clean her boss's office. The custodian had filed a grievance demanding six hours of back pay at overtime rates for compensation resulting from Susan's conference room clean-up activities. She had a right to clean around her regular work place (her desk) but not the adjoining conference room. After going through the regular grievance procedure, the custodian was paid and Susan was instructed to no longer clean the conference room. It was later learned that the custodian had on occasion flirted with Susan and had been consistently rebuffed. He told a friend that he would find a way to show her where she really stands.

Experienced managers can sense dissatisfaction and frequently prevent grievances by counseling, changing work assignments, or simply sharing information. A key to grievance prevention is the development of a climate of trust and confidence that minimizes the need for formalized complaints.

Although there is not a uniform set of procedures used by all organizations to settle grievance, Table 17.2 outlines features found in many contracts.

In reviewing Table 17.2, it should be kept in mind that there is a definite time period between each step in the grievance procedure and that arbitration is used only if management and the union cannot agree on an interpretation of contract provisions or if the union disagrees with management actions toward an employee. *Arbitration* involves using a third party, usually a member of the American Arbitration Association, to settle the grievances. Since arbitration is expensive, involves an "outsider," and means the final decision is uncertain, both unions and management usually strive for settlement before going to arbitration. Arbitration costs are normally shared equally by management and the union representing the employee.

arbitration

Grievance procedures are the primary tool in union-management relations. They are the regulators of actions by both sides and form a

Table 17.2 Typical grievance procedure

	Union Actions	Management Actions
Step 1.	Employee submits grievance to management	Management either settles or rejects grievance.
Step 2.	If not settled at first step, employee and steward submit grievance to next level of management.	Higher management settles or rejects grievance if not settled at first step.
Step 3.	Chief steward submits grievance to top management representatives, usually a labor relations specialist, for a formal hearing. In some cases a grievance committee of union and management members comprise third step.	Top management, usually represented by a labor relations specialist, hears grievance and settles or rejects if not settled at second step. In case of committee, committee settles or rejects.
Step 4.	Both sides jointly submit grievance and facts to an arbitrator (independent third party) for settlement. Arbitrator's decisions are binding on both parties.	

basis for rule clarification as well as redress of management actions toward employees. The number and types of grievances are frequently a barometer of the health of union-management relations.

Into the Future

Evidence already indicates that new work methods will increase the number of jobs where employees will be machine supervisors, programmers, and directors rather than assemblers, office clerks, inspectors, or manual technicians. Many of today's jobs will no longer exist or be significantly reduced in number by 1990, and by the year 2000 an entirely new cycle of jobs will emerge. These trends are reflected in an overall decline in union membership, as shown in Figure 17.1. Unions draw most of their strength from older industries.

New jobs mean new skills, different demands, and most importantly new relationships between management and employees. It is highly probable that traditional, authoritarian management approaches will continue to decline and that status and power differences between managers and employees will be far less evident than in the past. We predict that out of this, new relationships between management and unions will also emerge.

new jobs, new skills

A Short Look Backwards

We have deliberately avoided the legal and historical framework of union-management relations, as well as other important issues, in an attempt to illustrate a few factors that affect on-the-job human rela-

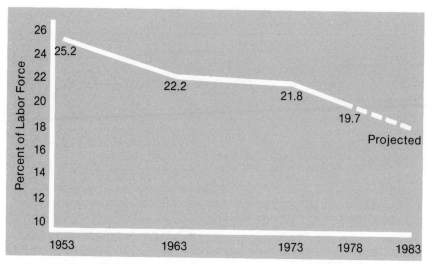

Figure 17.1 Union membership as a percent of the total labor force.

tions in a work environment. Unions are organizations with both formal and informal structures in much the same way as management. Well-organized unions with capable leadership are much more successful in achieving bargaining goals and influencing management policy than are those unions whose leadership is concerned primarily with personal gain. By the same token, management that is thoughtful, goal directed, with high expectations for itself and its employees, is also more likely to relate well with their workers as employees *and* as union members. It is unfortunate that management and union bottom-line thinking, which concentrates on short-range goals, immediate rewards, and a win-lose philosophy, all too often blocks real progress.

Quick Review

I. Why People Form Unions
   A. Unions have been in existence for at least 100 years before the American Revolution.
   B. Unions comprise about 20% of the total work force.
   C. Collective bargaining stems from the desire to influence management.
II. Unilateral and Bilateral Relations
   A. One-sided rule making is unilateral.
   B. Managers and employees who agree on rules both have made are governed by bilateral relations.
   C. *Quid pro quo* means give and take or "you scratch my back and I'll scratch yours."

III. Language of Labor Relations
   A. Language of industrial relations includes terms unique to collective bargaining.
   B. The language includes both terms in the contract and terms associated with negotiations and collective bargaining.
IV. Issues in Collective Bargaining
   A. Most labor-management contracts include twenty to thirty contract clauses, each dealing with a different issue.
   B. Issues include pay, benefits, schedules, seniority, grievance procedures, arbitration, and many related issues.
V. Individuals and Unions
   A. Employees may be faced with dual loyalties both to management and the union.
   B. Contracts may be used either as a means of improving employee relations or as a weapon by management or unions.
VI. Special Problems in Union-Management Relations
   A. Seniority is a major principle in union-mangement relations, protecting workers on the basis of their length of service.
   B. Seniority can cause problems in companies that have established affirmative action programs.
VII. Personal Security and Representation
   A. In addition to numerous other benefits, unions offer two important protections to workers: jurisdiction and grievance procedures.
   B. Jurisdiction is the protection of a worker's job through union membership in a given craft.
   C. Workers are also given the right to due process in which they are guaranteed a fair hearing.
VIII. Grievance Procedures
   A. Grievances are formal written complaints requiring management actions.
   B. Although there is no uniform set of procedures, most contracts spell out specific grievance steps.
   C. If union and management cannot settle an issue, it may be referred to arbitration and settled by a neutral third party.
IX. Into the Future
   A. New methods of work and new types of jobs will require a new relationship between labor and management.
   B. Status and power differences between workers and managers are likely to be much less evident than in the past.

Key Terms

Unions

Unilateral
  relationship

Bilateral relationship

Negotiation

Quid pro quo

Collective bargaining

Seniority

Contract

Jurisdiction

Grievance procedures

Due process

Arbitration

Discussion Questions

1. Union membership seems to be declining as a percent of the total labor force. Why? What do you predict for the future?
2. Labor unions have historically concentrated on manufacturing, mining, crafts, and other blue-collar employment for membership. Will this change? Why or why not?
3. Some states prohibit union contracts that require that employees become union members. Membership is completely voluntary in such instances. Do you agree with the right to work regardless of union membership?
4. What effect will increased use of robots and electronic devices in the work place have on unions?

Case Incidents

Dirty Diapers?

Although the "Dirty Diaper Laundry Company" serviced fewer homes, it was still doing considerable commercial laundry business with hotels, restaurants, beauty shops, and other firms using employee uniforms. Beverly Dunn had worked for "Dirty Diaper" for three years as a "Laundry Worker A," a classification every employee held after three years. Beverly was competent, hard working, and loyal. When supervisor Pat Showalter turned down Beverly's request for a transfer to other work, Beverly filed a grievance. She wrote in her grievance, "The contract clearly states that management will not discriminate." Beverly's steward, Bob Garrett, argued that no other employee had been a sorter for such a long period of time. It was a clear case of one employee being treated unfairly. Bob demanded that Beverly be transfered. Pat Showalter argued that all workers were classified alike and management could assign them anywhere they pleased.

1. Who is right? Was Beverly discriminated against?
2. How should Pat, Beverly's supervisor, handle this case?

3. How will Beverly's case affect the next union-management negotiation?

What's Fair Is Fair

John Crago stated briefly but firmly, "We will give a flat 70 cents per hour shift differential. Every person who works on the second shift will receive an added 70 cents per hour plus a paid lunch period." Marie Higgins retorted, "We want a 10 percent hourly increase, not a flat 70 cents per hour." "Since our base rate is $7.00 on the average," argued John, "70 cents per hour *is* 10 percent." "Not for everyone," countered Marie.

1. Why did Marie want a flat percent instead of 70 cents per hour increase?
2. Is 10 percent for shift differential too much or too little? Support your point.
3. How would this shift differential affect morale?

Exercise *Labor Unions*

1. Ask other students in your class if they belong to or have belonged to unions. Determine whether unions have benefited or not benefited their jobs.
2. List three benefits of a seniority system and three disadvantages. Is length of service a fair way of awarding employee benefits such as added vacation, increased sick leave, and choice of promotional opportunities within job classification?
3. Right to work laws prohibit people from being required to join a union although the place they work may be unionized. How many people in your class favor right to work laws?
4. Are union employees more secure and better paid than non-union employees? List three reasons for union membership and three reasons for not joining unions.

Endnotes

1. Based on interview with member of Red Bluff, California Police Department, November 1981.
2. Reported on "60 Minutes," 14 March 1982, CBS Television Network.
3. Douglas A. Fraser, "Justice Means Taking Risks and New Approaches," *Los Angeles Times*, 14 March 1982.
4. E. Edward Herman and Alfred Kuhn, *Collective Bargaining and Labor Relations* (Englewood Cliffs: Prentice-Hall, 1982), pp. 124–26.

18 Social Responsibility and Ethics

Learning Objectives

After reading this chapter, you should be able to:

1. Discuss the concept of social responsibility and its impact on business.

2. Explain how business and government are attempting to implement equal opportunity in the work place, and the problems they face.

3. Describe how companies deal with the issues of environmental, employee, and consumer protection.

4. Identify some of the ways companies handle alcoholism, drug abuse, and emotionally troubled employees on the job.

5. Describe the various ethical systems and the operational approach for making ethical decisions.

6. Understand the forces at work in the ethical decision cycle.

7. Discuss major ethical issues in the work place, including sexual harassment.

This chapter coauthored with Edward F. Thode, Department of Management, New Mexico State University.

Chapter Topics

Beyond Profits, Products, and Services

Social Change at Work

Protectors of Society

Troubled Employees, Alcoholism, and Drug Abuse

Right or Wrong—The Ethical Dilemma

Value Ranking and Ethical Decisions

General Concepts and Ideals

Sex in the Office—A Special Issue

Preview and Self-Evaluation

In a rapidly expanding electronics company, an employment interviewer accepts bribes from job applicants in exchange for making sure they are hired. Employees for a well-known clothing manufacturer are shown how to make clothes look right even when color patterns are incorrectly matched, seams not properly sewn, and shoulders on shirts and blouses of unequal height. Management of a midwestern chemical plant fails to inform employees that long-term exposure to certain fumes may cause permanent liver damage. A major paint company manufactures three different labels of paint, each selling for a different price but all containing precisely the same ingredient mix. Supervisors in a large production machine shop accept "hush" money from employees who sell marijuana on the side to other employees during work hours. Two major raw milk suppliers fail to report that their cows regularly eat grain previously treated with potentially toxic insecticides.

The social and ethical obligations of organizations both to society and to employees are often difficult to define clearly and even harder to police. In this chapter we will examine problems organizations face in establishing their ethics, appropriate social responsibilities, and their responsibilities to individual employees.

A few questions related to the special obligations of management are shown below. How many can you answer? When you have finished reading the chapter, try taking the quiz again.

Answer True or False

1. Today, "social responsibility" refers to business's obligation to achieve the goals of growth, profit, and survival.　　　　　　　　　　　　　　　　　T　　F

2. The concept of equal opportunity is an attempt to help women and minorities "catch up" with most white males.　　　　　　　　　　　　　　　　　T　　F

3. Under the Civil Rights Act, the concept of "protected classes" refers to specific job categories protected by federal law.　　　　　　　　　　　　　T　　F

4. Government environmental control regulations may conflict with the need to conserve energy.　　　T　　F

5. Ethics is not concerned with issues related to social responsibility.　　　　　　　　　　　　　　　　T　　F

6. Society in the future can be the only judge of whether today's organizations are socially responsible.　　T　　F

7. Each person's value rankings—their feelings of what is right and wrong—are different.　　　　　　　T　　F

8. Other people influence our ethical decisions.　　　T　　F

9. Sexual harassment includes all sexual approaches, even when both parties give their consent.　　　　T　　F

10. Sexual conduct is a problem in organizations only when it involves some form of sexual harassment.

ANSWERS: 1. F; 2. T; 3. F; 4. T; 5. F; 6. F; 7. T; 8. T; 9. F; 10. F.

Beyond Profits, Products, and Services

For just a moment stop and think about these very basic questions: Where does the wood, metal, glass and plastic of the buildings we use come from? Where do we get our clothes? Our food? Automobiles? Television sets? Furniture? Electricity? The answers are to a large extent the same. Many, if not nearly all, of the things we use, enjoy, and need in life are supplied by organizations. Organizations influence not only the lives of those who make up their work force but also society as a whole.

Perhaps more so than in other countries, Americans have recognized organizational influences that go beyond profits, products, and services. Through the actions of a combination of dedicated pressure groups such as the National Association for the Advancement of Colored People (NAACP), Ralph Nader's Consumer Advocates, the National Organization of Women, environmental protection groups like the Sierra Club, and many other associations and unions, people have become more aware of the social responsibilities of work organizations. Responding to public demands, federal, state, municipal, and local governmental agencies have enacted legislation that forces managers of organizations to be increasingly responsible for not only their own organizations but also the concerns of society as a whole.

areas of social responsibility

Although many top managers for many years have recognized the social impact of their organizations and have actively sponsored programs designed to improve the well-being of society as a whole, the concept of the social responsibility of management is relatively new. Management's primary social responsibilities fall into four major areas:

1. Promotion of equality of opportunity.
2. Protection of the environment and conservation of resources.
3. Concern for the health and safety of employees both on and off the job.
4. Promotion of ethical standards in their actions and those of their employees.

In addition, management is expected to participate actively in community projects and to promote services and legislation that will benefit everyone. These and other related social pressures have not only created tremendous burdens, but have also caused a reassessment of management attitudes and traditional management rights.

Social Responsibility

During most of its history, the United States was economically poorer than it is today. Subsistence, survival, and profits were more important goals for both organizations and individuals than they are now. As time passed and the country grew in economic strength, a phenomenon occurred that has had tremendous historical impact. A great middle class developed as the dominant segment of the country's population. The lines between the haves and have-nots became far less clear than before. No longer was there a clear division between rich and poor. In addition to survival needs, other societal goals for work organizations became increasingly important.

At first the new awareness of the social responsibilities of work organizations was highlighted by laws regulating monopolistic practices and restraint of trade. In addition, the responsibility for on-the-job safety shifted from the employee to the employer. A further emphasis was placed on regulating the relations of organizations with shareholders of its stock. Today, as individual income increases, new social objectives for work organizations are being directed, in some cases voluntarily and in others by legal mandate, toward the development and enforcement of equal work opportunities, environmental and pollution control, and consumer protection.

The old goals of profit, growth, and survival are no longer enough. *profit, growth,* Work organizations must be socially responsible. Although deplored *and survival are* by many managers, social responsibility is an increasingly important *not enough* part of managerial and organizational life. *Social responsibility* in simple terms is the acceptance by management of the reality that organizations must act in the public interest in their pursuit of profit and provision of goods and services. Public interest involves that which the public, not management, defines as of greatest importance. Social goals of equal opportunity, preservation of the physical environment, and concern for the users of products and services provided by organizations are all within the public interest as shown in Figure 18.1. When these are at least partially achieved, new goals will doubtless become apparent.

Realistically, social responsibility as seen by the general public is frequently in conflict with organizational goals. The question always remains, Whose interest is public interest?

Equal Opportunity

"When I first started in this business," remarked the personnel *providing equal* manager of a large multiproduct manufacturing company, "if a *opportunity* manager wanted all redheads over five feet eight inches tall, that's what we'd recruit and hire." "We had," the personnel manager continued, "a battery of tests each employee was required to take. If their scores weren't right, they wouldn't be hired. Promotions were based pretty much on who the manager liked. Our only women supervisors were in jobs that required running departments such as clerical pools and records keeping departments that were traditionally all women. In our factory, all supervisors were men, even in departments that were predominantly made up of women."

"Now it's different," the manager smiled. "We no longer have all black custodians, all white female clerks, and all white male supervisors. Everyone has an equal chance. Strangely, most of us don't care what sex or color gets a particular job. It's whether they can perform or not that counts."

Within organizations (and outside them as well) few issues have caused as much controversy as the legal and social mandate to provide equal opportunity. Although it is an honored moral value of our society, *equal opportunity* has been much abused. Equality is lost when people are either given or not given consideration for employment, training, or promotion because of their race, color, sex, age, size, national origin, physical handicap, religion, or any of the other non-job-related ways we classify people. Rewards are often given for how well people are liked rather than how well they perform. Self-reliance goes undeveloped when whole classes of people are dependent on public assistance because of lack of job opportunities.

With certain notable exceptions, the most opportune jobs, especially those with status and power, have been dominated by white males.

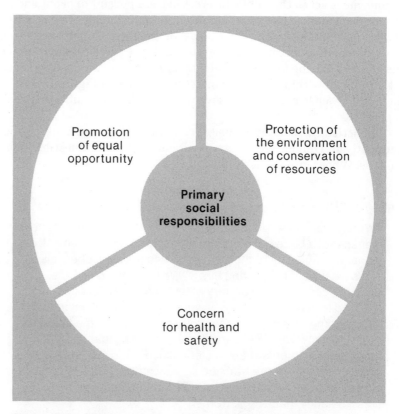

Figure 18.1 Management's primary social responsibilities.

Managers, and unions by virtue of their own value systems, have developed and perpetuated a tradition that for most of our history has suppressed the opportunities of many to achieve qualifications for the more highly skilled and highly paid jobs.

Social Change at Work

Few people will openly admit their own prejudices. Statements like "Some of my best friends are (black, Hispanic, Jewish, Moslem, Polish, etc.)," however, are a certain indication of bias. For many years, social psychologists have studied the values associated with esteem or feelings of self-worth that develop in both groups and individuals. If another person by virture of race, religion, color, national origin, life-style, accent, socioeconomic background, skill level, or any of a number of other characteristics is seen as being "different," that difference is often interpreted as inferiority. Visible differences, such as color and sex, as well as invisible differences, like religion and national origin, are important. While mistrust, suspicion, and prejudice have been very pronounced and still are between identifiable groups, changes in our social values are reducing some of the traditional preconceptions that people have about each other.

prejudice

Social value change is often slower than it seems. Prior to 1750, women in the colonial United States were for the most part treated equally to men in all respects. As a result of the influence of European customs during the latter 1700s, women were relegated to a different set of roles. They became housewives, childbearers, objects of admiration, and property of their husbands or fathers. They had little or no real influence. It wasn't until 1920 that women attained the constitutional right to vote. During World War II, women entered fields of employment traditionally held by men. But by 1950, they had been "demoted," for the most part, back to "women's jobs" as grade school teachers, nurses, garment industry workers, small parts assembly workers, textile mill's hands, clerical workers, retail salesclerks, and switchboard operators. Even in these assignments, opportunities for promotion were minimal. During the late 1960s and early 1970s, long-smoldering resentments surfaced. With help from a series of legal mandates and highly vocal organizations, women moved into male-dominated fields that offered greater opportunity.

social change

For blacks, Hispanics, and other minorities, the pattern has been much the same. Through carefully planned and ably led organizations such as the National Association for the Advancement of Colored People, the Urban League, and the Southern Christian Leadership Conference, blacks have been able to weaken many traditional barriers and influence the passage of laws that guarantee their basic constitutional rights. Other minority groups have experienced similar gains through similar organizations.

A primary concept of the equal opportunity movement is the commitment to "job-related" selection devices (interviews, tests, and evaluations). "Job-related" means, in essence, that an employer must not ask pre-employment questions or establish occupational requirements unless they can be proven to relate directly to the job for which the employee or applicant is being considered. As a result of a series of legal rulings, including the often reported *Griggs v. Duke Power Company* case that first challenged the necessity of a high school diploma and the passing of an intelligence test as requirements for employment, many organizations no longer require paper and pencil tests in their pre-employment screening. They are too difficult to prove related to the job.

preferential
treatment

The transition to equal opportunity has not been easy. To overcome past discrimination, organizations have voluntarily (or involuntarily, under court order), openly given preferential treatment to protected classes—women and minorities—even though the law specifically prohibits perferential treatment. Results have not always been satisfactory:

1. Open preferential treatment has at times, created deep-seated resentments within both the existing work force and the community.
2. Some women and minorities have taken personal advantage of civil rights laws by claiming discrimination when it has been doubtful that any unfair treatment existed.
3. Managers have often used women and minorities as showpieces in work areas that were formerly all white or all male in order to demonstrate equal employment. In the early 1970s, it was common practice to have a black or other minority group member in the front office, a person who was highly visible evidence that the organization was complying with equal opportunity requirements.
4. Job adjustment for people with a heritage of being denied equal employment opportunities for hundreds of years has been, in some cases, difficult. Attitudes of fellow workers, imagined injustices, and lack of confidence based on fear of failure have all contributed to major management-employee relation problems.

deal with
problems openly,
impartially, and
promptly

Sensitive managers have, in many cases, been able effectively to minimize the adjustment and attitudinal difficulties exhibited by both the existing work force and the new, nontraditional employee. The key to their success has been attending to both real and imagined injustices with careful, corrective efforts. Employees who know that they were hired because they are needed and that they are expected to perform and be rewarded or disciplined like other employees adjust more readily and make greater progress. An equally important factor affecting successful adjustment is the careful training of all levels of management to recognize potential personnel problems and to deal with them openly, impartially, and promptly.

Some managers and employees, unfortunately, seem blind to the reality of a changing work force. Their personal bias based on deep cultural traditions has impeded true achievement of equal opportunity. As a country, we have exercised our ability to discriminate against people all too well.

The Legal Framework of Social Policy

Since U.S. citizens share equally under the law the responsibilities and the protection of government, Congress, in 1964, reinforced the concept of equality and fairness by extending it into the work place.

Few laws have affected the responsibilities of organizations as dramatically as the federal *Civil Rights Act* of 1964 and its subsequent amendments in 1972. Under Title VII of the act, any employer or union of fifteen or more people is prohibited from discriminating against any person because of race, religion, color, national origin, or sex. Although many responsible organizations had voluntarily instituted nondiscrimination programs long before 1964, systematic exclusion of many U.S. citizens from the work force continued. Reinforced by state fair employment practice laws, investigative rulings of the federal Equal Employment Opportunity Commission, and court interpretations of equal opportunity laws, management has been forced to build work forces that are representative of the community as a whole. In effect, the Civil Rights Act has made work organizations primary agents of social change, a role often perplexing and sometimes in conflict with other organizational purposes.

legal framework

A major concern in many organizations has been the development of the concept of "protected classes." While the Civil Rights Act specifically prohibits preferential treatment, administrators of the law have held that because of past inequities, it may be necessary to set specific hiring, training, and promotional goals to build a more representative work force. Programs to implement this concept are called *affirmative action* programs. Under this interpretation of the Civil Rights Act, women, blacks, Hispanics, American Indians, and Asians have become protected classes. As protected classes, they may, under certain conditions, be given preferential treatment in employment and promotion. If an employer has no protected classes in a specific job classification, special recruitment to find qualified women or minorities may be undertaken. In many cases, the traditional "rule of three," in which the highest three test scorers are given preference in employment or promotion, is altered to provide opportunities for people who have previously been excluded from certain jobs. Those who scored lower than the top three have equal consideration with top scorers under the altered rules. Refusal by a work organization or union to take *affirmative action* in building a work force that represents the community at large can have severe consequences.

Civil Rights Act

When the employment service of a medium-sized Louisiana city found that few black applicants were qualifying for police and fire department openings, an intensive investigation was launched. Three major factors were found that contributed to the problem.

1. Some well-qualified black applicants were fearful of public reaction from other blacks and from white conservatives if the applicants became part of the police force.
2. Tests used for applicant selection were found in some instances to be culturally biased.
3. Many black people were suspicious of the motives of a city that had for almost two centuries denied them equal opportunity.

A special "public employee selection board" was established to recruit black applicants. To avoid possible legal entanglements with the "rule of three" provisions of the city's personnel regulations, oral interviews were weighed much more heavily than written tests in the selection procedure. After three months of concentrated effort, the selection board had developed "eligibility lists" of applicants that included a fair representation of the city's ethnic distribution. Special indoctrination and training sessions were developed for those selected to fill existing openings and for the previously all-white male work force as well. In the six years that the program has been in effect, there has been only minor public outcry over the procedures. The integration of the work force went far more smoothly than predicted. Recently, when one of the original black firefighters was promoted to the position of department chief, it was accepted as a routine, normal event. Before 1970, the event would have been unthinkable to many people in the city.

Special Problems

reality of affirmative action
Regardless of philosophical implications, the reality of affirmative action will be a part of employment and personnel activities for the foreseeable future. For both employees and managers, several special problems exist. From a management point of view, the doctrine of fairness is the most difficult. What the various laws affecting social policy state, and what courts have ruled, are of particular concern. Applications, interviews, and tests may ask only job-related questions. Most personnel specialists know that it is virtually impossible to construct any selection device that can be proven perfectly job related. The law states that an employer may not give preferential treatment to any employee, yet preferential treatment to protected classes is regularly assigned by the courts. Employers must know not only the law, but the way courts interpret the law's intent. A few of the major laws affecting personnel, not including the Fair Labor Standards Act and those that affect union-management collective bargaining relationships, are shown in Table 18.1.

From an individual employee's point of view, problems are often more complex than those encountered by management. Three true incidents exemplify some of the many different problems (the names of the companies and individuals have been changed):

> Sandra Holmquist was the first woman in Telo-Com Electronics' all-male market planning department. Although she was hired, admittedly, to break the sex barrier, her qualifications were excellent. Sandra's college training included both marketing and electronic technology. At twenty-seven she was attractive and hard working, but apprehensive about being accepted by the other employees. On several occasions, she was on the verge of quitting Telo-Comm because of both covert and open sexual approaches by her fellow workers. She was also told, not only by her fellow employees but also by women in other departments, that she had the job only because of her sex. When her immediate supervisor was moved to a higher-level job, Sandra was recommended for promotion to manager of technical market planning. Three days after assuming her new duties, a complaint was filed with the state Fair Employment Practices Commission alleging preferential treatment because of sex by Telo-Comm management. The Fair Employment Commission investigation concluded that Sandra was, indeed, qualified for her new assignment and that Telo-Comm had not violated the provisions of the Fair Employment Practices Act. Sandra has subsequently received additional promotions but still has nagging doubts concerning her full acceptance by other managers as well as employees.

Table 18.1 Major personnel-related laws

Equal Pay Act, 1963	Prohibits paying women less than men doing equal or similar work.
Civil Rights Act, 1964 (amended 1972)	Title VII requires equal treatment, regardless of race, color, religion, sex, or national origins, in all personnel actions. Applies to all employers or unions except for certain specific exemptions such as Native Americans and bona fide religious orders.
Fair Employment Practices Act	State-level equal opportunity acts.
Age Discrimination Act, 1967 (amended 1980)	Prohibits discrimination based on age for persons between 40 and 70 years of age.
Occupational Safety and Health Act, 1970	Mandates minimum safety and hygiene standards.
Worker's Compensation Laws	Enacted by all states; ensures employees of losses due to job-related injuries or illnesses.

Joe Mitsubi, a correctional institute parole officer, was told by his immediate supervisor that he would probably not be promoted, although his qualifications were outstanding. The Department of Correction's policy was to match supervisory parole officers ethnically with the majority of parolees. Since there were almost no prisoners with Japanese ancestry at Joe's assigned institution, there was no way for him to be "ethnically matched." He subsequently transferred to another agency within the state Government that needed a qualified management trainee.

Steve Morgan, who had a PH.D in anthropology, was told "confidentially" by several university deans of social science that they would like him on their staff, but their next hires were going to have to be either women or minorities. The U.S. Department of Health and Human Services was threatening withdrawal of funds for failure to hire minorities. Steve finally went to work for a friend in the construction business as a public relations manager.

Although it benefits many, the force of affirmative action has also created problems and sometimes, unpredictable injustices.

Problems in Attitudes

Few people will openly admit their own prejudices, and most of us at least profess a belief in equality and fairness. In spite of the force of law and the gradual reduction of racial, sexual, and national background barriers to job opportunities, the concept of preferential treatment to balance the ethnic and sexual composition of the work force has created deep resentment that is expressed in many forms.

Women and minorities have most often been the recipients of criticism, not because of what they themselves have done or not done, but because they are frequently perceived as receiving preferential treatment.

Although management may stringently try to balance a largely white male work force by giving minorities and women "nontraditional jobs," its actions may be interpreted as deliberately excluding eligible white males. Increasingly, young qualified males are protesting what they feel are discriminatory practices. Supreme Court rulings on discrimination against white males point out that preferential treatment of women and minorities is illegal; yet ethnically balanced and sexually representative work forces must be achieved.

problems of prejudice are still with us

Gradually, however, the stories of the Joes, Sandras, and Steves are disappearing. There is greater acceptance of women into previously male-dominated fields and acceptance of minorities in jobs from which they were previously excluded. The problems of prejudice and individual adjustment are still, unfortunately, with us. "Are they there primarily because they are female or minorities, or because of their qualifications?" and conversely, "Am I here primarily because I am female or a minority, or because of my qualifications?" remain important question.

Protectors of Society

Although the problem of equal opportunity has been a major one and to some extent will probably continue to be for the foreseeable future, it is not the only social issue management faces. Concern for the use of resources, protection of the environment, and safety and quality of products, as well as consumer reaction, are all part of management's expanding areas of responsibility. Managers are increasingly realizing that their actions and therefore their responsibilities extend far beyond their place of work.

> In Azusa, California, a process was developed to convert spoiled and unmarketable fruit into an excellent supplement to cattle fodder. Shortly after the conversion plant using the process went into operation, the surrounding area was enveloped in an overpowering stench similar to that of spoiled fruit. A local citizen's group sought and obtained a court injunction prohibiting the plant from further operation until controls for the odor could be installed.

Over the past twenty years, public concern for our environment has developed into a strong *environmental protection* movement. Various public and government groups have put increasing pressure on companies to control or eliminate pollutants.

However, a major deterrent to voluntary assumption of responsibility for environmental protection has been the frequently prohibitive costs. While covers on its processing tanks and filters on external ventilators can help odor control at the Azusa cattle fodder supplement plant, it may be far more difficult and expensive for a chemical manufacturer to dispose of waste products.

environmental protection

Management decisions can have significant impact on environmental problems, but the issue is complex. While work organizations are frequently blamed, a great deal of pollution is the result of consumer demand for convenience products. We don't want to give up our automobiles, canned drinks, no-return bottles, prepackaged food, double-wrapped gum and candy, or especially, jobs in companies that belch smoke and dump sewage into rivers. Pollution exists for many reasons. The question here, however, is, How can management take a leadership role in protecting the environment? In all probability, pollution of our air, water, and land will continue; but if it is not controlled, neither organizations nor society will survive.

On-the-Job Environmental Protection

Managers, as contributors to the shaping of society, may do a variety of things to encourage protection of the environment. Many companies have developed programs designed to encourage employees to ride in car pools, thus saving gasoline, reducing pollution, and congestion of highways. Some organizations have experimented with providing vans to selected people willing to pick up a number of other employees so all can ride in one vehicle.

Sponsorship of clean-up campaigns that encourage both employees and their children to become aware of pollution is another effective way of developing concern for environmental issues and the importance of individual action. Most significant, however, are the contributions management makes by setting in-house examples of waste control and cleanliness and demonstrating concern for its impact on the community.

Management can, and in many cases voluntarily does, act to control its organization's pollution problems. Organizations must, however, in addition to management action and example, conform to increasing legal requirements.

Management, Environment, and the Law

During the 1950s and 1960s, a growing awareness of damage being done to our environment began to stir the conscience of many people. Comedians joked endlessly about smog in Los Angeles. When people in nearly every large city in the United States finally realized that Los Angeles was not alone in its air pollution problems, the jokes were no longer funny.

In 1962, Rachel Carson's beautiful and touching *The Silent Spring* served as catalyst to encourage public action on environmental issues. Her book focused on the damage being done by the most widely used pesticide throughout the world, DDT. Once hailed as a means of saving humanity from hordes of insect infestations, which in many cases it did, DDT was found to be killing not only insects but fish and birds as well. Eventually, largely through public pressure, DDT was removed from use as a general insecticide.

pollutants   Managers whose organizations created pollutants of any kind came under legal and public scrutiny. In one instance, a public outcry was raised when it was found that industrial pollution was making Lake Erie incapable of supporting life. Companies that had traditionally disposed of industrial waste in streams that fed not only Lake Erie but also other bodies of water were forced, by law, to take stringent pollution control measures. Public concern for our physical environment grew steadily.

Many laws designed to protect the environment have been enacted by federal, state, and local governments over a number of years. A problem for management is determining which agencies have jurisdiction. In 1977, the Dow Chemical Company withdrew plans for building a giant chemical-processing facility in northern California largely because of difficulties in determining environmental protection measures and securing related permits. Over one hundred different government agencies were involved in water, air, and solid waste pollution controls.

To unify administration of environmental protection laws at the federal level, the *Environmental Protection Agency* was established in 1970 to coordinate government action in the areas of air, water, solid waste, toxic chemicals, pesticides, and radiation pollution control. Some of the agency's actions, especially in establishment of motor pollution control standards of automobiles and sewage treatment standards, have drawn sharp criticism. Managers of some organizations frequently cite environmental protection rulings as primary contributors to inflation and loss of productive capability.

Environmental Protection Agency

From a practical point of view, companies are often faced with difficult, conflicting demands and ever-increasing paperwork requirements from the hundreds of agencies with which they deal. On one hand consumers demand less expensive, better-quality products and services, yet those same consumers also blame management for failing to be concerned with the environment in which all of us live. Managers must plan operations that produce products, services, taxes, and jobs and at the same time meet society's demands for less pollution, better use of scarce resources, and greater corporate social responsibility.

conflicting demands

Despite all the uncertainties, we do know this: *Only society in the future can determine the true long-range effectiveness of today's social policies in work organizations.*

Shelling Out for Environmental Protection

There are times when the government seems to work against, not for, the environment. The Blue Diamond brand almond-processing plant came up with an ingenious plan for turning discarded almond shells into energy to help run the facility. The concept was the brain child of a joint effort between Imotek Corporation and the Almond Growers Association. It was to be the only large-scale bio-mass energy production unit of its kind.

But government experts vetoed the original design for controlling unwanted ash and odor by-products and instead specified a system that Imotek engineers felt would not work. After only a short time in operation, the plant began emitting a penetrating odor and spewing a fine brown ash into the air. The ash coated nearby neighborhood shrubbery and homes. Almost overnight, citizen pickets sprang up protesting the plant's pollution.

Imotek enigneers went to work on the problem. Within three months, they had modified the system back to their original design. This time it worked—without the help of government experts "protecting" the environment.[1]

Not all environmental control efforts have the happy ending of the Imotek story. Kaiser Steel Company's Fontana Plant began closing its facility in the spring of 1982. After many years as the West Coast's largest steel producer, the company cited two major reasons for the plant shutdown. Unreasonable union demands were originally thought to be the primary difficulty. After union employees moderated their requests, it was then noted that Kaiser had spent over $30 million in a failed attempt to meet federal environmental control standards. Further expenditures would be financially prohibitive and still could not guarantee that federal standards would be met.

Troubled Employees, Alcoholism, and Drug Abuse

Nearly every organization is faced with problems related to employees who are alcoholic, dependent on drugs, or suffer relatively severe long-term emotional difficulties. While there are no easy answers, most organizations recognize that it is frequently less costly to try to rehabilitate valuable, trained employees with such problems than to replace them.

costs of alcoholism

At Bechtel Corporation, a large international construction and engineering corporation, it is estimated that it costs $10,000 to replace a problem employee. TRW and Caterpillar both report similar figures, exclusive of training time.[2]

Of all employee problems, alcoholism has been most prevalent and most studied. The National Council on Alcoholism estimates that problem drinking costs American corporations between $13 and $20 billion dollars annually. Absenteeism, accidents, and sick leave usage by problem drinkers may be 16 times higher than the rate for average employees. Although these statistics are formidable, reliable studies indicate that rehabilitation programs have been successful in 50 percent to 75 percent of the cases.

treating problem drinkers

Many different approaches have been developed to handle alcoholic employees, with supervisory counseling and referral to outside agencies by far the most common. It is well known that threats of dismissal or demotion only encourage an employee to conceal the problem. Open, nonthreatening discussion seems to be a necessary first step toward achieving employee cooperation. Most organizations utilize competent outside agencies for actual rehabilitation. A close follow-up is usually made of employees completing treatment; and if a relapse occurs, another rehabilitation attempt may be tried. However, in some cases suspension and termination may be necessary. In most instances, large corporations report that an attempt is nearly always made to "save" the employee before termination.

Caterpillar Corporation reported that of 990 employees referred for treatment since their program began, 414 were completely rehabilitated. A follow-up study indicated a 50 percent decline in lost hours, a 31 percent decline in accidents on the job, and 75 percent fewer disciplinary actions for treated employees.

Drug and emotional problems are more difficult to recognize and treat than alcoholism. While there are no accurate statistics, the number of drug-related employee problems is increasing. At the present time, there are few policies other than termination for blatant use of illicit drugs such as marijuana, cocaine, and heroin, since in most cases, use of these substances is considered illegal under current law. Difficulties in determining when an employee is "hooked" rather than an occasional "joint" smoker compounds the problem. It is apparent that companies with some success in rehabilitation of alcoholics may need to take the same tactics in handling some types of drug users. *drug and emotional problems*

Emotional problems are usually recognized by noticeable changes in behavior such as increased irritability, withdrawal from social contact, excessive tiredness, fits of temper, forgetfulness, or unusual physical symptoms. Most emotional symptoms will pass in a relatively short period of time. When they persist, however, it is generally unwise for supervisors to assume the role of counselors or attempt to talk the employee out of their troubles. Like alcoholics, chronically disturbed employees should be referred, usually through appropriate medical or personnel services, to agencies that can provide expert counseling. Some corporations have developed widely publicized employee assistance programs or hotlines for troubled employees to use in seeking help. Unlike alcoholics, emotionally troubled employees will usually willingly seek and accept help rather than hide their problems.

A Hotline That Works

Control Data's dial-for-help program has been so successful that the company is now selling the plan to other organizations.

The program is administered by Control Data's Life Care Institute and provides a variety of telephone and face-to-face counseling. Workers can call into the 24-hour hotline to get help with any type of personal problem, whether or not it is job related. The hotline staff has dealt with everything from alcoholism to alimony. Over seven years, 30,000 of the company's 48,000 employees have used the hotline.

At the present time, thirty-seven organizations, including the National Basketball Association, are buying the Control Data program for their own employees.[3]

Right or Wrong—The Ethical Dilemma

From 1973 to 1980, when gasoline prices were soaring, oil companies came under sharp attack for disregarding public interests and deliberately profiteering at the expense of national inflation. Even now, with the current oil glut, these companies have never fully recovered from this criticism. Many people still view them as giant manipulators of government policy and the controllers of other segments of the economy.

corporate corruption

Oil companies are not the only ones who suffer from a declining public image. Almost daily, news items reveal instances of corporate kickbacks, bribery, cover-ups, deceptive advertising, and unfair treatment of employees. A substantial portion of society believes that business corporations, especially the large, highly visible ones, are interested only in profits and totally disregard the well-being of society. Not only are business organizations viewed with suspicion, but government agencies also suffer the same tarnished image. The General Services Administration has been accused of paying as much as $32 to have a key duplicated (usually no more than $3 at a local hardware store), issuing contract payments for work never performed, and continuing to accept kickbacks and bribes. Department of Agriculture grain inspectors, Federal Department of Transportation highway inspectors, and a host of other government officials have been accused of illegal and unethical practices that go uninvestigated and unpunished.

It is clear that social responsibility and ethics in organizations are part of the same general concerns. While social responsibility is directed toward issues related to the effect of an organization's actions on society in general, ethics deals with the somewhat clouded issues of what is right and wrong.

ethics defined

What Is Ethics?

Ethics concerns matters of right and wrong of good and bad. The original Greek word meant "character." The Romans had a corresponding word meaning "customs." We learn from ancient wisdom that character is judged by the customs of the particular group of people we are working or living with.

Ethics and morals are first learned from our parents and are "relearned" as we grow older as part of the development of our total system of attitudes and values. Our values and, thus, our concepts of right and wrong, are strongly influenced by the values of our parents and by our environment. A person raised in a midwestern farming community has different values from one raised in an eastern inner city. One whose father was a banker has different values from one whose father was a railroad engineer. Without making judgments about them, these differences must be recognized.

Values also differ because of cultural heritage. To take a minor and funny example, compare western and eastern United States traditions on wearing hats. The cowboy feels that it is the "right" thing to do to wear his beloved broad-brimmed hat in the house, even at mealtime. The Yankee would never think of wearing his hat in the house, and it would be a great "wrong" to wear his hat at the table.

This example makes the point that "right" or "wrong" is established by what are called *reference groups*, as well as by our early training. A major problem in the study of organizational ethics is that there are so many different reference groups, such as union members and CPAs, in our American society. The people we deal with in supervision and management come from many different kinds of reference groups. They have different values; they have different expectations. Dealing with the various value systems of employees poses numerous problems for managers at all levels and makes business and organizational ethics something few people want to talk about.

we learn what is "right" and "wrong"

Approaches to Individual Ethical Decisions

If you read summaries of what is written about ethics, you find that ideas of the "right thing to do" fall into four classes:

1. *A rigid set of rules.* In all ages, from the beginning of written history to the present, many people have said that the only right and safe thing to do is to follow a rigid set of rules which applies in all circumstances. It can easily be demonstrated that this is a very dangerous approach to follow, especially in business. Here is an example from civil society: It is universally accepted that to lie is wrong. If, however, you were a visitor in a totalitarian country and saw a well-known freedom fighter pass you on the street, a person you knew had been in jail, would you tell anyone, especially the police? Your answer would probably be no. You know that many people will lie to save the life of someone they consider worthwhile. The principle of absolute rules does not work as a rule of ethics.

set of rules

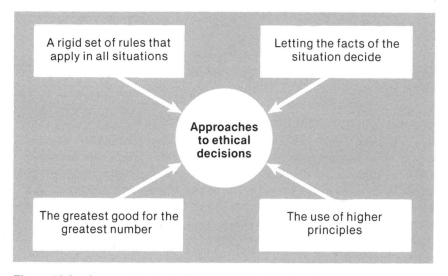

Figure 18.2   Approaches to individual ethical decisions.

greatest good   2. *The greatest good for the greatest number.* The greatest good for the greatest number is a rule of life that has been advocated for many years. Any viewer of television will see that many public figures adopt this principle. But any viewer of television will also see that many good persons reject this principle. The minority does have rights—the greatest good for the greatest number could mean slavery, oppression, or death for a certain number of people. This is intolerable in American society.

situation ethics   3. *Situation ethics.* A currently popular approach is to determine the rightness or wrongness of each individual decision by the facts of the situation. The "best" judgment of the decision maker results from the nature of the existing situation. In the extreme of this approach, each situation is decided independently of personal past experience or the past experience of others. This approach can be dangerous and unworkable because we cannot act today without being influenced by what we did yesterday. An individual should not decide and act independently of what others think and what others have previously done. While the situation *is* an important factor in any decision, the situation cannot dictate the rightness and the wrongness by itself. Workable principles must be applied. One of the early writers on situation ethics in the 1960s, Joseph Fletcher, was appealing to people to make the situation a factor, but not the only factor.[4] He was trying to move people toward the approach described in the next paragraph.

higher principles   4. *Use of higher principles.* Most values which our parents taught us or which we have learned in our lifetime can be ranked into a system. Some values rank higher to us than others. Each person's ranking is different. The most consistent and satisfactory system of ethics for modern man and woman is the commitment to a rank of values and the use of the highest values in making ethical decisions. It is to this fourth principle that the remainder of the chapter is devoted.

Why Managers Face Ethical Dilemmas

complex ethical problems of managers   Managers often face ethical dilemmas simply because they deal with a broad range of human behaviors and with many groups and cultures. They must obviously deal with individuals who adhere to codes of conduct differing from their own. This poses a very complex set of conditions. Few philosophers attempt to gauge the "rightness or wrongness" of managerial decisions. If philosophical underpinnings do not exist, we can, as managers and concerned individuals, adopt an operational approach and take actions, make decisions, and resolve differences. It cannot be overemphasized that a simplistic approach based upon mindlessly following "tried and true" advice often leads to unsatisfactory results.

Case I: The technical director of a paper company was called in by the vice-president of operations and told: "Go to the State Technical meeting next week and be sure to take the plant trip. The company you'll tour has a new process they have been keeping under wraps. We could use it—find out how they do it!" When the technical director arrived at the plant, the tour host told all concerned that the new process was a trade secret and requested guests to stay close to their guides. The visitors were not to see any part of the plant involved in the new process. Ignoring strong group tradition against violation of courtesies extended guests, the technical director "lost his way" and found the control room of the new process. He was discovered there by an executive of the competing company as he was frantically copying operating data. He never got another job.

Case II: The development projects manager of a major aerospace component company was not impressed when a young test engineer came to him with a problem. The young man had gone over his project engineer's head to complain that the concept and design for a new aircraft braking system were faulty and that performance tests were rigged to conceal the defect. Even though the project engineer in question was notorious for his inability to accept criticism, the superior manager followed company tradition and refused to investigate the project engineer's brake program. He told the complainer to forget about his worries; the project engineer could handle the matter. The company went ahead with rigged tests and test data. When the customer put the faulty brakes on a test aircraft, they heated to the point that they fused on landing, almost wrecking the aircraft and endangering the pilot. At that point, the test engineer and an associate resigned their jobs and told their stories to the authorities and the press. As a result, the company lost the contract and suffered a lot of bad publicity.[5]

The two cases just cited had unfortunate consequences because the decision makers blindly followed "rules" instead of analyzing the total situation and applying useful general concepts after such analysis. In Case I, the unfortunate technical director was afraid he would lose his job if he did not follow orders, but failed to recognize that the group tradition against violating the "guest rule" was so strong as to make him a virtual outcast if he did. In Case II, the superior manager made the mistake of not knowing his own subordinate and not knowing enough details of the task to properly evaluate the justifiable complaint of the junior employee. The lower status of the junior employee was interpreted as not only lower status but also lower credibility.

Value Ranking and Ethical Decisions

Honorable business decisions rest on the decision maker's strong sense of personal worth. Along with the forces in the individual, forces in the task, forces in the other people involved, forces in the environment, expectations of the group, and general concepts and ideals in the community all bear on an ethical decision. The relationships of these factors are shown in Figure 18.3.

Forces in the Individual

forces in the individual
We have already stated that one of the primary forces in any person is the set of experiences from early childhood. These forces are so important that many people believe that there would be no value system at all for an individual unless he or she had experienced strong inputs from parents and other closely associated adults. We know today that people who react in an "instinctive" manner are those who have not examined the values gained in their own childhood. An effective member of society must build on the best of what is learned in the first six years to develop his or her own value system. Another major set of forces in the individual is the experience in adolescence and early adulthood. The judgments of peers and superiors about actions have a major effect on our ideas of right and wrong. Finally, as we progress in early adulthood into positions of responsibility, the reactions from bosses, associates, and subordinates even further modify our idea of right and wrong and produce forces in us as individuals. These forces are often in conflict. This is the human situation. Every decision we make produces a reaction which produces a force within us.

Forces in Others

forces in others
Every situation we face is different. This is especially true of the forces in other people in the situation. These people may be our bosses, our associates, or our subordinates. They may be exactly the same people by name, but they have changed since the last time we dealt with them. A construction superintendent may be asked to work his crew an extra four hours after completing the normal eight-hour shift. He may say yes or no. There is a moral or ethical situation involved. It is well known that tired people are more likely to make mistakes. Construction is a dangerous occupation at best. The superintendent must wonder if the lives of any of his crew will be endangered by having to work an extra four hours.

If they have just come back from a restful weekend and have been working well, safely, and harmoniously, he may feel "right" in accepting the responsibility for the additional work. It will be an advantage to his firm, it will be an extra pay for his workers, and presumably it will not affect their well-being.

Suppose, to the contrary, this is the fourth day in a row that overtime has been requested. If the superintendent's employees have worked twelve hours each of the last three days, they are likely to be tired, out of sorts, and prone to make mistakes. They are the same peo-

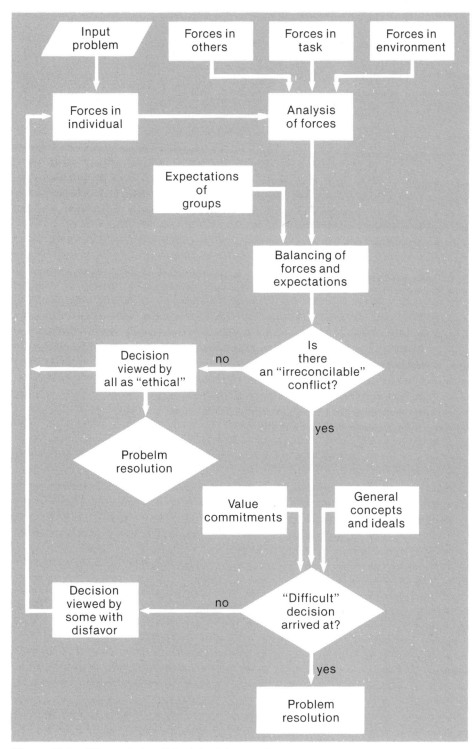

Figure 18.3 Elements in ethical decision cycle.

ple, but they have become predisposed to errors, they could hurt themselves, they could kill somebody. In such a case, it would be "wrong" for the superintendent to accept the requirement for an additional four-hour shift no matter how badly the company needed it.

Many of the most important firms in the United States, such as the Exxon Corporation or the DuPont Company, give great weight to forces in individuals before making a decision. The top management of Exxon Corporation, for example, gives major consideration to the personal situation (ages of children, health conditions, life-style, etc.) of second-level managers before reassigning them to positions of greater or different responsibility in the company. In a *Fortune* magazine interview, the former chairman of what is now Exxon Corporation stated that, in making such a determination, the company wanted to be sure that the best interests of the company and the best interests of the individual were served.

Forces in the Task

task forces To give an example of the forces in the task, let us look at coal mining, a very hazardous occupation. Miners and managers alike realize the dangers involved. Many miners and foremen die every year in industry accidents. The economy of the United States, however, requires continual mining of large amounts of coal. An ethical and responsible mining manager will not, because of hazards, avoid the assignment of managing a coal mine. The manager's principal obligation is to see that mining is carried out under optimum precautions to protect the lives of the miners as well as increase efficiency.

Forces in the Environment

environmental forces Business today operates in a confusing social and legal environment. The letter of the law, while an ideal, is often so confusing and, in the judgment of many, occasionally so wrong, that open defiance of it is sometimes considered to be an ethical action. Change through the judicial process may be hoped for. It also should be clear that mere adherence to the letter of the law does *not* make a person honorable or ethical. Most of us know of many scoundrels who have never broken the law, as written, but have violated its intent. It is nearly universally believed in the United States today that it is more important for business to adhere to the spirit than to the letter of the law. Many well-intended laws have such serious defects that it is possible for an unethical person to deprive fellow citizens of their just rights without violating the letter of the law. The managers in Case II had certainly violated the spirit of the law but suffered no punishment for it.

Another side to the legal situation today refers to "administrative laws." Ethical managers at all levels may be forced to make a "wrong" decision for their firm to avoid retaliation from those who enforce administrative law on the basis of personal interpretation. No law enacted by Congress or a state legislature may have been violated by making the "right" decision, but governmental forces may damage a person's firm so seriously that compliance is the only option. How to remain ethical and still deal with the unpredictable characteristics of administrative law is one of the biggest problems of today's manager.

Expectations of Others

We have already commented that the firm is made up of many groups of people among its managers, employees, customers, and stockholders. We have further noted that the values and expectations of these various groups are extraordinarily different. The modern firm exists in many different communities. The local plant or operation is one community; a large firm spread over the entire country is another community.

Many citizens of the city in which an organization is located have group expectations which differ from those of the firm's employees. The people that work for the firm have ties to the town, with its different expectations. Furthermore, they have ties to churches, fraternal associations, family groups, and ethnic groups. Each of these has different valuations from those of the firm, as well as different valuations from each other. Moreover, the employees may well be members of labor unions and one political party or another. Additional conflicts may arise because of the different values of these unions and parties.

group expectations

A common expectation within the labor force in a given firm may be something like, "Never rat on the boss, even though you think he or she is doing the wrong thing." Common expectations among professional and technical groups would include, "Sure it would be a good idea to have the plant open for technical personnel from competitive companies, as long as they realize they are our guests and stay away from designated COMPANY CONFIDENTIAL areas." The technical director in Case I became unemployable because of his violation of this group expectation. Common expectations of unions are that seniority will be honored above all else in the maintenance of employment. A common expectation of citizen groups is that the firm will "be a good neighbor" in encouraging its employees to take an active role in civic affairs and in complying voluntarily with environmental protection regulations. A common expectation of church-related groups is that the company will never deceive the public in its advertising or in public relation communications. All these differing expectations are not *necessarily* conflicting, but in some situations they *may* be.

expectations may be in conflict

General Concepts and Ideals

When we were small children, we were all exposed to absolute concepts such as, Always tell the truth. Another colloquial absolute goes like this: He who takes what isn't his'n must pay up or go to prison. Still an-

stealing, freeloading, and bribery

other is, There ain't no free lunch! We have already commented that these absolutes are of use to us and are necessary in building the value commitments by which a person may live. For example, we all know and honor the imperative, Thou shalt not steal, but is it wrong for the employees of a supermarket wrecked in a tornado to remove canned food from the ruins to distribute to starving survivors of the natural disaster?

There has been much publicity in the past year or so about bribery. We know nothing can be accomplished in certain countries abroad unless officials, minor or major, are persuaded with money to do their duty. If you are moving your household goods into a foreign country, is it wrong to pay a surcharge of 10 percent on top of all the legally imposed fees in order to see that the goods are delivered in time for you and your family to do the most effective job possible for your company?

Real conflicts occur in deciding the right thing to do in a given situation from a personal point of view. It is useful to look on a crucial statement by a twentieth-century theologian and philosopher, Paul Tillich, who once remarked, "Every event in our lives takes place in two worlds; the world of concrete realities and the world of ideal sentiments." We must balance the demands of both worlds.

greater goods   Earlier, we spoke of the underlying theme of this chapter, that there are greater goods (or "rights") and lesser goods (or "wrongs"). One of the greater goods is that we should *not* kill or harm other human beings. Yet we all know that there are times when it may be possible and necessary for us to violate this great good. In protecting our own life or the lives of those near and dear to us, it is right and proper for us to take human life. This is virtually a universal moral code in the United States. Widely, although less universally accepted, is that it is right to take a human life in the defense of our country. We must judge, in each instance, which is the greater good. But we must have our own firmly established system of values and priorities if we are to make such judgments and live with the consequences.

The Operational Approach to Ethical Dilemmas in Practice

The following case describes an incident which took place only a few years ago. In this case, the decision maker, an airline pilot, followed through entirely the procedure illustrated in Figure 18.3. In fact, it was a later discussion with him about the incident that resulted in the writing of this chapter and the paper which preceded it.[6] See if you can determine what the decision maker was thinking and how he balanced the forces in developing a desirable and ethically correct decision.

Case III: As has been well documented, major passenger airline pilots are truly operational managers. Their minor decisions, if incorrect, may cause opportunity losses of thousands of dollars. A major pilot error may cost tens of millions of dollars as well as hundreds of lives. Pilot-managers must have the ability to rapidly assess the many facets of a complex situation and arrive at an operational decision. In this case, the captain arrived for pre-flight check in a drunken state. The ground operational staff discreetly ignored his condition, but when the first officer arrived a few moments later, things were different. Drawing the older man aside, the first officer asked in a low but firm tone, "Captain will you turn yourself in, or shall I have to?" The captain proceeded immediately to the chief pilot's office and voluntarily grounded himself. Drying out took six months, but he has returned to flying for several years now without touching a drop. The two men have flown together often since the incident and are on good terms with each other. The younger pilot's only repercussions came from some other senior pilots who didn't like his violation of the axiom, Never blow the whistle on your boss!

Case III had a desirable outcome for all concerned. It did not result from applying a rigid, if valid rule, in this case, "Drunken pilots must not fly!" Rather, it resulted from the first officer's rapid operational assessment followed by a decision to force the captain to ground himself. The younger pilot had to assess the forces acting in four elements of the situation: (1) in himself, (2) in the other individual, (3) in the task, and (4) in the environment. He then had to determine their interactions and the ethical (or traditional) impact on each force and apply his value concepts in making a viable decision.

The first officer had three choices: (1) to ignore the captain's condition and trust to luck and his own skill as a pilot to carry the flight through, (2) to go to the chief pilot, or (3) to persuade the captain to do so himself. A number of first officers have "covered" for a drunken captain by getting the captain to agree to let them handle the takeoff and any landings before the captain sobered up. The first officer, in this case, recognized that the captain was an alcoholic. Covering for him would not help him in the long run. Passengers, furthermore, have the right to expect *two* competent, alert pilots up front. Going directly to the chief pilot was a last resort, because it would bypass the vital step in recovery from alcoholism in which individuals recognize for themselves that substance abuse may ruin them. Clearly, it was in the best interests of the airline, the public, the two individuals—and of the task of accomplishing a transcontinental flight—for the captain to ground himself. The copilot expected repercussions for violating "tradition," but he felt he could adapt to pressure. It would have been a worse violation of traditional authority for *him* to have gone to the chief pilot.

Sex in the Office—A Special Issue

One of the most troublesome issues involving both ethical values and principles of social responsibility is the use of power to gain sexual favors. Sex in the office has two sides. On one hand, it involves the use of threat or promise of promotion by a manager, usually a male, to obtain sexual compliance from an employee at a lower level. In 1980, the Equal Employment Opportunity Commission (EEOC) issued sex discrimination guidelines covering sexual harassment on the job. *Sexual harassment* includes such behavior as sexual advances, requests for sexual favors, or other verbal or physical conduct of a sexual nature directed toward an employee or applicant for work. Three general conditions generally define sexual harassment:

sexual harassment

1. Submission to or toleration of such conduct is an explicit or implicit term or condition of employment, appointment, promotion, or performance evaluation.
2. Submission to or rejection of such conduct is used as a basis for personnel decisions of any type.
3. The conduct has the purpose or effect of interfering with the employee's work performance or creating an intimidating, hostile, offensive, or otherwise adverse working environment.

problems for organizations

The other side of the problem concerns sexual conduct based on the willing consent of both parties. Public knowledge of the matter may be embarrassing to an organization because of unfavorable publicity and the impact on the organization's public image. A secretary who becomes pregnant and names her boss as the father, a male employee who claims his female boss propositioned him after they were discovered sharing a hotel room, and accusations against companies by suspicious husbands or wives are only a few of hundreds of types of sexual conduct at work based on mutual consent. One of the most celebrated such alleged relationships revolves around William Agee, chairman of the board of the Bendix Corporation, and Mary E. Cunningham.

> After graduating from Harvard University in 1979, Mary Cunningham rose from a minor management position at Bendix to vice president in a little over a year. William Agee, the Bendix Corporation's chief executive officer, was rumored to have personally promoted the attractive Ms. Cunningham. Although Agee had recently been divorced from his wife of 23 years, he strongly insisted that there was no romance involved and that he and vice president Cunningham were just close friends. After months of extensive publicity, Mary Cunningham resigned from Bendix and shortly thereafter was employed as a vice president for the Joseph E. Seagram Company.[7]

private affairs

Many people doubt the wisdom of corporate executives engaging in highly visible relationships that direct unfavorable attention to the organizations for which they work. Most employers would prefer to keep private affairs private. Like many other facets of organizational life, the proper course of action to take when conflicts between individual privacy and corporate image occurs is not clear.

Quick Review

I. Beyond Profits, Products, and Services
  A. Social responsibility falls primarily into three areas of concern:
    1. Promotion of equal opportunity.
    2. Protection of environment and conservation of resources.
    3. Concern for health and safety both on and off the job.
II. Social Change at Work
  A. Social value change is slower than technological change.
  B. The results of affirmative action programs have been mixed, at times achieving the goal of equal opportunity, at times resulting in further discrimination.
III. Protectors of Society
  A. Pollution is a troublesome byproduct of our affluent economy.
  B. Most companies resist complying with costly environmental protection measures.
  C. Concern for the use of resources, protection of the environment, safety and quality of products, and consumer protection are all part of management's expanding areas of social responsibility.
  D. Management must answer the question, "How much profit must be sacrificed for social goals?"
IV. Right or Wrong—the Ethical Dilemma
  A. Ethical systems can be grouped into four categories:
    1. Applying a rigid set of rules in all situations.
    2. Determining the greatest good for the greatest number.
    3. Basing one's ethical decisions on the circumstances of a particular situation.
    4. Using higher ethical principles as the basis for operational approaches to ethics.
  B. The many diverse groups and cultures with which management deals often present managers with ethical dilemmas and values conflicts.
  C. A simplistic approach to ethics generally leads to unsatisfactory results.
V. Value Ranking and Ethical Decisions
  A. Honorable business decisions rest on the decision maker's strong sense of personal worth.
  B. Several forces must be considered in an operational approach to ethics:
    1. Forces in the individual.

2. Forces in others.
3. Forces in the task.
4. Forces in the environment.
5. Expectations of others.

VI. General Concepts and Ideals
   A. Absolute concepts are useful to us in building our values commitments.
   B. Conflicts occur when absolute concepts and ideals clash with real-world situations.
   C. We must have a firm system of values and priorities to make judgments and weigh consequences.

VII. Sex in the Office—A Special Issue
   A. Sexual harassment includes sexual advances, requests for sexual favors, or other sexual conduct that interferes with a person's work or intimidates a person on the job.
   B. Public knowledge of sexual conduct between consenting employees can also create problems for the firm and damage its public image.

Key Terms

Social responsibility
Equal opportunity
Affirmative action
Environmental protection
Sexual harassment

Environmental Protection Agency
Civil Rights Act
Situation ethics
Ethical dilemmas
Willing consent

Alcoholism
Drug abuse
Reference groups
Prejudice
Ethics
Value ranking

Discussion Questions

1. Which is more important to modern management—social responsibility or profits? Explain your answer.
2. Equal employment opportunity has been enforced for twenty years. Should preferential hiring treatment still be given to women and minorities because of past discriminatory practices? Explain your answer.
3. Nearly all countries except the United States see bribery of public officials in business transactions as a normal part of doing business. Should U.S. companies continue to be prohibited from bribery practices in foreign countries? Why?
4. Illegal aliens working in the United States are not protected by the Civil Rights Act. Should they be protected? Why or why not?

5. At Capstone Manufacturing Company, employees are given rewards for reporting theft of company materials by other employees. Comment on Capstone's policy.
6. Highest unemployment rates are among young minority males. Explain why.
7. Some white males feel females, blacks, and Hispanics are given preferential treatment in employment selection. Is this true? If true, is it justified? Explain your position.
8. Has the environmental protection movement gone too far? Explain.
9. Is there really an energy shortage? In what ways should people prepare, if any?
10. Do any organizations you know practice some form of social responsibility? How?
11. Is it reasonable to assume that religious organizations with profit making businesses should be given tax free status? Explain.

Case Incidents

A Private War at the Public Works

At forty years of age, Chris Minanaro was an aggressive, intelligent, and unusually attractive executive. She was the only woman to hold the position of Public Works Director for the city of Three Rivers. All of the Public Works Agency's major service department managers were men. Two of the managers, Les Watkins and Walt Hinkle, were openly resentful of Chris's promotion to director. Each had applied for the director position at the time Chris was promoted. Both had stated their suspicions that Chris's relationship with the city manager was more than a working one.

"Besides being the city manager's playmate, the fact that she's Fillipino and female tells me she knows all of the city supervisors on a more than personal basis," stated Les Watkins in a meeting with other managers.

"That's right," echoed Walt Hinkle, "sex will get you where brains won't."

Two days later, Chris asked Les and Walt into her office for a private meeting. "I understand you two feel I was promoted because of my sex, not what I know," she began. "For fifteen years, I've worked my way up in the city because I wanted to succeed. I've earned everything I've got. How would you feel if I asked you two, 'How'd you like a promotion? Come up to my place tonight and do what I tell you and you'll get one.' How would you like that?" As Chris talked, she became coldly angry. "If I hear one more rumor or innuendo about me, that is started by either of you, you're going to be out on the street. You may even have to answer to me in court. I hope that's clear."

The next morning, Chris was notified by Alan Braden, Three City's personnel director, that a formal charge of sexual harassment had been filed against her by Watkins and Hinkle. "Chris, I know you didn't, but both swear that you stated, 'How'd you like a promotion? Come up to my place tonight and do what I tell you and you'll get one,'" Alan reported.

Chris thought back over her conversation with Watkins and Hinkle. "Alan," she replied, "the whole thing is taken out of context. What do I do now?"

"I'm afraid it's going to be rough," Alan responded slowly, "they've already released their side of the story to two reporters with the Three City's news."

1. What possible errors did Chris make?
2. What ethical and social responsibility factors are involved in the case?
3. Does Chris have a defense for herself? What can she do?

When Are Trade Secrets Fair Game?

Quicktype memory typewriters were successfully being marketed to schools, government offices, and some private businesses. As a comparatively small typewriter producer, it was constantly struggling to gain a larger share of the vast electronic typewriter market.

Shortly after Brad Ferris was hired as design engineer, he met with Beverly Langely, Quicktype's manager of Research and Development. "Just before I left Telecom Electronics," Brad began, "I was working on an interface between electronic typewriters and small computers. It's a simplified system that would make it possible to attach a Quicktype machine to any standard micro-or mini-computer so the typewriter could be used as either a printer or an input terminal. What do you think?"

"How far along is the design?" asked Beverly.

"Far enough to start prototype production," replied Brad enthusiastically. "It could give us a jump on the whole field of interface devices."

"You're right, and it sounds great," said Beverly, "but there may be some serious problems—at least ethically."

1. What are Beverly's ethical concerns?
2. Should Quicktype produce Brad's interface?
3. Identify a similar ethical dilemma. How can it be resolved?

Exercise   *Ethics and Social Responsibility*

1. How many students in your class have been, or know of some-
    one, who has been either the victim of discriminatory treat-
    ment or "reverse discrimination?" List the different types of
    occurrences.
2. What are some unethical practices observed by class mem-
    bers? Which ones do you consider most harmful?
3. List examples, in your community, of poor environmental pro-
    tection practices and inefficient use of energy.
4. Arrange a role-playing situation in class that demonstrates un-
    ethical practices by public officials.

Endnotes

1. Based on interview with Sue Sharp, Executive Assistant, California
    Almond Growers Association, February 19, 1982.
2. Adapted from unpublished paper "Alcoholism," Nick Correale,
    California State University, Sacramento, California, May 1982.
3. Adapted from *Forbes* Magazine, 22 June 1981.
4. Joseph F. Fletcher, *Situation Ethics, The New Morality* (Philadelphia:
    Westminster Press, 1966).
5. Kermit Vandiver, "Why Should My Conscience Bother Me?" in
    Organization and People, eds. J. B. Ritchie and Paul Thompson (St.
    Paul: West Publishing Co., 1976).
6. E. F. Thode and D.L. Costley, "A Contingency Approach to Managerial
    Ethics," *Proceedings, Southwest Division, Academy of Management,
    18th Annual Meeting*, San Antonio, March 1976.
7. Based on a story in *Time Magazine* and in numerous newspapers,
    February 8, 1982.

19 Career Development and Personal Success

Learning Objectives

After reading this chapter, you should be able to:

1. Understand the meaning of personal success.
2. Recognize factors contributing to career development.
3. Understand management's central role in career development.
4. Recognize the need to view an organization realistically.
5. Develop an appreciation for stages of career change and development.
6. Appreciate the value of periodic self-assessment.

Chapter Topics

Personal Success and Career Development

Success and Personal Development

Organizational Career Development Plans

Career Development and the Individual

Keys to Success

A Managerial Perspective

Preview and Self-Evaluation

For many years, success for most people meant a secure job with a reliable organization. People usually prepared for a lifetime career. Today few people work at the same job, career, or place more than a few years. Even those who remain with a single organization frequently find the nature of their work changed as new technology and societal requirements affect their organizations.

Success today is not measured solely in terms of money but may include life-style, job interests, geographic location, the degree of self-determination at work, and a host of other personal values.

While career success is still largely based on personal achievement, it is not always tied to salary or compensation. A struggling family in the Alaskan backwoods who has just sold its first cabbage crop may feel as successful as a more highly paid mid-manager in a large corporation.

In Chapter 19, we will explore some aspects of career development and personal success. To test your knowledge of the subjects, answer the following True-False questions before you read the text. Retake the quiz after reading the material.

Answer True or False

1. Career development is a continuous process.   T   F

2. Formal career development programs are available
   in most work organizations.   T   F

3. Managers who are developers of people usually
   make decisions for employees as a method of
   training.   T   F

4. Midlife crisis usually occurs around age 50 to 55.   T   F

5. Performance evaluation, no matter how carefully
   planned, does not substantially help in career
   development.   T   F

6. It is ultimately the company and management that
   make career development.   T   F

7. If a person works hard, he or she can be assured of
   job advancement and career devlopment.   T   F

8. A reality of organizational life is that knowledge of
   politics at work has little to do with success.   T   F

9. People should not stay with an organization or job
   they don't like and that offers little opportunity.   T   F

10. Research shows that geographic relocation rarely
    helps career advancement.

ANSWERS: 1. T; 2. F; 3. F; 4. F; 5. F; 6. F; 7. F; 8. F; 9. T; 10. F.

Personal Success and Career Development

A few years ago, Liam Hudson, a Scottish professor in Edinburgh, observed that some students did best in tasks that required following rules, utilizing systematic approaches to problem solving, and careful detail.[1] Such students seemed to be more comfortable with subjects such as conventional mathematics, accounting, physics, and analytical studies, which require logical, step-by-step reasoning. Hudson identified such students as *convergent thinkers*.

convergent thinkers

Other students Hudson observed were more imaginative, less organized and less precise, and seemed to rely more on their feelings than on logic. These students, called *divergent thinkers*, tended to be people oriented, better at creative tasks than convergent thinkers, more imagina-

divergent thinkers

tive, and better able to deal with ambiguity. But they were also less orderly and precise than their counterparts.

Hudson postulated that if his observations were correct, a number of predictions could be made. Divergents assigned to convergent tasks would not be successful. Convergents assigned to divergent tasks would at best be dissatisfied. Although there is not a great deal of research to support Hudson's hypothesis, David Kolb at the Massachusetts Institute of Technology has extended Hudson's original studies and has developed a strong body of evidence that people have different preferred learning styles.[2] Their styles of learning to some extent determine their job preferences.

work and learning styles

Our point in mentioning the Hudson/Kolb theories is that success in life and career may be at least partially dependent on choosing types of work that match our styles of thinking and learning. We are just beginning to understand some of the factors that lead to job success. It is likely that a number of personality elements ranging from our inherited physiology to our environments, learning, cultural values, early childhood development, family structure, and other life experiences affect the choices we make and our concepts of success and failure.

Success and Personal Development

Some people view success in terms of personal achievement, money, approval by others, power and influence, and competence. Others may equate success with self-determination, freedom of choice, and independence from organizational constraints. While there is no universal definition, our society seems to look at success in terms of progressive achievement, organizational advancement, stability, and movement into higher socio-economic brackets.

personal and societal views of "success"

It is becoming increasingly clear, however, that success defined by general societal values and success defined by individuals may be different. One mid-level executive with a major southcentral gas transmission corporation recently turned down a substantial promotion for several reasons.[3] "First," he stated, "I don't want to move, because I like my job. It has more variety and freedom than the new job could offer. In addition, this is where my children have their roots and where most of my friends live. The extra money and prestige isn't worth destroying my present life-style." While some people are able to successfully reject an offer of promotion, for others it is more difficult.

More Workers Refusing Promotions

Heywood Klien, staff reporter for *The Wall Street Journal*, reports that a number of managers are doing what was once unthinkable—refusing a promotion. He points out that resisting a promotion can brand an employee as disloyal or lacking ambition, but some managers see it as a way of managing their own careers. In some cases, managers turn down promotions into "dead end" jobs so they can later accept jobs that offer brighter future prospects. Others, however, want to avoid a difficult future boss or simply want to enjoy life more.[4]

Career development usually means continually acquiring increased knowledge, skill, and competency and as a result being promoted to successively higher levels in an organization. Employees, managers, and organizations share in the career development process.

Organizational Career Development Plans

As part of their long-range personnel planning, some companies such as Sears, Carborundum, Xerox, IBM, and a number of federal government agencies have utilized career management techniques. These include encouraging employee education and self-development, maintaining updated personnel information, providing specialized training, and carefully appraising performance to help employees identify strengths and areas needing improvement. Some also identify a progressive sequence of assignments for employees who demonstrate the desire and ability to work at increasingly more responsible tasks.[5]

career development plans

Formal career development programs are still, unfortunately, the exception rather than the rule. In all probability, most managers realize the value of assisting employees in development of their capabilities. A. L. Camp, a former director of manufacturing for Aerojet-General Corporation and subsequently the vice-president and president of Cleveland Tool Company in Cleveland, Ohio, once stated that he felt a manager's single most important task was to be a "developer of people."[6] Camp's basic philosophy hinged on encouraging all levels of personnel who demonstrated the desire and ability (1) to accept more responsibility; (2) to constantly set high but achievable goals; (3) to assess their own performance; and (4) to become less dependent on higher levels of management for key job decisions. Camp views management's roles in career development as coaching, providing performance assessment and feedback, and setting a climate for acceptance of personal responsibility.

managers as "developers of people"

While individual managers, especially those at upper organizational levels, are helpful in establishing a climate for career development, formal programs should be established. Such career development efforts must also be supported by organizational policy and top management commitment. Many organizations are beginning to realize the importance of *human resource planning (HRP)*. HRP involves the careful analysis of available personnel resource needs for the future, technol-

formal programs

ogy changes, market projections, and other related factors to determine potential organizational needs. It seeks to make the optimum utilization of existing people as well as projected new hires. A part of well-founded HRP efforts is the identification of training needs and advancement potential for individual employees. As computer programs in personnel become more sophisticated, career management can be more thoroughly integrated into overall human resource plans.

human resources planning

Although organizations have a major responsibility in providing career development programs, opportunities, and data for employees, ultimately, individual desire and energy make career development efforts work.

Career Development and the Individual

Thirty years ago, Abraham Maslow noted that some people are able to define their role in life more easily than others.[7] They identify what they *like* to do and what they *can* do. Once they have found a satisfying successful activity, they work at perfecting their skills. These *self-actualized* people are those who are able to fulfill their needs for competence, achievement and "doing what they should do."

self-actualized people

Not all of us, unfortunately, are able to easily identify career paths that will self-actualize us for long periods of time. However, identification of career goals is a necessary first step. While many people find careers largely by accident and coincidence, many others may find they are constantly seeking a type of work for which they feel suited.

There are several approaches that are useful. Many colleges and universities offer career counseling and testing services. Users of the career programs can more easily define their personal aptitudes, limitations, interest patterns, and potential marketable skills. Larger cities have private career counseling services which may be expensive but can also be helpful. In some instances, state and federal employment services will offer some degree of career advising.

career services

Once a career choice has been made, it is necessary to develop a personal career development plan. Randall Schuler notes that a successful personal career management plan should result in a realistic awareness of skills, abilities, weaknesses, needs, values, career opportunities, and a sense of self-esteem and self-worth.[8] Some possible steps that can be taken are to:

1. List the activities you like and dislike.
2. Evaluate skill levels needed for activities liked.
3. Obtain training and proficiency in a preferred activity.
4. Carefully survey potential job markets.
5. Apply for jobs that look challenging, even if it means relocating geographically.
6. Work hard.

7. Learn organizational politics.
8. If you change jobs, leave on friendly terms by your own choice.

"go to hell" funds

Years ago, some newspaper reporters were famous for developing a "go to hell" fund, which was the equivalent of a year's salary put aside in a separate bank account. If they felt they weren't achieving what they wanted at their work place, or felt they were incompatible with the boss, they could tell the job, and in some cases the boss, to "go to hell." They were financially secure at least for a year while they hunted for other work. While we do not advocate everyone having a go-to-hell fund, a reality of life is that for many reasons some jobs just do not work out the way we had hoped. People who are able to maintain contacts with other organizations, develop professional friendships, and make new contacts through membership in associations frequently find moving to another job easier.

Personal Values and Career Development

New employees often need to understand several key realities of work-life. These include the fact that most organizations require greater conformity than many new employees like; that some managers are both power and control oriented; that bright people are frequently assigned to dull jobs; and that economic necessity can often override other personal considerations.

realities of worklife

Few people in today's economic, technological, and socially complex world work at a single occupation, at one place, with the same skills more than a short period of their lives. As organizations change, both jobs and people change. It seems to make sense that personal career values must include the realities of organizational life and change. By *personal values* we mean those things that an individual feels are personally important such as interesting work, a sense of responsibility and contribution, some self-determination and independence, and good interpersonal relations with other members of the organization both management and nonmanagement. Expectations must be realistic; but if they are totally at odds with organizational style, it is frequently better to seek other work than to remain locked into an unsatisfactory and often stressful pattern of work.

personal values and career change

While many younger employees are competent, trained, energetic, and want to please, these characteristics alone are not enough to ensure success. Younger employees must also realize that every organization has its own political style. People either become part of a network of in-groups or find themselves excluded from these informal support networks. An isolated individual is more vulnerable and may become a victim of the *bleeding shark syndrome*. When a shark bleeds, it is often attacked by other sharks. Likewise, people in organizations who, knowingly or unknowingly, offend a member or members of a support network in-group may be constantly attacked rather than helped by others in the network.

bleeding shark

Time and Careers

Levinson model

In his book, *You Can't Go Home Again*, Thomas Wolf portrays the futility of trying to go back in time, to be as we once were, and to expect the world to remain the same. As people grow older, not only do their careers develop but their life directions change. Daniel Levinson and a group of colleagues developed what has become widely recognized as the *Levinson Model of Career Change.*[9] About every seven to ten years, our lives undergo major and sometimes traumatic changes. Some of these life stages are depicted in Table 19.1.

Table 19.1 Levinson's model of career change

Age	Major Change Event
16–22	*Pulling up roots.* Individuals assert independence and self-confidence. Some who prolong parental ties become underachievers.
22–29	*Entering adulthood.* Lifestyle and career are selected; jobs are established, and first encounters with career success, failure; realization of competencies occur.
29–32	*Change.* During this period, the career matures and many individuals seek change through a series of job relocations, geographic moves and redirection of lifestyle. At this point, they solidify their personal values and life direction.
32–39	*Career advancement.* During this period, the job often becomes the dominant feature of a person's life. Organization skills are frequently at their peak, and it is the period during which many make their most significant career moves. It is, unfortunately, frequently a period of family stress, and social readjustment in that career and organization become more important than social contacts.
39–43	*A midlife crisis.* This event may occur for some people during this period. Individuals may look back on their achievements with resentment, sadness, or, in some cases, pride. A growing number of people attempt to make radical career and lifestyle changes during the midlife crisis. Not everyone views this period as a crisis. For some, it is a period of increased renewal of goals and achievement.
43–50	*Openness and self-development.* Many people recognize this as a period of settling down. For many, careers have peaked, competencies and confidence have been developed, and there is a renewed interest in activities outside of work.
50 and above	*Maintenance and reflection.* After the age of 50 until retirement, many employees continue the pattern developed earlier but with increasing awareness that significant changes in lifestyle are unlikely and that promotions will come slowly, if at all. For some, it can be a period of high productivity and renewed interests in a diversity of activities. For others, it may become a period of "working for Friday" so weekends can be enjoyed more than day-to-day job routines.

There are many models of career change patterns other than the one popularized by Levinson. All have a common element: as people mature, their career interests and directions change. While changes are not universal in that no two people are affected precisely the same way, there seem to be reasonably consistent patterns of development and change for most people.

Allness and Resistance to Change

One of the more difficult individual career problems originally identified by William C. Haney, is the development of an attitude of *allness*.[10]   *attitude of allness* Allness occurs when individuals begin to believe that they know all about a particular subject or occupation and as a result become unwilling either to accept change or to examine alternative ways of doing things. Individuals who say, "This is the way I've always done it and always will," are expressing allness. Their mind is made up; they don't wish to consider new facts.

Allness is all too common in many management people who have been at the same or similar organizational levels for many years. In their view of the world, things and people are unchanged and unchanging. New problems are solved in old ways. Attitudes, values, and beliefs remain frozen. Often only traumatic personal experiences can break the all-wall and let established managers be shaken loose from the secure but ineffective allness behavior.

Nonmanagement employees, especially those with well-established patterns of behavior, may also exhibit the same type of allness that characterizes some managers. They resist change, criticize new methods, complain about different approaches, and refuse to consider the potential benefits of new work methods and new technologies, or the impact of evolving societal values.

When organizations are dominated by allness, they often follow policies that can ultimately lead to bankruptcy and massive loss of jobs. Management has historically suffered from the shortsightedness of allness. Ford Motor Company, headed by Henry Ford III, fired Lee Iacocca largely because of Iacocca's desire for change. Iacocca went on to become the most recognized automotive manufacturing and marketing leader at Chrysler Corporation; he successfully led the movement toward revitalization of the U.S. automobile industry. Many people wondered why Ford continued to slide downward as Chrysler edged upward as a leader in the automotive field. Allness stops not only careers but companies as well.

Self-Fulfilling Prophecy

Some ancient philosopher is credited with saying, "We are what we   *thinking success* think we are." Many researchers and psychologists have written that self-image is a vital determinant of success.

Their research indicates two important and closely related concepts. People who think they will succeed have a greater chance of success than those who think they will fail. Similarly, people who others think will succeed have a greater chance of success than those others think will fail. Athletic coaches who believe their teams are winners are more likely to be successful than those who feel their teams are failures. By the same reasoning, the coach who thinks, "My teams are the best," has an edge on those who are doubtful of their team's ability.

winners   In organizations, individual managers who are winner oriented have winning oriented employees. They are the group most likely to be high achievers and may be the ones to excel and earn recognition as the best. Few, if any, careers are built on timidity, lack of confidence, and fear of failure. Winners are people who believe they are winners.

Esprit de Corps

Tucson, Arizona, has what is probably the country's best garbage collection corps. Led by an enthusiastic ex-"ecology technician," the ultra-modern refuse collection system is well disciplined and technically superior, and recognized as the best large city unit of its kind. Tucson's mayor, city council, and managers of the sanitation workers' staff as well as non-management employees all know that their success stems largely from the fact that they *believe* they're the best and others take pride in their achievements.[11]

Career Development Assistance

Many organizations have developed approaches to help employees in their career development. In Illinois, the State Department of Personnel uses its Performance Appraisal System (Figure 19.1) as a basis for career development. California's State Department of Finance has inaugurated a self-assessment approach that may be applicable in many other states to help employees assess their personal strengths and weaknesses as potential managers (Figure 19.2).

Unfortunately, many employees do not take advantage of personal development opportunities when they are offered. Active encouragement by managers is necessary. In many instances, as shown in Figure 19.1 and 19.2, personal development is tied directly to the employee's formal performance evaluation in order to emphasize both the need and advantages of additional training and experience.

State of Illinois
DEPARTMENT OF PERSONNEL
Springfield, Illinois

INDIVIDUAL DEVELOPMENT AND PERFORMANCE SYSTEM

1. EMPLOYEE'S NAME - LAST, FIRST, MIDDLE	2. DEPARTMENT, BOARD OR COMMISSION	3. DIVISION OR INSTITUTION
4. EMPLOYEE'S SOCIAL SECURITY NUMBER	5. EMPLOYEE'S PAYROLL TITLE	6. TIME IN CURRENT TITLE _____ YEARS ___ _____ MONTHS
7. PERIOD OF REPORT FROM TO	8. TYPE OF REPORT ☐ FIRST PROBATIONARY ☐ FINAL PROBATIONARY ☐ ANNUAL ☐ SALARY INCREASE ☐ LAYOFF ☐ DISCHARGE ☐ OTHER (SPECIFY) _____	

GENERAL INFORMATION

An objective centered performance evaluation system provides for the collaborative review of employee performance and for the establishment of appropriate work and developmental objectives.

The form itself is a neutral instrument. The value of the system will be determined by the amount of effort individuals are willing to devote to the objective setting and evaluation processes. This evaluation system requires continuous communication between the employee and the supervisor.

The system is an attempt to make the process of evaluation more rational. It helps the employee and supervisor understand more fully what is involved in doing their jobs as well as clarifying the relationship of their work to the work of others around them. This approach helps reduce the problem of misunderstanding by requiring that the employee and supervisor meet and jointly agree to a set of objectives, in order of importance, for the employee's job. The individual gets direct feedback on how he is progressing through the use of the quarterly review sessions. The organization benefits by being better able to plan and coordinate its functions for more effective and economical delivery of services.

The objectives of the organization and the objectives of the individual should be integrated as closely as possible. Those employees who see their own objectives being accomplished, while at the same time achieving the objectives of the organization, are more interested, more motivated and, therefore, more effective in performing their jobs.

The establishment of employee objectives is a five-step process which may be illustrated as follows:

1 EMPLOYEE'S ROLE Discuss areas of re-responsibility relating to objectives and self-development needs.	2 Prepare list of objectives for discussion with supervisor. Discuss and agree on work objectives for this period.	3 Prepare plans of action to meet objectives for approval of supervisor. Perform the job to be done.	4 Review progress and discuss any problems with supervisor.	5 Make self-evaluation and evaluate results for annual appraisal. Prepare list of objectives for next period.
INFORMATION TO BE SHARED Organization objectives; major job responsibilities; self-development needs	OBJECTIVE SETTING	PLANS OF ACTION FOR JOB TO BE DONE	QUARTERLY PROGRESS REVIEW	EVALUATE PERFORMANCE ANNUALLY. RESET OBJECTIVES.
1 SUPERVISOR'S ROLE Communicate and discuss appropriate objectives.	2 Prepare a list of objectives with employee. Discuss and agree on work objectives for this period.	3 Approve plans of action for achieving work objectives and review with higher management.	4 Review progress. Make adjustments as required. Provide coaching and assistance.	5 Evaluate performance and results for annual appraisal. Prepare list of objectives for next period.

Each employee will be counseled by his supervisor and a copy of this form filed in the individual's personnel folder not less than once every twelve (12) months. Results of quarterly progress review sessions need be recorded only on copies retained by the employee and the supervisor.

A minimum of three (3) copies of this form will be required--one for the supervisor, one for the employee, and one for the personnel files. Additional copies may be required if needed. If employee position is at a level (unskilled, etc.) that does not lend itself to objective setting, indicate by inserting "N/A" (Not Applicable) wherever necessary.

DP-201R (2-74)   Page 1 of 4

Figure 19.1 Illinois Individual Development and Performance System: Performance Appraisal Form.

PART I. APPRAISAL OF OBJECTIVES.

Supervisor is to list and evaluate all objectives for which the employee was held accountable during the last reporting period. Mark the appropriate column for each objective.

	Objectives		
	EXCEEDED	MET	NOT MET

PART II. GENERAL APPRAISAL OF EMPLOYEE PERFORMANCE

Complete items 1 through 8 for all employees and items 9 and 10 when applicable. Differences between ratings by employee and by supervisor must be discussed.

		TO BE COMPLETED BY EMPLOYEE			TO BE COMPLETED BY SUPERVISOR			
		EXCEEDS EXPECTATIONS	MEETS EXPECTATIONS	NEEDS IMPROVEMENT	EXCEEDS EXPECTATIONS	MEETS EXPECTATIONS	NEEDS IMPROVEMENT	INSUFFICIENT OPPORTUNITY TO OBSERVE
1. JOB KNOWLEDGE:	Consider overall knowledge of duties and responsibilities as required for current job or position	☐	☐	☐	☐	☐	☐	☐
2. PRODUCTIVITY:	Evaluate amount of work generated and completed successfully as compared to amount of work expected for this job or position	☐	☐	☐	☐	☐	☐	☐
3. QUALITY:	Rate correctness, completeness, accuracy and economy of work - overall quality	☐	☐	☐	☐	☐	☐	☐
4. INITIATIVE:	Self motivation - consider amount of direction required - seeks improved methods and techniques - consistence in trying to do better.	☐	☐	☐	☐	☐	☐	☐
5. USE OF TIME:	Uses available time wisely - is punctual reporting to work - absenteeism - accomplishes required work on or ahead of schedule	☐	☐	☐	☐	☐	☐	☐
6. PLANNING:	Sets realistic objectives - anticipates and prepares for future requirements - establishes logical priorities	☐	☐	☐	☐	☐	☐	☐
7. FOLLOW-UP:	Maintains control of workloads - allocates resources economically - insures that assignments are completed accurately and timely	☐	☐	☐	☐	☐	☐	☐
8. HUMAN RELATIONS:	Establishes and maintains cordial work climate - promotes harmony and enthusiasm - displays sincere interest in assisting other employees	☐	☐	☐	☐	☐	☐	☐
9. LEADERSHIP:	Sets high standards - provides good managerial example - encourages subordinates to perform efficiently - communicates effectively	☐	☐	☐	☐	☐	☐	☐
10. SUBORDINATE DEVELOPMENT:	Helps subordinates plan career development - grooms potential replacements - gives guidance and counsel	☐	☐	☐	☐	☐	☐	☐

Page 2 of 4

Figure 19.1 Illinois Individual Development and Performance System: Performance Appraisal Form. (*cont'd.*)

EMPLOYEE'S NAME - LAST, FIRST, MIDDLE

PART III. REMARKS BY SUPERVISOR.

Comment on employee's outstanding achievements. When "not met" is checked in Part I or "needs improvement" is checked in Part II describe the reasons for this rating, and what remedial steps were taken.

PART IV. EMPLOYEE OBJECTIVES FOR NEXT REPORTING PERIOD.

To be established by the employee with input, advice, and agreement of the supervisor. Objectives should be set for each major area of job responsibility, ranked in priority order, and be as measurable as possible. Personal development objectives may be included.

Page 3 of 4

Figure 19.1 Illinois Individual Development and Performance System: Performance Appraisal Form. (*cont'd.*)

PART V. EMPLOYEE'S COMMENTS.

   Employee may comment on all or any part of the information contained in this document, including the evaluation process. If the employee does not concur with the evaluation, check the appropriate box and explain reasons for disagreement.

PART VI. SIGNATURES.

EMPLOYEE'S SIGNATURE	PAYROLL TITLE	DATE

☐ I DO NOT CONCUR (USE PART V FOR COMMENTS)

SUPERVISOR'S SIGNATURE	PAYROLL TITLE	DATE

☐ I HAVE PERSONALLY DISCUSSED THE CONTENTS OF THIS DOCUMENT WITH THE EMPLOYEE AND WE HAVE AGREED TO THE OBJECTIVES SET.

NEXT HIGHER LEVEL SUPERVISOR SIGNATURE (REVIEW)	PAYROLL TITLE	DATE

AGENCY HEAD SIGNATURE (REVIEW)	PAYROLL TITLE	DATE

PART VII. QUARTERLY PROGRESS REVIEW. (This can be initiated by either the employee or the supervisor.)

   The employee and supervisor are to meet quarterly to review progress toward previously agreed upon objectives. If the original objectives need to be adjusted, use the space below to document the change. The employee and supervisor should date and initial the document at the time of each review.

1st quarter
Date _____
Initials:
Emp. _____
Sup. _____

2nd quarter
Date _____
Initials:
Emp. _____
Sup. _____

3rd quarter
Date _____
Initials:
Emp. _____
Sup. _____

(DO NOT WRITE BENEATH THIS LINE)

For use only if third party consultation is required.

Figure 19.1   Illinois Individual Development and Performance System: Performance Appraisal Form. (*cont'd.*)

STATE OF CALIFORNIA

INDIVIDUAL DEVELOPMENT PLAN
FOR FUTURE JOB PERFORMANCE OF PERMANENT EMPLOYEES
STD. 637 (10/78)

EMPLOYEE'S NAME _(LAST, FIRST, MIDDLE INITIAL)_	DATE OF THIS PERFORMANCE DISCUSSION	
CIVIL SERVICE TITLE	POSITION NUMBER	DATE OF LAST PERFORMANCE DISCUSSION
STATE DEPARTMENT	SUBDIVISION OF DEPARTMENT	EMPLOYEE'S HEADQUARTERS

PERFORMANCE OBJECTIVES -- Goals for further improvements in job performance during the next year in order to meet or exceed standards for the employee's present job or to develop employee skills.	PLANS FOR ACHIEVING OBJECTIVES -- Specific methods by which the employee can work toward accomplishing his or her performance objectives (in-service training courses, college courses, rotation, special work assignments for training purposes, etc.).

I HAVE PARTICIPATED IN A DISCUSSION OF OVER-ALL JOB PERFORMANCE

SIGNATURE OF EMPLOYEE	DATE	SIGNATURE OF SUPERVISOR	DATE
▶		▶	

(Over)

Figure 19.2   California Department of Finance Career Development Form.

PERFORMANCE APPRAISAL SUMMARY

OF PAST JOB PERFORMANCE OF PERMANENT EMPLOYEES

STD. 637 (2/78) — REVERSE

PERFORMANCE FACTORS	I	M	E*	COMMENTS*
1. **QUALITY OF WORK:** Consider the extent to which completed work is accurate, neat, well-organized, thorough, and effective.				
2. **QUANTITY OF WORK:** Consider the extent to which the amount of work produced compares to quantity standards for the job.				
3. **WORK HABITS:** Consider the employee's effectiveness in organizing and using work tools and time, in caring for equipment and materials, in following good practices of vehicle and personal safety, etc.				
4. **RELATIONSHIPS WITH PEOPLE:** Consider the extent to which the employee recognizes the needs and desires of other people, treats others with respect and courtesy, inspires their respect and confidence, etc.				
5. **TAKING ACTION INDEPENDENTLY:** Consider the extent to which the employee shows initiative in making work improvements, identifying and correcting errors, initiating work activities, etc.				
6. **MEETING WORK COMMITMENTS:** Consider the extent to which employee completes work assignments, meets deadlines, follows established policies and procedures, etc.				
7. **ANALYZING SITUATIONS AND MATERIALS:** Consider the extent to which the employee applies consistently good judgment in analyzing work situations and materials, and in drawing sound conclusions.				
8. **SUPERVISING THE WORK OF OTHERS:** Consider the employee's effectiveness in planning and controlling work activities, motivating and developing subordinates, improving work methods and results, encouraging and supporting employee suggestions for work improvements, applying policies, selecting and developing subordinates in accordance with State Personnel Board and departmental affirmative action policies.				
9. **PERSONNEL MANAGEMENT PRACTICES:** Consider the extent to which the employee understands and applies good personnel management practices including affirmative action and upward mobility. Does the employee contribute effectively to the implementation of State Personnel Board and departmental equal employment opportunity policies and to the attainment of affirmative action goals?				

GENERAL COMMENTS OR COMMENTS ON OTHER FACTORS

*The supervisor may make "Comments" only, or may use rating categories only, or may use either or both methods of appraisal on any performance factor, as he or she prefers. The rating categories are:

I - Improvement needed for performance to meet expected standards.
M- Performance fully meets expected standards.
E- Performance consistently exceeds expected standards.

Figure 19.2 California Department of Finance Career Development Form. (*cont'd.*)

EMPLOYEE CHECK LIST
FOR
APPRAISAL AND DEVELOPMENT INTERVIEW

On_____we will have an "A. & D." discussion.

During our appraisal and development discussion we will talk over your present job—what your duties and responsibilities are and how well you are fulfilling them—and also plan constructively for your future job development.

Attached is a copy of the form we will complete. You may use this form as a work sheet to prepare for our discussion.

This check list can help you plan for our meeting. The following questions will give you some idea of the things we might talk about during our discussion.

PRESENT JOB

1. Are all of my duties and responsibilities clear?

2. Do I, and my supervisor, have a common understanding of what I am supposed to do, and how well I am supposed to do it?

3. Is there anything about my present job that I do not like? Can anything be done to change this?

4. How well am I doing my job? What, specifically, do I do best? What, specifically, do I not do so well?

5. If I were filling out my appraisal form, what comments would I make, and what check marks would I make? (Perhaps you should write these down.)

FUTURE JOB DEVELOPMENT

1. What are my long-term job goals and objectives? My specific short-term goals?

2. What, specifically, could I do in my present job, or in my present civil service classification, that should help me obtain these goals?

3. What specific things can I do to take advantage of the strong points I listed under 4 above, and to build up the things which were not so strong?

4. What job assignments that might be available would help make me more useful to the Department?

5. What training do I need to do my present job better?

6. What outside study or education do I need to prepare myself for my next job?

DAS-PM 011 (8/74)

Figure 19.3   Personal Development Check List.

Keys to Success

Two dominant factors seem evident in much of the literature related to career development. Perhaps the most important is the necessity for continual assessment of personal skills, knowledge, attitudes, effective interpersonal relations, and the degree to which personal goals are being met. Awareness of personal limitations and strengths and development of strategies to offset weakness as well as accentuate strengths is an important ingredient of career management.

viewing the organization realistically

In addition to self-assessment, a realistic view of organizational life is equally necessary. A common error made by some inexperienced entrants into career programs is the belief that they can change an organization's style or that if conditions are unsatisfactory, they will soon improve. New workers must recognize that if opportunities are limited, if the political climate is distasteful, or if a low level of trust and confidence exists within the organization, it may be time to leave. Voluntarily changing jobs is, in some cases preferable to continuing in a situation where career opportunities are limited and personal needs unsatisfied. We are not advocating impulsive job-hopping, but rather periodic evaluations of whether the present job and organization are meeting your personal and career needs or have the potential for meeting those needs in the future.

job change

A Managerial Perspective

Arthur Elliott Carlisle has written of an interview conducted with an oil refinery manager named McGregor.[12] McGregor is an extraordinarily successful manager who has an unusual management style. He insists that those employees who report directly to him solve their own operating problems. As chief executive of the refinery, McGregor refuses to make decisions his lower-level managers are hired to make. Once a week, McGregor holds a meeting with his immediate staff and asks them to review the decisions they've made and the number of employees they have helped. McGregor insists that employees get help from others with whom they work, not the general manager.

solving your own problems

Each of his submanagers has learned McGregor's technique of refusing to solve problems he was not hired to solve. The submanagers insist that supervisors solve their own work problems. Supervisors transmit the same type of downward decision making to their employees. In McGregor's plant, every employee and manager is reponsible for identifying and finding solutions to work problems within their sphere of operations and expertise. It is more than participation. Active involvement, not only in routine assignments, but in decisions directly affecting productivity, quality, costs, schedules, facilities usage, and a variety of other factors is a job requirement. Decisions are reviewed after they are implemented. Mistakes are discussed openly, and seldom made more than once. Promotions are based, at least in part, on the quality of decisions.

McGregor recognized that a supply of qualified subordinates had to be developed for the future and that time was a scarce commodity. He designed and implemented a managerial system, "that had as its hallmark self-development for his employees, and efficient operation for his employer, and time for himself to actively consider the impact of future developments on his unit." McGregor had built a successful management system by insisting people take responsibility for their own jobs. *personal responsibility*

While not every manager is a McGregor and many companies require different approaches than oil refineries, development of employees can have many benefits. McGregor's employees were the ones most avidly recruited for promotional positions by the company's other refineries. His plant is known as the most well run and efficient. McGregor also has more time to pursue his favorite recreational activity—playing golf.

Perhaps the most important lesson to be learned from the McGregor story is that the development of people means, in the final analysis, providing the methodology for encouraging and even insisting on self-development. *self-development*

Quick Review

   I. Personal Success and Career Development
      A. Career choices may be linked to the way people think.
      B. Convergent thinkers tend to be precise, controlled, and well organized.
      C. Divergent thinkers tend to be people oriented, imaginative, creative, intuitive, and not well organized.
  II. Success and Personal Development
      A. Success as viewed by society and as viewed by individuals may be different.
      B. Career development usually means continually acquiring increased knowledge, skill, and competency.
 III. Organizational Career Development Plans
      A. Formal career development programs are the exception rather than the rule.
      B. Human resource planning seeks to determine the most effective use of individuals and the potential employment needs of the organization.
      C. It is ultimately individual effort that makes career development work.

IV. Career Development and the Individual
   A. Self-actualized people are able to define and fill career needs.
   B. A successful career management program involves a realistic awareness of skills, abilities, weaknesses, needs, and a sense of self-worth.
   C. Personal career values must acknowledge the realities of organizational life. Competency, training, energy, and the desire to please do not necessarily guarantee career success.
   D. Levinson believes we go through a major change in our career development about every seven to ten years.
   E. Allness is the belief by a person that he or she "knows it all" and no longer needs to consider new ideas.
   F. The self-fulfilling prophecy states that "we are what we think we are."
   G. Many organizations have developed career identification and planning assistance to help employees advance and grow.

V. Keys to Success
   A. Continual assessment of skills, knowledge, attitudes, and interpersonal relations are necessary to successful career development.
   B. A realistic view of organizational life and the willingness to change are necessary career development ingredients.
   C. All career development is ultimately self-development.

VI. A Managerial Perspective
   A. In some companies, all employees and managers are responsible for identifying and solving their own work problems.
   B. Such programs demonstrate that developing people means providing the means for and insisting on self-development.

Key Terms

Career development
Personal success
Convergent thinkers
Divergent thinkers
Human resource
   planning

Self-actualized
   person
Personal values
Bleeding sharks

Career change
Allness
Self-fulfilling
   prophecy

Discussion Questions

1. What does career development and career management really mean?
2. David Hall once wrote that if you know where you're going, you are more likely to get there. What did Hall really mean?
3. Employee development—career management programs are expensive and require expanded personnel records. In your opinion, are they worth the money and effort? Why or why not?
4. How can employees be encouraged to update their personnel files?
5. What can prevent an employee from taking advantage of company career enhancement programs in order to qualify for work with another organization?

Case Incidents

When Hard Work Isn't Enough

In 1978, Laron Wilson was hired by the State Department of Transportation as a junior management analyst. Laron's job involved analyzing reports to determine compliance with regulations, compiling data for use in efficiency evaluations, and reviewing written procedures. After a year of hard work and some recognition for his work, Laron wrote a budgeting report that was eventually read by the head of the department. As a result of his study, Laron was promoted to the position of "management analyst," a low level supervision assignment.

Laron worked hard at his new job, and earned a reputation as a top-notch analyst. He avoided office friendships, talked to his immediate supervisor only when necessary, and took almost no time away from his desk. "Hard work will do it," he thought.

Eventually he was promoted to senior management analyst, and seven years later found himself in the same job. "I've worked hard, kept my nose clean, and out of people's way," he complained to a friend after work. "What went wrong? Why have I been passed over for management assignments?"

1. Why did Laron advance rapidly during the early part of his career?
2. What could have caused Laron's attitude toward success after his first promotion?

3. Explain why Laron failed to obtain a management promotion, even though his work was excellent.

The Word Processing Trap

Valerie Hill was classified as a "word processing specialist" for Compquick, Inc., a computer software company in Fort Wayne, Indiana. She was competent, intelligent, and liked her work—until it began to dawn on her that the job was really a dead end. Unless she could get reclassified or promoted, Valerie felt she would be stuck the rest of her working life staring at the display screen of a word processor. She wasn't sure which direction to go. Her immediate supervisor was Sue Harper, manager of Procurement, who seemed to like the purchasing business. But Valerie wan't sure that she would enjoy a career in purchasing.

"It's hard to decide what to do," she confided in Curt Langley. "I'm sure I don't want to be a word processing specialist all of my career, but it's what I'm trained for and what I do well."

"There's a few things you may want to try," replied Curt. "Compquick has a career development program, but you've got to get the process started yourself."

1. What suggestions other than getting into Compquick's employee development program is Curt likely to have made?
2. Is Valerie stuck in her present job? Explain.
3. What are some personal considerations that Valerie will have to take into account in planning a career change?

Developing Employee Development

As chief executive officer of Contrax Corp., a medium-sized business forms and reports company, Christine Martinez felt that some sort of career development program for her employees would help not only the employees but the company. Contrax had expanded from its origins in Denver to the eleven states of the central West. As services and products multiplied, many new management, professional specialist, and administrative opportunities would be available. Rather than depend solely on outside recruiting to supply critical personnel needs, Christine strongly supported the concept of internal development and promotion. As a starting point, she needed someone to plan and monitor the internal personnel development effort.

Christine called Stan Salzman on the telephone. "Stan," she began, "we've got an important project and you're going to be in charge. What do you know about employee career development?"

1. As a starting point in putting a career development effort to-gether, where must Stan start?
2. What criteria is Stan likely to use in choosing people for partici-pation in the career development program?
3. Identify responsibilities individual employees have in develop-ing their own careers at Contrax Corp.

Exercise *Self-Assessment*

Complete the "Career Development Form," Figure 19.2 in your text. Compare your responses with another person in your class. What strengths and weaknesses in your own background can you identi-fy? What additional training do you need?

Endnotes

1. Liam Hudson, *Contrary Imaginations* (Middlesex, England: Penguin Books, Ltd., 1966).
2. David A. Kolb, et al., *Organizational Psychology: An Experiential Approach*, 3d ed. (Englewood Cliffs: Prentice-Hall, 1981).
3. Personal interview with Harry A. Todd, Sr., July 1981.
4. Heywood Klien, *Wall Street Journal*, 18 May 1981.
5. Randall S. Schuler, *Personnel and Human Resource Management* (St. Paul: West Publishing Company, 1981), p. 359.
6. Interview with A. J. Camp, 1978.
7. Abraham Maslow, *Motivation and Personality,* 2d ed. (New York: Harper & Row, 1970).
8. Schuler, Ibid.
9. Daniel K. Levinson and others, *The Seasons of a Man's Life* (New York: Knopf, 1978).
10. William V. Haney, *Communication and Interpersonal Relations: Text and Cases,* 4th ed. (Homewood: Richard D. Irwin, Inc., 1979).
11. Extracted from "20/20," ABC Television Productions, New York, 14 May 1982.
12. Arthur Elliott Carlisle, *Organizational Dynamics 5,* Summer 1976, pp. 50–62. Full text quoted in, *The Managerial Experience*, William F. Glueck, Lawrence R. Jauch, and Sally A. Coltrin (Hinsdale, Ill.: Dryden Press, 1980).

Appendix

Organizational Evaluation Questionnaire

I. Working Conditions

   A. *Physical Conditions*

      Do the employees have adequate space to do their jobs?

      Do the employees have adequate tools and equipment to do their jobs?

      Are adequate safety precautions taken to protect the employees on their jobs?

      Are the environmental factors (light, air, etc.) comfortable for employees?

      Are there adequate provisions for non-job-related facilities (parking lots, restrooms, etc.)?

   B. *Orientation*

      Do the employees have adequate information to effectively perform their jobs?

      Do the employees fully understand work rules?

      Are the employees kept informed of changes in the organization?

   C. *Job Security*

      Are the employees assured of a job as long as they perform effectively?

      If layoffs occur are they done fairly and consistently?

      Do the employees understand the procedures for layoffs?

D. *Pressure to Produce*

Is there unreasonable pressure for better performance?

Do the employees have to find meaningless work to do in order to "look busy" to their superiors?

II. *Work Groups*

A. *Cooperation*

Do the employees work together as a team?

Do the employees help each other in their jobs?

Do the people in the organization get along well together?

B. *Training*

Do the employees need more training to do their jobs well?

C. *Job Performance*

Do the employees encourage each other to improve their job performance in output of *quantity?*

Do the employees encourage each other to improve the *quality* of their job performance?

III. *Social Groups*

What are the social groups within the organization?

What functions do the social groups perform for the employees?

What functions do the social groups perform for the organization?

IV. *Status*

What are the status symbols within the organization?

What are the functional status indicators?

What are the dysfunctional status indicators?

V. *Economic Rewards*

A. *Pay*

Are the employees paid fairly compared to similar organizations?

Are the employees paid fairly compared with others in the organization?

Do the methods of pay accomplish their goals?

What is the basis for pay increases?

Do the employees accept pay increases as fair and adequate?

B. *Benefits*

Does the organization assist employees in preparing for their retirement?

Does the organization assist employees in their insurance programs?

Does the organization have a good sick-leave program?

Does the organization assist employees in the cost of educational activities?

VI. *Management Policies and Administration*

A. *Communication of Information*

Do all individuals in the organization understand the organization's objectives and policies?

Are there areas where policies do *not* exist or are *not* understood?

Are the employees given information concerning the organization's financial situation?

Are the employees always informed of important changes before they occur?

B. *Fairness of Policies and Administration*

Are policies and rules applied equally to all employees?

Are there employees who receive unjust discipline?

Does the organization have rules that are not necessary?

C. *Advancements and Promotions*

Are advancements and promotions based on merit?

Are the employees who receive advancements and promotions the most deserving in the organization?

Are qualified employees allowed to transfer to better jobs within the organization?

What are an employee's chances for advancement in the organization?

Are the employees confident that they will receive advancements and promotions when they are capable of handling the job?

VII. *Satisfaction with the Nature of Work*

   A. *Freedom*

Are the employees free to use their own ideas performing their jobs?

Are the employees allowed to set their own pace on the job?

   B. *Growth*

Are the employees able to learn new skills on their present job?

Are the employees able to further their educations while with the organization?

   C. *Responsibility*

Are the employees responsible for decisions related to their jobs?

Are the employees responsible for planning and organizing their jobs?

   D. *Achievement*

Are the employees able to use their abilities on their jobs?

Do the employees gain personal satisfaction from doing their jobs?

   E. *Influence*

Are the employees able to influence the manner in which their jobs are performed?

Are the employees' recommendations used in decisions concerning their jobs?

F. *Interest*

Do the employees find their work interesting?

Does time pass slowly for employees?

VIII. *Supervision*

A. *Communication*

Do the supervisors let people know where they stand?

Do the supervisors like to obtain employees' ideas for improving their jobs?

Are the supervisors easy for employees to talk to?

Are the employees free to make constructive criticisms of their supervisors?

Do the supervisors give clear and understandable instructions?

Do the supervisors give employees all the information they need to do their jobs well?

B. *Trust*

Do the supervisors live up to the promises they make to employees?

Do the supervisors give honest answers to the questions of the employees?

Are the supervisors fair in their dealings with employees?

C. *Job Competence*

Are the supervisors effective organizers?

Are the supervisors able to evaluate the employees' work?

Are the supervisors effective planners?

Are the supervisors well trained in human relations?

Do the supervisors possess the technical qualifications to do their jobs well?

D. *Consideration*

Are the supervisors considerate of the employees' needs and interests?

Do the supervisors genuinely look out for the interests of the people in their areas?

E. *Delegation of Responsibility*

Do the supervisors allow employees to make decisions on their jobs?

Do the supervisors like employees to make decisions without checking with them first?

Do the supervisors expect outstanding job performance from employees?

F. *Recognition*

Do the supervisors attempt to gain recognition for employees who deserve it?

Do supervisors reward those who perform their jobs well?

G. *Supervisor-Employee Relationship*

Do the supervisors bring out the best in the people in their areas?

Would the employees prefer to have different supervisors?

Glossary

Brief Key Term Definitions

achievement motivation: The need to get things accomplished. Usually the need to be part of an organization that excels or to gain personal goals.

achievement-oriented leadership: Leadership that is goal directed rather than based on personal power or survival needs.

adaptation: Tendency to, over a period of time, become accustomed to repeated events, sensations, styles, or rules. For example, a person may become adapted to background noise at work and learn to ignore it.

adaptation level: The degree to which a person is able to adjust to his or her environment. Some situations allow rapid adaptation, while others are more difficult.

affiliation motive: The need to associate with others; to receive approval, acceptance, friendship, or love.

aggression: Usually "attack" behavior; expressions of hostility, or in some cases intense determination to achieve a particular goal.

agreement: In labor-management relations, a contract governing wages, hours, and conditions of work legally binding on all parties. Labor contracts govern all personnel matters between union employees and management.

allness: The belief by a person that they know all about a subject, thing, job, event, or person. Unwillingness to accept new or different information or concepts.

approach-approach conflict: Internal conflict or stress that occurs when a person is required to choose between alternatives that are equally desirable.

approach-avoidance conflict: Internal conflict or stress that occurs when a person has a strong desire to act, change, or choose but is fearful of the consequences, or the consequences are uncertain.

arbitration: In labor-management relations, a procedure using a neutral third party to resolve grievances that management and labor are unable to solve. Costs of arbitration are usually split evenly between management and the union.

artifacts: Adornment worn or displayed that tells something about a person such as jewelry, clothing, or office decor.

association theory: Sometimes known as behaviorism. The belief that specific behavior is associated with specific types of events or stimuli.

authority: The right to act, decide, choose, give orders, or institute change. Most authority comes from organizational position and is delegated downward. However, the consent of the governed is authority derived from the people and granted to leaders.

avoidance-avoidance conflict: Internal conflict or stress that occurs when a person is experiencing or faced with undesirable conditions and any alternative seems equally undesirable. "Out of the frying pan, into the fire."

behavior: Any act by a person either overt (visible) or covert (hidden). All behavior is a response to some internal or external stimulus.

behavior modification: A technique for shaping or directing behavior by rewarding correct behavior and ignoring or, in some cases, punishing incorrect behavior.

behavioral theory: See *association theory*.

bilateral relations: Personnel rule making by both managers and employees, usually associated with labor agreements between union and managers.

bleeding sharks: A person or persons in trouble at work and attacked rather than helped by others.

bureaucracy: A system or organization with highly structured divisions of labor, specialization of work, rules, regulations, reporting systems, and controls.

career change: Change in type of work, organization, level of management, or geographical location as a result of new technology, promotion, change in interests, reduction-in-force, termination, development of new competencies, or change in life-style.

career development: All of the actions necessary to enhance career goals such as training, specialized experience, gaining expertise and skills, and learning to be self-directed.

career management: A systematic, planned approach to career development.

change: Any alteration of events, people, circumstances, or situations. Differences that are a function of time.

change diffusion: The ripple effect of change. Every change has a tendency to cause or direct other changes. This process is known as diffusion.

change direction: Change may be either upward (as in prices), downward (as in loss of sales) or in several directions at once (computers cost less but do more).

change rate: The speed at which change occurs; technical change generally occurs rapidly while social change generally occurs slowly.

change recognition: A developed ability to foresee significant change and plan to use it to best advantage. Change recognition allows planning for the future with a higher degree of certainty.

change resistance: The tendency to reject change that is externally imposed or over which a person has no influence. Resistance to doing or thinking differently.

chronemics: Use of timing as a nonverbal communication. Being late or early to meetings is an example.

civil rights: Right of every person regardless of race, color, religion, national origin, or sex to fundamental opportunities, liberties, and responsibilities guaranteed by the constitution.

climate: See *organizational climate*.

closure: The tendency to perceive things in whole and continuous patterns. First noted by Gestalt psychologists.

coercive power: Power that comes from threat, ability to punish, disapprove, withhold promotion or pay, or to demote, terminate, or assign punitive tasks.

cognitive theories: Personality and learning theories that state people choose their reactions to both internal and external stimuli based on interpretations of the stimuli and the expected consequences of their responses.

communication: The act of understanding and being understood. Sending, receiving, decoding, and interpreting messages.

communication channels: Any of the verbal and nonverbal sources of communication.

communication links: The number of people or steps between the originator of a message and its receiver. Each link weakens the probability of message accuracy.

conformity: Following rules precisely. Obeying group norms or slavishly copying the actions, dress, or speech of others.

constructive discipline: Disciplinary action designed to train or correct rather than punish.

convergent thinking: Thinking and actions which are precise, well ordered, dependent on rules and regulations, with close adherence to detail. Low tolerance of ambiguity.

coordination: Actions taken to inform and assist to ensure that people are working in an organized, planned, smoothly flowing work pattern.

creativity: Generation of new ways of acting, new explanations, unique methods of solving problems, or any activity that utilizes a previously unknown or unused approach to a human activity.

credibility: The degree of confidence, trust, honesty, truthfulness, knowledge, and/or skill assigned to an individual or group.

decoding: Interpretation of either verbal or nonverbal messages.

defense mechanisms: Any behavior adopted to protect a person's symbolic self, self-image, or ego.

delegation: Assigning tasks and the authority to complete those tasks.

destructive competition: Competition based on the concept of winning at all costs regardless of consequences to others.

direct communication: Face-to-face communication or voice-to-voice communication. Any communication directly between two people.

directive leadership: Leadership style based on giving orders, directing activities of others, or setting goals for others to achieve.

divergent thinking: Thinking and learning that is more dependent on feelings, intuition, and creativity than that of convergent thinking. Less dependent on rules, precision, detail; comfortable with ambiguity.

due process: The right to a fair hearing, to present both sides of a story, to face an accuser, to be treated without one-sided, arbitrary action.

effectiveness: Getting things accomplished correctly, on time, within costs.

efficiency: Getting things accomplished correctly in minimum time, minimum costs, with optimum utilization of resources.

emotion: Psycho-physical reaction to situation or other people. Feelings that result in physical changes such as increased heartbeat, sweating, eye dilation, tenseness, etc., and/or feelings such as joy, fear, disgust, desire, etc.

empathy: Understanding another person from that person's point of view. Understanding feelings and ideas from another's frame of reference.

encoding: Converting ideas, perceptions, and feelings into symbols, such as words on pictures, that may be used in message transmission.

environmental protection: Any action taken to preserve or improve air, water, land usage, or other natural aspects of the world.

equality of opportunity: Nondiscrimination in job opportunity because of race, color, religion, natural origin, sex, or in some cases, age and physical handicap.

esteem needs: Needs for approval, recognition, status, approval, feelings of self-worth, ego satisfaction.

ethical dilemmas: Conflicts between ethical values, each of which may seem positive or acceptable. Usually based on a conflict of needs. (If bribery of an official in a foreign country is accepted in that country in order to obtain business, should an organization engage in bribery?)

ethics: Personal values of correct and incorrect behavior, honesty. Societal values of honesty, truthfulness, fairness, and equity.

expectancy theory: The theory that behavior is directed by the value of a potential outcome and the anticipated consequence of the action.

expectation: Anticipation of the outcome or consequences of an event or set of circumstances.

expert power: Power that is derived from special knowledge, skills, ability to solve problems or provide needed information.

extinction: Disappearance of behavior because of the lack of reinforcement.

feedback: Literally, the response to a signal or communication. In organizations, the reaction to a decision or communication. In communication, the reaction and response from one communicator to another.

Fiedler's contingency approach: Fiedler's theory that as conditions change so should management styles. The style of management is contingent on conditions present. In times of high stress authoritarian styles may be appropriate. As conditions improve, a move toward participative styles is necessary. In very good conditions additional "tight ship" methods may be needed.

flexibility: The condition or ability to change as conditions and environments change.

formal: For official use. Usually refers to policies, procedures, signed memoranda.

formal status: Status because of job title, level of responsibility, or degree of authority.

frame of reference: Personal perception or viewpoint based on one's experience, cultural values, attitudes, beliefs and values.

frustration: Reaction to a blocked need, unresolved conflict, unsolved problem, or incomplete or unstarted effort.

goal: A desired outcome of a planned series of actions.

goal-directed behavior: Actions centered on specific goals.

goal orientation: Behavior that is consistently directed toward well-defined goals.

goal-setting systems: Formal written procedures for defining and implementing goal-directed behavior.

great man theory: The theory that leaders are born, not made.

grievance: A written formal complaint from an employee to a supervisor.

grievance procedure: A systematic series of steps for resolving grievances.

group: More than two people gathered together with coordinated efforts to achieve common goals.

group dynamics: The ever-changing relationships among group members. Interaction among group members.

group pressure: Unwritten, informal pressures by group members to force individual members to conform to group norms.

hot stove rule: A system that calls for immediate corrective action, or in some cases punishment, when a rule infraction occurs.

human potential: The belief that every person can achieve more, do more, and develop their full capabilities.

inference: "Jumping to conclusions." Development of a belief about an event, person, or circumstance without full knowledge of factual data.

innovation: Utilization of existing resources in new and different ways. Developing unique solutions or approaches to problems. See *creativity*.

institutional power motivation: The use of personal power to achieve goals of the organization or institution rather than the use of power for personal self-serving reasons.

interaction theory: Recognition that no event occurs by itself. People constantly give and receive from their environment, other people, and activities.

internal change: Change that occurs within an organization. May involve people, technology, organizational format, climate, product or service orientation, and types of work.

jargon: Language associated with a particular job or type of work that has little or no meaning to those not associated with the work. The word "scupper," for example, has little meaning to people outside the building trades.

job enrichment: A technique popularized by Frederick Herzberg for improving performance by providing greater employee control and responsibility for all aspects of assigned tasks.

job overload: Increasing the number of tasks, amount of work, or level of responsibility beyond an employee's ability to perform.

kinesics: Body language including posture, body movements, facial expressions, pointing behavior, eye blinks, and any other physical movements.

language and meanings: Meanings are in people, not in words or language. Language is a symbolic encoding and expression of concepts, feelings, information, sensations, and perceptual interpretation. It is not reality.

leader-member relations: In Fiedler's leadership theory, leaders must have effective relations with group members to be successful. Power position and task orientation are also leadership factors according to Fiedler.

leadership: The act of obtaining voluntary compliance from others. Influencing others because they want to be influenced or because they believe and support the leader's perceived power.

legitimate power: Power derived from a job title, position in organization, status symbols, or in some societies, age.

levels of abstraction: In communication theory, generalizations based on incomplete information. The first level is based on contact or observation. Each subsequent verbal or pictorial representation of the event is an additional abstraction level.

line organization: Organizational components and its members directly involved in producing the end product or service of the organization.

management by objectives: A management system based on achievement of well-defined, attainable, time-limited, quantitative goals and objectives at every level and by every person in an organization.

managerial grid: A system developed by Robert Blake and Jane Mouton for measuring mangement style based on both concern for people and concern for task accomplishment.

message isolation: In situations where multiple messages are being given, the necessity for selecting only those with significant meaning.

morals: Basic values of right and wrong; good and bad. Usually cultural or religious in origin, as opposed to ethics, which is societal in origin.

motivation: Internal causes of behavior. Drives, needs, desires, that precede and cause activities.

multiple channels: In communication theory, the concept that understanding is enhanced by communicating through as many sensory modes as possible, including speech, touch, vision, and odor.

natural work units: Tasks that are related to each other by skill, knowledge, or required expertise.

need hierarchy: Maslow's theory that lower order needs must be at least partially satisfied before higher level needs become operational. Physiological and safety needs, for example, usually must be satisfied before social and psychological needs are important to an individual.

need satisfaction: The theory that all behavior is designed to satisfy a need or a set of needs.

negotiations: The process of give and take between management and unions (or any other parties) in reaching agreement based on compromise.

nonverbal communication: Communication based on media other than spoken words or written material. Includes paralanguage, proxemics, kinesics, pictorial representation, chronemics, etc.

norms: Expected (normal) behavior of a group.

nothing jobs: Jobs that have little interest or value to workers other than the pay received for their performance.

objectives: Those goals an individual or group decides must be accomplished. Good objectives are specific, measurable, assigned to individuals or groups and are time limited (scheduled).

organization climate: The feeling, tone, spirit, or degree of voluntary cooperation found in organizations.

organizational centrism: A belief which sometimes develops that a particular unit of an organization is more important to the success of the entire organization than are other units.

organizational structure: Division of work as well as levels of responsibility and authority in work organizations.

path-goal theory: The theory that leaders must clarify goals and show followers how goals must be reached.

paralanguage: Use of voice tone, inflection, timber, amplitude, and emphasis to give meaning to spoken phrases.

participation: Involvement by all members of organizations in key decision process. Sharing of power between managers and employees.

perception: Interpretation of sensory awareness. The act of interpreting what is seen, heard, smelled, tasted, felt, or sensed in other ways such as anticipation based on past events.

perceptual processes: The awareness and interpretation of both external and internal stimuli. Involves awareness, organization, and interpretation of data in whole and continuous patterns.

performance evaluation: The assessment of a person's performance in achieving job objectives.

performance feedback: Providing performance evaluation both formal and informal.

permissive leadership: Leadership that allows both individual and group contributions and decisions independent of leader's desires. A form of nonleadership.

personal development: Individual improvement of skills, knowledge, expertise, and long-range perspectives.

physiological needs: Needs for biological survival such as food, air, water, warmth, sleep, elimination, etc.

placebo effect: Change based solely on belief, incorrect information, attitudes, or values rather than fact.

power: The degree of influence an individual has over another individual or group.

power motivation: Motivation based on the need to control, direct, shape, and alter. May be negative or positive.

politics: Behavior deliberately aimed at gaining or increasing power, agreement, or support.

positive reinforcement: Feedback and rewards for correct or desired behavior.

prejudice: Bias toward another, usually based on race, color, religion, national origin, sex, or physical disability. An attitude rather than a fact.

primitive power: Self-serving, negative use of power.

proxemics: Use of space, distance, and arrangement to communicate deep-seated personality factors.

psychological contract: Mutual expectations of employees and managers that are unspoken but real. Managers expect productivity, quality, attendance, pride, honesty, etc. Employees expect fair treatment, proper assignments, help when needed, participation, etc. As long as expectations are met, the contract is in force.

psychological distance: Recognition of role differences between managers and nonmanagers creates both status and power differences. The distance is necessary, but can, if too wide, lead to distrust and suspicion.

psychological needs: Needs for recognition, esteem, worthwhileness, status, and responsibility—ego satisfaction needs.

psychological noise: Distortion of communication caused by emotion, inferences, values, beliefs, perception of situation, or previous experiences.

quality circles: A technique for encouraging genuine participation through worker-manager problem-solving groups that meet on a regular basis.

quality of work life: An organizational philosophy that concentrates on development of a work climate that views both managers and employees as responsible for success or failure of the enterprise.

It holds that strong supportive relationships between employees and managers are necessary for optimization of goal achievement.

quid pro quo: Something for something. You scratch my back, I'll scratch yours. Do me a favor; I'll do one for you.

referent power: Power that comes when people refer to a person, use that person as a model, or adopt his/her beliefs, philosophy, or attitudes.

reinforcement: Reward or punishment immediately following an action or behavior that tends to shape future behavior. Rewarded behavior is usually repeated, punished behavior is usually avoided.

responsibility: The obligation to perform, act, carry out job assignments, meet work expectations, act on perceived needs, or take a position on a set of principles.

reward power: Power derived from giving both tangible rewards such as money and promotion or intangible rewards such as approval and recognition.

ringi: A Japanese technique for decision concensus similar to the Delphi method. Everyone must agree before the decision is implemented.

role: Behavior that is shaped by the situation, expectations of others, learned experiences, and observations of others.

role ambiguity: Uncertainty of appropriate behavior in a situation or psychological-social setting.

role conflict: When requirements are added to a role that were not anticipated or desired. A work group leader may understand both employee and management points of view and why they differ. Conflict occurs when the leader must take either management's view or that of the employee's.

role expectation: The expectation of behavior of others or self in a particular psychological-social setting.

safety needs: Need for protection, security, certainty, absence of risk.

self-actualization: Self-fulfillment. Defining and doing those things that are personally satisfying. Maslow's highest need.

self-fulfilling prophesy: Reality that is shaped by beliefs. Making things come out the way we believe they'll come out.

selective awareness: In perception theory, the observation that we are aware of only some things in our environment and totally unaware of others.

selective exposure: In perception theory, the observation that we are exposed to only a relatively few of the factors present in our environment.

seniority: Length of service in a job, department, or organization.

sensory stimulation: Stimulation through the senses and emotions.

sexual harassment: Any act, proposal, or suggestion of compliance in sexual conduct as a condition of work or promotion. Any sexual proposal or suggestion that interferes with the performance of work.

situation ethics: Appropriate behavior in terms of fairness, honesty, and correctness determined by situation.

situational leadership: Leadership style and skills determined by situation rather than by personal characteristics.

social change: Changes in attitudes, values, beliefs, and lifestyles by a majority of a given population.

sociobiology: The belief that there are genetic predispositions to much of human behavior. Behavior is both limited and enhanced by genetic factors.

staff: That part of an organization whose members are engaged in support, advisory, planning, legal, or other functions not directly associated with the end product or service of the organization. In some cases, the word "staff" is used to denote employees of the organization or a special group of employees.

status: The perceived rank of a person when compared to others. Perceived social worth of an individual in a particular society, group, or organization.

status awareness: Sensitivity to status differences in organizations, social group, and society in general.

status compression: The tendency for status differences to become less far apart over a period of time or as social values change.

status perception: Assigning status based on the way a person is seen rather than knowledge of position, power, wealth, or other status characteristics.

status symbols: Symbols associated with position, power, wealth, educational level, socioeconomic condition, or other status designators. Symbols include dress, office size and furniture, location, type of automobile, etc.

stereotyping: Assigning behavioral characteristics to people because of race, national origin, heritage, job title, organizations, geographic origins, etc.

steward: An elected union employee representative who represents both the employee and the union in grievance resolution or other conflicts with management. Stewards are usually employees who function as representatives on an "as-needed" basis.

stress: A tension reaction to threat, fear of failure, attainment of goals, compressed schedules, poor interpersonal relations, or any of a variety of other anxiety or emotion-inducing job factors.

stress carriers: People who are crisis oriented and induce stress in themselves and others as a usual behavior pattern. Can also apply to situations typically stress-inducing.

stress management: The act of controlling and directing stress as an energizing rather than a destructive force. Also, the act of creating working environments without undue or destructive stress.

supportive climate: A work climate that emphasizes voluntary cooperation, mutual assistance, analysis rather than criticism, and providing help and information when needed.

survey feedback: An organizational development technique that utilizes survey data that is summarized and given to the survey respondents who in turn interpret the data and suggest actions.

symbolic value: Worth and desirability based on symbols rather than reality. Desk size, office location, job title, office equipment, type of automobile, etc., all have greater symbolic value than real value.

symbols and reality: The concept that symbols are not reality. Words (symbols) are not the things they describe. Maps (symbols) are not the territories they depict. Pictures (symbols) are not the objects drawn or photographed.

task structure: Activities directed toward accomplishing a task, set of tasks, or series of objectives. According to Fiedler and others, a necessary component of effective managerial leadership.

technological change: Change in organization, jobs, and society because of introduction of new technologies. Introduction of automobiles, telephones, and computers are examples of technological changes affecting society at large.

Theory X: Douglas McGregor's label for traditional management assumptions that people do not like work, shun responsibility, are not normally creative, and must be controlled.

Theory Y: Douglas McGregor's label for management assumptions that work is as natural to people as play and that under the right conditions, people enjoy work, seek responsibility, are normally creative, and are self-controlled.

Theory Z: William Ouchi's label for management and employee assumptions that organizational success is dependent on managers and employees working in partnership, each sharing responsibility for the organization's achievements or failures.

tiger teams: Task forces of employees and managers working as teams to solve specific problems or to generate new ideas.

traits and abilities: Early studies of leadership attempted to identify specific characteristics (traits) and skills (abilities) common to all leaders. Such studies have yielded very little useful results.

union: An organized group of employees who collectively bargain with management to reach bilateral agreements on issues of wages, hours, and conditions of work.

valence: In expectancy theory, the attractiveness or desirability of a particular goal or incentive. The strength of a behavior is directly related to the valence of the goal or incentive.

value: Anything that has personal worth or meaning. Values are based largely on religious, moral, and societal precepts learned at an early age and modified throughout a person's life.

value ranking: Deciding which values are most important in a person's life. If telling a lie will prevent another person from being hurt, is it more important to be truthful or to prevent hurt? The response depends on a person's value ranking.

withdrawal: A psychological retreat from conflicting, boring, or threatening situations. Fantasy (daydreaming), falling asleep, physically leaving, and suicide are all withdrawal behaviors.

work redesign: A technique of rearranging, changing, adding to, or deleting specific tasks to make a job more challenging, more interesting, and affected employees more productive.

Index

†